History Teaches Us to Hope

For Marvin,
With my sincere
regards,

Charles P. Roland

HISTORY
TEACHES US TO
HOPE

Reflections on the
Civil War and
Southern History

CHARLES P. ROLAND

Edited and With an Introduction
by John David Smith

THE UNIVERSITY PRESS OF KENTUCKY

Publication of this volume was made possible in part by a grant from
the National Endowment for the Humanities.

The University Press of Kentucky

Scholarly publisher for the Commonwealth,
serving Bellarmine University, Berea College, Centre College of Kentucky,
Eastern Kentucky University, The Filson Historical Society, Georgetown College,
Kentucky Historical Society, Kentucky State University, Morehead State University,
Murray State University, Northern Kentucky University, Transylvania University,
University of Kentucky, University of Louisville, and Western Kentucky University.
All rights reserved.

Editorial and Sales Offices: The University Press of Kentucky
663 South Limestone Street, Lexington, Kentucky 40508–4008
www.kentuckypress.com

11 10 09 08 07   5 4 3 2 1

Library of Congress Cataloging-in-Publication Data

Roland, Charles Pierce, 1918-
  History teaches us to hope : reflections on the Civil War and southern history / Charles P.
Roland ; edited and with an introduction by John David Smith.
    p. cm.
  Includes bibliographical references and index.
  ISBN 978-0-8131-2456-8 (hardcover : alk. paper)
  1. United States—History—Civil War, 1861-1865—Historiography. 2. United States—
History—Civil War, 1861-1865—Causes. 3. Secession—Southern States. 4. Generals—
Confederate States of America—Biography. 5. Command of troops—Case studies. 6.
Southern States—History. 7. Southern States—Civilization. 8. Roland, Charles Pierce,
1918- 9. Historians—Southern States—Biography. 10. Historians—United States—
Biography. I. Smith, John David, 1949-   II. Title.
  E468.5.R65 2007
  973.7'11—dc22   2007034581

This book is printed on acid-free recycled paper meeting the requirements of the American
National Standard for Permanence in Paper for Printed Library Materials.

Manufactured in the United States of America.

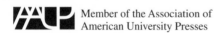 Member of the Association of
American University Presses

To my grandchildren and their children and thus ad infinitum

—CPR

Contents

Part Four: The South in Fact and in Myth

Foreword

On April 23, 2006, a tour bus neared the General Albert Sidney Johnston Monument on the Shiloh Battlefield. For those aboard, a long-anticipated moment was at hand. The driver parked the bus, opened the door, and lowered the steps. It was raining and chilly, but no one thought of remaining on board. Quietly we followed the guides to the base of the monument. Then, as they moved aside, Dr. Charles P. Roland stepped onto the monument's pediment, to stand squarely above the name "Johnston" emblazoned on the stone footing. The biographer of Albert Sidney Johnston had come to speak about the great "soldier of three republics" at the site of his death. Holding his umbrella overhead, Dr. Roland began to speak. He held no notes, speaking instead from heartfelt knowledge. He began by telling us that he had at home in Lexington, Kentucky, an old photograph of himself, at age eight or nine, sitting then where he stood now.

Then Roland spoke of his subject's life, Johnston's crowning moment, and his untimely death on this battlefield on April 6, 1862. Roland spoke for perhaps forty minutes. The rain never ceased. For those of us there the time was as brief as a snapshot—a moment frozen in time.

Professor Roland's life and work are marked by superb historical scholarship, writing, and teaching. His professional skill and artistry are enriched by his participation in great historical events. The historian's calling is framed in his engaging manner and humane liberality. He is a true doctor of letters.

As a youth he witnessed some of the last of the "old South." He saw the Depression and the coming of war. He was in the ranks of the great generation of citizen-soldiers of World War II. In the U.S. Army, in England, France, Belgium, and Germany, he was Captain Charles Roland, 99th Infantry Division. He saw the worst of the Battle of the Bulge, and he crossed the Rhine on the captured bridge at Remagen. At war's end he began what he calls his "odyssey" from war to academe. His journey brought him recognition as one of our most distinguished historians of the South, and of what he calls the "American Iliad." Since he began his odyssey, Roland's teaching and writing have influenced countless lives. He also carried his calling beyond academe, into the world of historical tourism, on both sides of the Atlantic. I came to know him under the auspices of the McCormick Civil War Institute of Shenandoah University, where he has been our principal lecturer for over a decade. Wherever Roland lectures and provides commentary, he arrives well before the day on which he is to speak, in order to meet and get to know his audience. He remains with the group until the event has come to its close, taking home to Lexington newly formed friendships. Roland doubtless exhibited the same qualities in the Army, and in academe.

When Professor Roland finished speaking on that rainy day in April, he led his listeners to the ravine where General Johnston died. Once we gathered, he answered several questions. Then Professor Roland led us in conversation that spanned and then went beyond the general, Shiloh, even the "American Iliad." The teacher meant to sharpen our perspective and deepen our understanding of the context of these great events. By the time we filed back to our bus, an hour had passed. I believe that the spirit of that single hour at Shiloh will be found in the pages that follow here.

Brandon H. Beck, Director Emeritus
McCormick Civil War Institute, Shenandoah University

Introduction

Charles P. Roland, Historian of the Civil War and the American South

John David Smith

Charles Pierce Roland, Alumni Professor Emeritus of History at the University of Kentucky, ranks as one of America's most distinguished and respected historians of the Civil War and the American South. A Tennessee native, he studied history at Vanderbilt University (B.A., 1938) and, after distinguished service as a combat officer in World War II (Roland received a Purple Heart and a Bronze Star for meritorious service), he continued his training as a historian at Louisiana State University (M.A., 1948, Ph.D., 1951). At LSU Roland worked with three renowned historians of the South and the Civil War era—Bell Irvin Wiley, Francis Butler Simkins, and T. Harry Williams.[1] Many years later Wiley remembered Roland as one of his best former graduate students, one of several men recently discharged from the Army who "had had some time to gain perspective; they meant business, they knew what they wanted, and they knew how to go about it. They were delightful."[2] Over the years Roland repeatedly cited Wiley as a master historian who influenced his thinking as a scholar.[3] In 1991 Roland dedicated his *An American Iliad* to Wiley, the only teacher he has so honored.[4]

Roland taught at the university level for thirty-six years, dividing his teaching equally between Tulane University (1952–1970) and the University of Kentucky (1970–1988). He directed nine doctoral dissertations at each institution. Over the course of his long career Roland also served as the Victor Hugo Friedman Distinguished Visiting Professor of Southern History at the University of Alabama (1977), as the Harold Keith Johnson Visiting Professor of Military History at the Army Military History Institute and Army War College, Carlisle Barracks, Pennsylvania (1981–1982), and two terms as visiting professor of military history at the U.S. Military Academy (1985–1986, 1991–1992). For his service at West Point, in 1986 Roland received the United States Military Academy Commander's Medal for Outstanding Service.

Because of his dedicated work as advisor, consultant, lecturer, and researcher for the Department of the Army (in 1985–1987 he chaired its Historical Advisory Committee), it recognized Roland by bestowing upon him two awards, the Department of the Army Outstanding Civilian Service Medal and Citation (1982) and the Secretary of the Army's Decoration for Distinguished Civilian Service (1992). Members of the historical profession also honored Roland, electing him president of both the Louisiana Historical Association (1969–1970) and the Southern Historical Association (1981).

Popular audiences nationally and internationally know Roland as a lively and engaging speaker on topics ranging from the causes of the Civil War to the tactical elements of the Battle of the Bulge. Though almost ninety, he maintains an active speaking schedule that would tire a person half his age. Several groups have acknowledged his accomplishments as a lecturer and promoter of history, especially of the Civil War era. In 1986 the Kentucky Civil War Round Table, in which over many years Roland has played and continues to play a leadership role, awarded him its Townsend-Hamilton Award for distinguished accomplishments in Civil War history. Similarly, in 2000 the Chicago Civil War Round Table presented Roland with its prestigious Nevins-Freeman Award for outstanding contributions to American history during the period of the Civil War. The next year Roland garnered the William Woods Hassler Award from the Civil War Education Association for "exceptionally meritorious contributions" to the field of Civil War studies.

Much of Roland's success, and his reputation as one of America's leading scholars, results from his long list of major publications. A dogged researcher, gifted stylist, and keen interpreter of historical questions, Roland has published nine books and scores of journal articles, essays, and book reviews.[5] Taken as a whole, his work features skillful phrasing, comparative analysis, and careful attention to irony, paradox, and subtle and nuanced change. Roland's book-length publications fall roughly into three overlapping chronological periods.

Roland made his initial mark as a Civil War historian while teaching at Tulane. His first book, *Louisiana Sugar Plantations during the American Civil War* (1957), examined the vicissitudes of life—for sugar planters as well as their slaves—during the war. Because historian J. Carlyle Sitterson had recently published *Sugar Country: The Cane Sugar Industry in the South, 1753–1950* (1955), Roland encountered difficulties in finding an American publisher. To his good fortune, E. J. Brill, the distinguished publisher founded in the Netherlands in 1683, accepted his manuscript, published it handsomely, and distributed it internationally.

In keeping with the scholarship of his day, Roland wrote *Louisiana Sugar Plantations* largely from the perspective of the planter class, not the slaves; he focused more clearly on the experiences of the white masters than of the black slaves and the freedpeople. For example, Roland described the sugar planters as "men of sound wit who tempered their lives with vigorous play, set the pace for the area in which they lived, and made the plantation ideal supreme." In 1862, as Federal armies enveloped Louisiana's sugar parishes, the alleged romance of plantation life turned into horror. "Mansions stood empty and pillaged," Roland wrote, "with idle sugar houses falling rapidly into ruin. Cane fields were littered with rottenness. Desolation brooded over the plantation country." Louisiana sugar growers saw no future for themselves or their cash crop in a world without slaves. "Bred in this conviction," Roland explained, the once proud sugar barons "permitted *a priori* condemnation to blind them to the possibility of any good in the new order, just as Federal authorities were led by their preconceptions to exaggerate its immediate virtues."[6]

Though by today's standards *Louisiana Sugar Plantations* appears seriously outdated in approach, argument, and method, contemporaries considered it a pathbreaking work and gave the book a warm reception. The Louisiana Library Association bestowed upon Roland its Literary Award, for "the most distinguished book on Louisiana published during 1957."[7] *New Orleans Times-Picayune* columnist and local historian Charles L. "Pie" Dufour pointed to Roland's "exacting research," and wrote that his book underscored the economic, political, and social power of Louisiana's sugar elite. Dufour praised Roland's portrayal of plantation white females as multitalented mothers, hostesses, managers, and businesswomen.[8]

Academicians also greeted Roland's book enthusiastically. Vanderbilt University's Herbert Weaver noted that in his book Roland concerned himself "with both those who experienced the ruin of war and those who might be considered the authors of the ruin." Weaver also credited Roland with contributing "significantly to the understanding of the grim tragedy suffered by this gay and colorful region."[9] While historian Raleigh A. Suarez of McNeese State College considered Roland's book "a well-written, interesting narrative," he nevertheless questioned its originality: "the conclusions reached by the author are not unexpected," he said.[10] Historians James G. Randall and David Donald disagreed. In their *The Civil War and Reconstruction* (1961) they cited Roland's *Louisiana Sugar Plantations* as "a pioneer work" in the generally ignored field of southern agricultural history.[11]

Grounded on research in plantation records, journals, diaries, and parish archives, *Louisiana Sugar Plantations* remained the standard work on the topic until C. Peter Ripley's *Slaves and Freedmen in Civil War Louisiana* appeared in 1976. It is important to note that Roland published his pioneering book decades before the appearance of a substantial revisionist historical literature that positioned the slaves' agency, slave resistance, and the emancipation process at the center of Civil War era social history.[12] In 1996 Roland acknowledged that "the unavailability of contemporary slave accounts" constituted "the most glaring gap in my sources." This "deficiency," he added, "robs the book of an adequate description of their [the slaves'] feelings and motivations."[13] Even so, to a certain degree, Roland, by focusing on the destruction of slavery in Louisiana's sugar parishes, foreshadowed the "new" emancipation studies, most notably the work of historian Ira Berlin and the University of Maryland's Freedmen and Southern Society Project.[14] Four decades after its original publication, Louisiana State University Press published a new edition of Roland's book, revising its title as *Louisiana Sugar Plantations during the Civil War.*[15]

While teaching at Tulane in the 1960s, Roland also published two other classic Civil War titles—*The Confederacy* (1960) and *Albert Sidney Johnston: Soldier of Three Republics* (1964). Historian Daniel J. Boorstin invited Roland to write his book on the Confederacy for his prestigious University of Chicago History of American Civilization series. Boorstin designed the series volumes as compact and informed syntheses, not monographs, and aimed the books at general readers and students, not professional historians. Roland's *The Confederacy* ranked as one of the most enduring volumes in Boorstin's series, going through several paperback printings. By the mid-1970s it had sold around forty thousand copies.[16]

Narrating the Confederacy's rise and fall, Roland underscored the complex factors that led to secession, the strengths and weaknesses of Confederate nationalism, and the ultimate causes of the South's defeat. In less than two hundred pages of text Roland examined virtually every aspect of the southern Confederacy, including its diplomacy, its shining military victories, and the dark shadows of its downfall. Anticipating future scholarship, he devoted a chapter to "A Divided South and Total War." Though he praised President Jefferson Davis's unflagging devotion to the Confederate cause, Roland faulted him for failing to formulate "a unified command or a national strategy worthy of the national army which he fashioned with foresight and resourcefulness." According to Roland, Davis's gravest error was his failure to concentrate southern forces "against exposed fractions of the enemy." Recognizing Davis's mistakes, Roland found it "questionable that the Confederacy would have triumphed had these errors been avoided; failure to avoid them made defeat certain."[17]

Generations of college students and Civil War enthusiasts enjoyed Roland's fast-paced, succinct, and well-written *The Confederacy*. Reviewers agreed that it was the best short treatment of the Confederate war, though they acknowledged that Roland's book was less detailed and comprehensive than E. Merton Coulter's *The Confederate States of America, 1861–1865* (1950) and Clement Eaton's *A History of the Southern Confederacy* (1954). One reviewer, Samuel Shapiro, found Roland's slender work preferable to the competition. Writing in *Commentary,* the publication of the American Jewish Committee, Shapiro judged Roland, like fellow historian C. Vann Woodward, "a liberal Southerner who is not blind to his section's faults." Shapiro found *The Confederacy* "free from the retrospective patriotism and denigration of the Negro that mark E. Merton Coulter's earlier book on the same subject." Shapiro also considered Roland's descriptions of the wholesale death and suffering that resulted from the war "useful correctives to the habit of many [Civil War] Centennial celebrants of regarding the War as simply a vast and enjoyable kind of game."[18]

Historian E. B. Long noted *The Confederacy*'s "admirable balance of military and non-military events."[19] Another scholar, Mary Elizabeth Massey, observed that though Roland's work replaced neither Coulter's nor Eaton's books, Roland nonetheless made an important contribution by examining conditions on the home front and in southern cities and towns.[20]

Writing in the *Journal of Southern History,* historian Rembert W. Patrick remarked that Roland paid insufficient attention to the inadequacy of the South's transportation system. On balance, however, Patrick rated *The Confederacy* "a readable summary for the laymen and a resumé of basic interpretations for the historian."[21]

Historian James W. Silver agreed with Massey's and Patrick's evaluations, but balked at what he considered the neo-abolitionist tone of Boorstin's preface and identified "about a half-dozen questionable statements" in Roland's text. Silver nonetheless judged *The Confederacy* "the best short statement on the Confederacy . . . written in an extremely graceful, simple style which makes its reading a delight." Silver complimented the book's "fine balance," though he warned that "the patriots may insist that it is weighted on the internal decline of the Confederacy, with perhaps more attention to the opposition to the [Jefferson Davis] administration than is merited."[22]

Despite the strengths of Roland's book, by the 1980s Emory M. Thomas's *The Confederate Nation, 1861–1865* (1979) had superseded it in terms of breadth of research and level of argument. In fairness to Roland, however, he never intended his short book to be more than a brief survey, and it had a long and useful life. Roland's *The Confederacy* accomplished another important function: it served to introduce him as a leading Civil War historian to a broad national audience, especially to those who tended not to read the scholarly articles that he began publishing in the 1950s and continued to publish in the following decade.[23]

One of Roland's early articles, "The Generalship of Robert E. Lee," garnered him considerable attention. Roland's essay had stemmed from a symposium at Northwestern University in the fall of 1961 organized by his longtime friend historian Grady McWhiney. Though still an emerging scholar, Roland received the invitation to speak at Evanston because, McWhiney recalled, "I wanted someone who would defend Lee satisfactorily. . . . I knew [Roland] well and was confident he would deliver an outstanding paper."[24] At Northwestern Roland found himself in exceedingly good company; the other invited speakers included the nationally acclaimed authorities on the Civil War Bruce Catton, David Donald, and T. Harry Williams. Though Roland's paper was generally well received, including a favorable mention by the renowned Lincoln scholar Don E. Fehrenbacher, one critic, Dudley T. Cornish, judged him too zealous in praising Lee's alleged military genius. According to Cornish, "Professor Roland labors his argument, belabors Lee's critics, and wears the reader down with thirty-nine impassioned pages (and forty-seven footnotes)."[25] More recently, historian Joseph T. Glatthaar has credited Roland's essay with foreshadowing and demolishing much late twentieth-century criticism of Lee's generalship. "What emerges," according to Glatthaar, "is the finest brief essay on Lee that exists today."[26] This article would be but the first of Roland's many contributions on Lee.

Three of Roland's other early articles focused on another Confederate general, Albert Sidney Johnston, the subject of Roland's research for more than a decade during the late 1950s and early 1960s. Many scholars and Civil War enthusiasts consider Roland's third book, *Albert Sidney Johnston: Soldier of Three Republics* (1964), to be his most original and important work; most agree with historian Grady McWhiney that Roland's biography stands as "the definitive treatment of the Confederate president's favorite general."[27]

Unquestionably, his study of Johnston's life exceeded in depth of research, sophistication of analysis, and grace of exposition either of Roland's previous books. *Albert Sidney Johnston* was a mature, substantial work by a rising star in the historical profession. In his narrative of the first moments of the battle of Shiloh of April 6–7, 1862, Roland's lyrical prose evoked an intense familiarity with the local terrain and an almost eerie sense of one who had experienced the tranquil calm before battle. "The sun rose brilliant," he wrote, "upon a country of fresh-leaved oaks, brightened throughout with the white blossoms of dogwood and here and there with the soft pink of farmhouse peach orchards."[28]

Roland in fact seemed almost destined to write about Johnston, the Kentuckian who graduated high in his class at the U.S. Military Academy, who served with distinction in the U.S. Army, who fought for and served in the government of the Republic of Texas, and then, finally, who fought and died for the Confederate States of America. Johnston commanded Confederate forces in the strategically vital but vast and vulnerable western department and died in combat at perhaps the most critical moment of one of the war's most important early contests—the battle of Shiloh. As Roland explained in the preface to his biography, "Shiloh was hallowed ground to me in my childhood. Born and bred in West Tennessee . . . I visited there often. I went there on family occasions, on school excursions, to religious revival meetings. Shiloh's historic sites . . . were forever branded into my memory. So were Shiloh's historic figures—Johnston and Beauregard,

Grant and Sherman. I listened to the saga of valor at Shiloh; I looked upon
the spot where Albert Sidney Johnston fell at the head of the Confederate
Army; I pondered the effect of his death upon the outcome of the battle.
His presence seemed to abide at Shiloh." Upon arriving at Tulane, Roland
had discovered a large cache of Johnston's private papers in the university's
library. "I felt compelled to write the story of his life," he recalled.[29]

Not only did Johnston's biography pose a natural project for Roland to
pursue, but the historical profession eagerly awaited a scholarly work on
the career of the general that one reviewer dubbed "the *beau ideal* of the
Confederate cause."[30] In 1878 Johnston's son, William Preston Johnston,
had published *The Life of Gen. Albert Sidney Johnston,* a filiopietistic defense of his father's actions during the disastrous February 1862 loss of Fort
Henry on the Tennessee River and Fort Donelson on the Cumberland River
and the battle of Shiloh. Roland sought to write an objective, fair-minded
account of the man whom Jefferson Davis and many others considered to
be one of the greatest military minds in the new Confederacy.

Because Johnston fell so early in the war, most of Roland's study naturally focused on his long antebellum career. After graduating from West
Point in 1826, Johnston entered the U.S. Army and fought in the Black
Hawk War before joining the Republic of Texas as commanding general
(1836–1838) and secretary of war (1838–1840). Johnston fought brilliantly
with a volunteer division in the battle of Monterrey in the Mexican War
(where he befriended Jefferson Davis, then of the Mississippi volunteers),
and in 1849 he rejoined the U.S. Army as paymaster of troops along the
Texas frontier. In 1855 Johnston commanded the elite Second U.S. Cavalry (a unit that included such future Civil War generals as Robert E. Lee,
William J. Hardee, George H. Thomas, George Stoneman, and John Bell
Hood) that unsuccessfully pursued the Comanches. Two years later the
Army gave Johnston the difficult and delicate assignment of suppressing
the early stages of a rebellion by Mormons and asserting federal authority
in Utah Territory. In 1861, when Texas seceded from the Union, Johnston
commanded the Department of the Pacific. He resigned his commission to
cast his lot with the new Confederate army. Davis appointed Johnston a full
general, giving him the daunting responsibility of defending Department
No. 2—a five-hundred-mile defensive perimeter from the Appalachians in
the east to the western border of Arkansas.

In *Albert Sidney Johnston,* Roland narrated Johnston's prewar career
with a deft touch, blending description with judicious analysis and draw-

ing upon sources unexamined by previous scholars. Perhaps Roland's most original contributions were his analyses of Johnston's sense of personal honor, his commitment to family and friends, his financial worries, his devotion to the Republic of Texas, the complexities of Johnston's civil-military assignment in Utah, and his self-control in the midst of adversity. Aside from providing a thorough account of Johnston's pre–Civil War career, Roland's major achievement in *Albert Sidney Johnston* was his balanced assessment of the general's performance as a commanding general and his place in Civil War history—what today's scholars term "historical memory."

After weighing the evidence, including contemporary post-action reports and postwar recollections by Generals Pierre G. T. Beauregard and Ulysses S. Grant, Roland concluded that Johnston blundered in virtually every phase of the Confederates' disastrous losses of Forts Henry and Donelson. Though he credited Johnston with the "moral courage" necessary to abandon Kentucky and Tennessee and thereby to hope to fight another day, Roland ultimately held the general responsible for the debacles. The Fort Donelson campaign, according to Roland, could "hardly be matched in the annals of warfare." He judged the performance of the local officers a mélange "of courage and timidity, of decisiveness and vacillation, of brilliance and stupidity—a tactical comedy of errors turned into high tragedy for Johnston and for the South." In surrendering the forts, Johnston's subordinates squandered away one fourth of his army east of the Mississippi River and left Nashville virtually indefensible. Johnston faced insurmountable odds and received little support from the central Confederate government in Richmond or the state governments, Roland explained, but when the smoke of battle cleared, Johnston "failed to act with the audacity and decision required by the crisis that he faced."[31]

Following the humiliating defeats on the Tennessee and Cumberland rivers, Johnston orchestrated the strategic retreat of his army south of the Tennessee River to the important rail center of Corinth, Mississippi. There he was determined to recover military advantage, to redeem his reputation, and to save the Confederate west. Concentrating troops from throughout the region, Johnston began a bold counteroffensive, mobilizing a large army with hopes of catching Grant's divided Federal army by surprise just across the Tennessee line at Pittsburg Landing on the west bank of the Tennessee River.[32] Roland agreed with Johnston's critics that by delaying his attack until April 6 he committed "another strategic miscalculation."

Nonetheless, the historian defended the general, explaining that as an officer in World War II he had "observed entanglements and delays" in the movement of troops "reminiscent of Johnston's march" from Mississippi to Tennessee. "Yet these modern organizations had every advantage over Johnston's army in training, transportation, communications, roads, and maps."[33]

Despite the delay, Johnston nevertheless caught Grant's troops totally unprepared; Roland termed this "one of the greatest strategic surprises in all military history." As the early morning sun lit the West Tennessee countryside, Confederate troops advanced forward across a three-mile-long front. Shiloh would become the greatest battle yet fought in the Civil War. During the ferocious combat that ensued, Johnston personally directed units into position, inspired men into combat, and boosted morale. While admonishing General John C. Breckinridge's Tennessee troops to advance, a minié ball penetrated Johnston's right leg below the knee, tearing the popliteal artery. He bled to death within fifteen minutes. Confederate command then passed to General Beauregard, who continued the advance until 6:00 P.M., when he ordered the Rebel troops to cease the attack and withdraw for the night. "This decision," according to Roland, "was a grave mistake; Beauregard ought either to have risked all in a desperate assault on the last Federal position, or to have led his army back to Corinth during the night of the sixth." Reinforced that night by General Don Carlos Buell's fresh troops, Grant pushed the demoralized Confederates back to Corinth. The South had allowed a stunning victory to slip from its grasp.[34]

Evaluating Johnston's place in history, Roland avoided the carping, conjecture, and speculation of the general's contemporaries and his son's biography. He credited Johnston with anticipating many of the concepts of modern warfare: the bold maneuver to conceal weakness, the importance of the relationship between military strategy and politics, the new and increasingly vital role of railroads, the use of cavalry in reconnaissance and as a protective screen, and the importance of replacing rearguard troops with slaves to maximize the number of effectives for the battle. Roland faulted Johnston for misjudging the amount of support he would muster for the Confederate cause in Kentucky and for dividing his army (and thus losing so many troops) at Fort Donelson. In the end, Roland maintained that death denied Johnston, unlike Grant, General William T. Sherman, and other Civil War military leaders, the opportunity to learn from his mistakes and to grow as a combat commander. "Had Johnston lived," Roland concluded, "he doubtless would have emerged from Shiloh with vastly enhanced prestige, regardless of the outcome of that contest, for he demonstrated there that he had the will and courage to fight, and that in moments of crisis his judgment and determination transcended that of fellow Confederates."[35]

Contemporary reviewers welcomed Roland's *Albert Sidney Johnston* enthusiastically. For example, Robert W. Johannsen of the University of Illinois described the book succinctly as "complete, well-rounded and scholarly," and complimented the author's "excellent use of Johnston's papers."[36] Warren W. Hassler Jr. also praised Roland's "wide research—especially in manuscript sources," and described his book as "fluently written, and sober in its judgments." He predicted with considerable prescience that Roland's biography "will long remain the standard work on this stalwart soldier of three republics."[37] The University of Maryland's David S. Sparks complimented Roland for "rescuing Johnston from his over-zealous friends, as well as from his severest critics." This "called for meticulous scholarship, discriminating judgment, and a thorough grounding in military and political history." Sparks, who agreed with Hassler that Roland's "splendid" work would prove to be "definitive," nevertheless remarked: "It is so good, in fact, that one closes the book with the distinct impression that this is a biography that deserved a better subject."[38]

Generations of readers obviously have disagreed with Sparks's remark. Recently historian Gary W. Gallagher has pointed out that on two occasions—in 1981 and 1995—Roland's *Albert Sidney Johnston* appeared in compilations of the key one hundred Civil War titles published. "In a field," he adds, "where new books appear at a staggering rate, even superior studies seldom retain preeminence for more than a few years. Roland's life of Johnston is an exception."[39] And through the years Roland has continued to defend Johnston from critics, such as historian James Lee McDonough, who have disparaged the general's role at Shiloh. In 1978 Roland admitted "that Johnston unquestionably made a number of serious misjudgments and was, at times, guilty of indecisiveness, especially in connection with the ill-fated defense of Forts Henry and Donelson. . . . Certainly there is room for criticism, and every student of Johnston's operations is entitled to his own conclusions." Having said this, however, Roland vindicated Johnston's "command decision" to surprise Grant at Shiloh. "Will, audacity, steadfastness, insight into the opponent's character and mood, and intuition or 'hunch'—these are among the qualities that distinguish a great command decision from an ordinary one."[40] In 2000 Roland, drawing heavily upon his earlier book, published a 112-page summary, *Jefferson Davis's Greatest General: Albert Sidney Johnston.* This short, nicely illustrated work is especially well suited for undergraduate students and Civil War buffs.[41]

Roland's move to the University of Kentucky in 1970 signaled another transition—one that proved to be only temporary—from his research and writing on the Civil War to the field of southern history.[42] Though identified during his years at Tulane as an authority on Louisiana history, the Civil War, and the Old South, during his tenure at Kentucky Roland expanded the range of his publications to include a sweeping survey of southern history, a more limited interpretive study of the region's history since 1945, and several important essays on southern culture, identity, and economic and urban growth.[43] At Kentucky he taught various courses on the Old and New South, but not on the Civil War or on military history. His nine doctoral students at that university completed dissertations on the history of the South, not on the Civil War. Years later Roland explained that his election as president of the Southern Historical Association resulted from his overall scholarly accomplishments but as "the immediate reward" for two books on the South: *A History of the South* (4th ed., 1972), a work he coauthored with the late Francis Butler Simkins, and *The Improbable Era: The South since World War II* (1975).[44]

Roland of course had studied with the legendary Simkins at LSU and ranked as one of his foremost former doctoral students. The senior scholar, who died in 1966, had a long and distinguished career. He published, among other works, *The Tillman Movement in South Carolina* (1926), *South Carolina during Reconstruction* (with Robert H. Woody, 1932), *The Women of the Confederacy* (with James W. Patton, 1936), *Pitchfork Ben Tillman, South Carolinian* (1944), and *The South Old and New: A History 1820–1947* (1947; second edition, 1953), and its revised and expanded third edition, *A History of the South* (1963). His coauthor James W. Patton wrote that on various occasions the iconoclastic Simkins had been accused of having "Carpetbagger ancestors" and being "a Bilbo with a Ph.D." Whether or not one accepted Simkins's arguments, Patton explained, "he remains a significant figure in Southern historiography, a stimulating writer, a superb raconteur, and a warm personal friend."[45]

Simkins, who earned his doctorate under William A. Dunning at Columbia University in 1926, spent most of his teaching career at Longwood College in Virginia.[46] Roland admired Simkins's scholarship, especially his independence of thought and critical verve, and appreciated his eccentricities. In 1963 he reflected on his mentor: "His books and essays have enriched the literature on the region. His scalpel book reviews have dissected scores of writings about the South, and have cleanly parted sound scholarship and exposition from superficiality and jargon. His lectures—whether formal in the classroom or casual 'under the campus oaks'—have kindled the minds of thousands of students. The keenness of his intellect, the warmth of his friendship, the courtliness of his address, and the innumerable striking eccentricities of his manner have united to endear him to a host of associates and admirers. Professor Simkins is a personage among Southern historians."[47] In 1954, twenty-seven years before Roland received the same honor, Simkins served as president of the Southern Historical Association.

During his day, historians considered Simkins a historical gadfly and Roland's intellectual lineage to him is an important aspect of the younger historian's professional life. Early in his career Simkins sympathized openly with African Americans, at one point preferring to serve as a field researcher for Carter G. Woodson's Association for the Study of Negro Life and History rather than teaching at a college for southern white women. "Being a white South Carolinian of Conservative traditions," he informed Woodson in 1924, "I am sorry to say that I do not believe that the negro of the South has a happy future. The white democracy, hating culture . . . owns everything and seems to cherish a furious aversion for the race which makes its bread. They are using a moderate but certain pressure to eliminate the race."[48]

Soon afterward Simkins emerged as a leading revisionist historian on Reconstruction, interpreting the post–Civil War decade as a period of much-needed reform for southerners black and white. "Historians of the South should adopt a more critical, creative, and tolerant attitude toward so important a period in the annals of their section as Reconstruction," Simkins wrote in 1939. "This will promote truth and scholarship in the austere sense of those terms."[49] Simkins's most important thesis, however, concerned the idea (which he shared with Wilbur J. Cash and others) that the American South was distinctive and complex—a contradictory amalgam of individualism and collective identity, violence and religious orthodoxy, radicalism and political conservatism, state socialism and laissez-faire capitalism, intemperance and social control, sectionalism and nationalism, and of what Roland termed "drawling speech, feminine women, and hot biscuits." Though Simkins became more conservative, more committed to southern "traditions" over time, he consistently espoused the idea of "the enduring South," a concept, Roland explained, that ran through his mentor's successful textbook like a leitmotif.[50] Well into the 1970s Simkins remained best known among scholars for his theme of "an everlasting South."[51] James S. Humphreys, Simkins's biographer, correctly identifies contradictions, what he terms "traditionalist and modernist aspects," in the historian's many writings. According to Humphreys, Simkins possessed both "a complex personality" and an "eclectic mindset."[52]

At the behest of Simkins's widow, the publisher Alfred A. Knopf asked Roland to revise, update, and serve as coauthor of the fourth edition of *A History of the South*. Roland welcomed and found flattering this assignment because he had first read his mentor's text while a graduate student at LSU. "It was," Roland recalled, "in my opinion, the most comprehensive, most insightful, and most brilliantly written single volume history ever produced on the region."[53] For its day, the 1947 edition of Simkins's work filled the need for a college history textbook. Simkins's text offered a bold reinterpretation, emphasizing the South as "a cultural province conscious of its identity," a self-concept of regional distinctiveness shaped largely by slavery and, later, by the perceived need by whites to maintain racial control over blacks. Simkins devoted roughly two-thirds of the book to the New South because previous historians generally had ignored the region's history since 1865.[54] Written before the advent of the 1950s civil rights movement, Simkins's original text retained the imprint of historian Ulrich Bonnell Phillips, whose *American Negro Slavery* (1918) and *Life and Labor in the Old South* (1929) had continued to map the terrain of southern historiography through the World War II period. To revise Simkins's classic text was a great honor, a daunting responsibility, and, in the immediate aftermath of the civil rights era, a political challenge.

The assignment was complicated, for example, because Simkins's original treatment of slavery went little beyond Phillips's earlier analyses. "In actual practice," Simkins wrote, "restrictions upon Negroes were not so severe as the laws provided." The bondsmen and women found ways to circumvent the rigid slave codes. "Southern forests were too deep and nights too dark to prevent the slaves' moving about." They learned to read and write, married, and maintained families. Having said this, Simkins admitted that "humane considerations . . . were almost entirely subordinated to the protection of property rights in slaves and of white society against possible Negro violence." Simkins's comments on the freedpeople during

Reconstruction harkened back to the interpretation espoused by his mentor, William A. Dunning. According to Simkins, the ex-slaves "demonstrated a distressing tendency to move to cities and to become vagrants lacking responsibility. . . . Unaccustomed to their obligations, the freedmen wandered from place to place, subject to disease and death, neglecting family ties and at times committing crimes." As for the New South, Simkins credited white churches with smoothing the way for gradual integration during World War II. He found "Negro leaders . . . bitter over denials to their race." Though the government did take steps to eliminate segregation in public accommodations and in the military, Simkins noted that blacks "belligerently demanded that the Federal government order a nation-wide abandonment of segregation." In his final analysis, Simkins identified little hope for black southerners who, surrounded by white racism, lacked initiative. In the decades since Reconstruction, he wrote: "it appears doubtful that in the years since Reconstruction Negro progress has outweighed Negro retrogression. As long as the black man is the victim of caste, the politician, capitalist, and labor leader will refuse to share any real power with him. Accordingly, he will be forced to remain a mere beggar for favors from a country not consciously unkind in its attitude. Perhaps the Negro will continue to improve materially, but he will need far more self-assertion and self-reliance before he attains the status of a respected American citizen."[55] Though these passages clearly reveal Simkins's "traditionalist and modernist aspects," contemporary reviewers generally glossed over his contradictions and applauded Simkins's *The South Old and New.* Frank L. Owsley and William M. Brewer, however, were exceptions; they criticized Simkins from decidedly different perspectives.

An expert on the Old South, especially its plain folk, and Confederate diplomacy, Owsley was one of the Vanderbilt Agrarians who took their stand against industrialization and the alleged "progress" of the 1930s. He defended his beloved region from what he considered the twin evils of Modernism and the Yankees' love of Negroes. Tearing into Simkins in the *Sewanee Review,* Owsley charged that his treatment of the antebellum South reflected "boredom and haste"; Simkins in fact knew "more about the Old South than most of the authorities" he cited. Beyond this, Owsley found infuriating and inexplicable Simkins's "carrying the torch for the colored man," a bias that diminished sections of the book that established him as "a brilliant and entertaining historian." Owsley found Simkins Janus-faced. "At times he seems to feel that race adjustment is something that Federal legislation—imposed on the South by non-Southerners—can accomplish; that folkways can be repealed by act of Congress. Yet at other times he is convinced that neither God nor man can change the Southern people. Like the Chinese, they absorb all foreign bodies, whether people, laws, or alien customs." Owsley found Simkins's southern distinctiveness thesis, "conceived in a mood of disgust and ill-conceived pride," almost schizophrenic.[56]

Writing in the *Journal of Negro History,* Brewer also noted Simkins's flashes of brilliance and liberalism, but assailed him for writing totally, like Phillips and historian Avery O. Craven, from the perspective of white southerners. "Negro crime and poverty appear," Brewer wrote, "in contrast to those of southern whites without consideration of the degraded slave background of enforced degeneracy and the peonage-servitude substitutes since nominal freedom." Brewer pitied Simkins because his surroundings and his circumstance blinded him from a critical view of the southern past. The "sectional bias and chauvinism" that Brewer identified in Simkins's text resulted because "the author is afraid to peer very far from behind the curtain of unreconstructed Southernism."[57]

Other historians found less to fault in *The South Old and New.* Thomas Perkins Abernethy considered it a "remarkable book for a Southerner to have written about the South," yet found the work "somewhat lacking in careful analysis and consistency of approach."[58] Duke University's Charles S. Sydnor noted facetiously that Simkins's obvious ignorance of the varieties of catfish "impeaches the author's competence to write about southern history." More seriously, Sydnor remarked that Simkins's treatment of black southerners might "irritate several groups: conservative southerners by his frank exposé of the hardships and handicaps imposed on the Negro by the southern white man; liberal reformers, because he has little faith in their doctrinaire theories; and many Negroes, because he holds the Negro partly to blame for his present plight."[59] A northern reviewer judged Simkins's book "a valuable synthesis, interpretative and timely." He added: "The romanticist will find it too realistic; the reformer will find it too historical."[60]

To Simkins's credit, he substantially revised the 1953 edition of his text, retitled *A History of the South.* The revision included five new chapters covering the South's formative history before 1820 and the division of the last chapter of the first edition into three chapters that brought the narrative up to 1952. Reviewer Robert S. Cotterill praised Simkins for "painstakingly" revising the entire previous text while retaining the thesis that "the region remains today psychologically unchanged, despite material changes."[61] Wendell Holmes Stephenson, dean of southern historiography of his day, observed that in his analyses of blacks—whether as slaves, freedpeople, or twentieth-century laborers—Simkins rejected modern scholarship, specifically Melville J. Herskovits's *The Myth of the Negro Past* (1941), that credited them with drawing upon their African background to resist what Marxists termed their "proletariat" status. Simkins, Stephenson explained, believed that the blacks had retrogressed after emancipation and that by nature they were an imitative people. "There could be no radical revolt because the black man inherited no distinctive culture of his own."[62] In his 1964 survey of southern history textbooks, Carl N. Degler noted that the third edition of Simkins's *A History of the South,* published a year before, included an additional chapter and that it remained an important and influential work for college classes. Degler pointed out, however, that by emphasizing that black southerners exhibited American, not African, characteristics, Simkins essentially undermined his own thesis of southern exceptionality.[63]

In agreeing to revise Simkins's classic text, Roland thus inherited an imposing job. Few tasks pose more pitfalls, emotionally and intellectually, than revising the work of one's *Doktorvater.* He had to rework his mentor's book, excising and adding text, reformulating it for college students not of the World War II era, but rather of the post–civil rights and Vietnam War eras. His revision of *A History of the South* ultimately established Roland as a leading historian of the South (historians already recognized his contributions as a Civil War scholar). But it no doubt was a challenging assignment.

Roland began believing that Simkins's "work deserves to be kept alive" and hoping his mentor "would applaud the independence of judgment that I have exercised." Roland prepared the new edition determined to bring the scholarship up to date and, especially, to expand the book's coverage up to the 1970s. Leaving several of Simkins's original chapters unchanged, Roland only emended the text "where recent scholarship has indicated a clear need."[64] A 1975 press release quoted Roland saying that he only made "some minor revision of the other [Simkins's original] material." The most significant changes, however, appeared in the final three chapters—"The Southern Economy since World War II," "The Civil Rights Conflict," and "Change and Continuity in the Recent South"—that Roland contributed.[65] During the previous quarter-century, Roland explained, the South had experienced dramatic changes. "In describing these, I have possessed the advantage of having witnessed the culmination of those new social, economic, and political forces that have shaped the era."[66]

Roland made clear that he subscribed fully to Simkins's argument that the South was distinctive—"a region with a mind and culture of its own"—what in 1947 his mentor had termed "a cultural province conscious of its identity." The South's special identity, Roland explained, endured Confederate defeat, Reconstruction, Populism, the Depression, World War II, and even the Civil Rights Revolution. Like Simkins, Roland believed that the South as an entity survived despite what he termed its "assimilation of national ideals and techniques." Roland's research upheld Simkins's comment in the 1963 edition of *A History of the South* that "the South is an attitude of mind and a way of behavior just as much as it is a territory." Though the South changed over time, in 1972 Roland insisted that the "old landmarks of sectional distinctiveness remained clearly visible; the changes themselves came about in a manner that was peculiar to the South." And the South's regional distinctiveness spawned strengths and weaknesses, Roland said. He revised Simkins's book with hopes that it would spark constructive criticism and self-reflection by northerners and southerners alike.[67]

Close examination of Simkins and Roland's edition suggests that Roland did indeed integrate modern scholarship into his revision, but, especially in the early chapters, that he retained much of what his mentor had originally written. In the examples from the 1947 edition quoted above (the chapters on slavery, Reconstruction, World War II, and the status of black southerners), with but two exceptions Roland reprinted Simkins's words verbatim. Whereas Simkins had written that blacks "*belligerently* demanded that the Federal government order a nation-wide abandonment of segregation," Roland deleted the inflammatory term "belligerently" and retained the remainder of the sentence. Roland totally revised Simkins's pessimistic conclusion about the status of blacks, replacing it with a more nuanced analysis informed by the writings of historians C. Vann Woodward and George B. Tindall and Swedish sociologist Gunnar Myrdal. Though Roland acknowledged improvements in twentieth-century race relations, he underscored the ubiquity of white racism and the power of the color line well into the post–World War II period. "Underneath the stagnant surface of Negro life and the calm surface of white life," he wrote, "ran powerful conflicting currents that were destined to bring the region and the nation to the most severe domestic crisis since the era of secession, Civil War, and Reconstruction."[68]

Unquestionably, Roland added new factual material, fresh bibliographical citations, and analyses that brought Simkins's 1947 text in line with 1970s-era scholarship. One chapter, "The Slave System," for example, exhibited considerable revision. Gone were Simkins's offensive references to the blacks' "genius for imitation" and their "jungle lore."[69] In his edition Roland included information gleaned from the works of such leading contemporary scholars as Kenneth M. Stampp, Carl N. Degler, Leon F. Litwack, Richard C. Wade, and Robert S. Starobin. Chapters on Reconstruction and the post-Reconstruction era featured the work of Stampp, as well as other influential historians, such as Woodward, V. Jacque Voegeli, Dewey W. Grantham, and William J. Cooper Jr. It is essential to remember that Roland revised Simkins's work more than three decades ago, long before the appearance of an avalanche of revisionist scholarship on virtually every aspect of southern history, especially on slavery and the Reconstruction era. Several years after his book appeared, when reviewing another southern history textbook, Roland commented on the methodological problems involved with integrating "new points of view . . . reflecting the experiences of modern America and the rest of the modern world" into an existing work.[70] The task posed more difficulties than the uninitiated might suppose.

The last three chapters of Simkins and Roland's text provide the most accurate barometer of how Roland merged his own research with Simkins's southern distinctiveness thesis. Assessing, for example, the condition of black southerners following World War II, Roland identified some progress during the war, but concluded that the South lagged behind the rest of the nation in moving toward equal rights for all Americans. This would change slowly, Roland explained, over the next twenty-three years, as black southerners asserted themselves in demanding equal rights. "By the summer of 1968," he wrote, "blacks throughout the land possessed and, to a degree were exercising, the right to vote, hold office, and serve on juries; and to attend schools with whites, occupy jobs formerly reserved for whites, own homes in customarily white neighborhoods, and be served in previously restricted stores, hotels, restaurants, and places of amusement." The rapid pace of social change in the post–World War II South, Roland observed, "would perhaps have astounded the most optimistic abolitionist of the pre–Civil War era."[71] It also set the South apart from the rest of the nation.

As in civil rights, the South also experienced "a veritable revolution" in virtually every aspect of its post–World War II social, economic, and political life. Based on his close reading of regional demographic and statistical data, Roland identified a marked economic upswing in the South from the 1950s onward. Economic incentives lured industry to the region, and southern industrial production rose from a volume of goods valued at more than $33 billion in 1947 to an amount valued at more than $79 billion in 1959. "This," Roland explained, "represented a rate of industrial growth higher than that of the nation as a whole." The region's number of textile mills, food processing plants, petrochemical and metals plants, and other enterprises soared in what formerly was the land of cotton. Thanks to the influx of national corporations and the development of a means to concentrate frozen citrus juices, Florida came to possess the second-fastest growing economy in the nation. Southern economic development also translated into southern urban growth. As Roland explained, the number of southern cities with populations of one hundred thousand or more increased from twenty-one in 1940 to thirty in 1950. "Once-stagnant places like Charleston, Wilmington, Alexandria, and Augusta nearly doubled in size and throbbed with trade and industry."[72]

Roland was quick to note, however, that despite the South's economic surge, "it still remained in 1970 a poor cousin of the affluent American society." In that year the differential between the region's and the nation's per capita income was $295 greater than it had been in 1948. Comparing average incomes of southerners and nonsoutherners led Roland, like President Franklin D. Roosevelt before him, to conclude that "the South continued to be the nation's 'Economic Problem No. 1.'" Economically, then, the South since 1945 "remained what it had persistently been throughout its history: the nation's economic enigma. It was a region of comparative want in the midst of immense natural riches: a land becoming and not a land become."[73] Roland's last chapters of A History of the South breathed life—fresh information and analysis—into Simkins's venerable but dated work.

Perhaps not surprisingly, Simkins and Roland's A History of the South, essentially a college textbook, received little critical engagement from scholars. In his 1978 article "Redeemers Reconsidered," historian James Tice Moore mentioned that compared to other historians, Roland presented "a more critical view" of C. Vann Woodward's revisionist argument that the "Redeemers" of the post-Reconstruction South were "new men"—former Whigs, not ex-Jacksonians, capitalists not agrarians.[74] Unlike Woodward,

Roland argued that the Bourbons "sought defensive formulas for sectional interests in the catchwords of an earlier American liberalism, and thus became proclaimers of the archaic virtues of Jeffersonian and Jacksonian political principles." Having made this point, however, Roland admitted that many Redeemers willingly surrendered "inherited tenets of agrarianism and states' rights in return for the South's participation in the great wave of industrial development that was bringing plenty to other sections of the United States."[75]

In her review of Simkins and Roland's text, Ball State University's Sharon E. Hannum credited Roland with significantly improving Simkins's earlier edition. Roland acknowledged slavery's central role in fashioning southern sectionalism, removed Simkins's antagonistic comments toward President Abraham Lincoln, and chronicled the region's vast economic and political metamorphoses up to 1970. "He notes elements of continuity as well as change and concludes that a distinctive South still exists," Hannum concluded. "Many changes in this edition," she added, "are revisions in tone. Roland is more detached from the subject than Simkins was; accounts of race relations are no longer defensive or edgy. Roland is more cautious than Simkins in his generalizations. Simkins clearly understood the whites' resistance to change; Roland appears to understand the blacks' aspirations for change."[76]

Monroe Lee Billington of New Mexico State University, who in 1975 had published *The Political South in the Twentieth Century*, found less value in Roland's revised work. "A comparison of this edition," Billington wrote, with Simkins's 1963 edition, "reveals that Roland made precious few changes. . . . He did not exorcise Simkins' book-long thread of implicit racism, so offensive to many people in an age of rising racial consciousness, and his revisions of the last three chapters . . . were relatively insignificant in relation to the entire Simkins volume." Billington sensed in fact that Roland "did not dovetail well with Simkins not only in regard to basic assumptions and frames of reference but also in subject matter and conclusions."[77]

Unlike Billington, Hannum praised the new edition of *A History of the South* for providing a more balanced account of the history of black southerners. "Roland has carefully excised the racist passages and revised Simkins's sometimes patronizing descriptions of blacks," she reported; but nevertheless "a few offensive passages remain." In Hannum's opinion, Roland should have qualified the statement that during Reconstruction "for

the first time in Southern history, rape was recognized as a real problem"
with "a note that so long as all the victims were black, white men did not
perceive that any 'problem' existed." She also found fault with Roland's
use (like Simkins's before him) of the term "southerner." For Roland, Hannum charged, "a 'southerner' is white, a 'southerner' is also male." She also
chided Roland for devoting "six short paragraphs" to the history of southern women. "What little is said consists of banalities about manners for the
white women and about miscegenation for the black ones."[78]

In 1973, when recommending Roland for a research fellowship, Bell
Irvin Wiley, the distinguished Emory University historian who in 1948 had
supervised Roland's master's thesis at LSU, appraised the fourth edition
of *A History of South*. Wiley, thoroughly conversant with Simkins's earlier
editions as well as Roland's latest edition of that text, explained: "The revision is vastly superior in every respect to the Simkins version. The research
is sounder, the interpretations are richer and more judicious and the style is
more graceful. The final chapters, covering the period since 1952, prepared
by Professor Roland, are models of excellence from standpoints of scholarship and style. They could stand alone as a separate book and a superior
one. Indeed, it is no exaggeration to state that Professor Roland's revisions
and additions transformed a good book into a superb book. Unquestionably the revised work is the very best book-length survey of the American
South."[79] Though Wiley, as a close friend and referee for Roland's grant
proposal, certainly could not qualify as an unbiased evaluator, his enthusiastic, unqualified praise nevertheless suggests how one of the most respected historians of the day judged Roland's edition of *A History of the South*.

Wiley also was prescient, because as Roland was completing his revisions of the Simkins volume, an editor encouraged him to expand the final
chapters of *A History of the South* into a separate volume on the history of
the recent South. Roland agreed to undertake this project and in 1975 the
University Press of Kentucky published his *The Improbable Era: The South
since World War II*. As Roland explained recently, "The central theme of
this work holds that though the post–World War II South experienced the
most striking changes of any region of the country, it nevertheless remained
the most distinctive of all the regions."[80] In making this argument, Roland
agreed with journalists Wilbur J. Cash and Edwin M. Yoder Jr. and the
southern sociologist John Shelton Reed that citizens of the region exhibited a special mentality—"a sense of uniqueness that . . . the native Southerner feels in his bones."[81] Roland elaborated upon this theme in his 1981

Southern Historical Association presidential address, "The Ever-Vanishing South," and continued to espouse the idea of southern distinctiveness throughout the 1980s.[82]

Freed from having to revise and "dovetail" his interpretations with Simkins's work, Roland's *The Improbable Era* clearly was *his* book, a masterful comprehensive and balanced interpretive synthesis. In an interview in 1975, Roland explained that he actually began collecting material for what became *The Improbable Era* in 1952. "Most of what I say . . . comes from my class notes, a constant update of my lectures."[83] Roland thus confronted the perils of writing "contemporary history"—what reviewer Bennett H. Wall described in 1978 as "the difficulty of writing the history of one's own time." Though he disagreed with some of Roland's emphases and some of his conclusions, Wall nevertheless proclaimed *The Improbable Era* "a fine book" and predicted that "the author bids fair to become the South's premier historian."[84]

In eleven terse and fast-paced chapters, Roland examined the South of the 1950s, 1960s, and 1970s, focusing on the interplay of cultural, economic, political, and social forces—all in 193 pages of text. Reflecting his deep interest in and mastery of a broad range of topics, he devoted individual chapters to southern religion, literature, education, and music and the visual arts. Roland drew heavily and imaginatively on census data, newspapers, popular magazines, personal interviews, and secondary accounts, again underscoring "the paradox of southern continuity in the midst of immense regional change." He explained that in their economy, racial accommodations, politics, education, religion, music, and the arts southerners had exhibited dramatic change since 1945. "Outwardly," Roland wrote, "they resembled closely their counterparts throughout the country. Yet there remained subtle inner distinctions," he said, that separated southerners from other Americans. "Southern courtesy, southern food, southern speech, southern athletic chauvinism, and southern sectional consciousness persisted in the midst of expanding tastes and altered mannerisms."[85]

Southern economic life offered but one example. Southerners, according to Roland, "as a whole enjoyed the greatest prosperity of the region's history" in the decades following World War II. Instrument manufacturing plants, food processing establishments, textile and clothing mills, aluminum and petrochemical plants—all symbolized the region's postwar industrial boom. Factory growth, and the concomitant expansion of southern cities, contributed to new levels of agricultural productivity, for example,

in tree farming, cattle growing, and poultry culture. Despite these "unde-
niable gains," Roland nevertheless again described the postwar South as
"a poor cousin of the affluent American society." In the 1970s the region
remained "relatively poor"—less industrialized than the nation's leading
industrial centers and "primarily extractive, producing minerals, fibers, and
fuel for the national industrial machine."[86]

Though blacks gained the least from the South's postwar economic
rise, according to Roland "they were the principal actors in a second Reconstruction" that revolutionized race relations and brought legal equality
to the region. Underscoring white southerners' commitment to racial supremacy, to keep the South what historian Ulrich Bonnell Phillips termed
"a white man's country," Roland chronicled desegregation's "painful progress through the network of measures designed to prevent or delay it."
While he noted the intransigence of white conservatives who employed
violent and legal means to postpone racial change, Roland celebrated liberals, black and white, northern and southern, who led the crusade for racial
justice. "The preeminent black heroes in the drama" of school desegregation, according to Roland, "were the handful of children who first actually attended the white schools. . . . Threatened, jeered, ostracized, and
abused, they demonstrated remarkable courage and persistence." While
many factors shaped regional politics into the 1970s, Roland insisted that
"race was still the most acute social, economic and political concern of the
South." Roland thus followed a historiographical genealogy from Phillips
to Simkins, underscoring the power of race in defining the region's distinctiveness. Even after the overturn of Jim Crow, Roland insisted, "the vast
majority of the members of the two races lived as far apart in the 1970s as
they had in the 1940s. Possibly they lived farther apart." "Paradoxically,"
Roland added, "where things had changed the most they seemed to have
changed the least."[87]

Roland's *The Improbable Era* also illuminated clearly the tension between continuity and change in post–World War II southern history. "Southern politics in 1960," he observed, "was remarkably similar to southern
politics in 1940." By the mid-1970s, however, the "Politics of Transition"
had shifted to "The Politics of Accommodation" as incipient Republicans
and black voters challenged "the two most distinguishing observable characteristics of the old politics—Democratic solidarity and white exclusive-
ness." Reacting negatively to the Democrats' commitment to civil rights,
in the 1960s white southerners gradually embraced Republican candidates

on the state and local level and President Richard M. Nixon's "southern strategy" that slowed the pace of school desegregation. As a reward, Roland explains, the South, always a bastion of patriotism, "was the most patient region . . . with the president's deliberate withdrawal from Vietnam, and . . . the region most reluctant to impute guilt to him in the Watergate and related scandals." Despite changes in the southern political landscape (South Carolina's J. Strom Thurmond switched from the Democrats to the Republicans, Alabama's George Wallace launched his American Independent party, and blacks won elected offices throughout the South), Roland insisted that the region retained its "traditional attitudes" and "political cohesiveness grounded upon ancient economic and social interests." For example, despite their marked political successes, in 1972 the number of blacks in elective office represented only 1.3 percent of all positions in the region.[88]

Most reviewers greeted Roland's *The Improbable Era* enthusiastically. For example, historian Richard S. Kirkendall of Indiana University described *The Improbable Era* as a "small book on a large subject," and Roland as "a historian and a very good one." Kirkendall noted that Roland "writes from a southern liberal's point of view"; he obviously welcomed the end of segregation and the rise of black voting "but does not wring his hands because the South is not totally new."[89] Political scientist William C. Havard of Virginia Tech praised Roland's thesis of southern homogeneity and also his analysis of "the recent convergence of South and North . . . as well as . . . the continuing points of divergence." Havard especially liked Roland's sense of balance—"in no case are the developments overplayed; appropriate qualifications are continuously made with respect to the contingent nature of all historic trends and the persistence of the bad as well as the good in the changing patterns of southern life."[90]

Writing in the *Greensboro Daily News,* historian Alexander R. Stoesen praised Roland's book as "one of the most comprehensive and lively studies of the recent South available." He noted the author's enthusiasm for the region and his optimism for its future. While Stoesen found disquieting Roland's remark that "the Benighted South appeared to be blending into a Benighted Nation," he predicted that such cynicism would appear "with recurring frequency in the future."[91] Historian Kenneth K. Bailey interpreted Roland differently; he judged *The Improbable Era* "manifestly not another epitaph for Dixie. Throughout," he wrote, "Roland emphasizes the stubborn survival of regional traits." Bailey went on to praise Roland's "sensible restraint and mollifying qualifications, never claiming to pronounce final verdicts, and without distorting the presentation overall."[92]

Other reviewers, however, identified weaknesses in *The Improbable Era*. An unidentified critic in the *Virginia Quarterly Review* noted that Roland's "point of view" was "rather to the left of the Southern center" and was "never vigorously asserted," and that *The Improbable Era* lacked "a unifying theme."[93] Political scientist Frances M. Wilhoit predicted that social scientists would fault *The Improbable Era* for emphasizing narrative description at the expense of interpretive analysis while historians would find Roland's documentation "woefully inadequate." Nonetheless, Wilhoit complimented Roland's work as the latest and best analysis of southern exceptionalism; "the very clarity and ease of style help conceal the density of thought and concentrated labor that went into it." He added, "if it is true that Roland's reach exceeds his grasp, one cannot fault him on his acute sensitivity to historical nuance and complexity or on his keen sense of historical irony."[94]

Writing in *The Cresset*, a publication of Valparaiso University, James E. Combs charged that in his analysis of southern distinctiveness and mythology Roland described more than he explained. "It would help us understand [President] Jimmy Carter and his region if these persistent myths had been explored in more detail." Though Robert A. Divine of the University of Texas praised Roland's sympathetic and insightful treatment of the South (*The Improbable Era* was "a calm, serene catalogue," he said), he nevertheless faulted the author's lack of passion for his subject. "In describing the racial turmoil of the 1960s, for example, Roland gives us all the facts but none of the emotions; he fails to convey the commitment of the Mississippi Freedom Workers in the summer of 1964, the national revulsion over Bull Conner's police dogs and Sheriff Clark's cattle prod, and the outcry provoked by Stokely Carmichael's advocacy of black power."[95] Another critic, David Buice of Louisiana Tech University, also criticized Roland for being too unimaginative, for not conveying "the agonies and the pathos which are so much part of the South's recent past." In Buice's opinion, *The Improbable Era* resembled "a slightly overcooked slice of beef—not really bad, but not what it could have been either."[96]

Perhaps the most devastating review of *The Improbable Era* appeared in the *Journal of Economic History*. There economic historian Gavin Wright of the University of Michigan challenged Roland's "enthusiastic account" of southern economic growth since World War II and dismissed his "equivocal clichés" regarding the persistence of southern traditions amid staggering change. Wright faulted Roland, "a professor of history," for failing to frame the postwar decades "in historical perspective. The book is instead one of several which have recently appeared, providing essentially journalistic accounts of the remarkable changes which have occurred in the South." Wright posited that Roland erred in looking for continuity in the South's recent economic past. Rather, it was "spurred by external shocks and demands, the most obvious of which are war, technological change and federal policies." According to Wright, following the war "well-educated northerners" traded places with "poor southern farmers," thereby changing the very basis of "a regional economy." Moreover, Wright explained, the South exhibited "a remarkable economic homogeneity, rooted in slavery and its aftermath." He lamented that the examination of southern economic questions had "passed from the economists to general thinkers like Charles P. Roland."[97]

Such scathing criticism had no impact on Roland's career, which soared in the 1970s and 1980s. Before his retirement from Kentucky in 1988, Roland became the self-described "architect"—conceptualizing, developing, refereeing, and editing—of a monograph series on the American South for the University Press of Kentucky. New Perspectives on the South, one of the first series of its kind, became a prototype for other series on the South published by university presses. Roland based it on Daniel Boorstin's University of Chicago History of American Civilization series, the successful series in which his *The Confederacy* had appeared in 1960.[98] Between 1979 and 1997, Roland published thirteen books in New Perspectives on the South. Several of the books received prizes; all gave Roland immense pride.[99] Long associated with the University Press of Kentucky, as a member of its press committee and as chair of its editorial board, Roland recently commented that he considered "the Press one of the most creative and distinguished departments of the entire state university system."[100]

Following completion of *The Improbable Era*, Roland immersed himself in another ambitious project in the field of southern history—a biography of Albert Benjamin "Happy" Chandler (1898–1991), the larger-than-life former Kentucky governor, U.S. senator, and national commissioner of baseball. Roland, only vaguely familiar with Chandler's life and contributions before moving to Kentucky, discovered that "it was virtually impossible to live in Kentucky without learning about him; he had been one of the most important, and one of the most controversial, political figures in the state's history, and possibly the most colorful of its citizens."[101] During the 1970s Chandler remained seemingly ubiquitous—in newspapers, on the radio, on television, on the sidelines at Kentucky football games, and, along with Roland, on Kentucky's athletics board. Roland, a close student of southern politics, race, and culture, seemingly was the natural biographer of Chandler, who conducted several controversial political campaigns, reformed Kentucky government, integrated Major League Baseball, and desegregated the commonwealth's public schools. In a 1980 speech at Transylvania University, Roland described Chandler as "the very incarnation of the Horatio Alger tradition in American life—the tradition of rising from rags to riches through pluck, proper conduct, hard work, and unflinching determination." Aware of his subject's "volcanic energy," power, and "flaming anger," Roland promised to investigate all aspects of Chandler's career, including accusations of impropriety.[102]

Roland spent almost two decades researching Chandler's life—studying his enormous collection of private manuscripts and interviewing not only Chandler, but also his many friends and enemies, including Alabama governor George Wallace and Kentucky's most successful former football coach, Paul "Bear" Bryant. Though Roland planned to devote his retirement years to the Chandler project, other opportunities (teaching at Carlisle Barracks and West Point) and other projects (a narrative history of the Civil War) took precedence. In 1991, after working on the Chandler project for many years, and after having published *An American Iliad: The Story of the Civil War* (1991), he informed a journalist that he was "cranked up" to finish his book. While he admitted to having had "some burn out" on the book over the previous five to six years, Roland remarked that Chandler's death in June 1991 provided access to important documents and interviews hitherto unavailable to researchers. Even so, Roland refused to commit to a completion date for the book. "People think I have a manuscript in the deep freeze," he quipped. "I don't. It's still a long way off."[103] Once he began drafting the book, however, Roland realized that the task would require yet more research and, after completing roughly 20 percent of the manuscript, he abandoned the work. "But this came slowly and painfully," Roland recalled. "I clearly realized that I was suffering a severe case of burn-out. Finally, and reluctantly, I decided to turn the project over to someone else, someone who possessed the energy to finish it." Roland selected Thomas H. Appleton Jr., one of his top former doctoral students at Kentucky, "to complete the biography as a collaborative work in his name and mine."[104]

During his alleged "retirement," Roland still had energy enough to lecture nationally and internationally and to complete several books. In the mid-1970s, upon receiving an invitation to speak at a military history conference at the University of Alabama on GI Joe, the proverbial common soldier of World War II, Roland began redirecting his longstanding interest in military history into an autobiographical mode. The speaking engagement at Alabama required Roland to relive and rethink his experiences as a combat officer during the 1940s, framed within more than three decades' worth of historical research and reflection on the meaning of life. In 1993, for example, when commenting on the work of another author, Roland mused over his experiences as an infantryman at war—"the doubts, fears, and struggles within the soul as well as the flashes of self-fulfillment, exhilaration, and valor."[105] Much to his surprise, Roland's "GI Charlie" talk (as it is known affectionately by his former doctoral students) became an instant hit. Over the years Roland presented the speech numerous times, including at such venues as the Army War College, the U.S. Military Academy, the Command and General Staff College, at many colleges and universities, and at a conference held at the Roosevelt Institute at Middelburg, The Netherlands.[106]

Roland believed that the opportunity to speak on his own history as "GI Charlie" exerted "a powerful effect on my subsequent career." His visiting appointments at the Army War College at Carlisle Barracks and at the U.S. Military Academy immersed Roland in worldwide strategic issues and forced him to retool in the field of general military history. Roland recalled that the West Point cadets "appeared to appreciate particularly my ability to draw upon my own war experiences for analogies to the events they were reading about." He left West Point convinced that students in general unwisely rejected the study of military history. "It's being very shortsighted not to consider the history of war," Roland said in an interview. "Students can profit by studying it as a whole—not just strategy and tactics, but also the whole political, economic and social picture."[107]

Roland's teaching stints at Carlisle Barracks and West Point signaled not only a revival of his interest in military history, but also his shift from writing about the South and his return to working on the Civil War. Roland in fact taught his first course on the Civil War during the 1981–1982 academic year at Carlisle Barracks, repeating that course upon returning to Kentucky and later at West Point. Gradually his class lecture notes began to take the shape of a book manuscript. "I think it was sitting inside me and I didn't recognize it," Roland recalled in 1990. "It represents, more than

anything else I've done, a whole career of reading and reflecting on the
Civil War."[108]

By the late 1980s he began writing what became a ninety thousand-
word "concise" history of the Civil War for college students and general
readers. Roland's *An American Iliad: The Story of the Civil War* appeared
in 1991, published simultaneously by McGraw-Hill (paperback; second
edition, 2002) and the University Press of Kentucky (hardback; second
edition, 2004). Aware that this assignment would require tight exposition, Roland also realized that there was an overabundance of Civil War
titles—that since the war had ended in 1865 more than a book a day had
been written about that conflict.[109] And, as Roland had explained in 1974,
towering above all Civil War textbooks was a hard-to-replace classic, *The
Civil War and Reconstruction* (1961, 1969) by James G. Randall and David
Donald.[110] "I will not be giving any factual information that somebody at
some time hasn't already said," Roland informed a reporter in 1988. "It's a
matter of focus and emphasis, and what I'd call interpretive spin."[111]

One feature of Roland's "interpretive spin" was his argument that in
terms of heroism and sacrifice, a direct parallel exists between the American Civil War and the famous Greco-Trojan war of between 1300 and 1200
B.C. recorded in Homer's epic poem *The Iliad.* Another "interpretive spin"
was Roland's framing the war's tactics and strategy within the context of
the influential writings of nineteenth-century military theorists Antoine-
Henri Jomini and Karl von Clausewitz. In an interview in 1991, Roland
explained that in *An American Iliad* he sought to provide a compact, ac-
cessible, up-to-date interpretive synthesis, with military history at its core.
"My book," he explained, "is based on a lifetime of reading, reflection, and
research, and I put into it what seemed to me the truth about the Civil War.
But I am perfectly aware that there will be people who will dispute my
conclusions and there will be historians who will demonstrate that what I
have written is subject to different interpretations."[112]

Roland divided the second edition of his 266-page undocumented
work into sixteen chapters. Whereas most historians get entangled in the
complex thicket of events leading up to the war, Roland treated the period
from the Compromise of 1850 through the firing upon Fort Sumter in three
chapters—in an amazingly concise forty-two pages. Commenting on the
quick pace of his early chapters, a reviewer of the first edition quipped:
"Roland clearly was eager to get the war underway."[113]

Whether or not this was the case, Roland's book is a model of terse prose. Despite *An American Iliad*'s emphasis on military history, Roland nevertheless balanced the remaining thirteen chapters almost equally among treatments of military campaigns, the respective home fronts, diplomacy, and political and institutional history, together with an interpretive conclusion and a short afterword. The author crafted *An American Iliad* as a summary of "modern scholarship," and though he repeatedly mentioned other scholars' arguments and "schools" of opinion among historians, Roland rendered his own conclusions directly and concisely. "The story of the Civil War," Roland insisted, "is the epic story of the American people. It is their Iliad." Slavery, in the author's opinion, drew "the most persistent and ominous stress line" between North and South. The South's racially defined labor system "shaped and contributed to all other sources of tension and added a burning moral and emotional element of its own."[114]

As in *The Improbable Era,* in *An American Iliad* Roland exhibited his talent in drawing precise word portraits, for selecting telling anecdotes, and in fashioning succinct phrases. These exhibited the skills of a polished writer, not just those of an accomplished historian.

For example, in Roland's opinion, President Abraham Lincoln's contemporaries portrayed him "as a gangling, rustic Ichabod of a man who cultivated popularity among the masses with his salty comments and anecdotes." Lincoln's rival, President Jefferson Davis, "was tall, erect, and slender, his bearing unmistakably military; though his features were too sharp to be called truly handsome, they were distinguished; southerners considered them genteel." Davis's often-absent second-in-command, Vice President Alexander Stephens, "was a man of diminutive and sickly body and wizened countenance, but with a keen and comprehensive mind." Roland characterized Confederate general Robert E. Lee as "the incarnation of the cavalier tradition so dear to the southern heart." In addition to his distinguished lineage, his outstanding education, and his legendary prewar military record, Lee, according to Roland, was "a strikingly handsome man of Jovelike bearing." When, in 1876, President Ulysses S. Grant ordered South Carolina's paramilitary Rifle Clubs to disband, they obliged. "But," Roland explained, "they at once reappeared under such innocent names as the First Baptist Sewing Circle, the Hampton and Tilden Musical Club, or the Allendale Mounted Baseball Team which counted 150 players, all heavily armed."[115]

As for "focus and emphasis," Roland traversed a traditional historiographical path, from secession, through the Confederacy's rise and fall, and into Presidential and Radical Reconstruction. Along the way Roland put his own footprint on the interpretation of the war. It "forever changed the course of American history, and thereby of world history," he said.[116]

In terms of the importance of Fort Sumter, Roland advanced a variant of historian Charles W. Ramsdell's famous thesis—that Lincoln and Davis each sought to manipulate the other into firing the war's first shot. Roland also maintained that once the war began, "intangibles of war, such as the nature of the war aims, the spirit of the population and the soldiers, and the boldness, originality, skill and inspirational qualities of the military and civilian leaders," worked to the South's advantage and tempered the North's apparent superiority in manpower and war materiel. Northern and southern commanders manifested both Jomini's "rational" and Clausewitz's "friction" theories of war and, according to Roland, the conflict itself "developed a body of tactical and strategic precepts of its own." As for Lee's importance to the South, Roland hinted that perhaps the general might have better served the Confederacy as a military advisor in Richmond than as head of the Army of Northern Virginia. In February 1865, as the end of the war neared, the Confederate congress (enthusiastically) and Davis (with much reluctance) appointed Lee general in chief. According to Roland, Davis had little reason to worry. "Lee was a reluctant generalissimo." He wanted no part of a dictatorship.[117]

Roland defended Lincoln from criticism both from his contemporaries and from later historians. In his opinion, as leader of a nation torn asunder by civil war the president had few constitutional precedents to follow; circumstances thus "necessitated both authoritarian decisions and delicate compromises." Davis also frequently had to interpret and shape constitutional questions in response to crises. In the Confederacy, Roland said, states' rights ideology became an albatross; it "ran counter to that of southern national control and worked against the concentration of Confederate military resources." Though the new central southern government "lacked the time and opportunity to develop formal political parties," politics nonetheless emerged—"politics in a form that may have been more destructive of unity and morale than a presidential election and partisan politics would have been." Agreeing with historian Frank L. Owsley, Roland concluded that the Confederates' "King Cotton diplomacy" proved little more than "a fatal miscalculation." The Yankees ultimately outmaneuvered the Rebels both at home and abroad, mobilizing better leadership, a more integrated national policy, and superior military strategy. The South succumbed, Roland explained, because it "failed to generate the necessary skill, unity, and will. Union victory was the result of a superiority in the sum of its war-making capacity, including numerical, material, and nonmaterial resources."[118]

In his analysis of Confederate military defeat, Roland shunned the "historical presentism" some historians employed that glibly defined the victorious North as strategically "modern" and the defeated South as strategically "old-fashioned." In retrospect, he wrote, adopting a "western concentration" might appear as a plausible alternative to Confederate strategy. In fact, however, the South's multiple disadvantages—in numbers of men and war materials and in its political, economic, and social structure—prevented the Confederacy from fighting a prolonged conventional war against the North, "western concentration" or not. Nor would the abandoning of its cities and the implementing of guerrilla warfare have yielded better results for the Confederates, Roland insisted. He doubted "that after four years of voluminous bloodshed and property destruction, and decisive defeat in the field, the majority of southern people would have been willing to undertake an endless guerrilla war." Prolonged irregular warfare "would have provoked an indefinitely extended federal military occupation accompanied by martial law." Roland speculated that the aftermath of guerrilla warfare "would have resulted in wholesale executions and imprisonments, civil strife between southern classes and factions, widespread confiscation and redistribution of property, and arming of the freedmen to bolster the counterforce and constabulary." In Roland's opinion, not only would guerrilla warfare have failed militarily in achieving southern independence, but it would have obliterated "the southern way of life."[119]

Though a reviewer in New England wondered why Roland would publish "yet another in a seemingly endless series of Civil War books," most critics greeted *An American Iliad* warmly, understanding that Americans apparently had an insatiable appetite for books on the war.[120] In 2005, historian Mark Grimsley of Ohio State University remarked that Roland's interpretation of the Civil War as America's epic moment had increasingly become the mainstream interpretation of America's bloody internecine conflict.[121] As the British historian Susan-Mary Grant wrote, "Roland is not the only historian [of the American Civil War] to see himself as a modern-day Homer."[122]

As Roland had predicted, however, scholars and partisans often differed over his book's merits. *The Rebel Rouser,* the newsletter of a Dallas,

Texas, Sons of Confederate Veterans camp, observed that Roland's opening chapter "evidences historic myopia by obsession with slavery as THE
cause of the War."[123] Ironically, another critic, historian Joseph Logsdon of
the University of New Orleans, charged that Roland sided with "the earlier
revisionist school" of Civil War historians that "avoids any discussion of
the dynamics of the American slave order." Logsdon noted that Roland,
"by cleverly sidestepping the initiation of the war by aggressive proslavery
leaders . . . avoids the need to focus on the workings of the southern slave
society."[124] And in his glowing review in the *Richmond News Leader,* Virginia Tech historian James I. Robertson Jr. "hoped that *An American Iliad*
will right some of the wrongs of several presentations of late."[125]

The majority of historians agreed with Gary W. Gallagher and Emory
M. Thomas, who argued, respectively, that *An American Iliad* was "the best
short introduction to the war" and "the best brief history of the United States
and the Confederate States at war."[126] Another leading historian, Frank E.
Vandiver of Texas A&M University, commented that "years of study give
Roland a maturity of judgment rare among Civil War students." He complimented the breadth and depth of his slim book. "Art, science, and literature
have their place in Roland's narrative, as do geography, philosophy, even
basic psychology." According to Vandiver, though *An American Iliad* was a
textbook, it included original arguments based on deep research. "Not large,
this is nonetheless a big book because of its new interpretations and refreshing style—it ranks as an important contribution to Civil War studies."[127]

Other historians, however, offered fainter praise in their evaluations of
Roland's book. In *Civil War News,* Richard A. Sauers identified a number
of factual mistakes in the book.[128] Historian Max R. Williams charged that
in his textbook Roland perpetuated the erroneous statement first made by
Frank L. Owsley in 1925 that North Carolina governor Zebulon B. Vance
had hoarded ninety-two thousand uniforms in the state's warehouses.[129] In
his detailed review of the second edition of *An American Iliad,* Stephen
S. Michot of Nicholls State University called Roland's coverage of Native Americans in the Civil War "nonexistent," and he listed several in-
accuracies—from an incorrect rendering of Confederate deployments in
Roland's map of Shiloh, to the author's erroneous analysis of Grant's assault on Lee's flank at Second Cold Harbor. Michot also described what he
termed "an in-balance" in Roland's battle coverage. In Michot's opinion,
the Trans-Mississippi Confederacy received scant and, in places, incorrect
attention.[130]

Earl J. Hess of Lincoln Memorial University noted interpretive errors in *An American Iliad* that resulted, he observed, from Roland's "failure to keep abreast of some of the important new interpretations of the war." Hess considered most serious "Roland's failure to discuss the reasons for fighting." Hess charged that Roland relied on Bell I. Wiley's early scholarship and ignored recent works that probed the ideology of Civil War soldiers. "Roland," according to Hess, "concentrates on telling what happened, not why it happened. There is no substantive discussion of popular thought about the issues of the war, no indication of the people's justification for its prosecution, and of their attitudes toward its results." Hess also identified a bias toward Robert E. Lee over Ulysses S. Grant in Roland's account. "Grant partisans (myself included)," he said, "will fume."[131]

As Hess remarked correctly in his review of *An American Iliad,* Roland did indeed hold Lee "as an army commander . . . without superior, possibly without peer."[132] He first exhibited his interest in and high regard for the Confederate general three decades earlier, in his 1961 lecture at Northwestern. When, in the mid-1990s, Stackpole Books asked Roland to write a short interpretive book on Lee, he jumped at the chance. The historian explained recently that he published his *Reflections on Lee: A Historian's Assessment* (1995) as a response to books published in the 1970s and 1980s that he believed to be "harshly critical of Lee." Roland explained: "They accused him of being so enamored of Virginia or so myopic that he was unable to see the Civil War as a whole; or that he was so wedded to Napoleonic military concepts that he was unable to adjust his strategy and tactical thinking to the age in which he fought: that he employed eighteenth-century tactics against nineteenth-century technology. I considered these criticisms to be tendentious and unbalanced, using speculative arguments to sustain their points of view."

In his brief, 130-page, undocumented book Roland aimed his historiographical ire at two historians in particular—Thomas L. Connelly, author of *The Marble Man: Robert E. Lee and His Image in American Society* (1977), and Alan T. Nolan, whose *Lee Considered: General Robert E. Lee and Civil War History* appeared in 1991. In his book's bibliographical essay Roland explained that he found Connelly's "psychobiographical" method and Nolan's "presentist judgments and prosecutorial methods" unpersuasive. Roland, who insisted that he did not "whitewash Lee's mistakes," nonetheless argued that the general "accomplished as much as, if not more than, anyone else could have done with the limited resources at his command; that he was a great general and a great human being, and that these two qualities were mutually reinforcing."[133]

Roland devoted the first eighty pages of *Reflections on Lee* to surveying the Virginian's life—from his birth in 1807 at Stratford on the Potomac River to his surrender in 1865 of the Army of Northern Virginia at Appomattox Court House. Laudatory of Lee as a Christian soldier and the beau ideal of the chivalrous southern gentleman, he characterized the general as "America's great tragic hero, in the classical use of the term, doomed by a fatal flaw in one of his cardinal virtues, loyalty." Roland, influenced by historian C. Vann Woodward's famous essay "The Search for Southern Identity," described Lee as "a marvelously gifted soldier and an ardently devoted patriot, yet he defended the most unacceptable of American causes, secession and slavery, and he suffered the most un-American of experiences, defeat."[134]

Though appreciative of Lee as a man and warrior, Roland nonetheless recognized that the general was a mere mortal; at times he exhibited indecision and poor judgment and erred. Commanding Confederate forces in western Virginia in the fall of 1861, he committed two mistakes, Roland explained. "In his unwillingness to issue peremptory orders to his subordinates or to remove them when they hesitated in obeying his instructions, he lost promising opportunities for striking the Federals an effective blow. In prematurely assuming the defensive in the Kanawha Valley, he lost a chance of defeating [General William S.] Rosecrans there." Lee returned to Richmond in late October as less than a conquering hero. His critics dubbed him "Granny" Lee.[135]

Roland also took Lee to task in his performance as commander of Confederate forces during the South's invasion of Pennsylvania in July 1863. While he noted that Lee was sick and probably was suffering from exhaustion at the battle of Gettysburg, Roland nevertheless held the general responsible for Confederate defeat in this pivotal battle. "Lee's frontal assaults at Gettysburg," Roland charged, "violated his own tactical doctrine, which he had once written explicitly to [General Thomas J. "Stonewall"] Jackson, instructing him to avoid attacks against an enemy in position, and instead to conserve his troops by turning the enemy out of position." For all his admiration of the venerable Confederate general, Roland wrote that at Gettysburg he "unquestionably overestimated the ability of flesh and blood to prevail over fire and iron." Having sketched Lee's military career, Roland next devoted thirty-five pages of *Reflections on Lee* to a tightly argued "Evaluation" of his overall "generalship."[136]

Aware that the mere questioning of Lee's military prowess often set off fireworks among professional historians and Civil War enthusiasts alike, Roland evaluated the topic evenly, dispassionately, and with characteristic restraint. When the smoke of battle cleared, however, it was obvious that Roland was not among what he later termed "the Lee disparagers."[137]

He found little merit, for example, in the British general J. F. C. Fuller's 1933 criticisms that Lee failed logistically (in supplying his army) and strategically (in failing to concentrate his forces temporarily in the vicinity of Chattanooga). Responding to the first point, Roland said that Fuller "offered no convincing explanation of what Lee . . . could have done to remedy the inadequacy of the southern commissary and transportation systems." Roland then identified a host of correctives to Fuller's second argument. Concentration, he explained, "would have required surrendering indefinitely to the enemy the entire upper South and the Atlantic coastal states, a proposition that would have been outrageous to President Davis and to the southern population in general. An equivalent strategy today would call for the surrender of everything in the United States above the Potomac, Ohio, and Missouri Rivers and west of the Rocky Mountains. Fuller's plan ignored the political, economic, social, and psychological realities of southern life. Lee, on the other hand, insightfully adapted his strategy to those very factors." Roland conceded that "as a sand-table exercise in strategy, Fuller's plan may have been sound," but it failed to take into consideration the red-clay realities of the Confederate experience.[138]

In his "Evaluation" Roland next dissected arguments espoused by what he obliquely termed "some recent students," apparently unwilling to mention Connelly, Nolan, or other contemporary historians by name and to cite specific references to their works. Instead Roland explained in general terms that Lee's modern critics reproached him as too wedded to past military doctrine, as incapable of adapting to new modes of warfare, as too prone to throw Confederate armies into pitched battles, as ignorant of the relationship between military campaigns and civilian affairs, as slack in maintaining discipline, as too likely to issue discretionary orders instead of peremptory commands, and as failing to develop a modern staff system.[139]

Roland responded, admitting that, yes, in some ways Lee was "old-fashioned." During his invasion of Pennsylvania, for example, he ordered his men not to loot or to molest private property. But Roland insisted that had Lee adopted a strategy predicated on "the tactical defensive," it "would have been a recipe for certain defeat. It would have surrendered the initia-

tive to the enemy, permitting him to concentrate his vastly superior numbers against Lee and to select the place and time of battle." As in his *An
American Iliad,* in *Reflections on Lee* Roland also dismissed arguments
that Lee should have abandoned conventional warfare and adopted guerrilla tactics. Such a plan, Roland wrote, "would have visited indescribable
physical, political, economic, and social havoc upon a South that already
lay crushed by the war of armies." Regarding Lee's use of discretionary
orders, Roland concluded that while this "mode of command caused Lee
to suffer some defeats, it gained him even more victories." And for Lee's
alleged failure to employ a modern staff system, Roland commented that "a
stronger staff would have alleviated Lee's burden of communications, but
that it would have enhanced the effectiveness of his generalship cannot be
demonstrated." In fact, Roland added, "the relative smallness of Lee's army
is what made his command methods work so well so often. He ought not be
faulted for failing to invent something that he did not need."[140]

On balance, Roland considered Lee's "greatest shortcoming" not his
generalship, but rather his "lack of an implacable revolutionary purpose."
To have staged a coup d'état against Jefferson Davis's administration would
have violated Lee's character, his sense of duty, honor, and responsibility.
"He was too American to play Napoleon," Roland argued. Rather than become a "generalissimo," Lee instead "remained deferential, possibly excessively so, to Davis." Lee's personal qualities—qualities that might have
enabled him to become a dictator—made him loved by his men and idol-
ized by the southern people. Instead of leading a counterrevolution, Lee
followed the orders of his constitutional commander in chief and fought
until the cause was indeed lost. Roland exonerated Lee of criticisms that
he senselessly sacrificed too many Confederate lives. "He was obliged to
fight as long as the civil authorities chose to do so, and as long as his army
had the capacity to do so. It possessed this capacity until just before the
end."[141]

Roland's *Reflections on Lee* found an appreciative but not uncritical
audience. On the one hand, historian Daniel E. Sutherland of the University of Arkansas praised Roland for providing an "evaluation that pulls no
punches and ignores no controversy."[142] On the other hand, in a collection
of essays on Lee's generalship published in 2004, Peter S. Carmichael cat-
egorized Roland's book as among those "excessively laudatory treatments
of Lee published in the last fifteen years and containing almost no original
research."[143]

Historian Steven E. Woodworth took the middle ground, noting that Roland offered "the mature judgment of a very senior and very highly respected Civil War historian." While he considered Roland's biographical sketch of Lee among the very best, Woodworth nevertheless judged Roland's "Evaluation" necessarily controversial. "Many will disagree with some of the conclusions offered." If indeed the lawyer Alan T. Nolan, to use Roland's terms, employed "prosecutorial methods to indict Lee's character and motives," Woodworth wrote, "then Roland himself is surely counsel for the defense."[144]

Brian S. Wills of Clinch Valley College recognized the "formidable task" that Roland assumed in tackling Lee historiography, noting that the historian's early work on the Confederacy's western theater assisted him in providing a balanced assessment. "His is a quiet reassessment," Wills explained, "devoid of venom or vitriol, even when he clearly disagrees with another writer's conclusions." But Wills considered *Reflections on Lee* "somewhat enigmatic," clearly "sympathetic to his subject, but strangely apologetic in placing the general in the context of his times, particularly in the latter's expressions on race." It was to Lee's credit, Wills observed, that he altered his views regarding African Americans as the war ended and Reconstruction ensued. Yet Roland "seems troubled that Lee's beliefs about race leave the general open to modern criticism." Roland, according to Wills, also failed to examine critical aspects of Lee's biography, including the general's relationship with his father, Henry "Light Horse Harry" Lee. After digesting Roland's book, Wills admitted savoring it more as "hors d'oeuvre than main course."[145]

Historian Michael C. C. Adams of Northern Kentucky University found Roland's book less appetizing. In 2003 Adams cited Roland's *Reflections on Lee* as an example of the tendency to interpret Lee as "a model American"—that Lee's "views were typical of the time." In Adams's opinion, "to be a continuing American hero, we should ask whether his views were the best, the most enlightened, that were in circulation in his era." In contrast to Lee, Adams said, Abraham Lincoln considered slavery an evil and (unlike Lee) worked to prevent its extension into the federal territories. "It is worth remarking that some of those who cannot judge Lee harshly as a man of his time manage to come down pretty hard on John Brown, who was also acting out ideas in common currency and who had the support of men of intellectual stature like Henry David Thoreau and Thomas Wentworth Higginson." Adams also challenged Roland's interpretation of Lee as a "tragic figure," yet one whose views nonetheless were legitimate. "One cannot have it both ways," Adams said. "More over, the tragic hero in person must recognize before dying that fatal flaws have led to doom. Unfortunately, Lee never seems to have expressed regret either for his views on slavery or for his decision to leave the Union and fight for the Confederacy after a lifetime in federal blue."[146]

In 2003, after decades of debating Lee's generalship, Roland refused to alter his opinion of the man. "Obviously," he informed an interviewer, "Lee is a great favorite of mine." But Roland only reluctantly compared the Virginian to other generals, especially to Grant. "These men fought under such vastly different circumstances, not just in numbers, but also in all sorts of supplies and armaments, and also even in the nature of their mission," Roland explained. Upon reflection, Roland admitted that he believed Lee to have been superior to Union general John Pope at the battle of Second Manassas and to Union general Joseph Hooker at Chancellorsville. At times, Roland continued, Lee "out-generaled" Grant; at other times Grant "out-generaled" Lee. "To bring it down to modern parlance . . . I guess if you could set these two men out on an absolutely level playing field . . . and you had them run through the exercise ten times, I'd put my money on Lee to win more times than he lost."[147]

Readers of Charles P. Roland's eighteen articles, chapters, essays, and speeches gathered in this anthology will be "winners" because they will be treated to a sampling of the work of one of America's foremost historians and premier historical stylists. The contributions appear in four sections. The editor has arranged Roland's essays and speeches topically. Aside from silently correcting typographical errors and editorial inconsistencies, the editor presents Roland's pieces virtually as he wrote them. The author's use of personal pronouns and his omission of documentation remain in several of the speeches.

Part One offers glimpses of Roland's autobiography, including two selections from *My Odyssey through History* and "A Citizen Soldier Recalls World War II," a version of his "GI Charlie" speech.[148] Collectively, Roland's first-person reflections underscore his identification with the traditional values of the South, his love for family, friends, teachers, colleagues, and students, and his patriotism. Above all, the autobiographical pieces illustrate Roland's modesty and his belief in contingency and serendipity—that his many opportunities and successes resulted from accident and chance, not from predetermination or hard work.[149]

To paraphrase President Abraham Lincoln's famous remark to a fellow Kentuckian, in his autobiographical reflections, Roland claims not to have controlled events but rather that events have controlled him.[150] The historian Michael J. Birkner has likened Roland's self-effacing autobiography to that of Forrest Gump, Winston Groom's 1985 fictional character. According to Birkner, "think of Forrest Gump with a high IQ."[151] Readers will find Roland's recollections of his youth, education, and courtships to be charming; his experiences as a combat infantryman in World War II are riveting. Few academic historians possess Roland's background as a civilian soldier caught in the cross fire of war. Yet readers will join historian Robert F. Durden in regretting that Roland paid "short shrift to his distinguished record in southern and especially, Civil War history and to his teaching career, first at Tulane and then at the University of Kentucky."[152]

Part Two presents five of Roland's contributions on the causes of the Civil War and the war itself. In the previously unpublished "Why the War Came" (a lecture first presented at the Deep Delta Civil War Symposium at Southeastern Louisiana University), Roland cautioned against the role of "presentism" in historical analysis and took a stand against what he termed "the 'political correctness' lobby" that dictated that slavery be interpreted as *the* cause of the Civil War. Mindful of slavery's powerful role in shaping national politics before 1860, Roland argues that "slavery did not of itself cause the Civil War." Rather, the election of Lincoln in 1860 signaled to white southerners that a "change of attitude toward the institution [of slavery] and toward the relationship between the nation and states" had occurred. They feared that the Republicans would deny Congress, territorial legislatures, or the U.S. Supreme Court the authority to legalize slavery in federal territories. "This denial," Roland explains, "coupled with Lincoln's rejection of any compromise on the issue, convinced the citizens of the Deep South that their only protection lay in secession, a decision that brought the war."[153]

In "Louisiana and Secession" and "The Resort to Arms" Roland emphasizes the revolutionary nature of the breakup of the Union and the centrifugal force secession unleashed. "The black funnel of war loomed on the horizon," he writes. The previously unpublished "A Slaveowner's Defense of Slavery" (first presented at a symposium on secession sponsored by Kentucky's Campbellsville University) is a significant departure for Roland, written in an avant-garde genre that literary scholars term "creative nonfiction." The text and characters are imaginary, but "the argument and outlook are not," Roland says, "they have been gleaned by me from thousands of letters and diary entries of the time."

In his January 1861 letter to his friend Frederick Darcy of Illinois, the fictional character Frank Lawrence of Louisiana regrets that "secession is now inevitable." Lincoln's election, on a platform that "supports northern interests only," and "the Republican rejection of all efforts of the United States Senate to effect a new political compromise . . . have cut the ground from under the unionists of Louisiana and the other southern states." "Though I continue to hope for an amicable settlement of the issue," Lawrence notes, "I now hope against hope. The die seems fatally cast." "Louisiana Sugar Planters and the Civil War" summarizes the bitter fruit of secession, civil war, and humiliating defeat in the sugar parishes of Frank Lawrence's state. "From the mood of optimism and exultation that marked the days of faraway war," Roland writes, "they sank into despair as the conflict enveloped their plantations and their lives."

Part Three includes five essays on one of Roland's favorite subjects—Civil War leadership. One, "The Generalship of Robert E. Lee," was Roland's talk at the 1961 Northwestern University symposium. The remaining four articles appear in print here for the first time. In "Albert Sidney Johnston and the Defense of the Confederate West" (first presented at a seminar sponsored by the Civil War Education Association in Corinth, Mississippi) Roland concludes that the general's "electric presence at the front added a potent weapon to the Confederate attack." Had Johnston survived the battle of Shiloh, the author predicts, "he would have been an incalculable asset to the Confederacy." In "Robert E. Lee and the Leadership of Character" (first presented at a conference at the Virginia Military Institute) Roland argues that Lee's character was an even more important "source of his greatness" than his intellect. He identifies two sources of this trait—"the cult of Virginia gentility in which he was reared, and the profound religious faith he acquired from his mother."

Roland's "Alan Nolan Considered: or Lee in Caricature" provides the detail and exhibits a stridently critical tone absent from the author's *Reflections on Lee*. Whereas in that book Roland relegated mention of Nolan and his *Lee Considered: General Robert E. Lee and Civil War History* to his "Selected Readings," in this essay he engages fully with and rebuts Nolan's disparagement of Lee's military strategy. After responding to Nolan's thesis (that in order to protect the lives of his soldiers, Lee should have adopted a strategy of fighting only on the tactical defensive), Roland says: "Nolan's book represents an unrelenting indictment of Lee both as general and as man." Finally, in "Lee and Jackson: An Indomitable Team," Roland highlights the similarities between the two Confederate chieftains and how their talents complemented each other.[154] "Together," he writes, "Lee and Jackson forged what figuratively might be called a synergistic relationship in which the effect of the whole exceeded that of the sum of its parts, the performance of each man galvanized by the presence of the other."

Part Four, focusing on the tension between fact and mythology, between change and tradition in southern history and identity, includes five articles, all previously published. Roland first presented the often-cited "The South, America's Will-o'-the-Wisp Eden" at Longwood College in Farmville, Virginia, and later as his presidential address before the Louisiana Historical Association. In this essay he reviews the paradox of southern distinctiveness over the course of the region's history. "The South," Roland concludes, "has persistently been the nation's greatest economic enigma— a region of want in the midst of boundless natural riches. It has been, and remains today, a land becoming and not a land become—a garden spot that beckons only to recede like a mirage when approached. It is America's will-o'-the-wisp Eden." In "The South of the Agrarians" Roland applies his thesis of the enigmatic South to the 1920s. According to the author, the Vanderbilt Agrarians "lived in a South that was significantly behind the rest of the nation according to every measure of progress: a South that yet preserved a great body of its traditional beliefs and values: a South that bore a heavy burden of national scorn." Roland underscored that unquestionably "the Agrarians *were* southerners, and their response to the world situation was unmistakably a southern response as well as a philosophical one."

In his "Happy Chandler" Roland sketches the life of the colorful two-term Kentucky governor, U.S. senator, and baseball administrator. "Chandler offers a remarkable illustration of the power of the individual in a free society to conquer adversity through will and character," Roland writes. Though in many ways Chandler, known for his evangelical-like oratory and "good old boy" demeanor, typified the traditional southern politician, Roland interprets him as a reformer who invested heavily in Kentucky's highways and schools (he established the University of Kentucky medical school and hospital in 1956) and who enforced the U.S. Supreme Court's desegregation decision for the state. In "Change and Tradition in Southern

Society," a chapter from Roland's *The Improbable Era,* he observes, among
other things, the persistence of the South's regional character (de facto racial segregation, a penchant for personal violence, conservative Protestant
theology, enthusiasm for sports) amid dramatic post–World War II regional
change. And finally, in his 1981 Southern Historical Association presidential address, "The Ever-Vanishing South," Roland predicts that "the region's
unique combination of political, religious, cultural, ethnic, and social traits,
reinforced as they are by geography and history, myth and folklore, and
convention and inertia, will for a good while yet keep it distinctive."

Writing more than three decades ago, Roland praised a fellow scholar who
"presents his evidence with an old-fashioned but refreshing objectivity or
determination to be as honest and impartial as possible and to let the facts
speak for themselves."[155] For a half-century Roland too has subscribed to
these values, both in publishing history and in teaching undergraduate and
graduate students. In his memoirs Roland recalled that while he expected
his doctoral students to be independent thinkers, he "demanded only that
they diligently pursue the sources and support their conclusions with convincing evidence, logical reasoning, and clear and concise expression."[156]
As readers of the present volume will discover, since the 1950s Roland has
followed his own admonition.

Perhaps the most enduring quality of Roland's impressive oeuvre is its
breadth and depth. Few scholars have written as authoritatively about several eras (two centuries in fact) and have offered as sweeping and incisive
commentaries about past and contemporary history. His range as a scholar
is remarkable; so too his graceful and powerful prose. Charles P. Roland
will be remembered for his substantial corpus of scholarship on the Civil
War and his native South and its people. Years of study, reflection, and real
world experience convinced him that history "is a vital sustaining force in
society." Like Robert E. Lee, Roland found solace in the contradictions,
nuances, paradoxes, and subtleties of the past. "It is history," Lee wrote,
"that teaches us to hope."[157]

NOTES

I wish to thank the following persons for their assistance in researching and writing this introduction: Charles P. Roland, Ken Williams, Steve Wrinn, Joyce Harrison,

Matt Lockhart, Jeffrey J. Crow, Chuck McShane, Terry L. Birdwhistell, Deirdre A. Scaggs, Anne Miller, James Old, Anne Mitchell Whisnant, Cecilia Moore, Pete Carmichael, Jennifer Scism, Mimi Riggs, John C. Inscoe, Gary W. Gallagher, James S. Humphreys, Michael Parrish, Chrissy Wilson, Brent Tarter, Pat Mains, James I. Robertson Jr., Paul D. Escott, James C. Klotter, Stan Deaton, Kay Jorgensen, Jessica Brown, and Thomas H. Appleton Jr.

1. On Roland's career and achievements, see his candid, concise, and self-reflective autobiography, *My Odyssey through History: Memoirs of War and Academe* (Baton Rouge: Louisiana State Univ. Press, 2004). Roland published a chapter of this book as "Becoming a Soldier," *Register of the Kentucky Historical Society* 101 (winter/spring 2003): 75–92.

2. Orley B. Caudill, "An Interview with Bell Irvin Wiley," June 4, 1976, in *The Bell Irvin Wiley Reader,* ed. Hill Jordan, James I. Robertson Jr., and J. H. Segars (Baton Rouge: Louisiana State Univ. Press, 2001), 230. For Roland's appreciation of Wiley as graduate professor, historian, civil rights activist, and friend, see Charles P. Roland, review of Hill Jordan, James I. Robertson Jr., and J. H. Segars, eds., *The Bell Irvin Wiley Reader,* in *Register of the Kentucky Historical Society* 100 (winter 2002): 83–85.

3. See, for example, Charles P. Roland, review of Daniel Aaron, *The Unwritten War: American Writers and the Civil War,* in *American Historical Review* 80 (June 1975): 724; Charles P. Roland, review of Michael Barton, *Goodmen: The Character of Civil War Soldiers,* in *Journal of Southern History* 48 (August 1982): 436; Charles P. Roland, review of James M. McPherson, *What They Fought For, 1861–1865,* in *Journal of Southern History* 61 (November 1995): 812–13.

4. Charles P. Roland, *An American Iliad: The Story of the Civil War,* 2nd ed. (Lexington: Univ. Press of Kentucky, 2004), [vii].

5. Listings of Roland's publications appear in John David Smith and Thomas H. Appleton Jr., eds., *A Mythic Land Apart: Reassessing Southerners and Their History* (Westport, Conn.: Greenwood Press, 1997), 191–95, and in Roland, *My Odyssey through History,* 131–32.

6. Charles P. Roland, *Louisiana Sugar Plantations during the American Civil War* (Leiden, The Netherlands: E. J. Brill, 1957), 9, 56, 115.

7. "Louisiana Library Assn. Presents Annual Awards," *Shreveport Journal,* March 21, 1958, page 1A.

8. Charles L. "Pie" Dufour, "Plantations and the War," *New Orleans Times-Picayune,* March 23, 1958, page 4.

9. Herbert Weaver, review of Charles P. Roland, *Louisiana Sugar Plantations during the American Civil War,* in *Mississippi Valley Historical Review* 44 (December 1957): 559–60.

10. Raleigh A. Suarez, review of Charles P. Roland, *Louisiana Sugar Plantations during the American Civil War,* in *Louisiana History* 1 (winter 1960): 88–89.

11. James G. Randall and David Donald, *The Civil War and Reconstruction,* 2nd ed. (Boston: D. C. Heath, 1961), 760.

12. For criticism of Roland, see C. Peter Ripley, *Slaves and Freedmen in Civil War Louisiana* (Baton Rouge: Louisiana State Univ. Press, 1976), 210, and Eric Foner, *Reconstruction: America's Unfinished Revolution, 1863–1877* (New York: Harper and

Row, 1988), 4 n. 7. For insightful criticism of the emphasis on "agency" in recent slavery studies, see Peter Coclanis, "The Captivity of a Generation," *William and Mary Quarterly* 61 (July 2004): 544–55.

13. Charles P. Roland to John David Smith, November 15, 1996 (in possession of the editor).

14. On this scholarship, see John David Smith, "Review Essay: 'The world at first neither saw nor understood'—Documenting the Emancipation Experience," *North Carolina Historical Review* 71 (October 1994): 472–77, and John C. Rodrigue, *Reconstruction in the Cane Fields: From Slavery to Free Labor in Louisiana's Sugar Parishes, 1862–1880* (Baton Rouge: Louisiana State Univ. Press, 2001).

15. See Charles P. Roland, *Louisiana Sugar Plantations during the Civil War* (1957; reprint, Baton Rouge: Louisiana State Univ. Press, 1997). This edition includes a foreword by John David Smith.

16. Holman Hamilton, review of Charles P. Roland, *The Improbable Era: The South since World War II,* in *Kentucky Alumnus* 47 (summer 1976): 31.

17. Charles P. Roland, *The Confederacy* (Chicago: Univ. of Chicago Press, 1960), 91.

18. Samuel Shapiro, "That Tragic Land," *Commentary* 32 (October 1961): 360–64.

19. E. B. Long, "General Works," in Allan Nevins, James I. Robertson Jr., and Bell I. Wiley, eds., *Civil War Books: A Critical Bibliography,* 2 vols. (Baton Rouge: Louisiana State Univ. Press, 1969), 2:27.

20. Mary Elizabeth Massey, "The Confederate States of America: The Homefront," in *Writing Southern History: Essays in Historiography in Honor of Fletcher M. Green,* ed. Arthur S. Link and Rembert W. Patrick (Baton Rouge: Louisiana State Univ. Press, 1965), 257.

21. Rembert W. Patrick, review of Charles P. Roland, *The Confederacy,* in *Journal of Southern History* 27 (February 1961): 101–3.

22. James W. Silver, review of Charles P. Roland, *The Confederacy,* in *Mississippi Valley Historical Review* 47 (March 1961): 702. In his preface, Boorstin remarked that Roland's book enabled readers to "begin to be able to assess the truth of James Madison's prediction . . . that any country cursed with a servile population cannot win against a people wholly free." See "Editor's Preface," in Roland, *The Confederacy,* viii.

23. These included Charles P. Roland, "Difficulties of Civil War Sugar Planting in Louisiana," *Louisiana Historical Quarterly* 38 (October 1955): 40–62; Charles P. Roland and Richard C. Robbins, eds., "The Diary of Eliza (Mrs. Albert Sidney) Johnston," *Southwestern Historical Quarterly* 60 (April 1957): 463–500; Charles P. Roland, "Albert Sidney Johnston and the Loss of Forts Henry and Donelson," *Journal of Southern History* 23 (February 1957): 45–69; Charles P. Roland, "Albert Sidney Johnston and the Shiloh Campaign," *Civil War History* 4 (December 1958): 355–82; Charles P. Roland, "The Generalship of Robert E. Lee," in *Grant, Lee, Lincoln, and the Radicals,* ed. Grady McWhiney (Evanston: Northwestern Univ. Press, 1964), 31–77; and Charles P. Roland, "Introduction," in Richard Taylor, *Destruction and Reconstruction: Personal Experiences of the Late War,* ed. Charles P. Roland (1879; reprint, Waltham, Mass.: Blaisdell Publishing Company, 1968), pages xi–xiii. Roland's "The Generalship of Robert E. Lee" also appeared in Gary W. Gallagher, ed., *Lee the Soldier* (Lincoln: Univ. of Nebraska Press, 1996), 159–87.

24. Grady McWhiney, "Preface to the Louisiana Paperback Edition," in *Grant, Lee, Lincoln, and the Radicals,* ed. Grady McWhiney (1964; reprint, Baton Rouge: Louisiana State Univ. Press, 2001), viii.

25. Don E. Fehrenbacher, review of Grady McWhiney, ed., *Grant, Lee, Lincoln, and the Radicals,* in *American Historical Review* 70 (July 1965): 1134–35; Dudley T. Cornish, review of Grady McWhiney, ed., *Grant, Lee, Lincoln, and the Radicals,* in *Journal of Southern History* 31 (May 1965): 210–11.

26. Joseph T. Glatthaar, "Introduction," in McWhiney, ed., *Grant, Lee, Lincoln, and the Radicals* (2001), x.

27. Grady McWhiney, "Leadership—Confederate Army Officers," in *The American Civil War: A Handbook of Literature and Research,* ed. Steven E. Woodworth (Westport, Conn.: Greenwood Press, 1996), 349.

28. Charles P. Roland, *Albert Sidney Johnston: Soldier of Three Republics* (Austin: Univ. of Texas Press, 1964), 327. In 1987 the University of Texas Press issued a paperback reprint of this work.

29. Ibid., preface.

30. Warren W. Hassler Jr., review of Charles P. Roland, *Albert Sidney Johnston: Soldier of Three Republics,* in *Journal of American History* 52 (June 1965): 133.

31. Roland, *Albert Sidney Johnston,* 290, 292, 297.

32. Pittsburg Landing stood east of Shiloh Church, a small Methodist congregation. Northerners named the ensuing battle Pittsburg Landing; southerners called it Shiloh.

33. Roland, *Albert Sidney Johnston,* 309, 320 n. 88.

34. Ibid., 328, 338, 339.

35. Ibid., 350.

36. Robert W. Johannsen in Nevins, Robertson, and Wiley, *Civil War Books: A Critical Bibliography,* 2:86.

37. Hassler review, 134.

38. David S. Sparks, review of Charles P. Roland, *Albert Sidney Johnston: Soldier of Three Republics,* in *Civil War History* 11 (June 1965): 208.

39. Gary W. Gallagher, "Foreword," in Charles P. Roland, *Albert Sidney Johnston: Soldier of Three Republics* (1964; reprint, Lexington: Univ. Press of Kentucky, 2001), xii. The lists appeared, respectively, in *Civil War Times Illustrated* and *Civil War: The Magazine of the Civil War Society.*

40. Charles P. Roland, review of James Lee McDonough, *Shiloh: In Hell before Night,* in *Register of the Kentucky Historical Society* 76 (October 1978): 329–30.

41. Charles P. Roland, *Jefferson Davis's Greatest General: Albert Sidney Johnston* (Abilene: McWhiney Foundation Press, 2000). Also see Charles P. Roland, "Johnston, Albert Sidney," in *The Kentucky Encyclopedia,* ed. John E. Kleber (Lexington: Univ. Press of Kentucky, 1992), 476–77, and Charles P. Roland, "Johnston, Albert Sidney," in *Encyclopedia of the Confederacy,* ed. Richard N. Current, 4 vols. (New York: Simon and Schuster, 1993), 2:858.

42. On Roland's appointment to the Alumni Professorship at Kentucky, see press release, Department of Public Relations, University of Kentucky, September 10, 1970, Charles P. Roland Biographical File, University Archives, University of Kentucky (hereafter Roland Biographical File).

43. These articles included Charles P. Roland, "The South, America's Will-o'-the-Wisp Eden," *Louisiana History* 11 (spring 1970): 101–19; Charles P. Roland, "The Ever-Vanishing South," *Journal of Southern History* 48 (February 1982): 3–20; Charles P. Roland, "The South of the Agrarians," in *A Band of Prophets: The Vanderbilt Agrarians after Fifty Years,* ed. William C. Havard and Walter Sullivan (Baton Rouge: Louisiana State Univ. Press, 1982): 19–40; Charles P. Roland, "Sun Belt Prosperity and Urban Growth," in *Interpreting Southern History: Historiographical Essays in Honor of Sanford W. Higginbotham,* ed. John B. Boles and Evelyn Thomas Nolen (Baton Rouge: Louisiana State Univ. Press, 1987), 434–53; and Charles P. Roland, "Gang System," in *Dictionary of Afro-American Slavery,* ed. Randall M. Miller and John David Smith (Westport, Conn.: Greenwood Press, 1988), 283–84.

44. Roland, *My Odyssey through History,* 118.

45. James W. Patton, "The Historian," in *Francis Butler Simkins, 1897–1966: Historian of the South* (Columbia, S.C.: State Printing Company, n.d.), 33. Here Patton referred to the Mississippi demagogue Theodore G. Bilbo (1877–1947).

46. For a comprehensive and insightful intellectual biography of Simkins, see James S. Humphreys, "South Carolina Rustic: Historian Francis Butler Simkins, A Life" (Ph.D. diss., Mississippi State University, 2005). Chapter 12 includes an analysis of Simkins's *The South Old and New* and Roland's relationship with his mentor. Humphreys's work will be published by the University Press of Florida in 2008.

47. Charles P. Roland, "Foreword," in Francis Butler Simkins, *The Everlasting South* (Baton Rouge: Louisiana State Univ. Press, 1963), vii.

48. Francis B. Simkins to Carter G. Woodson, May 12, 1923 [*sic*], in *Papers of Carter G. Woodson and the Association for the Study of Negro Life and History, 1915–1950,* ed. Jacqueline Goggin, 34 microfilm reels (Bethesda: University Publications of America, 1999), reel 1. Simkins sent his letter to Woodson in 1924, not 1923.

49. Francis B. Simkins, "New Viewpoints of Southern Reconstruction," *Journal of Southern History* 5 (February 1939): 60.

50. Roland, "Foreword," ix.

51. See Forrest McDonald and Grady McWhiney, "In Search of Southern Roots," *Reviews in American History* 5 (December 1977): 454. Simkins titled the first chapter of the 1947 edition of his textbook "The Everlasting South."

52. Humphreys, "South Carolina Rustic," 404, 409, 414.

53. Roland, *My Odyssey through History,* 118.

54. Francis Butler Simkins, *The South Old and New: A History, 1820–1947* (New York: Alfred A. Knopf, 1947), vii.

55. Ibid., 44–45, 182, 472, 436.

56. Frank L. Owsley, "The Everlasting South," *Sewanee Review* 56 (autumn 1948): 716–20. On Owsley, see Fred A. Bailey, "*Plain Folk* and Apology: Frank L. Owsley's Defense of the South," *Perspectives on the American South: An Annual Review of Society, Politics and Culture,* ed. James C. Cobb and Charles R. Wilson (New York: Gordon and Breach Science Publishers, 1987), 101–14.

57. William M. Brewer, review of Francis Butler Simkins, *The South Old and New: A History,* in *Journal of Negro History* 33 (April 1948): 227–28.

58. Thomas Perkins Abernethy, review of Francis Butler Simkins, *The South Old and New: A History,* in *American Historical Review* 54 (October 1948): 157–58.

59. Charles S. Sydnor, review of Francis Butler Simkins, *The South Old and New: A History,* in *Journal of Southern History* 14 (May 1946): 263.

60. Harold J. Bingham, review of Francis Butler Simkins, *The South Old and New: A History,* in *Mississippi Valley Historical Review* 35 (September 1948): 305.

61. Robert S. Cotterill, review of Francis B. Simkins, *A History of the South,* in *Mississippi Valley Historical Review* 40 (March 1954): 764.

62. Wendell Holmes Stephenson, review of Francis B. Simkins, *A History of the South,* in *Journal of Southern History* 20 (May 1954): 241. In the last reference Stephenson quoted Simkins.

63. Carl N. Degler, "The South in Southern History Textbooks," *Journal of Southern History* 30 (February 1964): 48–57.

64. Francis Butler Simkins and Charles Pierce Roland, *A History of the South,* 4th ed. (New York: Alfred A. Knopf, 1972), vii–viii.

65. Paul Owens, press release, October 30, 1975, University of Kentucky Information Services, Roland Biographical File.

66. Simkins and Roland, *A History of the South,* vii–viii.

67. Ibid., viii, 618.

68. Ibid., 122, 260, 559 (emphasis added), 522.

69. See Simkins, *The South Old and New,* 35, 45.

70. Charles P. Roland, review of Clement Eaton, *A History of the Old South: The Emergence of a Reluctant Nation,* in *Register of the Kentucky Historical Society* 64 (October 1976): 321.

71. Simkins and Roland, *A History of the South,* 588, 616–17.

72. Ibid., 618, 572, 574, 576, 574.

73. Ibid., 581, 582, 587.

74. James Tice Moore, "Redeemers Reconsidered: Change and Continuity in the Democratic South, 1870–1900," *Journal of Southern History* 44 (August 1978): 359–60 and 360 n. 9. On this historiographical debate, see C. Vann Woodward, *The Origins of the New South, 1877–1913* (Baton Rouge: Louisiana State Univ. Press, 1951), and Sheldon Hackney, "*Origins of the New South* in Retrospect," *Journal of Southern History* 38 (May 1972): 191–216.

75. Simkins and Roland, *A History of the South,* 311.

76. Sharon E. Hannum, review of Francis Butler Simkins and Charles Pierce Roland, *A History of the South,* in *Journal of Southern History* 39 (February 1973): 97–98. In *The South Old and New,* 120, Simkins described Lincoln as a politician who employed "ambiguous words" and then who as president "with eloquent benignities on his lips, forced the South back into the Union without slavery."

77. Monroe Billington, review of Charles P. Roland, *The Improbable Era: The South since World War II,* in *West Virginia History* 37 (July 1976): 329–30.

78. Hannum review, 97. For the comment on rape, see Simkins and Roland, *A History of the South,* 291.

79. Bell I. Wiley to University of Kentucky Research Foundation, February 23, 1973 (copy in possession of the editor).

80. Roland, *My Odyssey through History,* 118.

81. Charles P. Roland, review of John Shelton Reed, *The Enduring South,* in *American Historical Review* 81 (October 1976): 954.

82. See Roland, "The Ever-Vanishing South," 3–20; Roland, "The South of the Agrarians," 19–40; and Charles P. Roland, review of Richard N. Current, *Northernizing the South,* in *Register of the Kentucky Historical Society* 82 (summer 1984): 296–98.

83. Owens, press release, October 30, 1975.

84. Bennett H. Wall, review of Charles P. Roland, *The Improbable Era: The South since World War II,* in *Register of the Kentucky Historical Society* 76 (January 1978): 53–54.

85. Charles P. Roland, *The Improbable Era: The South since World War II* (Lexington: Univ. Press of Kentucky, 1975), 188–89, 184.

86. Ibid., 11, 26, 28.

87. Ibid., 30, 42, 58, 176, 177. For Phillips's famous remark, see Ulrich B. Phillips, "The Central Theme of Southern History," *American Historical Review* 34 (October 1928): 30–43.

88. Roland, *The Improbable Era,* 73, 74, 96, 74, 91.

89. Richard S. Kirkendall, review of Charles P. Roland, *The Improbable Era: The South since World War II,* in *North Carolina Historical Review* 53 (July 1976): 336–37.

90. William C. Havard, review of Charles P. Roland, *The Improbable Era: The South since World War II,* in *Political Science Quarterly* 91 (autumn 1976): 541–42.

91. Alexander R. Stoesen, review of Charles P. Roland, *The Improbable Era: The South since World War II,* in *Greensboro Daily News,* August 1, 1976, page B3. For Roland's comment, see *The Improbable Era,* 190.

92. Kenneth K. Bailey, review of Charles P. Roland, *The Improbable Era: The South since World War II,* in *Journal of American History* 63 (September 1976): 466.

93. Anonymous review of Charles P. Roland, *The Improbable Era: The South since World War II,* in *Virginia Quarterly Review* 52 (spring 1976): 44.

94. Francis M. Wilhoit, review of Charles P. Roland, *The Improbable Era: The South since World War II,* in *American Historical Review* 81 (October 1976): 1000.

95. James E. Combs, review of Charles P. Roland, *The Improbable Era: The South since World War II,* in *The Cresset* 41 (January 1978): 23–24; Robert A. Divine, review of Charles P. Roland, *The Improbable Era: The South since World War II,* in *History: Reviews of New Books* 4 (August 1976): 186.

96. David Buice, review of Charles P. Roland, *The Improbable Era: The South since World War II,* in *Louisiana History* 18 (spring 1977): 253–54.

97. Gavin Wright, review of Charles P. Roland, *The Improbable Era: The South since World War II,* in *Journal of Economic History* 36 (December 1976): 982.

98. Roland, *My Odyssey through History,* 119–20.

99. The series volumes are Bill C. Malone, *Southern Music, American Music* (1979); J. V. Ridgely, *Nineteenth-Century Southern Literature* (1980); John B. Boles, *Black Southerners, 1619–1869* (1983); Albert E. Cowdrey, *This Land, This South: An Environmental History* (1983); Thomas D. Clark, *The Greening of the South: The Recovery of Land and Forest* (1984); James C. Cobb, *Industrialization and Southern*

Society, 1877–1984 (1984); Gilbert C. Fite, *Cotton Fields No More: Southern Agriculture, 1865–1980* (1984); Robert F. Durden, *The Self-Inflicted Wound: Southern Politics in the Nineteenth Century* (1985); Dewey W. Grantham, *The Life and Death of the Solid South: A Political History* (1988); Lawrence H. Larsen, *The Urban South: A History* (1990); Roger Biles, *The South and the New Deal* (1994); Margaret Ripley Wolfe, *Daughters of Canaan: A Saga of Southern Women* (1995); and J. A. Bryant, *Twentieth-Century Southern Literature* (1997).

100. Roland, *My Odyssey through History,* 120.

101. Ibid., 122. Also see Cindy Palormo, "A True Statesman: A. B. 'Happy' Chandler and His Contributions Are the Topic of Historian's Book," *Kentucky Kernel,* April 5, 1984, Roland Biographical File.

102. Charles P. Roland, "Happy Chandler," *Register of the Kentucky Historical Society* 85 (spring 1987): 138, 154, 157, 140. Also see Charles P. Roland, "Albert Benjamin Chandler," in *Kentucky's Governors,* ed. Lowell H. Harrison, updated ed. (Lexington: Univ. Press of Kentucky, 2004), 168–76.

103. Art Jester, "Roland Plans to Start Again on Biography of Chandler," *Lexington Herald-Leader,* June 23, 1991, Roland Biographical File.

104. Roland, *My Odyssey through History,* 122–23.

105. Charles P. Roland, review of Leon C. Standifer, *A Rifleman Remembers World War II,* in *Register of the Kentucky Historical Society* 91 (spring 1993): 240.

106. Roland, *My Odyssey through History,* 116–17. Also see Roland's "Becoming a Soldier" and *My Odyssey through History,* 28–90.

107. Roland, *My Odyssey through History,* 117, 120–21; Steve Baron, "Charles Roland in Retirement: Time to Write . . . But He'll Miss the Students," *Communi-K* [University of Kentucky], March 21, 1988, page 2, Roland Biographical File.

108. Art Jester, "The Civil War Condensed," *Lexington Herald-Leader,* November 8, 1990, page D4, Roland Biographical File.

109. Baron, "Charles Roland in Retirement," 2. The second edition of Roland's text included new opening and concluding chapters, as well as revisions regarding women, African Americans, and the northern and southern home fronts.

110. Charles P. Roland, review of Robert H. Jones, *Disrupted Decades: The Civil War and Reconstruction,* Robert Cruden, *The War that Never Ended: The American Civil War,* and Emory M. Thomas, *The American War and Peace, 1860–1977,* in *Civil War History* 20 (June 1974): 159.

111. Baron, "Charles Roland in Retirement," 2.

112. James Russell Harris, ed., "On War and History: Charles P. Roland Discusses *An American Iliad,*" *Register of the Kentucky Historical Society* 89 (autumn 1991): 363–76.

113. Kenneth W. Noe, review of Charles P. Roland, *An American Iliad: The Story of the Civil War,* in *Journal of Mississippi History* 53 (May 1991): 151–52.

114. Roland, *An American Iliad,* xii, 1–2.

115. Ibid., 88, 33, 70–71, 263.

116. Ibid., xi.

117. Ibid., 38, 45, 49, 73, 240. Ramsdell's thesis appears in "Lincoln and Fort Sumter," *Journal of Southern History* 3 (August 1937): 259–88.

118. Roland, *An American Iliad,* 101, 112, 115, 167, 250.

119. Ibid., 253, 254–55.

120. Anonymous review of Charles P. Roland, *An American Iliad: The Story of the Civil War,* in *Manchester* (N.H.) *Union Leader,* November 16, 1990, page 34.

121. See Mark Grimsley, review of Alice Fahs and Joan Waugh, eds., *The Memory of the Civil War in American Culture,* in H-Net Reviews, September 2005, www.h-net .org/reviews/showrev.cgi?path=289371137437090, accessed September 9, 2006.

122. Susan-Mary Grant, "'The Charter of Its Birthright': The Civil War and American Nationalism," *Nations and Nationalism* 4 (1998): 165.

123. Anonymous review of Charles P. Roland, *An American Iliad: The Story of the Civil War,* in *The Rebel Rouser* (Dallas, Texas) 18, no. 12 (December 1990), n.p.

124. Joseph Logsdon, review of Charles P. Roland, *An American Iliad: The Story of the Civil War,* in *North Carolina Historical Review* 68 (July 1991): 367.

125. James I. Robertson, review of Charles P. Roland, *An American Iliad: The Story of the Civil War,* in *Richmond News Leader,* January 23, 1991, page 13.

126. Gary W. Gallagher quoted in Jester, "The Civil War Condensed," page D1; Emory M. Thomas, review of Charles P. Roland, *An American Iliad: The Story of the Civil War,* in *Lexington Herald-Leader,* November 25, 1990, Roland Biographical File.

127. Frank E. Vandiver, review of Charles P. Roland, *An American Iliad: The Story of the Civil War,* in *Journal of Southern History* 58 (August 1992): 547.

128. Richard A. Sauers, review of Charles P. Roland, *An American Iliad: The Story of the Civil War,* in *Civil War News* (September 1992), pages 6–7.

129. Max R. Williams, "The General and the Governor: Robert E. Lee and Zebulon B. Vance," in *Audacity Personified: The Generalship of Robert E. Lee,* ed. Peter S. Carmichael (Baton Rouge: Louisiana State Univ. Press, 2004), 130 n. 40.

130. Stephen S. Michot, review of Charles P. Roland, *An American Iliad: The Story of the Civil War,* in *South Carolina Historical Magazine* 106 (April/July 2005): 184–85.

131. Earl J. Hess, review of Charles P. Roland, *An American Iliad: The Story of the Civil War,* in *Georgia Historical Quarterly* 75 (fall 1991): 639–40.

132. Roland, *An American Iliad,* 253.

133. Roland, *My Odyssey through History,* 123–24; Charles P. Roland, *Reflections on Lee: A Historian's Assessment* (Mechanicsburg, Pa.: Stackpole Books, 1995), 124–25. In 2003 Louisiana State University Press published a paperback reprint edition of *Reflections on Lee.*

134. Roland, *Reflections on Lee,* 1, and chapters 1–4. See Woodward, "The Search for Southern Identity," in *The Burden of Southern History* (Baton Rouge: Louisiana State Univ. Press, 1963), chapter 1.

135. Roland, *Reflections on Lee,* 33.

136. Ibid., 64.

137. Charles P. Roland, review of Russell F. Weigley, *A Great Civil War: A Military and Political History, 1861–1865,* in *Register of the Kentucky Historical Society* 99 (winter 2001): 78.

138. Roland, *Reflections on Lee,* 85–87. See J. F. C. Fuller, *Grant and Lee: A Study in Personality and Generalship* (New York: Charles Scribner's Sons, 1933).

139. Roland, *Reflections on Lee,* 89–97. On the question of Lee as a modern general, see Gary W. Gallagher, "An Old-Fashioned Soldier in a Modern War? Robert E. Lee as Confederate General," *Civil War History* 45 (December 1999): 295–321.

140. Roland, *Reflections on Lee,* 89–97.

141. Ibid., 98–99.

142. Daniel E. Sutherland, review of Charles P. Roland, *Reflections on Lee: A Historian's Assessment,* in *Register of the Kentucky Historical Society* 94 (winter 1996): 83.

143. Carmichael, "Preface," in Carmichael, ed., *Audacity Personified,* xi–xii.

144. Steven E. Woodworth, review of Charles P. Roland, *Reflections on Lee: A Historian's Assessment,* in *Civil War History* 42 (September 1996): 247–48. Woodworth quoted Roland, *Reflections on Lee,* 125. Like Roland, historian James M. McPherson invoked the courtroom metaphor in assessing Nolan's *Lee Considered.* McPherson wrote that in his book, Nolan "has shed the role of historian for that of courtroom prosecutor." See James M. McPherson, "How Noble was Robert E. Lee?" *New York Review of Books,* November 7, 1991, page 12.

145. Brian S. Wills, review of Charles P. Roland, *Reflections on Lee: A Historian's Assessment,* in *Journal of Southern History* 63 (May 1997): 418.

146. Michael C. C. Adams, "Review Essay: Robert E. Lee and Perspective over Time," *Civil War History* 49 (March 2003): 68–69.

147. Kenneth H. Williams, ed., "Slavery, the Civil War, and Jefferson Davis: An Interview with William J. Cooper Jr. and Charles P. Roland," *Register of the Kentucky Historical Society* 101 (autumn 2003): 455–56.

148. Roland published different versions of this essay as "A Citizen Soldier Recalls World War II," in *Military Leadership and Command: The John Biggs Cincinnati Lectures, 1987,* ed. Henry S. Bausum (Lexington, Va.: The VMI Foundation), 101–18, and in Charles F. Brower IV, ed., *World War II in Europe: The Final Year* (New York: St. Martin's Press, 1998), 221–35.

149. On Roland and "serendipity," see Art Jester, "A Personal 'Odyssey,'" *Lexington Herald-Leader,* January 18, 2004, page E6.

150. See Abraham Lincoln to Albert G. Hodges, April 4, 1864, in *The Collected Works of Abraham Lincoln,* ed. Roy P. Basler, 8 vols. (New Brunswick: Rutgers Univ. Press, 1953), 7:282.

151. Michael J. Birkner, review of Charles P. Roland, *My Odyssey through History: Memoirs of War and Academe,* in *North Carolina Historical Review* 81 (October 2004): 490–91.

152. Robert F. Durden, review of Charles P. Roland, *My Odyssey through History: Memoirs of War and Academe,* in *Journal of Southern History* 71 (November 2005): 959. Roland presented tantalizing but exasperatingly brief and restrained insights into his years at Tulane and Kentucky in "In the Classroom Again," *My Odyssey through History,* 107–25.

153. In December 1860 Lincoln rejected Kentucky senator John J. Crittenden's proposed constitutional amendment extending the Missouri Compromise line to the Pacific (and thereby guaranteeing slavery in Federal territories south of the 36°30' line) and requiring vigorous enforcement of the 1850 Fugitive Slave Act. To this President-

elect Lincoln replied: "Let there be no compromise on the question of *extending* slavery. If there be, all our labor is lost, and, ere long, must be done again. . . . Have none of it." See Lincoln to Lyman Trumbull, December 10, 1860, in Basler, ed., *The Collected Works of Abraham Lincoln,* 4:149–50.

154. Roland first presented this essay at Lee Chapel, Washington and Lee University, on April 17, 1998, in a lecture series sponsored by the Stonewall Jackson House.

155. Charles P. Roland, review of Joe Gray Taylor, *Louisiana Reconstructed, 1863–1877,* in *Journal of American History* 62 (December 1975): 704.

156. Roland, *My Odyssey through History,* 127.

157. Ibid.

Part One

The Man, The Soldier, The Historian

In the Beginning

I was born April 8, 1918, in the little town of Maury City in western Tennessee. The event occurred, as I was later informed, in a small wooden house that stood on a street so undistinguished that the townspeople called it simply "the lane." Today, the street bears the name Park Avenue, an upgrading of nomenclature for which I am in no sense responsible.

My ancestry was respectable but neither wealthy nor famous. I am under the impression that my forebears were largely of Scotch-Irish stock. Some of my kinspeople have traced certain of them back to the late colonial period in North Carolina. Decades afterward they joined the great trek west and settled in southwestern Tennessee and northeastern Mississippi, where most of them have continued to live.

I came quite naturally by the urge to teach. Both my paternal grandfather and my father were teachers. My grandfather, Isaac Newton Roland, taught in a private high school in the rural community of Essary Springs, about seventy-five miles south of Maury City. According to all available accounts, he was a splendid instructor. During World War II, when I was stationed at a camp in Texas, I met an elderly man at church one Sunday. When we were introduced, he asked, "Are you akin to Professor I. N. Roland?" I explained the relationship. He revealed that he had been a pupil of my grandfather's in the Essary Springs school. Upon learning later that I planned to become a teacher after the war, he bestowed upon me this blessing: "I hope you will be as great a teacher as your grandfather was."

My grandfather met and married a student in the school, Mary Margaret Nelms, who became my grandmother. She was a tall and stately woman, and she held a strong sense of personal rectitude.

My father, Clifford Paul Roland, was the first of three children, all boys, born to the I. N. Rolands. He was born July 4, 1893. He was a healthy, handsome child. A photograph made when he was about two gives him a decidedly serious look. He would grow up to be a handsome man; a girlfriend of mine once told me that she and her friends agreed that none of my father's sons was as handsome as he. Somewhat crestfallen, I concurred. He was a generally serious and reserved man, but with a strong sense of humor and a deep love of life. He was highly intelligent and especially gifted in mathematics, and he was a conscientious student in all fields of learning. He was also a good athlete, particularly in basketball and baseball.

My maternal grandfather was Burton Paysinger. Born a few years before the Civil War, he retained fearful childhood memories of the conflict. He received only about two years of formal education, but this was sufficient to ground him far more thoroughly in reading, writing, and ciphering than are most high school graduates today. He acquired a lifelong love of words and was a natural orator and storyteller. He was fiery and impulsive. He was a cotton farmer and he served as a magistrate on the county court. He enjoyed whiskey and chewing tobacco.

My maternal grandmother's maiden name was Josephine Hurley. She was petite and, from my earliest memories of her, was quite hunched in the shoulders. She was quick of mind and tongue, and was said to have been a pretty girl and a light-footed dancer in her youth. We grandchildren called our Paysinger grandparents Ma and Pa because an older cousin had done so.

My mother, Grace Pearl Paysinger, was three years younger than my father. In her, I could see strong elements of both of her parents. She was pretty, bright, impulsive, and fiery. When she was about nine years old, the Paysingers sold their farm in McNairy County, Tennessee, and moved to Essary Springs in order that the children could attend the private school that was now being run by my grandfather Roland. My mother was a fast learner and soon caught up with all the pupils who had been ahead of her in her grade in school.

She first saw my father shortly after moving to Essary Springs. As she later put it, in meeting him she met her Waterloo. Apparently, they fell in love at first sight; they were married in 1916 after a long courtship. When my father walked down into the field where Pa Paysinger was plowing and asked for my mother's hand, Pa's only words were, "Well, Clifford, she's got a mighty high temper." The wedding was something of an early flower-child affair. Because one of my mother's sisters was seriously ill, the event could not take place in her home; instead, they met the presiding official by the roadside under a large oak tree where the ceremony occurred.

My father had attended a private college by the name of The National

Teachers' Normal and Business College in the town of Henderson, Tennessee, which was on the Mobile and Ohio Railroad about thirty-five miles northeast of Essary Springs. He had been teaching school for two or three years in the village of Sardis, Tennessee, near the Tennessee River. He now accepted a position as co-principal of the high school in Maury City, about forty miles northwest of Henderson. He also coached the school's various athletics teams. My parents moved to Maury City shortly after their marriage. I was born there two years later; our family lived there until I was three.

My memories of life in Maury City are, of course, too dim to be reliable. According to community lore, one of the more sensational of these experiences occurred when I was an infant too young to remember it consciously. The story is that a teenaged girl engaged by my mother to babysit me had great difficulty stopping me from squalling. Finally, in desperation, she resorted to what the army would call a field expedient; she bared one breast and put me to it. I quieted instantly and was soon fast asleep. The experience may have affected me for life.

I do recall faintly some of the especially happy or especially painful episodes of my life there. For example: my parents playing the card game of Rook or eating homemade ice cream or watermelon with their friends, all the while engaged in laughter and lighthearted conversation; or an occasion when I inadvisably sampled the fiery-hot red peppers being grown in my mother's garden by the porch, an experience I was wise enough not to repeat.

In 1921 my family, which now included another son, Grady Paul, moved to Henderson, where my father had accepted a position on the faculty of Freed-Hardeman Junior College, the successor to The National Teachers' Normal and Business College. He would remain at Freed-Hardeman for the rest of his career. He retired from his service there on July 4, 1983, his ninetieth birthday. The school was affiliated with the Church of Christ. Most of the faculty were ministers in the church as well as teachers in the school, and in deciding to come there he decided also to enter the ministry.

My father's new position on the Freed-Hardeman faculty plus his role as a Church of Christ minister altered sharply the social and religious ambience surrounding the family. The college held a rather sternly puritanical outlook on life; it frowned on games of cards and on "mixed bathing," the term it applied to aquatic activities in which males and females swam together. Dancing was considered to be an unmitigated sin, one that would lead to horrendous lasciviousness. No longer did my parents engage in Rook parties; nor did they engage in any other social affairs except those related to the school, church, or family. The demands of the ministry caused my father to give up coaching. These restrictions and constraints would bear heavily on me as I grew older.

I went through the usual experiences of a young child in a small southern town of that era. I survived the severe childhood diseases that were popularly known as whooping cough and red measles, and the relatively mild diseases known as chicken pox and German measles. I had the best medical attention available at the time, but the best could be taxing. It included, for example, an annual purging. Every spring, our family physician would prescribe a "round of calomel to clear out the system," which had to be followed by a dose of castor oil. This procedure did indeed clear out the system! This occurred whether or not there were any symptoms that would have justified the ordeal, which seemed to me to be worse than any condition it might have cured or averted. All members of my family also faithfully took quinine to ward off malaria.

In Henderson, the Roland family grew with the addition of a daughter, Margaret Josephine (namesake of both grandmothers), Hall Carmack, and Isaac Nelms. I loved my siblings but seemed to be compelled to bedevil the two of them nearest my age. I once got Josephine (Jo for short) up on top of the house by way of a ladder that someone had carelessly left in place. I was unable to get her down, and my parents were not immediately available. Fortunately, a passing college student rescued her.

I constantly provoked fights with Paul. I also led him into all sorts of mischief. The very first words of every Henderson acquaintance of mine when encountered in later years were: "You and Paul were the worst kids I ever knew." In my maturity I have come to believe that jealousy was the cause of my picking on Paul. He had replaced me as the baby of the family. Also, he was more attractive than I. He possessed a round face with cheeks like big red apples; my face was sharp and pale by comparison. Invariably, some of the first words spoken when the family visited relatives were: "Isn't Paul cute?" Then, turning to me, "I do declare. Charles looks a little peaked, doesn't he?"

Josephine, five years my junior, posed a different kind of threat to my security. She was a girl. I soon began to derive great pleasure out of teasing her. She was a perfect target because she reacted so predictably and in a manner so gratifying to me. I honed my teasing talents to the point that I could send her screeching out of the room merely with a gesture or a knowing glance in her direction. I once appropriated her menu for a party she was planning for herself and her girlfriends. The menu called for a dime's worth of candy and seventeen glasses of cocoa-malt, a favorite family beverage that was thought to possess marvelous health-promoting qualities. The mention of that menu fifty years later would send her into blushes and gales of embarrassed laughter.

I entered the Freed-Hardeman elementary school at age five. For a long time afterward, I believed my parents started me early because of my precocity. After I became a parent, I began to suspect they were motivated at least in part by the need to get me out of the house for a while each day. Unquestionably, they had good cause for wanting to do this.

I was definitely not a good pupil. There is little doubt that today I would be diagnosed as being hyperactive; I had certain twitches and motions that may have been symptoms of what is now identified as Tourette's syndrome. To say that I had an attention deficit would be a gross understatement; I had an attention void. In all probability, I would today be put on medication. I was indescribably bored with most of my classes, notwithstanding that my teacher was a quite pretty young woman who was just out of college and who aroused in me all sorts of unidentifiable sensations.

I was unable, or unwilling, to memorize the information required by the tests. Arithmetic was a profound mystery to me. My lack of aptitude in the field is still a mystery to me, since both of my parents and all of my siblings were especially good in it. Fortunately, reading came easy for me. Also, both my teacher and my classmates gave me high marks for my ability as a narrator or raconteur, though these activities often got me into trouble for talking when I should have been silent.

Girls presented a serious distraction. They seemed to be the repositories of all beauty and brains. The ancient saying that little girls are made of sugar and spice and everything nice, and little boys of snaps and snails and puppy dog tails, I accepted as eternal verities. The girls came to school in immaculate dresses and shiny patent-leather shoes, their hair done in flawless braids or curls. The contrast between their appearance and mine was too painful for contemplation. One day while in the first grade I slipped up on a golden-haired little angel and stole a kiss; she ran home to her mother in tears. I felt like the troll who had emerged from under the bridge.

The intellectual contrast was as striking as the physical one. The little girls almost always got their tests back with big red 100s marked on them. They were downcast when they received a 99. If I had received a grade that high I would have known somebody had shuffled the papers.

Corporal punishment, both at home and in school, was a prevalent condition of growing up when I was young. In my early years my parents whipped with switches; later, my father whipped with his belt. There were periods when I was whipped at least once a day, some days, more than once. "Spare the rod, spoil the child" was the accepted wisdom in parenting. Strangely, despite the present view that such practice constitutes child abuse and inflicts permanent psychological trauma, I never felt abused, ceased to love my parents, never questioned their love for me. Whether the experience crushed or otherwise dismembered my personality, I leave to others. How much effect the punishment had on my behavior at the time is debatable.

In addition to the whippings at home, I was also whipped quite often in school. Yet I continued to misbehave regularly both places. When I was a teenager I received lashings at school hard enough to leave stripes that were clearly visible across my back for days when I was swimming with my cohorts. I wore the stripes as proudly as an army sergeant wears those on his chevron.

I was wounded by one of Cupid's arrows while in my early teens. My first actual romantic encounter occurred in the unlikely environs of the Freed-Hardeman College tennis courts. I found myself by accident in close proximity to a charming, sloe-eyed young brunette of about my own age. Before I knew it, we were embracing, kissing. To my utter bewilderment, she suddenly disengaged and fled, leaving me in a state of suspended animation.

Notwithstanding the frequency of domestic punishments, I can see that I was blessed with a secure and bounteous home. I never wanted for nourishing food or comfortable clothing and housing. There were always toys and other gifts at Christmas. This was possible during the Great Depression of the early thirties because Freed-Hardeman College resorted to barter in lieu of nonexistent cash; the faculty accepted goods and produce from parents in payment of their children's tuition fees. Also, in our home there was always parental love, albeit of a painful application on countless occasions.

Speaking of Christmas, in the Church of Christ it was an altogether secular occasion. We shot fireworks on Christmas the way most Americans elsewhere shot them on the Fourth of July. The bombardment began weeks in advance and gradually reached fortissimo on Christmas Day. By dawn that morning the town of Henderson sounded somewhat like the battle of Gettysburg.

In spite of my unimpressive performance in school, I managed to acquire an acceptable knowledge of the basics in education. My formal schooling was immensely reinforced by reading and by a certain amount of travel. When I was seven or eight my parents purchased a second-hand set of the youths' encyclopedia named *The Book of Knowledge.* Its many volumes (thirty, as I recall) contained snippets of almost every imaginable branch of literature and learning. Through the years I may have read every word of the entire work.

I also had ready access to a set of world classics that my father owned and kept in his home library. They were published in separate little volumes. Admittedly, they were a bit mature for me, but I read many of them anyway, including Homer's *Iliad* and *Odyssey.* Such of their expressions as "rosy-fingered dawn" and "wine-dark sea" struck a responsive chord in me. I read with intense satisfaction how the suitors of the wife of the absent and wandering Ulysses, pretending to be Ulysses, failed the test of identity to which they were subjected. Only Ulysses could draw the bow of Ulysses.

Another important source of my intellectual development lay in certain of the popular novels of the time. I devoured the novels of Zane Grey telling of the exploits of bold western riders and the Tarzan novels of Edgar Rice Burroughs with their story of a muscular young superman who was reared by the great anthropoid apes of Africa.

Unquestionably, the supreme literary influence on my youth was the King James Bible, in which I did a considerable amount of obligatory reading, but which came to me primarily through quotations—innumerable, reiterated quotations in sermons, Sunday school classes, and Freed-Hardeman's compulsory daily chapel exercises. After almost eight decades many of these striking passages still ring in my mind: "The heavens declare the glory of God and the firmament sheweth his handiwork"; "Consider the lilies of the field, how they grow; they toil not, neither do they spin: And yet . . . Solomon in all his glory was not arrayed like one of these."

An unintended enhancement in my early formal education—a piece of serendipity—was the result of the presence in the Freed-Hardeman elementary and high school of a number of pupils from a wide portion of the nation, including such faraway and exotic regions as Florida, Illinois, and

Texas, as well as such closer places as the cities of Nashville and Memphis. What I did not understand at the time but have come to believe is that at least some of them were there to receive a discipline that their parents were unable or unwilling to exercise at home. In other words, Freed-Hardeman served them somewhat as a reform school. Hence, among them were a number of previously undisciplined and highly mischievous (if not miscreant) boys and girls. They lived in the college dormitories, thus further developing their questionable knowledge and skills by contact with the older residents. All of this gave the Freed-Hardeman lower schools an extraordinary degree of versatility, energy, and color.

I profited immensely from these associations, though my parents would have been horrified by a lot of what I was learning. The most memorable of these youthful boarding pupils was a boy named Baskin Fuller (nicknamed Bosey) from Florida. Bosey was four or five years older than I. He was handsome, bright, articulate, and altogether charming; he probably grew up to be a highly successful lawyer, doctor, engineer, or business executive. He was also the quintessential corrupting influence according to the accepted Freed-Hardeman (or Roland household) point of view. He possessed a seemingly inexhaustible stock of gamy jokes and stories, and an equally ample repertory of sexual information (and misinformation) that he generously passed on to all of his youthful acquaintances. Since I received virtually no information on this subject at home, I looked to Bosey as my tutor in the course.

When I was in the seventh grade it was merged with the eighth grade because of the smallness of the enrollment in both at Freed-Hardeman. As a result, I went through both seventh and eighth grades in a single year. I was able to handle this speed-up all right in everything but arithmetic, where I had always been weak.

There was another result of the speed-up: I would graduate from high school just a month after turning sixteen years of age. This would put me into college about two years younger than most of my associates there, thus placing me at a social disadvantage because of my relative immaturity.

I was greatly stimulated by the visits our family made to places of historical interest and societal importance. By all odds the place that left the greatest impression on me was Shiloh. In the days when there were virtually no public recreation areas, the National Military Park commemorating the great Civil War battle that occurred there, and located only an hour's drive from my home, was a favorite spot for visiting. I went there on countless family or school occasions. I picked up Civil War musket bullets from the ground. I once startled a colleague mildly by saying that I may have made my very first trip to Shiloh before I was born.

Shiloh, of course, was more than just a recreation area. It was the site of an episode of immense tragic historic significance. The scores of cannons and monuments scattered across the fields and throughout the woods offered striking testimony to the events that occurred there. The place was hallowed ground to me. I drank in its historic scenes, the Hornets' Nest, the Sunken Road, the Peach Orchard, the Bloody Pond; I listened in awe to the saga of valor describing the fray. I stood under the great white oak tree where Gen. Albert Sidney Johnston, the Confederate commander, was found mortally wounded, and I listened to my grandfather say that Johnston's death had robbed the Confederates of victory there, perhaps of victory in the war. How could anyone, including me, know as I sat at age eight or nine for a Freed-Hardeman College group photograph on the Johnston monument that I would one day write the story of his life.

The other family visits that ranked almost with Shiloh in my consciousness were the annual Essary Springs community reunions. Hundreds of people came from hundreds of miles; a din of animated conversation and laughter floated over the place; mountains of food lay on rustic wooden tables under the trees; a constant line of people dipped and drank water from the spring (Essary Spring) that flowed into the Hatchie River a few feet away. We drank the water as a social ritual even when we were not the least thirsty; drank it until we were waterlogged and forced to seek relief wherever. Youngsters shot marbles and played ball; youths flirted and courted; the older folk told and retold stories of family, church, and community. The entire event was one of hearty bucolic conviviality.

My early years were lived without benefit of the so-called "miracle" drugs that would become prevalent during and following World War II. Fortunately, I inherited a body that was resistant enough to be spared all of the dread diseases of the period, such as polio, tuberculosis, meningitis, typhoid fever, scarlet fever, and the like. I had friends who died or were permanently disabled or weakened by one or another of these maladies.

My early years were also lived without benefit of organized athletics for children. We boys learned to swim by trial and error in a little nearby stream that bore the suggestive name Sugar Creek. Throughout its normal course the creek was perhaps twenty feet wide and two feet deep. But here and there were holes as much as seven or eight feet deep that served us admirably as swimming pools. Though I have been privileged to swim in many elaborate artificial pools, in both the Atlantic Ocean and the Pacific Ocean, in the Gulf of Mexico, Lake Pontchartrain, Lake Michigan, and the beautiful Barton Springs near Austin, Texas, I have never had greater aquatic pleasure than I enjoyed in muddy little Sugar Creek.

We wore no swimsuits. We "skinny dipped," shedding our scanty summer clothes as we raced the last few hundred feet to the creek and shouted, "Last one in is a [whatever insult or epithet came to mind]." One of our keenest pleasures occurred in a swimming hole that was close to the trestle bridge where the railroad crossed the stream. We "flashed" the passing passenger trains shamelessly. Startled women looked with open-mouthed indignation, startled girls with open-mouthed amusement. Between swims and flashing the trains, we reenacted the Tarzan story in a thick woods that grew along the creek bank. Still nude as at the moment of birth, we swung like monkeys from tree to tree, emitting the high-pitched, triumphal cries of our hero.

We played baseball, basketball, and football on vacant lots and in nearby cow pastures. We chose sides in a procedure that was explicitly and humiliatingly based on merit; the self-appointed captain of each team selected his players according to a descending scale of ability. The boy who was by general agreement the weakest baseball player in town happened to own most of the baseball equipment, including bats, balls, and a catcher's mask, mitt, and body protector. Though we had to allow him to play in order to get the use of the equipment, he was invariably chosen last, and with the proviso that the captain be permitted to take his last strike at bat.

As I grew older I played on the Freed-Hardeman high school and college teams. I was the Henderson boys' tennis champion (sixteen and under), and my partner and I were the town senior doubles champions though I was still young enough to qualify for the boys' competition. I was the number two player on the college tennis team. In football I was known as a "scatback," a light but swift and shifty runner. I played safety on defense, which meant that I returned the other team's punts. I have a distinct and scary memory of skipping around and watching the ball as it floated and wobbled high in the air above me, at the same time listening to the rumble of the big, beefy opposition players as they bore down on me like a herd of buffalo. In baseball I was a pitcher, with a local reputation of throwing a "fire-ball." One of my dearest friends later in life accused me of intimidating the batters by throwing the first pitch dangerously close to their heads.

In order to supplement the family income at the height of the Great Depression, my father decided to convert the five-acre plot of land on which we lived into a vegetable and fruit farm and dairy. He also had a nonfinancial motive in doing this. Reared on a farm and steeped in the Jeffersonian philosophy that those who work in the soil with their hands are God's chosen people, he hoped to develop his children's characters in this manner. As teenagers, Paul and I ran the dairy, milking five cows apiece by hand, and carrying out the many other chores that went along with the enterprise. We also delivered the raw milk to customers after our mother had strained and bottled it.

We cultivated the small farm during the summer under an arrangement that we would work every morning and have the afternoons free to swim or play tennis or baseball. I could say what Abraham Lincoln is quoted as having said: that my father taught me how to work, but not how to enjoy it. Whether these activities enhanced our characters I cannot say, but they developed our muscles and probably kept us out of a degree of mischief.

I particularly relished visiting with one of my Corinth, Mississippi, aunts, who was the mother of three vivacious daughters in my general age range. I traveled back and forth from Henderson on a single-coach diesel-electric train known locally as the Dinky. My cousins imparted to me many social virtues, and some of what were looked upon in my family circle as social vices. They taught me how to dance the Charleston, sort of. The choreography occurred in a most unlikely place: the bandstand of a renowned Civil War battle site, Battery Robinett of the battle of Corinth. The lessons were accompanied by rhythmic chanting and handclapping and sometimes by the jazz music of a portable windup phonograph.

As all of us grew older, our escapades grew more daring. I took my first drink of alcohol, a minimal sip of beer, in company with the three cousins and the boyfriends of the two eldest. This took place at a rustic beer joint just across the Tennessee line, because Mississippi was "dry," while beer was allowed in Tennessee. Many years later State Line, Tennessee, with a cluster of disreputable establishments allegedly featuring gambling and prostitution, would become the locale of violence in the popular movie *Walking Tall.*

When I was about fifteen the youngest of the cousins, who was approximately my own age, began to arrange dates for me with her girlfriends. She coached me in advance concerning my upcoming date's qualifications, tastes, and whims. My visits to Corinth were filled with excitement and fun.

My first two years of college were spent at Freed-Hardeman. I was an indifferent student as a freshman, barely managing to pass the required mathematics courses, earning C's in most courses, and no grade higher than a B. Mainly, I studied girls, all of whom were older than I and seemed far more sophisticated. My scores weren't very high in that subject either.

In the fall of my second year something happened that brought a significant change in my life. I was sitting with a group of local friends of mine on the courthouse yard evaluating the girls as they came and went to the soda fountain of the City Drug Store across the street. A discussion of college came up. One friend said he was headed for Duke, another for the University of Alabama, one for "Ole Miss" (the University of Mississippi), several for the University of Tennessee. Someone turned to me, addressed me by my nickname, "Chick," and asked where I intended to go to school after graduating from Freed-Hardeman. I had not given the matter a thought, but I felt called upon to offer an answer in order to save face. Because my father had attended Vanderbilt to do graduate work, that school popped into my mind. "I'll be going to Vanderbilt," I replied archly.

The more I thought of that possibility, the more the idea appealed to me. That evening at the dinner table (we called the evening meal "supper") I suddenly announced my intention to attend Vanderbilt. This statement was followed by a long silence, but afterward my father sat me down for a solemn talk about my future. He pledged to find the means to send me to Vanderbilt if that was where I wished to go, then he added another condition. "Provided," he said, "Vanderbilt will accept you." The thought that I might not be accepted had not entered my mind. He explained forcefully that my Freed-Hardeman record up to that point would not be acceptable. That evening, for the first time ever, I began studying seriously. According to my memory, I received nothing but A's for the remainder of my Freed-Hardeman career.

Vanderbilt did accept me, though I have wondered at times whether the decision may not have been influenced by my father's position and associations, including his being a Vanderbilt alumnus, and in September 1936 I enrolled there. As events turned out, I found myself to be quite adequately prepared educationally for the Vanderbilt experience. French was the course that I was most anxious about. Had my year of studying the language at a small junior college equipped me for an advanced university course in it? My anxiety increased when the instructor at Vanderbilt turned out to be a native Frenchman. To determine whether all of the students were qualified for the course, he administered a test at the first class meeting. To my delight and incredulity, he announced at the next meeting that the highest score on the test was that of Monsieur Roland. This gave me a tremendous boost in morale (and egotism); never again did I doubt my ability to do acceptable work at Vanderbilt. My score in French was actually a tribute to my Freed-Hardeman instructor in the language, Mrs. Mary Nelle Hardeman Powers, an extraordinarily intelligent and inspiring teacher.

Notwithstanding my recently acquired self-confidence, the university intellectual atmosphere was extremely rarefied for my system. In evaluating my Freed-Hardeman courses for acceptance, a brisk young woman in the Vanderbilt dean's office told me that only a portion of my Bible courses would receive credit and that the credit would count in lieu of "Bib Lit" (Biblical Literature). What I had studied as the inerrant revealed Word of God was thus transformed in the twinkling of an eye into nine quarter hours of "Bib Lit"! My course in the history of the American frontier, taught by the department chairman, Professor William C. Binkley, was a genuine eye-opener. I had always studied history as a body of fixed facts. Exposed to Frederick Jackson Turner's "frontier hypothesis" (that the American frontier experience had given the nation a unique character) and to my professor's commentary on the hypothesis, I learned to examine all historical "facts" critically and through a set of corrective lenses.

Vanderbilt offered me an excellent education, and I profited immensely from it. A number of professors, in addition to Dr. Binkley, are especially memorable. Frank Owsley was my major adviser, and I took his splendid course in the history of sectional controversy. Donald Davidson and John Crowe Ransom stood in on many occasions for the instructor in one of my courses in English literature.

In studying under these three professors, I was being exposed to some of the most brilliant, creative, and controversial scholars in the nation. Davidson and Ransom were members of the celebrated group of southern writers who called themselves "The Fugitives" and were leaders in the school of literary interpretation known as the New Criticism, which placed its decisive emphasis on form, structure, paradox, and imagery. Owsley, one of the most distinguished and original of all historians of the South, had joined Ransom, Davidson, and a number of other thinkers who in 1930, under the group name "Twelve Southerners" (widely known as "The Agrarians"), published the book *I'll Take My Stand*. It was a southern literary manifesto against the progressive, industrialized society that they deplored as a threat to the southern way of life, the environment of the entire earth, and universal classical values. Ransom captured the philosophy of the book brilliantly in a single sentence in the preface that described the modern progressive society as being constantly engaged in a losing war with nature, "winning Pyrrhic victories at points of no strategic importance."

Was I aware of the privilege of sitting at the feet of these men? Not in the slightest. I admired them as interesting classroom teachers and I liked them personally, but I was too ignorant to be cognizant of their importance as intellectuals. I was also too callow to care. Not until I was a graduate student a decade of years and a world of experiences later did I come to appreciate them for what they were.

My social education at Vanderbilt was fully as important as my intellectual education. Measured by the standards of campus life of the times the school and its student body were decidedly conservative; measured by today's standards, they represented the Stone Age. The boys were clean-shaven and wore neckties to class. The girls came to class looking like dolls—modest dolls, for they wore knee-length skirts and hose that exposed no flesh beneath the hem of the skirt. The prime enforcer of the girls' dress code was Dean of Women Ada Belle Stapleton. She cut a formidable figure. A woman of imposing height and girth, she had the eye of an eagle and the tongue of an adder. She was known to order girls back to their rooms to don the proper attire, or to remove exactly half of their rouge and lipstick. She was also known to stop boys on the campus who failed to tip their hats to her and have them do so "by the numbers." A hippie among the Vanderbilt students of the day would have been as unimaginable as a Bolshevik.

I had two great summers during my college career. The first was between my sophomore and junior years (before going to Vanderbilt) when I served as a counselor at a boys camp—Camp Elklore—in the beautiful hilly and wooded country near the town of Winchester in Middle Tennessee. In addition to being in charge of a cabin housing ten or twelve young teenagers, I taught tennis and swimming. Between my junior and senior college years I held a summer job with the National Park Service, working as a guide at the Chickamauga-Chattanooga National Military Park. I loved both of the summers' experiences.

I was a middling good student at Vanderbilt, with grades about half A's and half B's. After proving to myself the first year that I was capable of making A's in French, I eased back to a comfortable B in the language. My proudest moments came during the senior seminar my last year. Professor Owsley was in charge of the American history quarter of the course. For it I wrote a research paper on the battles for Chattanooga during the Civil War. Since I had served throughout the preceding summer as a guide in these battlefields and had given countless lectures on the campaign, writing this seminar paper was "a piece of cake." I received a grade of A on it.

Writing the paper for the European quarter of the course was a different matter. Not only had I not been a guide or lecturer on any European topic; the instructor in the course was a Professor Cruikshank, who was known to be a particularly severe grader. I had been happy over eking out a modest B in his lecture course. From his list of acceptable seminar topics, I chose one on the Norman conquest of the Sicilies, about which I knew nothing. I worked on it throughout the entire quarter, collecting bits of information wherever the reference librarian and I could find them. I turned in the paper in a quite diffident mood; a grade of B would have made me decidedly happy. Instead, I received an A and was told by the professor that mine was the superior paper of the seminar. I went away rejoicing.

My social life was much freer at Vanderbilt than at Freed-Hardeman. I became a dedicated dancer, began to imbibe alcohol in strict moderation, and to smoke cigarettes accordingly. Because my funds for social purposes were extremely limited, I did not date Vanderbilt girls—who, I understood, expected to be wined and dined. Instead, I dated girls who were in school at Peabody College across the street from Vanderbilt; they were training to become schoolteachers and expected less to be spent on them. I also dated high school girls, who were delighted to be brought to the Student Union dances held periodically in the gymnasium.

It was my good fortune to form a friendship with a student who was destined to become one of the nation's most popular celebrities. Her name was Fanny Rose Shore; she became the radio, movie, and TV singing star Dinah Shore. I knew who she was before I met her directly. Everybody on campus knew Fanny Rose, knew her as an attractive, outgoing, friendly, and talented young woman. She sang on a weekly program of a local radio station. She and I were enrolled in a large Political Science course in which the professor seated the students alphabetically. This arrangement put the two of us side by side on the back row and we quickly became classroom buddies.

One day she said to me, "I saw you playing tennis. Would you teach me to play tennis?" Would I teach her? You can bet I would! We made a date and I reserved a campus court. I was utterly intimidated by her appearance on the court. I played tennis in an ordinary pair of wash trousers and a street shirt with its sleeves cut off and hemmed by my mother. She appeared in tennis attire de rigueur, carrying a fancy tennis equipment bag with an expensive racquet and a can of fresh tennis balls. Once we were on the court, I saw immediately that someone else had beaten me to the job of teaching her how to play the game. We played on a few subsequent occasions, but her social calendar was too busy for such a casual arrangement to last very long.

An amusing incident occurred between us at the end of the Political Science course. One of the course requirements was the preparation of a research term paper. Near the close of the term she confided to me exultantly that she had recently interviewed the governor of Tennessee as a part of her research. My own work seemed to me to be awfully pedestrian compared with such a spectacular feat. On the day the papers were to be turned in she said to me, "Let me see your paper. Here's mine." We exchanged papers. After just enough time for her to scan my opening paragraph, she returned my paper with the exclamation, "My God! I'm not even gonna turn mine in!" She did turn hers in and probably received a good grade on it, for she was a quite competent student. We graduated together in the spring of 1938.

I was happy to be out of college, because I was tired of school work. But I still had little awareness of the realities of life. I took for granted that my parents would continue to support me. For a while they did. To acquire a modest amount of spending money I took a job that summer lifeguarding at Chickasaw State Park near Henderson. I also continued to live at home, eat most of my meals there, and drive my parents' automobile when I needed wheels, including the frequent occasions when I was on dates either with Henderson girls or with girls in the nearby town of Jackson.

One day my father casually informed me that he had spoken to a friend in Memphis who was the district sales manager for a national life insurance company. They had discussed my gifts as a salesman, and he had assured my father that I amply possessed the qualifications for such a career. Suddenly I could see dollar signs floating before my eyes, along with a wardrobe of modish attire and an automobile of sleek design, possibly a Terraplane like that of one of my friends. I signed a formidable contract and began diligently studying sales manuals and forms. This was an easy task after the taxing reading demands of my college courses. I continued to live at home and freeload off my parents.

I soon discovered that actually selling insurance was quite different from reading about selling it. In college I had been articulate, some would say loquacious, in discussing my coursework; now I felt embarrassed and tongue-tied when I attempted to explain the advantages of my product to an impatient potential customer. Two months went by without a sale except two small policies purchased by my father: one for my brother and one for me. I began to entertain serious doubts about my ability to do this kind of work; eventually, I quit trying to make sales and began sitting at home in an attitude of defeat.

Again my father came to my rescue. He set me on a course that ultimately would be my life's work.

A Citizen Soldier
Recalls World War II

In the early fall of 1944, my military unit, the 99th Infantry Division—a draftee division—was ordered overseas to the European theater of operations. I, having been drafted a few days after the Japanese attack on Pearl Harbor and rushed through basic training and Officer Candidate School, was now a captain, serving as the operations officer of the 3rd Battalion, 394th Infantry Regiment. I was also a member of the advance party of the division. Our mission was to precede the main body of the unit to Europe and make arrangements for its arrival.

To our delight, the advance party sailed on the great British liner *Queen Mary*. To our keener delight, Prime Minister Winston Churchill was a fellow passenger, returning from his Quebec conference with President Franklin D. Roosevelt. Churchill and his entourage occupied a restricted portion of the ship, and we did not get a glimpse of him until the last afternoon at sea, when he came down to the grand ballroom and gave a brief inspirational talk spiced with humorous asides. He received a booming ovation.

Other than Churchill's address, the voyage was uneventful, for which I was extremely grateful. There is, however, an interesting footnote to the story of the trip. In our initial safety briefing aboard ship, we learned that the famed Queens, the *Queen Mary* and her sister the *Queen Elizabeth*, sailed alone. They were too swift for enemy submarines to harm them, we were assured; escorts would slow them down and make them more vulnerable. I at first accepted this explanation with a grain of doubt. The doubt vanished when I learned that Churchill was along; the authorities certainly would take no risk with his safety. Considering the fact that throughout the war the renowned vessels repeatedly crossed and recrossed the ocean without mishap, one must conclude that they actually were relatively secure from the submarine menace.

Imagine my surprise when I learned years later in reading the published diary of Sir Charles Moran, Churchill's physician, that the lion-
hearted prime minister himself was rather preoccupied with the threat of
a submarine attack on us, questioned the ship's captain as to how long we
would remain afloat if torpedoed, vowed not to be taken alive by the Germans, and had a machine gun placed in his lifeboat. Obviously, my presence aboard the *Queen Mary* did not kindle in the great war leader the sort
of confidence that his presence aboard kindled in me.

The main body of the division soon arrived in England, and in early
November we crossed the English Channel on LSTs (tank landing ships)
and landed at Le Havre, France. The most memorable event of the voyage
was a Sunday religious service at sea. It occurred in the tank hold of the
vessel. The battalion chaplain, First Lieutenant Edwin W. Hampton, spoke
and dispensed the elements of communion from a portable altar that rested
on the hood of a jeep. The soldiers sat in trucks or on truck hoods or half-
sat leaning against artillery tubes. The chaplain spoke to the accompaniment of the creaking and snapping of the chains and turnbuckles that held
the vehicles and guns in place against the rolling motion of the ship. He
discoursed on the obligations of good soldiers fighting in a noble cause,
then, elevating his right hand in a gesture of beatitude, he pronounced:
"The Lord bless you and keep you; the Lord give you strength in the day
of battle." How could any of us know that this kind man of faith would be
among the first to die?

By now I felt quite seaworthy. I had crossed the Atlantic without a
trace of seasickness. I considered myself immune to this malady. How
wrong I was! Caught in a Channel storm, our shallow-draft vessel pitched
and yawed like an unbroken mustang. I thought I would die before the voyage ended. It seemed endless. It lasted almost as long as the trip across the
Atlantic on the *Queen Mary*.

I staggered down the ramp at Le Havre about midnight, still nauseated
from the capers of the ship and as weak as a kitten from being unable to
retain any food. An icy rain was falling. At the foot of the ramp a flashlight
beam caught my eyes and an authoritative voice came out of the darkness.
"Captain, give your name, unit, and assignment." I recognized the voice; it
was that of the division commander, Major General Walter Lauer. "Captain
Charles P. Roland, S-3 [operations officer], 3rd Battalion, 394th Infantry,
sir." He then said: "You are hereby placed in command of troop convoy
Blue-5. Your destination is the town of Aubel, Belgium. You are to conduct

the convoy there with the utmost dispatch. My aide will escort you to the convoy and supply you with the necessary maps and information. Do you have any questions?" "No questions, sir," I replied with a note of false bravado. "Very well, move out."

I saluted as briskly as possible under the circumstances and walked to a waiting jeep with the general's aide. A multitude of emotions surged through me, all of them distressing. Seldom after becoming a commissioned officer did I wish to swap places with an enlisted man. Now, bouncing over the cobblestones in the darkness, in this exotic land far from my native heath, I felt terribly lost and inadequate. As we rode along beside the parked convoy of some twenty trucks, I envied the soldiers who sat in them, swaddled in their blankets and tenting, sleeping like infants who had just been fed and burped.

After three days and two nights on the road, in a journey that featured a number of episodes in which I became lost during the night and was obliged to leave the convoy parked while I wandered the streets of some blacked-out city in search of the route markers, we arrived at our destination, Aubel, Belgium. The date was November 11. Winter arrived at Aubel that same day in the form of a snowfall of several inches.

I was exhausted to the verge of collapse. My eyes were bloodshot from cold, grime, and loss of sleep, with a bead of pus standing in the inner corner of each. Most of the soldiers spent the night in tents pitched in a large open field that lay between the villages of Aubel and Henri Chapelle. A few of us were fortunate enough to spend the night in a farmhouse with a covey of young Belgian women who were eager to converse about an American crooner they identified as "Beeng Crows Bee" and an American city they called "Sheek-a-Go." I wished to be sociable. The spirit was willing, but the flesh was weak. Immediately following a hot meal, some eye drops and two APC tablets (reinforced aspirin) administered by the battalion surgeon, and a swig of sacramental wine that Chaplain Hampton mercifully supplied, I fell into a deep sleep that lasted until noon the next day, when I was awakened to receive further orders from the battalion commander.

The division was to move into the line at once, and, as the battalion operations officer, I was again to be a member of the advance party. My job was to learn the location of the designated battalion assembly area and the route leading into it and guide the battalion there. The advance party spent the night in the cellar of a shell-wrecked house in a town named Murringen.

The sounds of intermittent gunfire, muffled by distance, punctuated the night. I slept fitfully and had lots of time to meditate.

We moved into a quiet sector located in the Losheim Gap, which is on the eastern border, the German border, of the Ardennes region of Belgium. It was quiet because most of the Allied ground forces were concentrated north and south of us, awaiting the coming of spring to launch the final offensive to end the war. We had been placed here in order to give us a feeling for the front before being subjected to arduous combat. We were spread out for some twenty-two miles, and on our south flank lay a gap of several thousand yards between us and the next division.

The area was largely covered with fir forests whose cone-shaped evergreens standing in deep snow and sparkling with crystals formed a scene of marvelous beauty. It could have served as the model for a Hallmark Christmas card. We sustained a few casualties from long-range enemy fire and mines and from patrol activities. First Lieutenant Charles M. Allen, a particularly close friend of mine, was killed while leading a reconnaissance patrol at this time. He was the first fatality of the division. Yet we were not severely uncomfortable, nor did we appear, in general, to be in great danger. Intelligence reports from higher headquarters advised us that the enemy had only a handful of beaten and demoralized troops in front of us and that they were being supported by only two pieces of horse-drawn artillery.

What the enemy actually had along the Ardennes front, skillfully concealed a few miles behind their forward line, was an immense force of two armies poised to strike in a desperate counteroffensive planned by Hitler to abort the Allied advance in the west. To state the matter candidly, our top commanders were afflicted with what I have dubbed the "Shiloh syndrome": the sort of heedless preoccupation with one's own plans to the neglect of enemy capabilities and intentions that came near destroying General U. S. Grant's army at Pittsburg Landing in the American Civil War.

Hugh Cole's authoritative history of the battle of the Ardennes opens with a discussion of the situation on both sides on the eve of the encounter. He shows how the German attack was to be focused in the action of the Sixth Panzer Army against the green troops holding the attenuated American line in the Losheim Gap. At the end of his description he comes to my regiment. Here is what he says: "The fateful position of the 394th Infantry Regiment would bring against it the main effort of the I SS Panzer Corps and, indeed, that of the Sixth Panzer Army."

It came at dawn of December 16, in a thunderclap of massed artillery fire amid the blinding mist of the Ardennes winter. The shelling was followed by a surge of infantry supported by tank fire. All that day and night and the following day we were assaulted front and flank. Time appeared to stand still, as if we were caught in a red nightmare of sound and fury, of desperation and panic.

My mind seemed to reject the reality of what was happening, to say it was all make-believe, until some specific event would bring me back to myself. At one point my eyes fell on an enemy tank that had been stopped by our fire a thousand yards in front of the line. How like a child's toy it looked, until I fixed my binoculars on it and could plainly see the bodies of two crewmen hanging from their waists like rag dolls out of the smoking turret hatch. One of our young lieutenants danced a rubber-legged jig as he twisted slowly, making the blue bullet hole between his eyes clearly visible. One moment our battalion chaplain and his assistant were kneeling beside their disabled vehicle; the next moment they were headless, decapitated by an exploding shell as if by the stroke of a guillotine.

The entire division was in peril of destruction. Yet it held, at least for a precious two days. If in places there was panic, in others there was valor supreme. Lieutenant Dewey Plankers and his rifle platoon repeatedly beat off attacks in overwhelming strength at the community of Losheimergraben, where an east-west highway from Germany entered Belgium. This highway, running to Liege on the Meuse River and linking with routes to the great Allied base of Antwerp, was intended to be the enemy's major line of operations.

At the village of Lanzerath, which lay on a secondary road that ran past the south flank of our position, the eighteen soldiers of the regimental Intelligence and Reconnaissance platoon led by First Lieutenant Lyle J. Bouck Jr. held up an entire panzer column throughout the first day of fighting. At the Losheimergraben railroad station, which was located outside of the village of that name, the rifle company of Captain Neil Brown (Company L, 394th Infantry) and the battalion anti-tank platoon led by Sergeant Savino Travalini decisively repelled the attack of an enemy column that attempted to turn the division flank and seize the highway behind our front.

Lieutenant Plankers was credited with personally destroying one enemy tank (a dreaded Tiger) that ventured too close to the cellar in which his command post was located and attempted to thrust the muzzle of its 88mm cannon through a small vent in order to blast out the defenders. According to regimental folklore, Plankers dispatched the monster by launching an anti-tank grenade up the bore of its gun before it had time to fire. Sergeant Travalini used anti-tank fire to flush a group of German troops out of an abandoned railway car. He cut them down with rifle fire as they emerged.

During the first night of the battle, Sergeant Alvin N. Rausch of Company K somehow remained undetected in the cellar of a house that had been seized by the enemy. Miraculously, the position was still connected by field telephone with our battalion command post. Rausch reported the presence of German troops in the house above him and of tanks surrounding the house. But upon receiving this information, the division headquarters said the tanks were American reinforcements. Shortly thereafter, the telephone line went dead as Rausch was detected and made a prisoner by the Germans. Scores of comparable episodes occurred along the division front, some known and recorded, many lost to history.

Losheimergraben was now a shambles of blasted and smoldering houses, burning tanks and halftracks, and mangled bodies of both the enemy and our own soldiers—the tragic debris of war. Our unit organization and cohesion above the company level were virtually gone. The resistance was largely that of small units fighting independently for survival.

The German plan called for a complete breakthrough of our position one hour after the assault began on the morning of the 16th. But the battle raged furiously throughout the 16th and the morning of the 17th, with our regiment, along with the entire division, holding its place at all critical points. Hugh Cole lists the tenacious defense of the Losheim Gap among the major factors that defeated the German offensive.

Many units of the division received presidential citations for their roles in the defense. Those so distinguished comprised the 1st Battalion, 394th Infantry, which included Plankers's platoon, Lieutenant Bouck's I & R platoon, Captain Wesley J. Simmons and a portion of his company (Company K) that had been attached to the 1st Battalion, and the 3rd Battalion of one of our companion regiments, the 395th Infantry, which repulsed the fierce enemy assaults along another important highway that entered the division sector near its north flank. Doubtless many other units deserved equal honors, including, in my judgment, Captain Brown and his Company L of my own battalion. The entire 99th Infantry Division received the Fourragère of the Belgian government, with a citation that read "for extraordinary heroism" in combat.

Significantly, one of the most meaningful accolades to our regiment was not at all intended as an accolade. It came from the enemy, from the man who was considered by Hitler to be the toughest and most resourceful soldier of the Wehrmacht: Colonel Otto Skorzeny. Earlier, Skorzeny had staged a spectacular rescue of the Italian dictator Benito Mussolini and an equally daring abduction of the Hungarian regent, Admiral Miklós Horthy.

In planning the Ardennes offensive, Hitler placed Skorzeny in command of a special force that was supposed to follow close behind the attacking echelon at Losheimergraben, move through the anticipated breach, commit sabotage behind our line, and dash forward by vehicle along the highway to seize the Meuse River bridges. In his memoirs, Skorzeny recorded how on the first day of the battle he anxiously awaited word of the quick breakthrough that did not occur. Describing the situation that prevailed at midday, he wrote, "The Americans were defending themselves particularly stoutly. . . . The only news [from Losheimergraben] was of violent fighting, without any considerable gain of ground." Thank you for the compliment, Colonel Skorzeny.

But our open south flank was bypassed during the night of the 16th by a powerful enemy panzer column. By the afternoon of the 17th, our front line was shattered into a ragged series of disconnected and isolated pockets of resistance, and our communications with the division headquarters and supply base were open only intermittently. We had no rations left and almost no ammunition. Our situation was desperate beyond measure.

Eventually we were ordered back from this exposed and vulnerable position. After an exhausting cross-country march in deep snow throughout most of the night of the 17th and the following morning, we reached the town of Elsenborn, where the battered and depleted division was deployed along the forward slope of a commanding ridge, along with other units that were being rushed to that location.

Our first night in this position was unforgettable. The flash and roar of exploding shells was incessant as the enemy artillery blasted the approaches behind us and our own artillery blasted those in front. In all directions the landscape was a Dante's inferno of burning towns and villages.

We worked furiously throughout the night because we knew we had only a few hours of grace before the enemy would be upon us with renewed fury. We distributed ammunition and field rations, cleaned and oiled weapons, dug foxholes and gun emplacements in the frozen earth, planted anti-tank mines, strung barbed wire, studied maps and aerial photographs by shielded flashlights in an effort to determine where the most dangerous attacks would fall, plotted fire zones for machine guns, mortars, and artillery, installed field telephone lines to the various command posts, and set up an aid station to receive a fresh harvest of casualties. Everyone was aware that there would be no further withdrawal, whatever the cost. Moreover, I could sense in the demeanor of the troops at all ranks that this resolution was written in their hearts.

Our position on the Elsenborn Ridge became the very hinge of the northern shoulder of a great salient in the line, the bulge that gave the battle its well-known name, "Battle of the Bulge." We remained there for six weeks, repulsing all efforts by the enemy to dislodge us and seize that terrain, which was critical to the success of their plan. John S. D. Eisenhower, in his book *The Bitter Woods,* says the action of the 99th and 2nd Infantry Divisions in securing this position may have been the most decisive operation of the entire Ardennes campaign. In an allusion to the battle of Gettysburg, the historian Stephen Ambrose has called Elsenborn Ridge the Little Round Top of the campaign.

Enemy mortar and artillery fire went on here around the clock. It became impossible to take a step in the snow without touching one of the ugly, fan-shaped smudges left by the exploding shells. Our own artillery also fired continuously. One immense "time-on-target" concentration of our Corps artillery broke up the most threatening German attack before it could get launched. Our 3rd Battalion artillery liaison officer, Captain Henry Reath, a close friend of mine, played a key role in originating this massive bombardment.

The weather now became almost as formidable as the Germans. Night after night the temperature fell well below zero (Fahrenheit). The wind blew in a gale that drove the pellets of snow almost like shot into our faces. Providing hot food on the front line became impossible, and we were obliged to live exclusively on emergency, or canned, rations. Remaining stationary in the damp, cold foxholes, with physical activity extremely limited, we began to suffer casualties from trench foot, an affliction caused by prolonged exposure in such conditions.

Trench foot in its advanced stage becomes gangrenous. Amputation is then the only remedy. At one point we were losing more men from trench foot than from enemy fire. All troops were ordered to change socks daily and to exercise their feet and massage them vigorously for at least thirty minutes at a time. We got clean socks by swapping our dirty ones for them. The dirty ones were then sent back to the kitchen facilities miles behind the line, where they were washed and dried to be returned to us for the next exchange. This down-to-earth but essential laundry and logistical operation occurred daily for more than a month. Platoon leaders and sergeants were to visit every foxhole and personally see that the massaging and changing were carried out. Officers were subject to court-martial if their units developed an excessive number of trench foot cases within a week.

In time, the combination of extreme cold, fatigue, boredom, and hazard became maddening. A few men broke under the strain, wetting themselves repeatedly, weeping, vomiting, or showing other severe physical symptoms. Only with a raging fever was a soldier deemed sick enough for temporary relief from front-line duty. Otherwise, the cure-all APC tablets had to suffice. Men began to wound themselves one way or another in order to get away from the front. Sometimes this was intentional; sometimes it occurred through gross negligence born of fear, exhaustion, and misery. Men who committed self-inflicted wounds were also subject to court-martial.

At Elsenborn we received fresh troops to replace our heavy losses in the foregoing action, losses that amounted to one-third of the strength of the front-line companies. By Army policy, all units were kept constantly at full roster, or as nearly so as possible. This was done through a complex replacement system, except that the newcomers were not called "replacements." In an effort to avoid further demoralizing them by reminding them that they were taking the places of men who had been killed, wounded, or captured, they were designated by the euphemism "reinforcements." Only a Kafka could truly describe the depersonalizing effects of the system. Upon arriving in Europe from the basic training centers they were sent to "Replacement Depots," or "Repple-Depples," as they were quickly nicknamed by the soldiers, and from there up to the divisions on the front.

Before reaching this destination they had no unit assignment, no way of developing either personal friendships or organizational confidence and pride. They were interchangeable parts in the giant machine. We soon established a brief behind-the-line orientation program. But quite possibly some of the early replacement troops, a number of whom had so recently eaten Christmas dinner at home with their families, were killed in action before they had an opportunity to learn the names of the soldiers in the foxholes with them.

The marvel is that the draftee divisions were able to generate and maintain any esprit de corps at all. Formed originally by mixing men indiscriminately from throughout the nation (thus severing all personal, social, communal, and regional bonds), identified by anonymous numbers (for example, 394th Infantry Regiment, 99th Infantry Division), and replenished through the notorious Repple-Depples, their only source of morale, other than the shared experience of hazard and hardship, was the character and patriotism of the soldiers, rank and file. Fortunately, that proved to be sufficient.

The last day of January, still in the dead of winter, our troops left their maze of dugouts, foxholes, and connecting crawl trenches to participate in an Allied attack to straighten out what remained of the enemy salient in our line. In this action we sustained many casualties from anti-personnel mines planted under the snow by the Germans as they withdrew. These devilish contrivances shattered the foot or leg of any soldier who was unfortunate enough to step on one of them.

One of the bravest and coolest acts within my knowledge occurred in connection with these mines. Here and there, as the advance progressed, a soldier who had exploded one of them lay groaning in agony. First Lieutenant Samuel Lombardo's platoon of Company I, 394th Infantry, halted. Nobody moved when Lombardo gave the signal to resume the advance. Facing his "moment of truth" as an officer, he made his decision. Ordering the soldiers to follow him single file and to step carefully in his footprints, he led them through the minefield, providentially, without a casualty. From this time forward, his troops would have obeyed his orders to go anywhere.

After a brief return to our unit's former position on the Elsenborn Ridge we were pulled back into Corps reserve for a few days of rest and rehabilitation. Then we joined the general Allied advance through the Rhineland. In early March we reached the Rhine at the city of Dormagen, which is located some forty miles north of Cologne. With the broad stream between us and the enemy, we felt secure. The weather was now pleasant with the first touch of spring.

We had learned that somewhere south of us a bridge across the Rhine had been captured by one of our armored divisions. The war seemed about over. By early evening we were busy selecting comfortable houses for billets and liberating captive wine cellars. Some of the soldiers, in a gesture of disdain and whimsy, carried out a promise made earlier by walking down to the bank of the historic river and making a direct, personal contribution to its volume and ammonia content. A holiday mood began to take hold of the entire command.

But the mood ended abruptly. Fresh orders arrived from Corps, and within an hour or two we were on trucks, rolling through the night, destination unknown. We halted after midnight and bivouacked in an open field. Shortly, I was awakened and escorted to division headquarters to join an advance party. We rode in jeeps for a few miles, then dismounted and walked for a thousand yards to the crest of a low bluff. In the dawn light we could see the Rhine below us. Spanning the stream was a long bridge with an arched superstructure. Peering at our maps, we made out the name of a town that lay at the near end of the bridge. It was Remagen.

Later that day I had an opportunity to examine the bridge at close range and to read the improvised sign that hung above its western end. The sign said, boastfully but fittingly, "Cross the Rhine with dry feet, compliments of the 9th Armored Division."

That night we crossed the Rhine by foot on the captured bridge. My mind flickered back to the historic episode in which Caesar crossed the same stream at almost the same location to fight the same enemy two thousand years before. My reverie was cut short by the whistle and crash of hostile shells. How exposed and vulnerable I felt on that strip of metal high above the black, swirling waters. Walking forward became extremely difficult. I had the feeling that each projectile was headed directly at my chest. Actually, we who had gained the bridge were relatively safe. The shells were hitting in the approaches to the bridge amid the marching troops, who suffered many casualties. The German guns had been quiet until the head of the column reached the bridge. We were convinced that someone in the town was giving the gunners the signal to open fire.

For some two weeks we fought hard to secure the bridgehead until our armored units could cross and break out of it. Here we had the new experience of fighting against women soldiers. In their desperate effort to contain or destroy our bridgehead, the Germans brought up a number of anti-aircraft units armed with multiple-barreled, rapid-fire, 20mm guns that were operated by women in uniform. We jestingly called them "flak-wacs," but their activities were no joke. They aimed their weapons down at us, dealt us many casualties, and made our job significantly more difficult.

During the Remagen battle I had an occasion to witness another of the scenes that have remained most vivid in my mind: the battalion aid station in full activity. Located in a deep cellar, it was lit by gasoline lanterns suspended from hooks screwed into the overhead beams. Lining the floor on litters and covered with blankets were a score or more of wounded soldiers, waiting to be transported back to a field hospital. They were arranged in rows with narrow aisles between. Most were heavily bandaged: a head, a face, a torso, a limb. Tubes ran to many of them from bottles of blood plasma that hung from the hilts of bayonets that had been thrust down between the cobblestones of the floor.

The battalion surgeon and his assistants worked ceaselessly among the wounded. Most of the soldiers lay still and quiet, their pain eased by morphine or shock, or both. One man held up a taped leg and said that he had received a "million-dollar wound," which, half in sport and half in earnest, was what we called a wound that was severe enough to get one out of combat, but not severe enough to be permanently disabling.

In one corner, partitioned off with a tent canvas, lay a group of soldiers whose faces were covered with blankets. They had given, to borrow Abraham Lincoln's exalted words, "the last full measure of devotion."

The highlight of our noncombat activities in this situation involved Lieutenant Lombardo's platoon flag. Having come to the United States from Italy as a young boy, and being filled with an intense love of his adoptive country, he requested an American flag to be presented as we advanced into Germany. Told that none were available, he managed to make one. Using a white sheet that had been hung from the window of a German house as a sign of surrender, he and the members of his platoon found pieces of red, white, and blue cloth which they cut and sewed to the sheet to complete the stars and stripes. This flag crossed the Rhine with only one side finished, possibly the first American national emblem to be flown east of that river in World War II.

After the Remagen operation, the 99th Division participated in the closing of the Ruhr pocket, then in the sweep across Germany, moving in a truck convoy some 250 miles southeast and passing through the mountainous piles of rubble that recently had been the proud cities of that nation. We met our last serious resistance at the Danube, which we crossed under heavy mortar fire, and which inspired the composition by our troops of a crude parody of Johann Strauss Jr.'s famous waltz tribute to that river.

After the war in Europe ended I remained there for seven months in the army of occupation. In the middle of the summer the 99th Division was deactivated and a number of its soldiers, including me, were transferred to the 1st Infantry Division, a Regular Army unit, which had been selected to be the security and service organization for the Nuremberg tribunal that was to try the German war criminals. I was a member (a lowly one, but a member nevertheless) of the division reconnaissance detail that made a survey of the public buildings in Nuremberg and chose the ones where the trials were to be held and the prisoners detained. At the time of the survey, much of the city lay in ruins; the buildings selected were themselves badly damaged, with windows broken and gaping shell holes in the walls.

Later, in the detention area, I once got a glimpse of the prisoners. Among this eternally infamous group only Hermann Goering, with an expression at once jovial and arrogant, was recognizable to me.

In early December I boarded ship at Marseilles for home. That night, as we glided along the smooth surface of the Mediterranean, I lay for hours on a blanket spread on the deck, gazing at the stars. They seemed much closer and more luminous than I had ever seen them. I had the feeling that I could almost reach up and pluck them out of the sky.

Countless emotions surged through me as I recalled my experiences of the recent past. For a while I lay in somber reflection, contemplating a vision of Charlie Allen, Chaplain Hampton, and other friends reposing among the thousands of graves aligned row upon row in the great Henri Chapelle cemetery, which I had learned was located between the Belgian villages of Aubel and Henri Chapelle, near the very spot where my regiment had spent the snowy night before moving up into the line at Losheimergraben. An image from my early youth floated into my mind, an image of a bronze plaque at the Shiloh battlefield cemetery, and of the stirring verse embossed on its face:

On fame's eternal camping ground
Their silent tents are spread
And glory guards with solemn round
The bivouac of the dead.

Then the reality of the present moment began to sink in. I was going home! Going home alive and whole! How unimaginably fortunate I had been! An involuntary and unspoken prayer of thanksgiving ascended from me.

The return voyage across the Atlantic was stormy, and the ship I was on this time was no *Queen Mary*. My old nemesis, seasickness, revisited me with a vengeance. I fought it off by popping Dramamine pills until I was in a zombie-like trance.

I got home a few days after Christmas and was discharged from active duty in March. I returned clearly aware that the tumultuous events of the past four years had vastly and permanently changed my life. Only dimly was I aware how much they had permanently changed the world.

In Retrospect

In looking back over my life, I believe I could not have chosen a more satisfying profession than that of teaching and scholarship. These activities have precisely suited my taste and personality. I was extremely fortunate in being the offspring of parents and grandparents who imbued me with a strong thirst for knowledge and the means of acquiring a sound formal education. I was equally fortunate in being able to study under mentors who imparted to me the most precious gift a teacher can bestow: the capability to teach myself. Finally, I have been blessed with a patient and loving wife who has encouraged and supported me unstintingly; without her, I could not have done anything comparable to what I have done.

Though I have never entertained any desire to repeat my military service, I am convinced that it added a significant dimension to my career, especially to that portion dealing with martial history. It taught me self-discipline and perseverance, qualities that are necessary to any field of endeavor. It also gave me an insight into the nature of my fellow human beings, and particularly into that of war and soldiers, an understanding that cannot be gained from books. I learned at the existential level the true meaning of Clausewitz's famous dictum concerning the ubiquity of "friction" in war: a meaning captured perfectly in the World War II soldiers' pungent acronym SNAFU ("Situation normal, all fucked up").

My odyssey through the expanses of history has convinced me that it is a vital sustaining force in society. It records, of course, the full range of human motives and actions, ignoble as well as noble, and thus can lead its votaries into cynicism and despondency. But I support the view expressed by Robert E. Lee near the end of his life when he wrote that his experience of men had not disposed him to think worse of them or indisposed him to serve them, nor had the many errors and failures which he had come to recognize caused him to despair of the future. He said the march of Providence is so slow, the life of humanity so long, and that of the individual so brief that we often see only the ebb of the advancing wave and are thus discouraged. "It is history," he concluded, "that teaches us to hope."

I have not been an especially prolific scholar, but I take pride in the books and articles which I have produced. They are unique to my character and experience; nobody else could have written them as they are written. I take pride also in the students I have produced, particularly the eighteen graduate students who prepared their doctoral dissertations under my direction, nine at Tulane University and an equal number at the University of Kentucky. They represent a variety of points of view, some of which differ from my own. This does not upset me; I had no desire to clone myself in my students. Instead, I sought to encourage them to think for themselves and demanded only that they diligently pursue the sources and support their conclusions with convincing evidence, logical reasoning, and clear and concise expression.

Some of my students have surpassed me, or will do so, in the volume or excellence of their work. This pleases me because I look upon their careers as an extension of my own. I have read or heard it said that Socrates' greatest contribution was the production of his student Plato, and Plato's greatest contribution the production of his student Aristotle. What a bracing thought on which to end these memoirs!

Part Two

Secession and the Civil War

Why the War Came

I am under the impression that the authorities of the National Park Service have issued instructions that, henceforth, the subject of slavery as a cause of the Civil War will be emphasized in the lectures given by Park Service personnel interpreting the battles that occurred on the various sites of the national military parks. Aside from an old-fashioned scholar's natural aversion for history by directive or memo, I can see no reasonable objection to a lecture on the causes of the war, including slavery, although they may have had little or no direct connection to any battle being described. I used to teach a one-semester course that was largely devoted to the subject of the causes of the war. My initial reaction to the idea of including this subject in the park interpretation is: good enough, but how in the world can such a vast and complicated topic be adequately taught in the few minutes that can be allotted it on these occasions? I shall not presume to try to tell the Park Service how to conduct its affairs, but since I was invited to this symposium for the express purpose of commenting on the causes of the war, I trust I am at liberty to do so.

Let me begin by saying that I hope the decision by the Park Service is not a product of the "political correctness" lobby. Political correctness is an effort, often reinforced by rules, sensitivity training (otherwise known as brainwashing), and punitive measures designed to ensure favorable treatment and comfort to all the minorities within the population, and to present the findings of history or other scholarly disciplines in a manner that is congenial to liberal revisionist ideas about the past. Political correctness extends into the literature and classrooms of today, exerting pressure either subtle or gross to alter the discourse in a way that reflects these revisionist convictions. For example, certain revisionist historians of World War II are extremely critical of President Harry S Truman for his decision to drop atomic bombs on Japan. They believe the war against that nation could have been ended satisfactorily without resort to such weapons, and they ignore or dismiss all evidence to the contrary.

Please indulge me for a few minutes of discussion on the cause or causes of the Civil War. Theories on these matters have run through many phases. Was the war caused exclusively or primarily by slavery? In his famous second inaugural address, President Abraham Lincoln said slavery was "somehow the cause of the war." But "somehow" is a remarkably vague and elusive explanation. Lincoln did not venture into specifics on this point. Many revisionists of today do so. They give what, in my judgment, is a simplistic argument, that slavery was of itself the cause of the war.

Many other theories have been offered. Was the war a contest between democracy and aristocracy? Was it a Marxian struggle between an industrial, capitalistic, hired workers' society and an essentially agrarian and paternalistic society? Was it a sectional struggle for control of the nation's financial system? Was it a war between advocates of a centralized nation and those of a decentralized nation of virtually autonomous states? Was it a war between an essentially Anglo-Saxon society and an essentially Celtic society? Was it a war between a religious society and an atheistic society? Hear the explanation given by the South's foremost theologian at the time. The distinguished Presbyterian Reverend James H. Thornwell declaimed: "The parties in this conflict are not merely abolitionists and slaveholders. They are atheists, socialists, communists, red republican Jacobins on the one hand, and the friends of order and regulated freedom [southerners] on the other. In one word, the world is the battleground, Christianity and atheism the combatants, and the progress of humanity at stake."

Let me return to the argument that the Civil War was a contest between the North and the South for economic control of the nation. I am not offering this as my own argument; I wish simply to use it to illustrate the vastness and complexity of the subject. This argument was advanced in the 1920s by two Columbia University history professors, a husband and wife team, Charles and Mary Beard. It was discarded decades ago by the history profession. Recently it was resurrected in a heavily researched and forcefully presented article published in the journal *Civil War History*. The author employs all of the latest computerized research and analysis techniques; the manuscript was read critically but favorably by a covey of eminent Civil War historians.

The title of the article is "The Beards Were Right." The article itself argues just that. I shall spare you a discourse on its contents, but I do wish to repeat two quotations from it. The first is from Senator Joseph Lane, a Democrat from Oregon, who said in 1861: "There is a large party in this country embracing almost the entire northern population of the country, who hold that this is one great consolidated Government—a national Government; that all power is in this Government, and that whoever has control of it can use it to the oppression of those they choose to oppress; that they can administer justice to one portion, and refuse equality, and nobody has the right to complain."

Before someone objects that Lane was simply a Democratic vice presidential candidate appealing for southern votes, permit me to present the other quotation. It was uttered in the U.S. Senate in February 1863, which I would remind you was after the issuance of the final Emancipation Proclamation. The speaker was John Sherman, the powerful Republican senator from Ohio, and, incidentally, the brother of the famous general who wore the name Sherman. He was addressing the Senate in support of the passage of the national banking act, which subsequently passed into law. Here's what he said: "The establishment of a national currency, and of this system, appears to me all important. It is more important than the loss of a battle. In comparison with this, the fate of three million Negroes in the southern States is utterly insignificant. I would see them slaves for life as their fathers were before them if only we could maintain nationality. . . . I regard all those questions as entirely subordinate to this. Sir, we cannot maintain our nationality unless we establish a sound and stable financial system; and as the basis of which we must have a uniform currency." The establishment of the national banking system had long been one of the goals of the northern bankers and industrialists. I say again that I present this material merely for the purpose of demonstrating the enormous complexity of the discourse over the question of the cause of the Civil War.

Was it a war that actually had no fundamental cause, a war that could have been avoided by wise and patient statesmanship? A group of prominent historians of the 1930s and 1940s thought so. They believed it was the product of superheated rhetoric by politicians, journalists, and preachers. Revisionist historian Professor Avery O. Craven of the University of Chicago produced a book in 1939 bearing the indicative title *The Coming of the Civil War: The Repressible Conflict*. In other words, an avoidable conflict.

Affirmative answers have been given to all of the above arguments. Some evidence can be found for all of them. Possibly all are partially correct. This complexity of ideas reinforces my concern over the prospect of an official, "school-solution" mini-lecture on the subject. To give a further idea of its complexities and nuances, I should like to quote briefly from the writings or lectures of four eminent Civil War scholars.

The first of these is Professor William E. Gienapp of Harvard University, who has probed deeply into the political factors leading to the war. He is fully aware of the role of slavery in precipitating secession and, indirectly, the war itself. He says it is impossible to imagine the coming of the Civil War without slavery. I agree. But Gienapp is talking about slavery in the context of the American political structure and ideology.

Writing in 1996, Gienapp says that, in this context, the Civil War was a product of the democratic political system itself, and the southern secessionists probably had the better constitutional argument in the fierce debate that led to war. He concludes by saying, "Both sides went to war to save democracy as they understood it. For southern secessionists, at stake was the right of self-government and the fundamental rights of southern whites to control their own destiny. For the North, the war was a struggle to uphold the democratic principles of law and order and majority rule. . . . Well before the fighting started, the sectional conflict represented a struggle for control of the nation's future."

Let me turn to another highly acclaimed Civil War scholar, Professor James M. McPherson of Princeton University. Perhaps many students of the war would say that he is the preeminent expert on the subject. Certainly, no one has ever accused him of holding a pro-Confederate bias. In an essay produced in 1983, he wrote that the South's pre–Civil War vision of America departed less from the revolutionary model than did that of the North. "Thus when secessionists protested in 1861 that they were acting to preserve traditional rights and values, they were correct. They fought to protect their constitutional liberties against the perceived northern threat to overthrow them. The South's concept of republicanism had not changed in three-quarters of a century. The North's had. With complete sincerity the South fought to preserve its version of the republic of the founding fathers—a government of limited powers that protected the rights of property and whose constituency comprised an independent gentry and yeomanry of the white race undisturbed by large cities, heartless factories, restless free workers, and class conflict."

Next, I turn to the words of Professor Bell I. Wiley. I am personally acquainted with all of the four historians I am now quoting. I highly respect all of them. But I was intimately acquainted with Professor Wiley. He was my major professor at Louisiana State University when I was at work on my master's degree. We hailed from the same part of the world, West Tennessee. He grew up at Halls, Tennessee, I at Henderson; they were only about fifty miles apart. I wrote my master's thesis, "Louisiana Sugar Plantations during the American Civil War," under his supervision. I served for a term as his graduate research assistant while he was working on his great book, *The Life of Billy Yank.*

The renowned Civil War writer Bruce Catton called this work and its companion volume, *The Life of Johnny Reb,* the two works on the war that will truly live. Professor Wiley introduced me to scholarly research in Civil War history. I can say without blinking an eye that I am convinced that a more dedicated, honorable, judicious, fair-minded, and objective scholar never lived. He exercised the utmost effort to avoid bias in his scholarly conclusions. I believe he was remarkably successful in doing so. I invite anyone who doubts this to read his masterpieces on the common soldiers of the Civil War and his groundbreaking work on southern blacks during the war. They are as free of bias as any books ever written on the war.

With this tribute to Professor Wiley's qualities behind me, let me quote a statement from him, made some forty years ago, concerning Robert E. Lee's decision to fight for the Confederacy. First, let me point out that Lee looked upon slavery as an evil in society, and that he had no part in the decision of any state to secede. As a matter of fact, he opposed secession and was sharply critical of South Carolina when that state took its direful step to withdraw from the Union.

Yet Lee fought for the Confederacy. What did he say when he made this fateful choice? "I cannot draw my sword against my own people." Shortly after the war, in a correspondence with the famed British historian Lord Acton, Lee gave an expanded and more reflective explanation for his decision, saying he fought for the constitutional rights of the states against the encroachments of the national government. He went on to explain that he believed these rights to be the safeguard of the preservation of a free government. And I quote: "I consider [the constitutional rights of the states] as the chief source of stability to our political system, whereas the consolidation of the states into one vast republic, sure to be aggressive abroad and despotic at home, will be the certain precursor of that ruin that has overwhelmed all those that have preceded it." Lord Acton was a willing recipient of these sentiments because he had already reached similar conclusions from his general study of history.

Lee's expressed fears perhaps exaggerated the actual dangers inherent in the growth of the power of the central government in this country, but no man who ever knew him, including those who fought on the other side in the war, questioned his honesty or sincerity in saying what he said. Now let us hear what Professor Wiley had to say about Lee's decision to fight for the Confederacy. "Lee . . . was the product of a locality and an authority that was two and a half times as old as the Union. His first loyalty was to Virginia. As the intersectional crisis approached in 1860–1861, he condemned the extremists, north and south, who were threatening the permanency of the Union. But when the break came and he had to choose between Virginia and the nation, he chose Virginia. . . . There can be no doubt of Lee's sincerity." Parenthetically, doesn't it sound quaint today to be told that there were northern extremists as well as southern, threatening the permanency of the Union?

At this juncture, Professor Wiley introduced a comment that I believe bears significantly on much of the history of the Civil War that is being written today. He said, "As Americans of our time ponder the events that led to secession and war, cognizance should be taken of the fact that a man as sincere, as admirable, as unselfish, and as honorable as Lee could prefer the state—his state—above the nation. It is not fair to judge Lee on the basis of twentieth-century ideas concerning the Union, for his ideas about the relative position of the nation and the state—ideas deriving largely from his background, experiences, and associations—were quite different from those of present-day Americans reared in an intellectual atmosphere vastly different from those of a hundred years ago." How odd, outdated, and unfashionable Professor Wiley's words sound today! I shall return shortly to his comment about fairness in judging Lee. But for the moment, I go to the fourth scholar on my list.

A recent comprehensive, one-volume history of the Civil War is that of Professor Russell Weigley, one of the nation's foremost military historians. He is a native Pennsylvanian, and he taught at Temple University in Philadelphia.

In discussing the causes of the war, Weigley says the soldiers of both the Union and Confederate armies enlisted out of a commitment to their ideals of American nationalism. But, and here I quote: "Southern volunteers [and in the beginning, virtually all of the soldiers on both sides were volunteers] enlisted to preserve differing aspects of the same ideals [as those of the Northern volunteers], perceived differently through the prism of the particular institutions of the South, especially, but not only, slavery. They volunteered to protect the American Revolution's legacy of self-government." Isn't that arresting? "Legacy of self-government."

What is the point of giving these quotations from the four scholars? It is that not one of them assigned slavery alone as the cause of war, or even as the primary cause, though all of them were keenly aware of its presence and its role in bringing on the conflict. Though none of them explicitly mentioned states' rights, it comes as an unavoidable inference from what they did mention. The question, then, is, "What has brought such a change in attitudes toward the cause of the war?"

I believe Professor Wiley hit the mark dead center when he warned against the reading of today's attitudes into the history of earlier times. One of the more famed historians of the past generation, Professor Carl Becker, wrote of the tendency for every generation to rewrite history in its own image. It is perhaps inevitable that we hold up the past to the mirror of the present. But this should be done with meticulous discretion and with due regard to the actual records of the past. Otherwise, what we call "history" emerges as the fallacy of presentism: passing moral judgment on the past according to the values, biases, and arrogance of the present. I am convinced that presentism is rampant in much of the world of Civil War scholarship today.

Presentism is being applied to northern motives as well as southern. If slavery was the fundamental cause of the war, and the southern population went to war simply to preserve it, then the northern population must have gone to war to combat it. But the contemporary records of President Lincoln's words, the speeches and actions of the Union Congress, the writings of the more prominent northern journalists of the era, and, until recently, the conclusion of most American historians, reveal unmistakably that the northern population did not go to war for the purpose of abolishing slavery. They went to war for the purpose of preserving the Union. We've heard in the harsh words of Senator John Sherman of Ohio that he considered the fate of the slaves inconsequential in comparison to that of saving the Union. Yet the literature on the war that is appearing today increasingly comes to say or imply that the northerners went to war in a moral crusade against the sin of slavery. An article in a recent issue of *U.S. News* put it this way: "The Civil War was a fight over slavery. The South was for it, the North was against it." In a major historiographical work on the war published some three years ago, Professor Michael Les Benedict wrote intriguingly (and apparently approvingly) that the civil rights movement of the second half of the twentieth century enlisted most American historians in its ranks, making them alter their perceptions of the cause or causes of the war, so that no longer was it the northern determination to preserve the Union; it had now become "The Battle Cry of Freedom."

Is this what the visitors to our parks will be told? Is the war to be presented as a nineteenth-century morality play of northern saints versus southern sinners? I certainly hope not, for I believe there was enough sin involved for everybody to get a generous piece of it. For example, even American slavery itself, though practiced largely by the South in the nineteenth century, was, in many respects, a national sin. The slave traders who bought, transported, and sold the slaves to purchasers in America (the most brutal aspect connected with the entire institution of slavery) hailed disproportionately from England, New England, and other northern colonies and states. The foundation of many of the family fortunes of those areas lay in the slave trade—"blackbirding," it has cynically been called. I have learned only recently that the endowment of one of our great northern universities, Brown University, came in part from the slave trade. Doubtless there are others of a similar background. One of the bitter ironies of the history of slavery is that the efforts made in the United States constitutional convention to abolish the overseas slave trade were defeated by opposition from a coalition of delegates from the states of the Deep South and—guess where—New England. Also, one needs to point out that the booming cotton textile industry of New England and other northern states rested ultimately upon slave labor.

Lincoln was keenly aware of the northern complicity in slavery. Consequently, in his second inaugural address he quoted from the Bible, "Woe unto the world because of offences! for it must needs be that offences come; but woe to that man by whom the offence cometh!" To this point he seemed to be chastising only the Confederates, but then he said, since God now willed to remove the offence, he gave "to both North and South, this terrible war, as the woe due to those by whom the offence came." Both North and South!

Perhaps the most significant question to be asked about the Park Service discussion of slavery is: Will it be presented in the context of the much larger and more volatile and difficult subject of race? For I would remind my hearers that American slavery existed solely within that context. All American slaves were black; a white person could not legally be a slave.

Professor Gienapp says that if the American slaves had not been black, slavery would doubtless have disappeared peacefully before 1860. I have long believed this. Why is this such an important part of the slavery issue? It is important because it exercised a profound effect on how the institution was regarded in both the South and the North.

Remember, three-fourths of southern white families owned no slaves, yet they joined the slaveowners in support of the institution, even to the point of shedding oceans of their blood in the effort. Why did they do so? The basic answer is that they believed that Africans were innately inferior to whites and incapable of being assimilated into society as free citizens; that emancipation would result in the Africanization of the South, a reversion to barbarism, violence, and social degradation. Here are the words, harsh but candid, from a member of the non-slaveowning class who had risen to prosperity and high political position, Governor Andrew Johnson of Tennessee. "If you liberate the Negro," he said, "what will be the next step? Blood, rape and rapine will be our portion. You can't get rid of the Negro except by holding him in slavery." Other southern political figures from the non-slaveowning class held similar beliefs. They spoke for their people.

I have said that the question of race is important because it affected northern attitudes toward slavery also. Indeed, northern views of the role of blacks in the American society were strikingly similar to southern views, though because blacks were relatively few in the North, the issue was obviously less urgent there. One of the reasons blacks were fewer in the North was that they were not welcome there; in many instances they were not allowed. A number of northern states that were close to the South, and therefore especially subject to black immigration in one form or another, had laws that excluded them from settling in the state.

Ironically, Illinois, the home of Abraham Lincoln, had such a law. The few blacks who were already there when the law was enacted were not citizens, could not vote, could not serve on juries, could not send their children to public schools. In only five northern states could blacks vote; these were New England states where there were virtually no blacks. Lincoln served repeatedly in the legislature of his state and one term in the U.S. Congress. His greatest claim to fame before becoming president sprang from his outspoken opposition to the further spread of slavery into the federal territories of the West. Insofar as I have been able to ascertain, he never condemned his state's black exclusion law or any of the many other racially restrictive laws and practices of his and various other northern states. He openly said he opposed the granting of citizenship to Illinois blacks; he spoke vehemently against any prospect of the intermarriage of blacks and whites; and he said that he preferred the white race to predominate in society.

What about the federal territories from which Lincoln would exclude slavery? After all, this is the specific issue that precipitated secession and war. He said he wished the federal territories to be reserved for "free, white settlers." He repeatedly said he would make no move against slavery in the states where it was already practiced.

Almost as ironic as Lincoln's views were those of Congressman David Wilmot of Pennsylvania, whose proposal to exclude slavery from any territory wrested from Mexico in the war with that country came near splitting the United States a few years before the Civil War. Wilmot explained at the time, "I do not plead the cause of the slave." He said his proposal did not arise out of any "squeamish sensibility upon the subject of slavery, nor morbid sympathy for the slave. . . . The Negro race already occupy enough of this fair continent," he asserted. He said he was quite willing to call his proposal "the white man's proviso." In other words, his proposal to limit the spread of slavery was actually a proposal to limit the spread of blacks into the western territories.

It is perhaps impossible to analyze with accuracy the conglomeration of beliefs and emotions that moved Lincoln and the majority of the citizens of Illinois and other northern states in their political decisions. But one of the identifiable elements in both their opposition to the further spread of slavery and, ironically, their simultaneous acquiescence in its continued existence in the South was a fear of black immigration north if the slaves should be set free.

Eventually, emancipation became a secondary Union war aim, justified by Lincoln as a military necessity. But many of the battles of the war occurred before this came about. On the eve of the war, Congress passed a constitutional amendment, the original thirteenth amendment, guaranteeing slavery permanently in the states where it already existed. Lincoln gave his support to this amendment. If the Illinois soldiers who fought at Shiloh in April 1862 had been told when they enlisted that they would be waging a war for the purpose of abolishing slavery, many of them, possibly most of them, probably would not have joined up.

I should like to return briefly to the subject of states' rights, or southern rights, as an important cause of the Civil War. The fashionable view among certain revisionist historians today is that this was simply a rationalization concocted by southerners after the war for the purpose of downplaying slavery as the cause of their resort to arms: a fig leaf, as it were, plastered over the locus of southern sin.

I believe that the revisionist accusations justify a word on the history of the political doctrine of states' rights or southern rights. It had a long and honorable history apart from slavery. Ironically, the man considered by some to be the father of the doctrine, George Mason of Virginia, was an enemy of slavery and an advocate of emancipation. He was a member of the U.S. constitutional convention, but he refused to sign the document and opposed the ratification of it by his state. Hear one of the reasons that he gave for his opposition: "The majority [northerners] will be governed by their own interests. . . . The Southern States are the minority in both houses. Is it expected that they will deliver themselves bound, hand and foot, to the Eastern States, and enable them to exclaim . . . 'The Lord hath delivered them into our hands'?" In addition to urging the inclusion of a bill of rights, Mason called for provisions that, in effect, would give the South a brake on legislation it deemed injurious to its interests. His objections and recommendations clearly foreshadowed the full states' rights position taken by later southern spokesmen.

Thomas Jefferson and James Madison invoked states' rights in their resolutions condemning the Alien and Sedition Acts of the John Adams administration. They argued that all powers not explicitly delegated to the federal government were reserved to the states or the people, a proposition riveted into the Constitution by the tenth amendment to that document, a long-forgotten part of the Constitution.

The firebrand political maverick John Randolph of Roanoke, in opposing a cluster of acts by Congress in the early nineteenth century, scoffed at the idea that the states had surrendered any of their sovereignty by joining the Union. He said that to ask a state to give up a portion of its sovereignty was analogous to asking a lady to yield a portion of her chastity. A long line of South Carolina writers, including Thomas Cooper, Robert Turnbull, and finally John C. Calhoun, upheld states' rights as a necessary barrier to allegedly unconstitutional federal actions concerning such issues as the tariff, federal expenditures for internal improvements, and slavery.

The most fiery pre-secession assertion of states' rights had nothing to do with slavery; it involved the relationship of the state governments to the Native Americans residing in the states. In 1832, the Supreme Court of the

United States issued an order to the state of Georgia concerning its treatment of the Cherokees living there. Governor Wilson Lumpkin indignantly rejected the order and declared that he would suffer no court to interfere with a state's right to govern its own population. "If Georgia has not these rights," he said, "then I say let her name be blotted out from the map of free states. What! The political rights of Georgia, subject to the decision of a few superannuated life estate judges. . . . Submission to such a state of things would degrade the State below the level of the subdued remnant of tribes of the aboriginals themselves." President Andrew Jackson, a renowned Indian fighter himself, supported Lumpkin.

Nor was the states' rights ideology confined to southerners. During this country's War of 1812 with Great Britain, the focus of the states' rights sentiment lay in New England, where the war was extremely unpopular. Some of the New Englanders even went so far as to consider secession; and Congressman Daniel Webster of New Hampshire, the figure destined eventually to become the high priest of national sovereignty, said that if the U.S. Congress should pass a national conscription act, the duty of the state government would be that of interposing itself between the national government and the citizens of the state. In other words, he was advocating state nullification of federal law.

Astonishingly, in view of later developments, the textbook on the U.S. Constitution used at West Point during the cadetship of such future Confederates as Albert Sidney Johnston and other southerners (a work by a New Yorker named William Rawle) contained unmistakable elements of states' rights, including, explicitly, that of secession as an ultimate redress of grievance.

By the time of the Civil War, the belief in the constitutional protection of states' rights was ingrained in the South's political creed. Every southern state, in seceding from the Union, invoked the doctrine of states' rights, including that of secession. Even those southern political spokesmen and journalists who opposed secession at the time freely conceded that states possessed the constitutional right to secede in an extremity. Countless individuals, in making a choice to join the Confederacy, explained it in terms of defending constitutional rights. Congressman William Preston of Kentucky, for example, wrote his wife that he would never support secession out of a desire to preserve slavery, but that he believed it his duty to do so in defense of the constitutional rights of the states. Confederate soldiers' letters affirm overwhelmingly that they fought not to preserve slavery, but out of a sense of honor and duty in defense of their states and homes.

This raises the question for those who challenge such motives: If the American colonists were willing to go to war in defense of their belief in the rights of independence and self-government, and if the northern people were willing to go to war in the defense of their belief in the constitutional guarantee of the permanence of the Union, why is it unthinkable that the southern people might be willing to go to war in defense of their belief in the constitutional protection of states' rights, including the right to own slaves and to secede? Even Abraham Lincoln had previously believed in the generic right of a people to withdraw from the larger body politic. A few years before the Civil War he proclaimed this to be a universal right, a "most sacred right," he said, "one that will ultimately bring freedom to the entire world." Are we to believe that southerners were less capable than others of holding such exalted views?

If the United States had been an absolute despotism, neither the spread of slavery nor the opposition to it would have caused a war. Whatever the ruler decreed would have prevailed. But the United States was not an absolute despotism. It was a federal republic operating under a constitution that provided for the existence of a nation made up of component states. The document outlined generally the boundaries of authority of both national and state governments, but it could not establish them with complete precision, nor could it settle all disputes a priori, in advance. On any issue that kindled intense and sustained emotion, the ultimate authority could be decided only by a test of arms.

Let us return to Lincoln's statement that "somehow" slavery was the cause of the war. This observation becomes particularly apt when a belief in slavery is linked to an equally powerful belief in states' rights and the constitutional guarantees of those rights. Any perceived threat to them arouses a determination to protect them at all costs.

Slavery did not of itself cause the Civil War. After all, Americans had lived with slavery for over two hundred years without a resort to arms. The crisis of the times was precipitated by the northern change of attitude toward the institution and toward the relationship between the nation and the states. The rhetoric and announced positions of the Republican Party, an exclusively northern party, appeared to southerners to repudiate the rights and guarantees of the Constitution. New York Republican senator William H. Seward's statements that a "higher law" than the Constitution applied to the question of slavery in the federal territories, and that there was an "irrepressible conflict" between the advocates of slavery and those of freedom, rang ominously in southern ears.

The platform of the Republican Party in 1860 appeared to southerners to be in direct conflict with the Constitution in its denial of the authority of Congress, a territorial legislature, or, "any other power" [a thinly disguised reference to the Supreme Court of the United States, and possibly to the Constitution itself] to legalize slavery in a federal territory. This denial, coupled with Lincoln's rejection of any compromise on the issue, convinced the citizens of the Deep South that their only protection lay in secession, a decision that brought the war.

Louisiana and Secession

This exercise is not addressed to the substantive causes of secession: that is, the southern belief, whether right or wrong, that slavery was vital to the region's economic and social well-being; and the conviction, right or wrong, that Republican ascendancy posed a mortal threat to slavery. Instead, this essay is concerned with the unique course, and the paradox, of secession by Louisiana.

Louisiana in 1860–61 was perhaps the unlikeliest state of the Deep South to attempt a break from the Union. Ten years earlier the state legislature had refused as much as the gesture of sending delegates to the Nashville Convention, a gathering designed by John C. Calhoun to crystallize southern sectional awareness and political cohesiveness, and hoped by such fire-eaters as Robert Barnwell Rhett of South Carolina to pave the way for secession itself. An overwhelming majority of the leaders as well as the rank and file of both Whig and Democratic parties in Louisiana had endorsed the Compromise of 1850, a group of measures thought at the time to have settled the sectional issue. Among the state's major political figures, only the volatile Senator Pierre Soulé opposed the compromise, and even he in doing so felt obliged to make a statement affirming his allegiance to the Union.[1] His supporters in rejecting the compromise were so few that the New Orleans *Daily Picayune* dismissed them as a handful of South Carolina emigrants who were still under the influence of the Calhoun press of their native state.[2]

In addition to the non-slaveholding farmers of the hill and piney-woods areas of Louisiana—the earlier stronghold of Jacksonian Democracy—the state contained various groups who by interest and tradition were strongly unionist in sentiment. Much of the population of the Deep South's chief metropolis, New Orleans, fitted this description, including the merchants and bankers because of their economic ties with the North, and the European immigrants (who in 1860 comprised about 40 percent of the city's white residents) because of their newly kindled American patriotism, their lingering class resentment, and their opposition to slavery. Also, a significant portion of the New Orleanians were of northern birth and upbringing. Even among the group of Louisiana citizens having the greatest immediate vested interest in slavery—that is, the slaveowning minority itself—there was an important element with exceptionally firm ties to the Union. This was the sugar planters, who were the dominant economic, social, and political class of rural South Louisiana. Their welfare rested partly upon the federal tariff, a measure not expected to endure under the aegis of a politically independent Cotton Kingdom. Most of the sugar planters had formerly been Whigs, and had looked with alarm on any threat to national solidarity.

Moreover, the conduct of Louisiana voters in the critical presidential election of 1860 indicated convincingly that, in spite of the forces of disruption at work during the preceding decade, the majority of the state's population still opposed disunion. John C. Breckinridge, the candidate of the Constitutional Democratic party (a code name for the southern wing of the Democratic party), received Louisiana's electoral vote, but he won it with a decided minority of the popular vote. Together John Bell of the Constitutional Union party and Stephen A. Douglas of the National Democratic party (a code name for the northern wing of the Democratic party) won more than 55 percent of the state's popular vote. Bell alone drew almost as great a vote as Breckinridge. Nor did a vote for Breckinridge necessarily mean a vote for disunion, though doubtless most if not all the state's disunionists voted for him. Ironically, his heaviest vote came from the hill and piney-woods areas, the very areas that would take the strongest stand against secession when it actually came. This was partly because of the influence of Senator John Slidell's invincible Democratic machine, but it was also partly because these voters looked upon the Breckinridge platform as the nearest of kin to Jacksonian Democracy.

How then explain the state's sudden turnabout between the presidential election in November 1860 and the fateful decision to secede in January 1861? First, one must understand the conditional nature of Louisiana unionism. Insofar as can be determined, the bulk of the citizens of the state, whether unionist or states' rightist in political outlook, believed in the right of secession as an ultimate measure of self-preservation. Perhaps Governor Joseph Walker, in his 1850 inaugural, expressed the prevailing mood in saying he would look upon the dissolution of the Union as the greatest calamity that could befall the people of the entire nation. Nevertheless, he continued, if the antislavery agitation of the North should lead to actual aggression, or if the federal government should upset the equality of the members of the Union, then he would advocate making common cause with the other slave states in breaking away from the parent body.[3] Seen in this light, much of the Louisiana unionism was subject to change under the pressure of events.

This pressure became increasingly fierce as the Compromise of 1850 dissolved in the heat kindled by the events of the times. The leading voices of public and private expression in Louisiana, as in the rest of the South, vehemently condemned the personal liberty laws of the northern states, the contents of the novel *Uncle Tom's Cabin,* the antislavery activities in Kansas, the provocative announcements of Senator William H. Seward of New York, and John Brown's raid on Harpers Ferry—condemned them as wanton violations of either the letter or the spirit of the Compromise of 1850, and of sectional amity and national goodwill. The Harpers Ferry incident and the subsequent apotheosis of John Brown by many leading northern writers and ministers were especially inflammatory. In the words of a modern historian: "Every flag lowered, every poem published, every speech intoned, and every bell rung in honor of the hoary-headed abolitionist confirmed the suspicion of many Southerners that the North wished to destroy the South."[4] Governor Robert Wickliffe of Louisiana pointed to Harpers Ferry, and to what he called the northern sympathy for treason and murder there, and solemnly warned of an approaching crisis in the affairs of the state.[5]

Clearly Louisiana unionism had eroded heavily since the state's virtually unanimous endorsement of the Compromise of 1850. The conditions to this unionism which had been expressed on the eve of that compromise by Governor Walker seemed now about to be violated. The antislavery agitation of the North had indeed led to actual, if limited, aggression at Harpers Ferry; and, in the judgment of many Louisiana citizens, the forthcoming presidential election threatened to upset the equality of the members of the Union.

This, then, is the perspective in which the state's vote in the 1860 presidential election must be seen. The majority popular vote for Bell and Douglas, taken together, was indeed a unionist vote, but the vote of a qualified and shrinking unionism: a unionism ill prepared to survive a victory of the Republican candidate. Which, of course, is what actually occurred. Lincoln's election, in Louisiana eyes, marked the culmination of a political process long watched with rising apprehension. It placed in the executive position of the national government a man and party who represented only the interests of the rest of the country, and who were acknowledged enemies of the state's most sacrosanct economic and social institution.

Louisiana fire-eaters considered the Republican victory itself sufficiently dangerous to justify immediate secession. "Why, then, should we desire to consort any longer with a people, so antagonistic to us in feeling, principles and interests?" asked a Pointe Coupée editor. "Why, with one effort, not heave off this incubus, which is oppressing our energies, strangling our commerce, and dwarfing the natural growth of our national proportions?" A prominent New Orleans journal of southern rights persuasion branded treasonous anyone opposed to immediate separation. More rational, but also more ominous in that they represented the views of a great body of the state's unionists, were the words of two of the leading antisecessionist newspapers. Just before the election the *Daily Picayune,* which favored Bell, said: "[Lincoln and his party] will be the most moderate of national men in their professions, without abating a jot of the ultimate purpose of forcing the extinction of slavery. . . . It is for these future, progressing, insidious, fatal results, more than from an 'overt act' of direct oppression, that the triumph of Black Republicanism . . . is to be profoundly deprecated by every Southern man of every shade of party opinion." Immediately after the election the New Orleans *Bee,* which had favored Douglas, said: "The result [of the election] proved astounding. It showed the tremendous power and popularity of Black Republicanism. . . . What could be alleged against such convincing and irrefragable proof of Northern unsoundness? With what shadow of reason could Southern men be advised to submit and await the possible events of the future when abolitionism had swept every Northern Commonwealth, and had even displayed unexpected and growing power in some of the slaveholding States themselves?"[6]

Probably in no event would, or could, Louisiana have assumed the lead in the secessionist movement. The South Carolina Hotspurs would not have tolerated such effrontery. But the outcome of the presidential election unquestionably prepared the Louisiana mind to reconsider the sectional issue once the process of secession was actually under way. That the newly elected governor, Thomas Overton Moore, and the majority in the legislature represented the dominant Slidell sector of the Democratic party—the very sector that earlier had helped stage a southern bolt from the national Democratic convention in Charleston and the subsequent formation of the Breckinridge party—that these circumstances prevailed in Louisiana made inevitable the calling of a state convention on the question of secession. Although the governor himself had previously opposed the idea of secession, he now reversed his position, presumably at Slidell's instance, called a special session of the legislature, and recommended a state convention for the express purpose of seceding. On December 10, 1860, the legislature approved a convention and set January 7, 1861, for the election of delegates.

The present discourse has nothing important to add to Charles B. Dew's findings and perceptive comments on the election itself. The essential facts are that the immediate secessionists polled 52.3 percent of the popular vote, but because of the distribution of these votes within the legislative districts, and because slaves were included in the count for representation, the immediate secessionists gained a comfortable majority of the convention seats—80 of 130. But, curiously, the popular vote was almost 13,000 below that of the presidential election only two months earlier.[7] Who the stay-at-homes were, why they stayed at home, or whether their votes would have changed the outcome cannot actually be determined, though some scholars, including Jefferson Davis Bragg and Roger W. Shugg, have speculated that these citizens were opposed to immediate secession, but remained passive because they were resigned to it, and that their votes would indeed have altered the result. Yet the proportion of absentees was about as great in secessionist parishes as in the others. Voting was light in the secessionist parishes, presumably because of a lack of opposition, or because of the weakness of the opposition. Hence it may be argued that as many of the immediate secessionists as of their opponents failed to vote because they also believed the die was cast and therefore that their votes were not required for victory.

Without attempting to settle this question, I wish to suggest that the ultimate course of the state in withdrawing from the Union probably would not have been altered even if the immediate secessionists had not won the election. For, as all scholars agree, the great majority of those voters and delegates who opposed immediate secession were by no means opposed to secession itself. Rather, they were cooperationists: citizens who, according to the best informed analysis of the time, had despaired of obtaining satisfaction in the Union, and who differed from the immediate secessionists only in desiring a united southern movement instead of action by the state alone.[8]

Two forces, one external, the other internal, were at work in dissolv-
ing the final Louisiana opposition to immediate secession. The external
force was the collapse of all efforts to achieve an acceptable sectional compromise. Again, it is in the steady progression to secessionism of many
formerly unionist organs of expression that the effects of this breakdown
are most clearly discernible. For example, shortly before the presidential
election the New Orleans *Bee* had proclaimed its unionism under "every
conceivable circumstance," as it said; "whether the Presidential election
terminates in the choice of Bell, or Douglas, or Lincoln or Breckinridge;
whether the next Congress is Black Republican or Conservative; whether
Seward counsels irrepressible conflict, or Rhett strives to muster an armed
force to prevent Lincoln's inauguration; whether John Brown is canonized
in New England, or solemn sanhedrins of Secessionists devote the Union
to the infernal Gods. The real Union men," concluded this ringing editorial, "have not the slightest idea of breaking up the Confederacy," by which
archaic term, of course, it meant the Union.[9]

But the outcome of the presidential election caused the *Bee* to favor a
state convention on secession; and on the 14th of December, immediately
after the rejection by President-elect Lincoln of the Crittenden compromise proposals, the *Bee* wrote: "The North and South are heterogeneous
and are better apart. . . . We are doomed if we proclaim not our political
independence."[10] This metamorphosis offers a vivid Louisiana illustration
of the accuracy of Dwight L. Dumond's observation that the inflexible Republican opposition to the various compromise measures "broke down the
differences of opinion and united the two great parties [that is, the secessionists and antisecessionists] in the lower South."[11]

But the internal force was as important as the external in breaking
down these differences. This was the force of propaganda, indoctrination,
and coercion at the command of the radical secessionists. From forum,
press, pulpit, and fireside it bombarded the minds of the citizenry. Senator
Judah P. Benjamin, a former Whig and conservative, now joined his senior
colleague Slidell in advising the state to secede without delay. "We must
be blind indeed," warned Benjamin, "if we entertain the remotest hope that
widespread ruin, degradation and dishonor will not inevitably result from
tame submission to the rule which our enemies propose to inaugurate. . . ."[12]
Fire-eater newspapers redoubled their efforts, stigmatizing all opponents of
immediate secession with the label "submissionist." The clergy strengthened the separatist chorus. The Presbyterian minister Benjamin Morgan

Palmer's famous (or infamous, if you please) Thanksgiving Day sermon proclaiming divine sanction for secession was printed and spread throughout the state. Emissaries from South Carolina and Alabama (both now out of the Union) made impassioned appeals to the Louisiana convention. Vigilance committees harassed citizens thought to be unionist in sympathy.

The decision of the Louisiana convention itself was anticlimactic inasmuch as the election of a large majority of delegates pledged to immediate secession had already settled the issue. Yet the deliberations of the convention (if its hasty motions and exchanges can be called "deliberations") revealed the sharp turn that had taken place in the minds of Louisianians, not only since the presidential election, but since the election of convention delegates also.

The most significant recent development was the shift of many former cooperationists into a more radical attitude toward secession. This was indicated in the convention measures presented to delay the state's withdrawal from the Union, and in the fate of these measures. First there was the motion by Joseph A. Rozier of New Orleans calling for a convention in Nashville, Tennessee, of slaveholding state representatives to propose amendments to the United States Constitution for protecting slavery, and empowering the Nashville meeting to carry out the secession of the slaveholding states if the amendments should not be promptly ratified by the rest of the nation. Rozier's motion was defeated 106 to 24. This majority included the votes of all the immediate secessionist delegates plus more than half of those elected as cooperationists. The defecting cooperationists thus demonstrated they were no longer willing to support overtures of compromise or wait for separation by united southern action. If their votes on the subsequent proposals for delay would show they were not fully converted to immediate secession by Louisiana, their votes on the Rozier measure demonstrated clearly they had ceased to be cooperationists.

The second delaying motion was that of James O. Fuqua of East Feliciana Parish. It too is usually considered a cooperationist measure because it received the support of most of the delegates who had been elected as cooperationists. Shugg, for example, in his essay on the cooperationist movement in Louisiana says merely that Fuqua's motion called for an Alabama convention of slaveholding states to cooperate in establishing a southern confederacy.[13] Ralph A. Wooster in his work on the secession conventions says only that the Fuqua motion called for Louisiana participation in an Alabama convention "for consideration of" a union of slaveholding states, and "would have delayed secession until after consultation with the other southern states."[14]

Both of these statements are accurate insofar as they go, but both fore-shorten and distort the Fuqua proposal. It was not a true cooperationist measure; it was a conditional secessionist measure. What it actually called for was a declaration repudiating the principles of the Republican party, and for a resolution absolving Louisiana from all allegiance to the Union if the federal government should undertake to coerce a seceded state, in which event Louisiana would make common cause with the seceded state and "resist such coercive measure with all the force at her command." The motion provided meanwhile for the appointment of Louisiana representatives to the forthcoming Montgomery, Alabama, convention, with instructions to urge the immediate formation of an independent union of slaveholding states. The motion was defeated 74 to 47.

The final attempt to delay Louisiana secession was the motion of Charles Bienvenu of New Orleans that the decision of the convention be submitted to a statewide popular vote. It was defeated 84 to 45. On January 26 the convention adopted the secession ordinance 113 to 17. All but 7 of the delegates signed the instrument; this handful of dissenters may fairly be called the only unconditional unionists of the convention. "The deed has been done," wrote the once unionist *Daily Picayune*. "'We breathe deeper and freer' for it."[15]

The actions of the Louisiana convention indicate also that the delegates no longer looked upon secession as a feat necessarily to be achieved by ex-plicitly sanctioned constitutional procedures, or to be sustained by peaceful means. In other words, by the time the secession ordinance was adopted, the delegates (and doubtless their constituents) were aware they were en-gaged in revolution, and that the undertaking was likely to end in war.

True, in the beginning there was talk about the constitutional right of secession and the lack of danger in such a course. But these sentiments quickly disappeared. The war danger was all along a major argument of the cooperationists and unionists. Their feelings were powerfully voiced by the convention's most implacable opponent of secession, James G. Taliaferro of Catahoula Parish, who warned his colleagues of anarchy and war, and accused them of perpetrating revolution.

But there was no need for such unionist warnings. After the Republi-can victory in the presidential election, and especially after the collapse of the compromise efforts, the secessionists themselves increasingly admitted the revolutionary nature of their cause and the possibility, indeed the probability, of war in its behalf. As early as November 29, 1860, the New Orleans *Daily Delta,* a fire-eater newspaper, acknowledged the risks involved in secession, but concluded in words intended to be reassuring: "There is not a country of the civilized world which has not been compelled to pass through desolating wars and bloody revolutions."[16] Two weeks later the *Daily Picayune,* which by now was in transition from unionism to secessionism, described the rise of "what may truly be denominated a revolutionary sentiment in this State."[17] The messages of Governor Moore and Senator Benjamin to the convention, to say nothing of the governor's action in seizing the federal military installations in the state, were unmistakably revolutionary, as was the convention's decision not to submit the ordinance of secession to a popular vote. A secessionist delegate expressed the prevailing mood succinctly: "The time for argument has passed," he told the convention. "We were sent here to act. We are in times of revolution, and questions of form must sink into insignificance."[18]

By recognizing that the secession of Louisiana was indeed revolution, and that the convention delegates and most if not all the population were aware of this fact, we bring their actions into truer historical perspective, however unwise and tragic they proved to have been. We see in them not inexplicable aberrations from the social norm, but a pattern of behavior common to revolutions. For example, we better understand the role of the fire-eaters. They were what Crane Brinton calls the "eternal Figaros" in the anatomy of revolution: the essential agents of agitation and alarm.[19] We ought not then be surprised over the harassment and intimidation of unionists, who, in the eyes of the secessionists, were the Tories of the day. (Everyone knows how Patriots treat Tories.) We can more fully comprehend the haste of the Louisiana convention delegates, their refusal to submit the ordinance to a popular vote, though, according to so unsympathetic a scholar as Shugg, and certainly in my own opinion, they had nothing to fear by doing so. Revolutionary bodies do not customarily tolerate delays or risk plebiscites. Instead, they act, trusting their actions will be ratified, in Thomas Jefferson's immortal words, by the "Supreme Judge of the world."

NOTES

1. William H. Adams, *The Whig Party of Louisiana* (Lafayette, La., 1973), p. 206.

2. Avery O. Craven, *The Growth of Southern Nationalism, 1848–1861* (Baton Rouge, 1953), p. 106.

3. Charles E. A. Gayarré, *History of Louisiana,* 4 vols. (New York, 1854–1866), IV, 673–74.

4. Donald E. Reynolds, *Editors Make War: Southern Newspapers in the Secession Crisis* (Nashville, 1970), p. 12.

5. Gayarré, *History of Louisiana,* IV, 686–88.

6. Quoted in Reynolds, *Editors Make War,* pp. 141, 143, 156–57, 215.

7. Charles B. Dew, "Who Won the Secession Election in Louisiana?" *Journal of Southern History,* 36 (February, 1970), 22–32.

8. New Orleans *Daily Picayune,* January 1, 1861, as quoted in ibid., 21.

9. Quoted in Reynolds, *Editors Make War,* p. 153.

10. Ibid.

11. Dwight L. Dumond, ed., *Southern Editorials on Secession* (New York, London, 1931), p. xx.

12. Quoted in Willie M. Caskey, *Secession and Restoration of Louisiana* (Baton Rouge, 1938), p. 23.

13. Roger W. Shugg, "A Suppressed Co-operationist Protest Against Secession," *Louisiana Historical Quarterly,* 19 (January, 1936), 200.

14. Ralph A. Wooster, *The Secession Conventions of the South* (Princeton, 1962), p. 110.

15. Lane C. Kendall, "The Interregnum in Louisiana in 1861," *Louisiana Historical Quarterly,* 16 (July, 1933), 391–95, 402–05; Wooster, *The Secession Conventions of the South,* pp. 101–02.

16. Quoted in Reynolds, *Editors Make War,* p. 174.

17. Quoted in Jefferson Davis Bragg, *Louisiana in the Confederacy* (Baton Rouge, 1941), p. 21.

18. Quoted in Roger W. Shugg, *Origins of Class Struggle in Louisiana: A Social History of White Farmers and Laborers During Slavery and After, 1840–1875* (Baton Rouge, 1939), p. 167.

19. C. Crane Brinton, *The Anatomy of Revolution* (New York, 1938), pp. 82–83.

The Resort to Arms

The nation's response to secession was at first extremely uncertain. President Buchanan, who would remain in office until Lincoln's inauguration on March 4, 1861, was by nature a conciliatory man. He also had strong sympathies for the South, and the makeup and attitude of his cabinet reflected this persuasion. Southerners held a number of positions in the cabinet: Howell Cobb of Georgia as secretary of the treasury, Jacob Thompson of Mississippi as secretary of the interior, and John Floyd of Virginia as secretary of war. Outside the cabinet, such prominent southern political leaders as Senator John Slidell of Louisiana and Senator Jefferson Davis of Mississippi were among Buchanan's closest confidants. Unquestionably, these men influenced his behavior.

The President's own political thinking was murky. A literal reading of his 1860 annual message to Congress indicates incompatible views on the relationship between the nation and its constituent parts. He declared secession to be illegal but that the Federal government had no right to coerce a state to remain in the Union. Seward parodied the address as saying it meant that "no state has the right to secede unless it wishes to" and that "it is the President's duty to enforce the laws, unless somebody opposes him."

Buchanan can legitimately be faulted for indecision and a weakness of will. Certainly his behavior in the national crisis is unimpressive when compared with that of an Andrew Jackson or an Abraham Lincoln. But Buchanan feared, possibly rightly, that a coercive move or threat at that point by the Federal government would scatter rather than extinguish the sparks of secession.

He gave his annual address with its opinions on secession in early December 1860 before any state had actually withdrawn. His forbearance did not, of course, prevent secession by the seven states of the lower South. Possibly his views encouraged the states to withdraw; but, more likely,

117

they would have done so in any event, and his tolerance may very well have helped prevent secession at that time by the eight remaining slave states. Indirectly it may have helped prevent secession altogether by some of them. With at least a trace of reason he could believe he might by caution be able to contain the secessionist fire. In the last weeks of his term, after secession was a fait accompli and the southern members gone from his cabinet, he strengthened his hand by appointing staunch unionists in their stead.

Reinforcing Buchanan's insistence on caution was his hope for the adoption of yet another great political compromise that would prevent or limit secession. Both houses of Congress appointed committees to study the feasibility of such a move, and the likeliest of the proposals was submitted to the Senate committee on December 18 by Senator John J. Crittenden of Kentucky, who now held the seat once occupied by Henry Clay and who saw himself to be Clay's heir as the architect of political accommodation. The most important article in the Crittenden Compromise called for amending the Constitution so as to restore the Missouri Compromise line and extend it to the border of California, with slavery to be prohibited in federal territories north of the line but recognized and protected south of it.

Led by Senator Jefferson Davis, southerners on the committee expressed a willingness to accept the compromise if the Republicans would do so. This the Republicans refused to do, in part on the advice of President-elect Lincoln, who said privately he was ready to support a guarantee of slavery in the states where it already existed, but advised, ". . . entertain no proposition for a compromise in regard to the extension of slavery. . . . The instant you do, they have us under again; all our labor is lost, and sooner or later must be done over. . . . The tug has to come and better now than later." Thus the most promising of the compromise efforts failed. That in the long run it would have averted or curbed secession is problematical, but at the moment the rejection of the Crittenden Compromise played a significant part in causing such states as Georgia, Louisiana, and Texas to move for immediate withdrawal.

Compromise efforts attempted outside of the Federal government also failed. The most notable of these was made by the Washington Peace Convention, which met in February in the national capital on the invitation of the Virginia state legislature. With ex-President John Tyler in the chair, delegates from twenty-one states—none from the seceded states—drew up a set of proposals quite similar to the Crittenden Compromise, but containing certain articles designed to overcome Republican objections, especially a criticism by Lincoln that the Crittenden proposal would encourage southerners to seek the annexation of new slave lands south of the border. The Washington Convention would provide a sectional veto—a form of Calhoun's concurrent majority—in the creation of new federal territories by requiring majority votes of both the free-state and slave-state members of Congress. These proposals were unacceptable to both the Republican leaders and the delegates from the slave states of the upper South; hence, they also came to naught.

While the Buchanan administration agonized over the progress of secession, the seceded states moved decisively with their own plans. On February 4, delegates from six states met—joined later by those from Texas—in the senate chamber of the Alabama statehouse and began the work of forming a new southern nation. Among the group of fifty were many of the leading politicians, slave owners, and lawyers of the South. With Howell Cobb in the chair, they hurriedly drafted and adopted a provisional constitution for an interim government for a new political entity, which they named the Confederate States of America. The assembly itself became the congress of the provisional government, the college of electors for a provisional president and vice president, and the constitutional convention for the drafting of a permanent instrument of government. The provisional constitution provided that within one year a permanent government be elected and the permanent constitution be ratified by the states.

The most urgent task before the assembly was the election of a provisional president and vice president. Swiftly and, in light of subsequent Confederate history, with remarkably little political or personal jousting, the assembly unanimously chose Jefferson Davis as the provisional president and Alexander Stephens as provisional vice president. In selecting these men the delegates rejected the southern fire-eaters, one of the most prominent of whom, Rhett, was a member of the assembly, and another, William L. Yancey, was conspicuously present in the city. Fire-eaters were too volatile and dangerous; the situation called for moderates who could bring stability out of revolution, for a Washington and a John Adams instead of a Patrick Henry and a Samuel Adams.

Davis was a southern moderate who embraced secession only after his own state was withdrawn from the Union. He, like Lincoln, had been born into a Kentucky farm family. But Davis was reared in Mississippi where his family migrated when he was an infant, and where the Davises rose to become affluent cotton planters and slave owners. Although he had previously been moved by a powerful sense of American patriotism, he was imbued with the spirit of the plantation aristocracy and the state-rights political doctrines of Thomas Jefferson and John C. Calhoun.

Davis was educated in the classical tradition at Transylvania University in Lexington, Kentucky, and in the martial tradition at the United States Military Academy, class of 1828. After the tragic death in 1835 of his bride of only six weeks—Zachary Taylor's daughter—Davis resigned his commission and spent ten years in semi-seclusion as a planter and a student of history and government. Then he met and married a vivacious young woman, Varina Howell, of Natchez. Marriage energized him. Almost immediately he entered politics and was elected to the United States House of Representatives. Resigning his position there to rejoin the army in the Mexican War, he commanded a Mississippi volunteer regiment with such valor and skill that he emerged from the conflict the most illustrious military hero in the state's history.

In 1847 Davis went to the United States Senate, where he became perhaps the most articulate champion of the southern cause. Four years later he left that body to enter a contest for the governorship of his state. But he lost because of his adverse views toward the Compromise of 1850. Rescued from political eclipse when his friend President Franklin Pierce appointed him secretary of war, Davis rendered outstanding service in this position. In 1857 he was again elected to the United States Senate. He resigned from the Senate upon the secession of Mississippi and accepted command of the state's military forces.

Davis was tall, erect, and slender, his bearing unmistakably military; though his features were too sharp to be called truly handsome, they were distinguished; southerners considered them genteel. When on February 15 he arrived in Montgomery to take up his duties as provisional president of the Confederacy, he was introduced to an admiring crowd by the eloquent Yancey, who said, "The man and the hour have met." Few persons in the Confederacy would then have disagreed.

Vice President Stephens was a man of diminutive and sickly body and wizened countenance, but with a keen and comprehensive mind. A gifted politician, he served Georgia in the United States Congress from 1843 until he retired in 1859 to resume the practice of law. As a compelling Whig orator in the House of Representatives, he impressed his party and congressional colleague and friend Abraham Lincoln, who after listening to one of the Georgian's presentations in Congress said it was the best speech of an hour's length that he had ever heard. Both men opposed the Mexican War; this created a special bond between them.

Stephens was an enigma in the Confederate administration. He held both the Union and the Federal Constitution in great affection; he had supported Douglas in the recent presidential election; he had opposed the secession of Georgia. Yet he was an ardent advocate of states' rights, and he saw no inconsistency in his thinking. Ultimately, he would turn the doctrine of states' rights against the government of the supreme creature of those rights—the Confederate States of America. He was also an ardent believer in southern slavery; he identified the institution as the foundation upon which the southern republic rested.

The permanent Confederate constitution drafted by the convention and promptly ratified by the states was strikingly similar to the United States Constitution. The Confederate document differed primarily in certain phrases and provisions that in the past had led to sectional controversy. It made explicit the recognition of states' rights and the legality and permanence of slavery. The preamble contained no general welfare clause and declared the constitution to be the work of the people of the Confederate States of America, ". . . each State acting in its sovereign and independent character." It forbade any Confederate law impairing the right to own slaves in Confederate states or territories. But the importation of slaves, except from the United States, was prohibited. The constitution outlawed protective tariffs on imports and general appropriations for internal improvements. On the other hand, it reversed the United States Constitution in permitting a tax on exports, this being designed to favor the South in its domination of the world's supply of cotton.

The Confederate organic law also differed from that of the United States in establishing a single, six-year term for the president, empowering him to veto selected parts of appropriations bills without killing the entire bill, and allowing cabinet members, when authorized by the congress, to sit in that body for the discussion of measures pertaining to their departments. The constitution was silent on the right of secession, though such a right was implicit in its affirmation of state sovereignty in the formation of the Confederate government.

Davis set about at once to form an administration and, together with the convention acting as a congress, to begin the formidable task of breathing life into the new nation. He quickly appointed a cabinet with Robert

Toombs of Georgia as secretary of state, Christopher G. Memminger of South Carolina as secretary of the treasury, Leroy P. Walker of Alabama as secretary of war, Stephen R. Mallory of Florida as secretary of the navy, Judah P. Benjamin of Louisiana as attorney general, and John H. Reagan of Texas as postmaster general. The group included some of the South's foremost public figures, especially in Toombs and Benjamin (former United States Senators), and it gave adequate representation to the various states of the Confederacy. Southerners said the right men were in the right places.

By retaining the main features of the United States laws, changing them only where they did not conform to the Confederate constitution, and preserving the Federal administrative machinery and services—postal employees and mail delivery, for example—the Confederate government eased its transition into being. Significantly, one of its very first acts was to create a Confederate army by calling on the various states to provide quotas of troops and arms. Coming events would soon make this a decision of vast import. One of Davis's first acts was the dispatch of Confederate commissioners to Washington in a vain effort to arrange an amicable settlement there.

Meanwhile, the most sensitive issue facing both President Buchanan and the provisional Confederate leaders was the possession of federal properties—military posts, forts, arsenals, customs houses, post offices—within the seceded states. As the states withdrew from the Union they demanded, in accord with their affirmed sovereignty and independence, the surrender of all Federal installations inside them; in most instances the local officials, many of them southerners, acceded. A few, however, refused to do so. One of these was Lieutenant Adam J. Slemmer, the commanding officer at Fort Pickens, a redoubt guarding the entrance to Pensacola harbor. Another officer who refused to surrender was Major Robert Anderson, a Kentuckian of southern sympathies fated to be located at perhaps the most explosive spot on earth—the birthplace of secession, Charleston.

Anderson stood by his sense of honor in declining to give up Fort Sumter, a masonry works that lay in the harbor and both protected and threatened the city. President Buchanan rejected the demands for the fort's surrender made by South Carolina commissioners in Washington, and later by Confederate commissioners, and instead dispatched an unarmed ship, *Star of the West*, with provisions and reinforcements. When on January 9, 1861, the vessel was driven off by fire from the South Carolina shore batteries, the President chose not to retaliate or regard the incident as an act of war.

On March 4 Lincoln became President and inherited the secession crisis. He had no specific program for meeting it, but in his inaugural he set forth certain broad principles by which he would be guided. From a windswept platform in front of the Capitol with its dome still under construction, and before taking the oath of office from Chief Justice Roger B. Taney, whose Dred Scott decision he had vehemently denounced, Lincoln asserted his conviction that the Union is permanent, secession anarchy, and violence in the cause of secession insurrection. He said he intended to execute the laws of the Union in all the states, and to "hold, occupy, and possess" the Federal properties.

But he again reassured the South that he would not interfere with slavery where it was already legal, and he appealed to the citizens of the seceded states by promising not to assail them and saying there would be no conflict unless they began it. Then, earnestly and eloquently, "While you have no oath registered in Heaven to destroy the government, I shall have the most solemn one to 'preserve, protect, and defend' it. . . . We must not be enemies. Though passion may have strained, it must not break our bonds of affection. The mystic chords of memory, stretching from every battlefield, and patriot grave, to every living heart and hearthstone, all over this broad land, will yet swell the chorus of the Union, when again touched, as surely they will be, by the better angels of our nature."

In view of the situation at the Pensacola and Charleston forts, the most ominous words in Lincoln's address were his declaration of resolve to "hold, occupy, and possess" the Federal properties. How this was to be done, whether by force or diplomacy, and whether he intended to include those establishments already in the hands of the seceded states, he did not say. Coming events would supply the answers.

He was scarcely in office when he learned the Fort Sumter garrison was almost out of provisions and Anderson would be obliged to surrender unless soon resupplied. Lincoln found himself beset with messages from throughout the North urging strong action and with criticisms over his lack of a plan for dealing with the crisis. But the nation's top military officer, elderly General Winfield Scott, hero of the Mexican War, said the fort could not be reinforced, and he suggested that both it and Fort Pickens be surrendered in order to conciliate the slave states of the upper South and prevent them from withdrawing. Lincoln was tempted to give up Fort Sumter if by doing so he could avert the secession of Virginia. He is said to have remarked that a fort for a state would not be a bad business. His newly appointed cabinet was seriously divided on the question.

The cabinet represented all sections of the nation comprising the states loyal to the Union. It also contained some former Democrats as well as men holding a variety of points of view within the Republican party. William H. Seward was the secretary of state. Former governor of New York, recently United States Senator from that state, also recently considered the foremost Republican contender for the presidency itself, he was, to many citizens both North and South, including himself, "Mr. Republican." Salmon P. Chase of Ohio, another aspirant to the presidency, an ardent abolitionist, was secretary of the treasury. Simon Cameron of Pennsylvania, Republican boss in his state, was secretary of war. Gideon Welles of Connecticut, conservative, secretive, honest beneath his wig and behind his luxuriant whiskers, the forthcoming diarist who would supply future historians with much of what they know about the inner workings of the Lincoln administration, was secretary of the navy. Caleb Smith of Indiana was secretary of the interior; Edward Bates of Missouri attorney general; and Montgomery Blair, formerly of Missouri and now of Maryland, postmaster general.

Seward played a slippery game in the Fort Sumter affair. With a sublime spirit of condescension he assumed the role of mentor to the presumably naive and bumbling Lincoln. Behind the President's back, Seward gave the Confederate commissioners in Washington what they interpreted as assurances the fort would be surrendered, and on April 1 he sent a memorandum to Lincoln saying, "We are at the end of a month's administration, and yet without a policy either domestic or foreign."

Seward advocated abandoning Fort Sumter but strengthening Fort Pickens, and at the same time he presented another recommendation that must have left Lincoln breathless. Seward suggested a plan for reuniting the nation by issuing ultimatums designed to start a war between the United States and a number of the leading countries of Europe. He believed the spirit of American patriotism aroused by a foreign war would bring the errant southern states back into the Union. He patronizingly offered to shoulder the responsibility for such a policy. Lincoln rejected the recommendation and quietly but firmly rebuked Seward by saying that he, Lincoln, must make the decisions and bear the responsibility.

In the end Lincoln decided, with the support of most of the cabinet, to attempt to resupply Fort Sumter with necessities only and to send a flotilla of warships along with the relief expedition in the event the Confederates opposed the move. He issued instructions for this to be done. But in a bizarre cross-up of communications he signed conflicting orders for the strongest of the warships, the *Powhatan;* consequently, it sailed for Pensacola, thus rendering the Fort Sumter relief escort impotent. At the same time Lincoln notified the governor of South Carolina of the coming attempt and promised that no troops, arms, or ammunition would be sent into the fort if the relief effort was not resisted.

Word of the expedition brought the Confederate authorities to a fateful decision. By now the possession of Fort Sumter meant far more than merely assuring access to the Charleston harbor; it had become an important symbol of Confederate independence itself. If the fort was to be taken, now was the time to do it, before the garrison was strengthened by any form of relief.

On April 9 Davis assembled his cabinet and received a unanimous, or perhaps almost unanimous, recommendation in favor of aggressive action. The one person alleged to have objected was the unlikeliest of the group to have done so, the impulsive Toombs, who, according to one source said, "It is suicide, it is murder, and will lose us every friend at the North. You will wantonly strike a hornets' nest which extends from mountains to ocean; and legions, now quiet, will swarm out to sting us to death. . . . It is unnecessary, it puts us in the wrong. It is fatal." Whatever was said, Davis made the decision to act and had his secretary of war telegraph the Confederate commander at Charleston, General P. G. T. Beauregard, to demand the immediate surrender of the fort, and attack and take it if the demand was rejected.

At dawn on April 12, after receiving what he deemed an unsatisfactory reply to the surrender demand, Beauregard opened fire on the fort. The old Virginia fire-eater Edmund Ruffin, now a member of a South Carolina militia unit, was allowed the honor of pulling the lanyard for at least one of the historic opening shots. The bombardment went on for almost forty hours while the citizens of Charleston, many of them from the rooftops of the mansions along the waterfront, watched in excitement and awe. Meanwhile, the weakened federal relief expedition lay helpless outside the harbor, making no attempt to come to the fort's assistance. Anderson and his little garrison returned the fire gallantly but ineffectually. Finally, with the fort reduced to rubble, but, incredibly, without a single human casualty from the Confederates' fire, Anderson raised the flag of surrender.

Scholars have long debated who was responsible for the event that precipitated the war. Did Lincoln play a Machiavellian game in which he deliberately provoked the Confederates to open fire in order to place upon them the onus of aggression and unite the northern population behind a hitherto faltering administration? Did Davis calculatingly begin the war in a move to kindle a spirit of Confederate patriotism, develop support for an inchoate administration, and attempt to induce the remaining slave states to secede and join the Confederacy? There is some evidence for answering yes to both questions.

Davis explicitly mentioned the idea of provoking a hostile enemy action in connection with an effort to end the standoff at Pensacola. On April 3 he wrote the Confederate military commander there, Major General Braxton Bragg, saying, "There would be to us an advantage in so placing [the Federals] that an attack by them would be a necessity, but when we are ready to relieve our territory and jurisdiction of the presence of a foreign garrison that advantage is overbalanced by other considerations." These considerations now justified seizing Fort Pickens by force, said Davis, and he ordered that it be attempted if the risk was not excessive. Only after being informed the risk was too high did he discard the plan. His thinking on this occasion anticipated and made virtually certain his decision a few days later to attack Fort Sumter.

After the bombardment of Fort Sumter, Lincoln expressed satisfaction over the outcome and said to the commander of the unsuccessful relief expedition, "You and I both anticipated that the cause of the country would be advanced by making the attempt to provision Fort-Sumpter [sic], even if it should fail; and it is no small consolation now to feel that our anticipation is justified by the result." A few weeks later Lincoln told his Illinois friend Orville H. Browning, "The [relief] plan succeeded. They attacked Sumter—it fell, and thus, did more service than it otherwise could." The New York Times described the relief expedition plainly as a feint and boasted that its object was to place upon the Confederates the blame for beginning the war.

Certainly both Lincoln and Davis gave serious thought to the advantages in having the other fire the first shot if it came to that. Understandably, both would have preferred having possession of the fort without being obliged to fight either to hold it or gain it. But both were willing to fight, if necessary, in order to possess the fort, and both hoped the other would begin the fighting if it should occur. Davis was at the disadvantage of being required to attack the fort in order to attain his goal. Lincoln could hold it indefinitely, if not attacked, by simply resupplying it occasionally; if attacked, he would be a defender and not an aggressor. Given the attitudes of both men, each correct according to his own premises, hostilities were inevitable.

The intentions and motives that led to Fort Sumter are arguable, the results beyond question. Toombs's warning, if uttered, now proved remarkably accurate. In the North the attack upon the flag stirred a tidal wave of patriotic wrath and determination to avenge the act and punish its perpetrators. "It was," said a northern newspaper, "an audacious and insulting aggression upon the authority of the Republic, without provocation or excuse." Another journal interpreted the event as "precisely the stimulus which . . . a good Providence sends to arouse the latent patriotism of a people."

The day after the fort's surrender, Lincoln issued a ringing proclamation identifying the attack as insurrection and calling upon the several states for their militia to the aggregate of 75,000 troops to be used to suppress "combinations . . . too powerful to be suppressed by the ordinary course of judicial proceedings." He also summoned Congress to meet in a special session beginning July 4. Four days later he proclaimed a blockade of the ports of the seceded states.

The North's response was not confined to the Republican party. Although northern Democrats pursued throughout the secession crisis a more conciliatory course toward the South than did Republicans, the Democrats now came to Lincoln's support in his determination to put down insurrection. In a gesture of personal good will and national unity, the leading northern Democrat, Stephen A. Douglas, stood by and held Lincoln's hat during the inaugural address. The day before Lincoln issued his call for troops, Douglas visited him and pledged assistance in the cause of preserving the Union. Before Douglas's untimely death a few months later he declared, "There can be no neutrals in war; only patriots—or traitors."

The southern response to Fort Sumter, and especially to Lincoln's proclamation, was similar in vigor to the northern response. It came in a great outpouring of spirit and determination to resist coercion. Governor Francis Pickens of South Carolina spoke for his people when he said, "Thank God the war is open . . . we will conquer or perish." Rhett welcomed the coming of hostilities as a spur to southern unity and dedication. Davis in his inaugural address as provisional president had expressed the hope for amicable relations between the Confederacy and the Union. "But," he said, "if this be denied to us, and the integrity of our territory and jurisdiction assailed, it will but remain for us, with firm resolve, to appeal to arms and invoke the blessings of Providence on a just cause." He now replied to Lincoln's proclamation with one of his own, calling upon the Confederate states to muster 100,000 troops and inviting shipowners to apply for commissions as privateers to constitute a "militia of the sea."

Obliged to decide between participating in a war to coerce the seceded states or withdrawing and joining them, the four states of the upper South cast their lot with the Confederacy. Their ties of blood and culture with the South proved stronger than their political ties with the Union. In many respects the decision of Virginia was the most poignant and the most crucial. The Virginians held a strong spirit of American nationalism, priding themselves as being offspring of the very Founding Fathers of the Republic. In the beginning they were cool toward the idea of secession. Governor John Letcher was sharply critical of South Carolina's hasty action; and though the Virginia legislature authorized a special convention to consider the state's course in the crisis, the body was required to submit its decision to the people for approval. On April 4 it rejected secession by a vote of 88 to 45. Meanwhile, Virginia urgently sought ways for a compromise to save the Union.

Lincoln's proclamation changed the picture at once. Governor Letcher bitterly refused the call for Virginia militia. On April 17 the convention, still sitting to await the result of the Fort Sumter affair, voted 88 to 55 in favor of secession, and set May 23 as the date for the referendum. By this time the state was in effect out of the Union, having already ratified the Confederate constitution, been admitted to the Confederacy, and received regiments of Confederate troops, all contingent in theory upon the outcome of the popular vote. Not surprisingly, the outcome was a substantial majority in favor of what in fact had already occurred—secession.

The secession of Virginia from the Union touched off a secessionist movement within Virginia itself. The counties of the Alleghenies and westward, where slavery and plantation agriculture were only shallowly rooted, opposed the withdrawal of the state, and when it took place their representatives began a move that culminated in the formation of the state of West Virginia, which in 1863 would be recognized by and admitted to the Union. Here was a paradox within a paradox: that Confederate Virginia, the product of secession, would fiercely condemn the withdrawal of its western counties, while the Federal government, sworn enemy of secession, would applaud and abet it within a state.

Like Virginia, the three other states of the upper South had at first considered secession, then turned it down. All now rejected Lincoln's call for troops. Governor Henry M. Rector of Arkansas declared that the people of his state would defend it against northern "mendacity and usurpation," and on May 6 the state convention voted to secede. Governor John M. Ellis of North Carolina said the state would have no part in a war upon the liberties of a free people, seized the Federal properties in North Carolina, and began to call up volunteers for state defense. On May 1 the state convention unanimously adopted secession.

Governor Isham G. Harris of Tennessee said his state would furnish 50,000 troops, not to Lincoln, but for the defense of Tennessee and other southern states. During early May, Harris and the legislature entered into a military alliance with the Confederacy, declared Tennessee independent, and ratified the Confederate constitution, these actions to be dependent upon approval in a referendum set for June 8. The Tennessee referendum, like that of Virginia earlier, went heavily in favor of what was already accomplished—the withdrawal of the state from the Union.

By gaining the four states of the upper South the Confederacy added sufficient strength to enable it to make a powerful bid for success in a war for independence. The addition of this area increased the white population of the southern republic by almost 80 percent and the industrial output comparably. Virginia was the most important state to join the Confederacy, not only because of its large population and relatively heavy manufacturing capacity, but also because of its historic political stature and prestige. Confederate authorities paid homage to the Old Dominion by making Richmond their permanent capital.

The border slave states were fated not to secede, though all of them harbored strong Confederate sympathies. The refusal of the Delaware legislature to authorize a convention settled the issue there. Maryland was more sharply divided. Governor Thomas H. Hicks vainly sought to keep the state neutral, and the legislature, despite the presence of many secessionist members, refused to call a convention. Geographically the state was pivotal. Its withdrawal would isolate Washington from the Union, with consequences that were made vividly apparent when on April 19 a formation of Massachusetts troops in answering Lincoln's summons was attacked in the streets of Baltimore by a prosouthern mob. Lincoln quickly suspended the writ of habeas corpus and permitted the military authorities to arrest many southern sympathizers, including legislators, and to seize a number of strategically important positions in the state. These measures prompted the writing by James Ryder Randall of the stirring song "Maryland, My Maryland," with its outraged line, "The despot's heel is on thy shore." But Lincoln's move forestalled any formal attempt at secession by the state.

Determined and partially successful efforts to secede occurred in both Kentucky and Missouri. Governor Beriah Magoffin of Kentucky and Governor Claiborne F. Jackson of Missouri were secessionists who rejected Lincoln's call for troops. But both legislatures refused to authorize conventions to consider separation. Kentucky for some time attempted to remain neutral, but was soon invaded by Confederate troops and then by Union troops. Missouri quickly became a scene of civil strife between secessionists and unionists. Eventually, acts of secession were adopted and Confederate governments set up by delegations representing sections of both states; both were admitted into the Confederacy, and both sent representatives to the Confederate congress; both had stars in the Confederate flag. But the Confederate governments of Kentucky and Missouri reflected the will of minorities only, and military events would soon make them merely "governments in exile."

By holding the border slave states the Union may have retained the balance of power for deciding the outcome of the Civil War. The population of the region, counting West Virginia, was more than 40 percent of that of the Confederacy, and the strategic location of the area was of paramount value. Lincoln was said to have remarked he hoped God was on the side of the Union, but that it must have Kentucky. He is known to have said: "I think to lose Kentucky is nearly the same as to lose the whole game. [With] Kentucky gone, we cannot hold Missouri, nor, I think, Maryland. [With] These all against us . . . the job on our hands is too large for us. We would as well consent to separation at once, including the surrender of this capital."

The Confederacy also nurtured the long-held southern ambition to expand into the American Southwest. Two areas in particular were objects of Confederate design there. Treaties of alliance with the five "civilized Indian nations" of Indian Territory—the Cherokees, Choctaws, Chickasaws, Creeks, and Seminoles, in the present state of Oklahoma—accepted an Indian nonvoting delegate to the Confederate congress and provided for the future admission of an Indian state. Indian units served in the Confederate army, but with a single notable exception, most Confederate Indian troop activity was confined to Indian Territory. Confederate sympathizers in the southern part of the New Mexico Territory organized themselves into the

Confederate Territory of Arizona, sent a delegate to the Confederate congress, and received territorial recognition. Military defeat early in the war dashed Confederate hopes in the area.

By summer 1861 secession was an accomplished fact. Both North and South were preparing in dead earnest for the conflict that so long had been in the making. When Confederate President Jefferson Davis proclaimed June 13 as a day of prayer for victory, a semiliterate Louisiana plantation overseer scrawled into his journal this dread malediction: ". . . My prayer Sincerely to God is that Every Black Republican in the Hole combined whorl Either man women o chile that is opposed to negro slavery as it existed in the Southern confederacy shal be trubled with pestilences & calamitys of all kinds & drag out the Balance of there existence in misry & degradation with Scarsely food & rayment enughf to keep sole & body to geather and O God I pray the[e] to Direct a bullet or a bayonet to pirce the hart of every northern Soldier that invades southern Soil & after the Body has Rendered up its Traterish Sole gave it a trators reward a birth in the Lake of fires & Brimstone My honest convicksion is that Every man women & chile that has gave aid to the abolishionist are fit Subjects for Hell I all so ask the[e] to aid the Southern confedercy in maintaining ower rites & establishing the confederate Government Believing in this case the prares from the wicked will prevailith much—Amen—."

The editor of the *New York Daily Tribune* wrote with more polish but no less venom: ". . . we mean to conquer [the southern people]—not merely to defeat, but to conquer, to SUBJUGATE them—and we shall do this the most mercifully, the more speedily we do it. But when the rebellious traitors are overwhelmed in the field, and scattered like leaves before an angry wind, it must not be to return to peaceful and contented homes. They must find poverty at their firesides, and see privation in the anxious eyes of mothers and the rags of children." The black funnel of war loomed on the horizon.

A Slaveowner's Defense of Slavery

Live Oaks Plantation on Bayou Lafourche
Post Office: Napoleonville, Louisiana

January 20, 1861

To: Mr. Frederick T. Darcy
Postal Box 10
Freeport, Illinois

Dear Frederick:

I take pen in hand to respond to your kind letter of the fourth instant. I fully share your expressed views as to the deplorable and tragic condition in which our beloved nation now finds itself. I fully share your expressed views also that this condition has been brought about by the work of dangerous fanatics both in the North and in the South. Would that all the southern fire-eaters and northern abolitionists be hurled together into Satan's

---

NOTE: This is an article designed to show the attitude of southerners of the pre–Civil War era toward slavery and secession. I have chosen to write it in the form of a letter by a southern slaveowner to a northern friend. The persons and the letter are imaginary, but the arguments and outlook are not; they have been gleaned by me from thousands of letters and diary entries of the time, supplemented by information from published histories of the South and the nation.

No one southerner said all of them; the writer of the letter is a composite southerner who very well could have said them all. He and his friend to whom the letter is addressed were classmates at the College of New Jersey (today Princeton University). It was a favorite college for the sons of wealthy southerners, so much so that it was sometimes referred to, whimsically, as the outstanding southern institution of higher learning. Both of these imaginary persons were political moderates at the time of secession; both voted for unionists in the presidential election of 1860. The article is written, inasmuch as possible, in the didactic manner of a highly literate southerner of the time.

flaming pit of perdition. What the end holds in store for all of us can only be surmised with fear and trembling.

You ask me for a complete statement of my attitude toward the institution of slavery and toward the ominous secession movements now transpiring in the South; you say such a statement may be useful in your conversations with your friends and associates. I shall attempt to summarize my feelings.

To begin, I would remind you of what you already know: that slavery has been a part of the American scene almost from the very beginning of European settlement on this continent. In the year 1619, little more than a decade after the founding of Jamestown in the Virginia colony, a few Africans were sold to the settlers from a Dutch ship that dropped anchor in the harbor. Strictly speaking, these Africans were not then slaves, for the English laws of the colony did not recognize such a condition. They were indentured servants, and they worked in the fields along with the many white indentured servants being sent from England.

This system was soon transformed into slavery. The Africans were found to be ideally suited to the situation in Virginia and the other southern colonies. They seemed to have been formed by God or by nature for working in the heat of the southern climate. I suggest by God because there has been a persistent belief both in Judaism and in Christianity that the colored people of Africa are the offspring of Ham, the errant son of Noah, whose progeny was cursed by the Almighty for looking on his father's nakedness on an occasion when Noah was overcome with wine; it is alleged that Ham's descendants were anathematized both with blackness and with servitude. I suggest the Africans were suited to southern needs by nature in line with the teachings of the great European scientists such as Buffon, Humboldt, Agassiz, and Darwin that the different races of man have in one way or another been adapted to the variations of the environment.

As time elapsed, more and more Africans were imported into the southern colonies, and their numbers grew rapidly through a high birth rate. This proved to be of great financial benefit to the landowners; large holdings, plantations, began to develop out of African labor and the growing of tobacco, and later of rice, sugar, and cotton.

The white indentured laborers in the colonies received their freedom after a contracted period of work, and in time acquired land of their own or turned to occupations other than farming; the Africans, except, perhaps, for a few here and there, remained in permanent servitude because there were no contracts limiting their terms of service. As their numbers grew, the colonial legislatures began to enact laws that set them apart from the white settlers. The early laws forbade intermarriage between them and the whites and prohibited the Africans from serving in the colonial militia or owning arms without special permission.

By the 1660s, statutes recognizing the institution of slavery by name were enacted in the colonies. In time these laws developed into the systematic slave codes that are in place today. As you are aware, a similar situation occurred in the English settlements in New England and in other places north of Virginia, so that by the end of the colonial period, slavery, sanctioned by law, was being practiced in all thirteen of the English colonies that gained their independence to become the United States of America.

In the northern states, the institution established only shallow roots; it was not an important support of the economy; the number of slaves was small; and their presence was deeply resented by the more numerous non-slaveowning white workers—so much so that the famed founding father John Adams of Massachusetts said that the whites of his state would have eradicated it by exterminating the slaves if the courts had not freed them. Certainly, this is not a compassionate solution to the problem. During the era of independence, all of the states north of Delaware did in fact begin the process of emancipating their slaves.

Southern slavery received an immense stimulus from the invention of the cotton gin in the 1790s, a device that led to the spread of the cotton culture across the entire southern region of the nation, including the area beyond the Mississippi River as far as and throughout the eastern portion of Texas. Though significant amounts of other plantation crops are grown in this region (among the more prominent being tobacco, rice, and sugar), so dominant is the cotton interest today that the South is often called "the Cotton Kingdom." African slavery is the primary labor force for the production of all of the plantation crops.

The number of slaves has continued to increase accordingly. Many hundreds of thousands were imported from Africa and the islands of the Caribbean during the colonial period. Since the prohibition by Congress in 1808 of the further importation of slaves, the growth in their numbers has been largely by natural increase, notwithstanding that a trickle has continued through smuggling. Today there are approximately four million African slaves in the fifteen states where slavery is legal. Slaves constitute about one-fourth of the entire population of the region. But the density of their numbers increases to the south. In some of the states of the Deep South, their numbers equal or exceed those of the whites; in South Carolina, for example, they make up some two-thirds of the total population.

These figures demonstrate clearly the vast dependence of the South on slave labor. The abolition of slavery would strike a devastating blow to the plantation system and the general economy of the region. Nor is this the whole picture. The economy of much of the world outside the South would be seriously impaired also. It is common knowledge that most of the slave ships of the colonial period were of northern registry, thus adding significantly to northern wealth. I understand that at least some of the affluence of many of the more prominent northern families today is from this source, an enterprise that is colloquially, and doubtless whimsically, referred to as "blackbirding."

It is self-evident that the wealth of the cotton mill owners of New England, as well as of England and France, comes directly from slave-grown southern fiber. So important is this transaction that critics of the South utter as a warning, and friends of the South as a boast, the refrain "Cotton is King." Southerners in the present sectional crisis say, with misplaced assurance, I believe, "The world dare not make war on King Cotton."

But this is not the whole picture of the role of slavery in the society of the South. Three-fourths of the white families of the region own no slaves at all. You point out in your recent letter that they have little if any economic interest in slavery, and that, indeed, one could argue that the institution places them at an economic disadvantage because it obliges them to compete against slave labor. You understandably pose the questions: What is the attitude toward slavery of the non-slaveowning portion of the southern white population? Would they fight to perpetuate it?

My answer is three-fold: First, I need to make clear that the great majority of the white population of the South are independent farmers who possess and work their own land. The more energetic and ambitious among them aspire to become slaveowners and planters, just as the more energetic and ambitious workers in the North aspire to become either land or mill owners.

Second, the white independent farmers of the South, and the considerable number of herdsmen who graze and forage their herds of cattle and swine on the public lands, as well as another considerable number of southerners who live a more or less frontier mode of life by residing in the back country and hunting and fishing largely for a livelihood, feel no direct competition from slave labor. In most instances, the white workers in the few cities are able, by violence, if necessary, if not by local ordinances, to prevent slaves from competing for their jobs. I understand that the colored workers in the North experience similar treatment. Thus a great majority of non-slaveowning whites do not feel threatened or disadvantaged by slavery.

My third point in explaining the attitude of all southern whites toward the institution is more subtle than the others, but no less powerful. Indeed, it may be the most critical of all. Slavery provides the white society with a means, the most convenient and possibly the only available means, of policing and controlling the vast African population in our midst. This is no idle matter. We are convinced that the majority of the slaves are incapable of sustaining a civilization comparable to the white man's civilization, and that the abolition of slavery would plunge us into African barbarism and racial violence.

We believe that Thomas Jefferson spoke wisely when he said that if and when the slaves should be emancipated, they must be removed from the country to avoid bloodshed and anarchy. Removal of the Africans from our midst is, of course, the object of the American Colonization Society, which has been active for many decades and has had many distinguished Americans, northerners as well as southerners, among its members.

Obviously, white Americans generally agree with us on this point. Even if this view is not always explicitly set forth outside the South, it is implicit in your laws refusing citizenship to colored persons, denying them the privilege of voting or holding office, barring their children from your common schools, and prohibiting any additional of them to settle in your states. The admired French traveler and thinker, de Tocqueville, has noted that the animus against colored people is strongest in the area where slavery is not practiced.

It has not escaped our notice that your most prominent public figure, President-elect Abraham Lincoln, has supported the racially restrictive policies of his and your own state of Illinois and has declared repeatedly that he believes that the federal territories in the West ought to be reserved for free, white settlers only. He also is known to favor returning the colored people to Africa or colonizing them in some other location outside the United States, a solution that the revered Benjamin Franklin advocated earlier.

Regarding such proposals as settling them elsewhere, I must express strong doubts. I have discussed this matter with some of my more intelligent servants, and I am convinced that they would not willingly leave this country. They say, and accurately so, that they know little of Africa and its ways; that their people have been here for many generations, speak our language, practice our religion, are accustomed to our machinery and methods of making a living, and are attached to our land. Also, they profess, sincerely or not I am unable to say, to hold me and my family in deep affection and to have no desire to be parted from us and this place. I question whether the majority of the servants in the South would voluntarily return to Africa even as a condition of emancipation. The American Colonization Society has had but limited success in persuading free persons of color to do so.

It follows from these observations that slavery is unshakably sanctioned by all classes of southern white society. Though, as I shall explain presently, I have reservations regarding the wisdom or virtue of holding slaves, I am at a complete loss as to how the institution might be eliminated without creating greater evils than those which are intrinsic to it. Ironically, there is reason to believe that it is also sanctioned by a majority of the more than 300,000 free persons of color of the South, and by the thousands of colored slaveowners of the region. I am free to admit, however, that this statement about the attitude of the latter two classes is impressionistic and speculative on my part.

Finally, would the non-slaveowning whites fight to preserve slavery? I believe without a doubt that they would do so, and most fiercely.

You say you would like a statement from me concerning the treatment and living and working conditions of the slaves. I am pleased to comply. What I am about to say on this matter applies not only to me but to all of my friends and neighbors among the planters, and many, if not most, of my other acquaintances who own servants. We learned long ago that it was to our material advantage, as well as to that of our peace of mind and the salvation of our immortal souls, to treat our people humanely and provide adequately for their well-being.

This attitude is summed up in such of our sayings as, "A happy servant is a good servant," or "The best way to ensure that your servants will work diligently is to supply them with plenty of pork." It is universally known among us that the colored people have an immense preference for this form of meat. In fact, a number of servants whose owners relocated from Louisiana to Texas have run away from their new homes and returned to Louisiana. When apprehended and asked the reason for their conduct, they replied, "Too much beef out there; not enough pork."

In addition to the regular allotments of meat, cornmeal, and molasses, I assign to each of the servant families a plot of ground to be used as a garden for the growing of fruits and vegetables. I also permit my people to obtain money of their own by the sale of firewood to the passing steamboats and the sale of fruits, vegetables, game, firewood, and Spanish moss to the residents of Napoleonville here on the bayou who use the moss for the purpose of stuffing their mattresses and furniture. I regret to say that the servants too often squander their money on worthless trinkets sold to them at outrageous prices by the Yankee peddlers who infest the region along the bayou.

We house our servants in comfortable quarters and clothe them in wear that is suitable to our climate, though doubtless you would retort that no housing or clothing on earth is suitable to a climate that combines a temperature of 100 degrees with comparable humidity. I provide a plantation infirmary and engage the services of a qualified physician for my servants. Many of my acquaintances do the same. I would challenge anyone who is interested in the institution to visit my plantation and compare the living arrangements of my people with those of the common laborers in your mills and mines or in the construction camps for the building of your railroads. You have actually been a guest here, and you are aware of the conditions of which I speak.

I protect my servants from the more grueling and hazardous labor of clearing the swamps and digging the canals on the back side of my land. For these purposes I hire Irish immigrants who demand but a pittance of money or spirits for their labor and who cost me nothing if they are killed or maimed. It would be imprudent of me in the extreme to expose my $1800 prime field hands to such risks when I can get the work done so inexpensively by others. I may be charged with a lack of concern for the immigrants, but I feel I must yield to practicality in this matter. I have observed that a similar attitude prevails in the North regarding the immigrants, especially the Irish. Of course, I am addressing in this letter only the one issue of slavery, not that of immigrant laborers.

I would remind critics of slavery that the last federal census indicates that our servants enjoy longer life expectancy than do your working classes, especially the free persons of color and immigrants among them. I would call attention also to the published observation of Mr. Frederick Law

Olmsted, the renowned New York landscape architect who is an avowed and outspoken critic of slavery on various grounds, and who has traveled widely in the South and has observed the plantation scene firsthand. He has written that the living conditions of the servants here are quite as good, if not superior, to those of the workers in the mills of New England.

I would point out also the report of the famous English geologist Sir Charles Lyell, an opponent of slavery and an advocate of emancipation, after his journey throughout parts of the South. (Let me say as an aside that I do not approve of Mr. Lyell's efforts through the study of rocks to discredit Bishop Usher's biblical chronology of the earth. The good bishop shows clearly that God's word indicates that Creation occurred some four thousand and four years before Christ, and not eons ago as the rocks are said to suggest.) But back to Mr. Lyell's observations on slavery: he said he found the servants to be very cheerful and free of care, better fed than a large part of the laboring class of Europe, and although cheaply dressed, and often in patched garments, never scantily clothed for the climate.

He says that a colored woman, upon being asked whether she belonged to a certain family, replied merrily, "Yes, I belong to them and they belong to me." Mr. Lyell further reported that for days he was accompanied about the plantations by colored guides whom he found to be as talkative and chatty as children, usually, he said, boasting of their master's wealth, and of their own peculiar virtues.

Foreign observers in the North fully substantiate such comparisons. They report that in the New England textile mills the operatives work from daylight till dark six days a week for $1.50 a week plus board. One proprietor explained, "So long as they can do my work for what I choose to pay them, I keep them, getting out of them all I can." Those who are unable or unwilling to meet his demands are discharged and replaced with workers who can and will do so. I understand that the names of laborers who are dismissed are placed on a "black list" that warns other proprietors not to give them employment.

What are the living quarters of these wage laborers like? Here are the words of an observer in Boston: "The whole district [of cotton mill workers] is a perfect hive of human beings without comforts and mostly without common necessaries; in many cases huddled together without regard to sex, age, or a sense of decency." In New York City, laborers live as many as twenty to a room. Neither my desire for productivity nor my conscience would allow me to treat my servants so basely.

There is another aspect of our treatment of the servants that we believe distinguishes it from your treatment of wage laborers. We continue to support the servants at times when they are too ill to work or after they have grown too old for it. I maintain on my place a number of such servants, as do other proprietors of my acquaintance.

Nor do we neglect the spiritual well-being of our people. You are aware of the existence of the chapel I have constructed for the servants on my place; you have been present during some of their services. You know that, as a dedicated Episcopalian, I require them to follow the dictates of my faith, as does the Reverend Leonidas Polk, the bishop of Louisiana, who, by the way, is a graduate of the United States Military Academy and has vowed that if the present sectional confrontation should result in combat, he will lay aside his clerical vestments and join the armed forces of the South. He would present a most formidable combination as a soldier both of the Lord and of the South.

You know that I have the servants catechized according to the Reverend Charles Colcock Jones's oral catechism for servants, and that I bring in a fervent and eloquent pastor to deliver sermons to them. I feel that these are wise measures; they minister both to the salvation of the servants' souls and to their good behavior here on earth by emphasizing such biblical texts as "Render unto Caesar that which is Caesar's . . ." and "Servants, obey your masters."

I demand that my servants enter wedlock in their relationships between the sexes, and to abstain from promiscuity. I strictly forbid my drivers (all of whom are also servants) from tampering with the wives of others. Nothing is more destructive of harmony, good discipline, and productivity than a general condition of sexual license among the servants. In order to maintain marital stability among them, I prohibit the separation of husband and wife unless they agree to take twenty lashes of the whip for the privilege.

Servant marriages are conducted properly; I do not accept the practice of "jumping the broom handle" that occurs among the servants on some of the places. When the pastor is not available, I conduct the wedding service myself, according to the Episcopal form, of course. When I did so recently, I am told that the servants enjoyed a bit of amusement at my expense by saying they couldn't understand how a horse racer could also be a preacher. Though I believe they said this facetiously, I suspect they picked up the idea through their exposure to the Methodist claptrap of the servants on an adjacent plantation.

I should be less than candid were I not to admit that abuses against servants do occur. Not all owners are conscientious in their treatment of them. Some owners violate the chastity of the colored women. Some inflict unreasonable punishment on their people. This is not to be considered a general condemnation by me of corporal punishment. As already seen, I at times have my overseers administer physical chastisement; I know of no other way to deter petty crimes and misdemeanors or malingering by some of the servants.

The abolitionist bigots accuse us of using the whip to coerce our servants to toil in the fields. This is a gross libel. Permit me to point out that whipping for just purposes has traditionally been inflicted throughout the nation on recalcitrant white indentured servants, soldiers, school pupils even into adulthood, ordinary citizens convicted of certain offenses, and, of course, prison inmates.

I do, however, make every effort to determine the true nature of the servant's offense, and to make the punishment fit the crime. I never allow whipping to the point of drawing blood, and never in anger; all corrections of my servants are carried out in a gentlemanly manner in an effort to impress upon the culprit that it is being done as a deterrent to unacceptable conduct, and not out of caprice, vengeance, or passion.

It is a lamentable fact that many serious abuses of the colored people are perpetrated by the non-slaveowners, especially by the poorer and less-educated elements among them. A few evenings back, I discovered in town three of my neighbor's servants who had been put upon and savagely beaten by a group of poor whites who were probably intoxicated; the servants' clothes had been torn from them and they were terribly lacerated and swollen from the beating. It was a brutal affair. I am convinced that the institution of slavery as a rule protects the servants from such treatment because, if only out of interest in preserving their property if not out of conscience, the owners do all in their power to prevent it.

You inquire my views on the very principle of slavery. To this, I freely state that I disagree with what seems to have become a popular belief among a significant portion of the southern people: that is, that slavery is a positive good for a society. The renowned Professor Thomas R. Dew of the College of William and Mary has brilliantly expounded this idea by pointing out that such great civilizations of antiquity as those of Greece and Rome were based upon the institution, to which the great Aristotle gave his blessing. Leading theologians of the region such as the Reverends

James H. Thornwell and Robert Louis Dabney explain slavery as having been ordained by God. Such outstanding political figures as Senators John C. Calhoun and James Hammond of South Carolina defend the institution as a rational means of dealing with the universal and inevitable problem of class and racial conflict in society.

But I know that many of my acquaintances support me in my agreement with such fathers of the Republic as Washington, Jefferson, and Mason, who looked upon the institution as an evil. I am told also that Col. Robert E. Lee of Virginia has said the same about it. (You doubtless are acquainted with Col. Lee, who served with such distinction on General Winfield Scott's staff during the late war with Mexico that Gen. Scott later said the nation owed its victory more to Lee than to any other man; and that if called upon to recommend someone to command the nation's armies in a time of grave national peril, he would name Lee with his dying breath.) I also agree with something else Col. Lee is said to have said about slavery, that the white people of the South are the greater victims of it, because the slaves here are immeasurably better off than their kinsmen in Africa.

But we are not dealing today with an abstract principle. We are dealing instead with a very real and difficult situation. The institution was planted here at a time when all the nations of Europe were seizing territory from the native inhabitants and either exterminating or displacing and relocating them at the invaders' convenience, or in some way subjecting them to a form of servitude. Slavery was already deeply rooted in Africa among the native tribes; the renowned English explorer there, Mungo Park, reported that three-fourths of the entire population were slaves. It is a grim irony that the vast majority of the slaves brought to this continent were sold to the English and New England slave traders by Africans themselves. I do not recite these facts to justify the existence of slavery today, but to show that the introduction of the practice here, regrettable as it now appears to me to be, was but an incident of the vast territorial and demographic upheavals of the times.

The institution was recognized in the Constitution of the United States by description, though not by name. Subsequently, it was sanctioned by federal statutes and judicial decisions. But almost from the beginning of the nation's history, the presence of slavery provoked sectional controversy, especially when the question of its spreading into newly acquired territories arose. These controversies were defused temporarily by political compromise, particularly the Missouri Compromise of 1820, which divided the vast area of the Louisiana Purchase into slave and free territories, and the Compromise of 1850, which made a comparable arrangement regarding slavery for the lands acquired from Mexico in the late war.

These historic agreements were nullified by the Kansas-Nebraska Act in 1854, which opened the northern portion of the Louisiana Purchase to slavery, and the Supreme Court's Dred Scott decision in 1857, which declared acts of Congress limiting slavery in any federal territory to be unconstitutional. Legal as the southern people, including me, believe these developments were, they have led directly to the present crisis.

I have already discussed the essential importance of slavery to the southern economy and social tranquillity of today. There appears to be no way, short of bloodshed, of eliminating it. The southern fire-eaters and the northern abolitionists have brought the situation to that dire point.

As to my own present position on secession, I have strenuously opposed any move in that direction by Louisiana. I voted for Mr. John Bell, the Constitutional Unionist, in the recent presidential election, and I was gratified to see that the greater part of the popular votes of the state and of the South generally, if combined, went to Bell and to Senator Stephen A. Douglas, the northern Democratic candidate, rather than to Vice President John C. Breckinridge, the southern Democratic candidate who is, doubtless unfairly, regarded as being the one most favorable to secession. In other words, the majority of the people of Louisiana and of the South voted for candidates who are unmistakably unionists.

My opposition to secession at this time does not alter the view that I have expressed to you in the past, which is that a state or group of states have the right to secede at any time if a majority of the people in that state or group of states have the desire and the ability to do so. Nobody has stated that principle more eloquently than did Mr. Lincoln some years back when he was a member of the United States Congress. He considered the principle to be universal, said it was a "most sacred right," one that would ultimately bring freedom to the entire world. My objection to secession at the moment is that it is not the wisest or most expedient option for the South.

I, too, believe as you do, that a majority of the citizens of the entire nation are unionist and moderate in their views toward slavery. I am aware that Senator Douglas is a man who is sympathetic to the southern attitude in this matter, and that President-elect Lincoln has pledged to make no move against the institution in the states where it is already established. You say also that the rank and file of both Democrats and Republicans of your acquaintance are not abolitionists; that they support Lincoln's position.

But I fear secession is now inevitable. The election of Mr. Lincoln, a Republican whose platform supports northern interests only, and declares that neither Congress nor a territorial legislature nor any other power (meaning the Supreme Court) possess the right to legitimize slavery in a federal territory; and, following his election, the Republican rejection of all efforts of the United States Senate to effect a new political compromise: these events have cut the ground from under the unionists of Louisiana and the other southern states.

The rejection of the Senate's Crittenden compromise proposal, which would have divided the territories permanently into slave and free areas, is viewed here as a confirmation of the accusation that the Republicans endorse the expressed attitude of Senator William H. Seward of New York. You are, of course, familiar with Seward's declarations that there is an "irrepressible conflict" between the interests of slavery and those of freedom, and that the issue of slavery in the federal territories must be decided by a "higher law" than the Constitution of the United States.

It is also generally believed here, as I understand it is in the North, that Seward will be the power behind the throne, the real president, in a Lincoln administration. It is feared that the recent effort of the incendiary John Brown to incite a slave insurrection is but a sample of what lies in store for the South as a result of Seward's outlook. As I have informed you previously, every expression of veneration or sympathy for Brown has increased the conviction of southerners that the notion of an irrepressible conflict threatens the destruction of the South. I regret that Mr. Lincoln has refused to explain his own position more fully to the southern people, to repudiate the accusation that his views are identical to Seward's, saying that evil men would only misconstrue his words.

What makes the collapse of the compromise efforts the more tragic, in my opinion, is my conviction that two of the great statesmen of late, Mr. Henry Clay of Kentucky and Mr. Daniel Webster of Massachusetts, were correct in saying that there is no real threat of slavery expanding into the western territories; that it has already reached its geographic limits. I recall vividly the words of Mr. Webster, a lifelong opponent of slavery, in opposing a congressional prohibition of the institution in the lands obtained from Mexico. He said, "I would not take pains uselessly to re-enact the will of God."

The editorials of the newspaper the New Orleans *Bee,* formerly anti-secessionist and, in the recent presidential election, supportive of Senator Douglas, unerringly reveal the ominous shift in the southern attitude. Shortly before the election the *Bee* wrote a ringing unionist article, saying: "Whether the Presidential election terminates in the choice of Bell, or Douglas, or Lincoln or Breckinridge; whether the next Congress is Black Republican or Conservative; whether Seward counsels irrepressible conflict, or Robert Barnwell Rhett [the great South Carolina fire-eater] strives to muster an armed force to prevent Lincoln's inauguration; whether John Brown is canonized in New England, or solemn Sanhedrins of Secessionists devote the Union to the infernal Gods, the real Union men [in the South] have not the slightest idea of breaking up the [nation]."

But immediately after the announcement of the collapse of the compromise, the *Bee* wrote: "The North and South are heterogeneous and are better apart. . . . We are doomed if we proclaim not our political independence." Though I continue to hope for an amicable settlement of the issue, I now hope against hope. The die seems fatally cast.

On a more pleasant theme, I take this occasion to express again my profound nostalgia for our carefree days together in Princeton.

With sincere wishes for your continued health, prosperity, and happiness,

I am yr. obt. servant,
Frank Lawrence

Louisiana Sugar Planters
and the Civil War

As Egypt was said to be the gift of the Nile, the Louisiana sugar country may be said to be the gift of its waterways. Bounded on the south by the Gulf of Mexico, it was traversed by the Mississippi River, Red River, Atchafalaya River, Bayou Lafourche, and Bayou Teche. A land of legendary fertility enhanced by spreading live oaks and blossoming magnolias and featuring broad fields of lush sugarcane ripening in the semitropical sun, it was a unique and colorful region embedded within the underside of the southern Cotton Kingdom.

The population of the sugar country also represented a unique ethnic and cultural mixture of Creoles, Anglo-Americans, Cajuns, and African Americans the vast majority of whom in 1861 were slaves (150,000) who provided the labor to operate the 1,291 sugar plantations that lay along the streams. These plantations varied in size from small farms to magnificent estates comprising thousands of acres and worked by hundreds of slaves. The proprietors of the large plantations dominated the economic, political, and social affairs of the area.

They were the spokesmen of the region in the parish and state governments and in the halls of the United States Congress. U.S. Senator Judah P. Benjamin was a sugar planter as well as a lawyer and politician. Episcopal bishop Leonidas Polk was an extensive sugar producer. The planters' manner of life both affirmed and reinforced their position in society. Many of their dwellings were fashioned after the religious temples and government edifices of ancient Greece; many of the Creole planters favored homes that copied the graceful architecture of the French West Indies. An English traveler and writer observed of the sugar planters, "One might imagine a lord of the seventeenth century in his hall, but for the black faces of the serviteurs and the strange dishes of tropical origin."[1]

147

The planters lived the good life, subject to the vagaries of the weather and the New Orleans sugar market. One of them expressed the common mood of euphoria during a revitalizing rainfall when he jotted into his plantation journal:

Millions of tiny drops
Are falling all around;
They're dancing on the housetops
They're hiding in the ground.
It seems as if the warbling
Of the birds in all the bowers,
Had gathered into raindrops
And was coming down in showers.[2]

Secession created a rift in the minds of the sugar proprietors. As Southerners and slave owners they resented and feared all threats against the "peculiar institution." But as men of property and affluence they were apprehensive of the disruption that almost certainly would follow secession. Another concern set them apart from the cotton planters; their prosperity was enhanced by a Federal protective tariff, an advantage they were unlikely to enjoy in a Southern confederacy whose economy rested upon cotton.

When the secession crisis actually came, a majority of the sugar planters yielded to their emotions as Southerners and slave owners and played the lead role in taking Louisiana out of the Union and into the Confederacy. A majority of the sugar parishes sent "immediate secessionist" delegates to the state secession convention; the president of the convention was a sugar planter who was known as a "Creole Hotspur" because of his fiery determination to take the state out of the Union. One of the largest of the planters spoke for his class when he gave his benediction to the action of the convention in withdrawing from the Union. He said, "All honor to the men, who had the courage to take this first step, to prosperity which will be as permanent as earthly things may be."[3]

A sublime mood of confidence pervaded the planters' minds. According to the English traveler, they believed that with trusted slaves to till the soil and valiant sons to fight the battles, and with England and France to supply the money, the South could beat the rest of the world in arms. They asked, "Have you seen our President, sir? Don't you think him a very able man?"[4]

The planters' self-assurance remained unshaken throughout the early months of the Civil War itself. Its military events were far removed from southern Louisiana; affairs on the sugar plantations went on as usual—in some ways, better than usual. The 1861 crop was bountiful, and the landowners saved and planted an exceptionally large amount of seed sugarcane. The 1862 harvest of 459,410 hogsheads was one of the heaviest in the history of the industry.

Soon the realities of war began to be felt in the sugar country. In the summer of 1861 the Federal navy established a blockade of the mouth of the Mississippi River. The planters found themselves unable to market the bumper 1862 crop; sugar prices fell while the prices of manufactured necessities rose. From the New Orleans market came word that trading was dull and slow, and sugar "very irregular." The planters sought desperately to sell their produce throughout the Confederacy. By spring they knew that their efforts were largely futile. The early mood of confidence was now gone.

The Mississippi River, benefactor to the planters in peace, betrayed them in war. In the spring of 1862 a powerful combined Federal fleet and army invaded the sugar country via the great river. The master of Magnolia Plantation below New Orleans sat in his mansion and wrote with resignation, "The fleet are now passing the House. . . . Appear to be uninjured."[5] New Orleans was surrendered on May 1, and the occupation of the city and the plantation country along the lower Mississippi began. In the fall the occupation was extended to the country along Bayou Lafourche; the following spring it spread to that along Bayou Teche and the lower Red River.

Great numbers of the proprietors with their families and slaves fled before the invaders, leaving their plantations at the mercy of the soldiers, runaway slaves, and poor whites of the area. Northern soldiers described the scene vividly. One of them who participated in the campaign committed his impressions to a popular novel: "Space fails us to tell of the sacking of this rich land of plantations [along Bayou Lafourche]; how the inhabitants, by flying before the northern vandals, induced the spoliation of their own property; how the Negroes defiled and plundered the forsaken houses, and how the soldiers thereby justified themselves in plundering the Negroes; how the furniture, plate, and libraries of the Lafourche planters were thus scattered upon the winds of destruction."[6]

In an equally graphic description another Union soldier wrote: "I ride along the banked-up margin of Lafourche Bayou, by acres of abandoned plantations, through miles and leagues of cane fields." Near the town of Houma the observer was struck by the desolation of an estate that had been known for the owner's extensive library. He told how the planter had left everything he possessed "to the spoil of squatters, provost-marshals, soldiers, and camp-followers. . . . how the books [of the library] were scattered, mutilated, and consumed as fuel long ago." He contemplated sadly the sight of the derelict plantations as he rode along, "passing through miles of rotting cane, decadence of ungathered crops."[7]

Nor did the "winds of destruction" blow from the Northerners only; Confederate campaigners in the region foraged in a manner hardly less destructive. They seized the best of the plantation horses as well as all kinds of food and other provisions. A prominent Bayou Teche planter summed up his grievances against the Southern troops that had encamped on his property for a number of weeks: "They have left on my plantation, devastation and despoliation behind them—No discipline among them, and no regard to private property. Our troops have stripped me, by robbery, of nearly every resource for living from day to day and what is in reserve for me from the common enemy is yet to be ascertained. From a condition of ease comfort and abundance, I am suddenly reduced to one of hardship, want and privation."[8]

Where neither Federal nor Confederate forces were in control, guerrillas and Confederate deserters were the predators. They were especially active in the Opelousas area, robbing and vandalizing property, taking off everything that could be moved. The guerrillas opposed the invaders, but they also wrought havoc upon the local residents. The *New Orleans Daily Picayune* put the matter succinctly: They "do more harm to inhabitants that yet remain on the plantations, mostly females, than to the Federal forces."[9]

Perhaps the Red River area suffered most of all. As the beaten Union army of Major General Nathaniel Banks withdrew following the battles of Mansfield and Pleasant Hill in the spring of 1864, it applied the torch in addition to committing the usual acts of theft and vandalism. In the exaggerated but indicative words of an eyewitness: "It cannot . . . excite surprise in the minds of any, that the line of march of the army under General Banks can be traced like an Indian war trail, or the fire path of the prairie—by smoldering ruins of villages, dwellings, gins, and sugar houses—the conversion of a rich, beautiful and highly improved agricultural region into a vast wilderness."[10]

Plantations whose owners remained at home, a majority of the whole, fared better than those that were abandoned. Yet all were subject to wholesale foraging and pilfering; all felt the cruel hand of war.

Plantations suffered not only physical destruction and neglect. In addition, Federal authorities pursued a policy of confiscating the property of disloyal owners, especially the estates of men who were prominent in the secession movement or in Confederate service, including such figures as former U.S. Senator Judah Benjamin, now a member of the Confederate cabinet, and Braxton Bragg and Richard Taylor, generals in the Confederate army. Property estimated at $1,000,000 in value was promptly seized under this program. But most of the planters were able to retain the ownership of their plantations by taking an oath of allegiance to the Federal government. Some were sincere Unionists who had no objection to this procedure; many swallowed their bitterness and took the oath out of practical necessity.

Those proprietors who stayed on their plantations faced the staggering task of growing crops and making sugar in the midst of physical destruction and looting, the loss of motive power in the form of horses and mules, and the chaos of a society at war. This chaos grew out of the disruption of virtually the entire plantation labor force in the wake of the Federal invasion. The slaves began at once to trickle away from the plantations, at first individually and in groups of two or three slipping away during the night. Eventually the trickle swelled into a flood as the slaves employed their legs to obtain freedom. An observer of a marching Union column beset by swarms of laborers from the fields likened the scene to that of thrusting a walking cane into an anthill.

So numerous were these runaways along Bayou Lafourche that the commander of the Federal expedition felt unable to cope with the situation. He wrote in consternation to his superior:

What shall I do about the Negroes? You can form no idea of the vicinity of my camp, nor can you form an idea of the appearance of my brigade as it marched down the bayou. My train was larger than any army train for 25,000 men. Every soldier had a Negro marching in the flanks, carrying his knapsack. Plantation carts, filled with Negro women and children, with their effects; and of course compelled to pillage for their subsistence, as I have no rations to issue them. I have a great many more Negroes in my camp now than I have whites. . . . These Negroes are a perfect nuisance.[11]

The scenes of abandonment of the plantations by the slaves were repeated throughout the entire sugar country as the Federal invasion proceeded.

The planters, who had believed their slaves would remain loyal to them, watched in dismay as they fled into the Federal lines. A Bayou Lafourche plantation mistress called her laborers together to discuss their new demeanor. "They came slowly and reluctantly," she said. "I see before me now those dark stolid faces in which I read nothing—I was among a strange people, and was unprepared for a change so great—I looked vainly in familiar faces for the old expression—they listened attentively, there was no response, not a sound—it was ominous in so excitable a people." The next morning all were gone except a few old or sick ones.[12]

In general, the blacks were peaceful in their behavior in the hour of their liberation; they simply left the plantations and collected around the Federal camps. But the whites, aware of the bloodshed in the great earlier slave uprising in the French colony of St. Domingue, lived in fear of violence. The commander of the Federal expedition on the Lafourche wrote, "Women and children, and even men, are in terror. It is heart-rending, and I cannot make myself responsible for [the outcome]."

The whites had cause to fear; occasional incidents of violence by the blacks did occur. The Federal commander described some of these affairs and the dread they stirred in the entire white community. Another Union soldier reported the execution of a black, who, he said, had no more intellect than a pig, for the rare episode of criminal assault upon a white girl.[13]

The seizure of plantation livestock by both the Union and Confederate armies was a severe blow to the sugar country, and the proprietors sought in every way possible to make up for this loss. They appealed, with partial success, to the local Union military commanders to return a sufficient number of horses and mules to work the crop. Some of the proprietors appointed special cart men among their laborers and allowed them cash incentives to guard the remaining animals. The proprietors resorted to the purchase of army horses and mules that had been condemned and sold at auction. They entered into arrangements among themselves for moving their remaining animals from plantation to plantation to carry out the operations. Some proprietors substituted oxen for horses and mules. Such improvisations enabled them to keep up a faltering production throughout the war.[14]

The planters further reduced their sugar crop by turning a portion of their land to the growing of corn, cotton, and tobacco, which required fewer laborers and animals and were of greater use to the Southern population. The resort to cotton and tobacco was a failure, but the growing of corn seems to have been successful. A Union soldier wrote in 1863 that fields near Opelousas that were customarily planted in sugarcane were then planted in corn. Another Federal, after marching through immense fields of corn in the western part of the sugar country, scoffed at what he called the "ponderous articles" of Northern newspapers that talked of the simplicity of starving the South into submission.[15]

But in the mind of the planters the disruption of the labor system had the war's most devastating effect on the production of sugar. The slaves flocked away from the plantations and settled into great encampments in the vicinity of the Union lines. There they engaged in an immense jubilee of freedom, foraging for food and depending upon the Northern soldiers for handouts. They were a constant source of interest, amusement, and gratification to their benefactors. At night the camps glowed with bonfires that cast flickering shadows of the campers as they whirled and shuffled to the sounds of the banjo and fiddle.

Blue-clad soldiers freely joined the exercises and tripped "the light fantastic toe" with the "sable virgins of Africa." At intervals soldiers could be seen leading "sable nymphs" out into the darkness. Then the mood might suddenly change as cries of "Glory to God" and "Glory to Abe Limkum" rang out, and the dance subsided into a prayer meeting punctuated with expressions of thanksgiving to "Massa Limkum and the Limkum sogers." Inevitably, the result of the liaisons between the soldiers and the black women was a crop of infants. When one Union campaigner asked an elderly black woman how she subsisted after leaving the plantation, she replied, to his astonishment, that she was a midwife in one of the camps, and explained, "The darkey women fall in love with the Yankee soldiers, and I take care of the little mules."[16]

Living conditions in the improvised camps were appalling; immense numbers of blacks died of malnutrition, exposure, and their accompanying diseases. One sugar planter left a searing description of life in the runaway community just across the Mississippi from New Orleans. The blacks "lived in the most abject misery and degradation," he wrote; they were dying by the hundreds and being buried under the floors of the salt warehouses they inhabited. He said they presented a scene "Revolting to the sight and repugnant to every sense of Humanity. . . . They were huddled together and remained there living in the most Loathsome manner and committing the most dreadful excesses of Depravity and Lechery in connection with the soldiers of the camps—Presenting a spectacle of the most Revolting nature."[17]

The presence of the multitude of idle blacks was a burden and a nuisance to the Union military authorities who at the same time glimpsed the specter of starvation among the general population because of the lack of productivity on the plantations. They sought to solve both problems by sending the blacks back to work, not as slaves but as wage laborers. Beginning shortly after the capture of New Orleans, the military authorities issued orders compelling the planters and the blacks to enter into contracts that provided for wages, quarters, food, and clothing for the laborers but required them to settle on the plantations and perform the usual work of growing and harvesting the cane and making the sugar. Abandoned places were turned over to agents, with the profits to be given to the government. These arrangements, with numerous modifications, remained in effect throughout the rest of the war.

From the planters' point of view, the arrangements did not work. Born and bred in the conviction that blacks would labor effectively only as slaves, the planters could see no good in the new order. They filled their journals and the local newspapers with complaints and condemnations. A Unionist proprietor of generally moderate and balanced judgment recorded the attitude of his class in saying that the blacks spent much of their time hauling moss into town for sale, dawdled in the fields and sugarhouses, refused to obey the instructions of the overseer, allowed the fires to die out under the boilers, thus wasting cane and exposing the entire crop to a ruinous frost, and hired out the plantation carts and teams for their own profit. He accused them also of pilfering and stealing plantation items for sale. "Their religion does not prevent them from stealing, lying and other vices," he brooded. "The wish of the Negro is now the white man's law. A man had as well be in purgatory as attempt to work a sugar plantation under existing circumstances."[18]

Planters throughout the cane country continued to record similar condemnations of the free-labor system. They accused the blacks of laziness and dishonesty. One planter said that plows, harrows, hoes, axes, and saws disappeared from his place, along with hogs, sheep, and poultry. "Demoralization of the sexes is shocking," he railed. "They work less, have less respect, are less orderly than ever." At an emergency meeting in the fall of 1864 the major proprietors of Terrebone Parish agreed that free black labor was an unqualified failure.[19]

The planters' condemnation of wage labor was unquestionably exaggerated by their preconceptions against it. Their own testimony indicated that some of the blacks worked well under the new arrangement. But the overwhelming judgment held that in its initial stages it was devastating to the sugar industry. Certainly, the early exuberance of freedom reduced the effectiveness of the laborers. This was followed by their keen disappointment at being herded back upon the plantations as workers (a process in which the proprietors and the military authorities cooperated) instead of receiving land of their own, which they had been encouraged to believe would occur. Some of them complained that their new situation was no better than slavery. It is understandable that they were less productive than under the former discipline.

Under the war's combination of afflictions—destruction, abandonment, looting, confiscation, and erratic labor—sugar production staggered and almost, but not quite, died. From the bumper crop of 459,410 hogsheads in 1861–1862 it plummeted to approximately 3 percent of that figure in 1864–1865.[20]

Despite the severe hardships wrought by the conflict, life went on, including social life, in the sugar country. Weddings, dances, and all sorts of other entertainments continued to occur, though marred by the absence of most of the young men of the community.

A few examples suffice to illustrate the situation. A dinner party given on a Mississippi River plantation reflected both the grimness of war and the resilient spirit of the population. The hostess was a young widow whose husband had died in the siege of Port Hudson and who sought to smother her sorrow in gaiety. She invited all Confederate soldiers who were friends of her family and were home on furlough and all the young women of the neighboring plantations. The women were dressed in an assortment of out-of-fashion or improvised clothing; one wore a jacket made from a piano cover. They came by an assortment of transportation, some mounted in men's saddles, some riding double, some on plantation mules.

After hours of dancing, they dined on ham and roast turkey, which the resourceful hostess had managed to procure, followed by a dessert of cornmeal pound cake and eggnog spiked with fiery rum from plantation molasses. The party disintegrated at the appearance of a Union gunboat: the hostess scooped up and hid the family silver, the Confederate soldiers disappeared into the darkness, and the female guests beat an undignified retreat on their lowly mules.[21]

Sugarhouse frolics during the grinding season had always been a favorite form of diversion on the plantations, and where places were still in operation they continued to be held. The presence of Confederate soldiers invariably enlivened these occasions immensely. At a party on a plantation near Port Hudson the young women and their uniformed beaux wandered merrily through the sugarhouse in the light shed by "Confederate gas" (flickering pine torches). At one point the young women seized the syrup ladles from the hands of the black laborers, dipped up the sugary liquid, and ate it with relish. Others preferred to chew the cane pulp for its sweet content.

Eventually the party turned to games to enrich the entertainment. First came "Puss Wants a Corner." "Such racing for corners," wrote a participant. "Such scuffles among the gentlemen! Such confusion among the girls when, springing forward for a place, we would find it already occupied." Dignity vanished as the group seemed to revert to childhood. Some of the Confederate officers entered into the affair with gusto; others disapproved and sulked. Some appeared "timidly foolish and half afraid of the wild sport." Soon they would face the Union guns at Port Hudson, but here they were strangely unassertive in the midst of cavorting plantation belles.

Later the group turned to the game of "Forfeits." It provided amusement, excitement, and gay absurdity. A lieutenant unknowingly sentenced himself to ride a barrel. A young woman was obliged to make a love confession to her partner. Another had to make a "declaration" to one of the officers. The game was followed by more cane chewing and conversation. The party disbanded at midnight.

One of the most extraordinary social occasions occurred in connection with an extraordinary war episode, the destruction of the Confederate gunboat *Arkansas*. A group of high-spirited young women from the Baton Rouge area rode along the levee and observed the vessel as it lay burning and exploding in the Mississippi below them. When the crew showed up at a nearby plantation they were told that they could not be invited into the house because the owner was on parole by the Federal authorities, but were assured by the proprietor's daughter that if they "chose to order," they might do as they pleased, "as women could not resist armed men." They chose to order, and the entire group partied until the following day, with each young woman appropriating an officer, naming him Miriam's, Ginnie's, or Sarah's, as if he belonged to her. When the sailors left, they were given bottles of gin as a refreshment.

But social diversions could not erase from the planters' minds the knowledge of the ruin that surrounded them. From the mood of optimism and exultation that marked the days of faraway war, they sank into despair as the conflict enveloped their plantations and their lives. Rumors of military affairs on distant battlefields fluctuated wildly. A young woman wrote from a plantation in the vicinity of Baton Rouge: "News comes pouring in. Note we a few items, to see how many will prove false. First, we have taken Baltimore without firing a gun; Maryland has risen en masse to join our troops; Longstreet and Lee are marching on Washington from the rear; the Louisiana troops are ordered home to defend their own state—thank God! if it will only bring the boys back!"[22]

But when the word arrived that Vicksburg and Port Hudson had fallen, a proprietor wisely warned that this marked the beginning of the end for the Confederacy. Plantation women knew fully the dread and bitterness of the situation and often gave vent to these emotions. Left without men to defend them, many of them referred their case to heaven. "I do believe the Lord is on our side," wrote one. "Our sins may be flagrant, and we may need to be scourged with scorpions; but will God permit us to be overwhelmed?" She said that a rekindled religious faith among the women enabled them to sleep the "sleep of the just."

News of the death of sons and husbands in battle plunged the families of the sugar country into deep mourning. Their correspondence and plantation diaries reveal their lamentations. A desolate young widow whose husband died in the fighting at Vicksburg cried, "Why does anybody live when Paul is dead?—dead, dead, forever?"[23]

Impending defeat crushed the planters' spirits. "I stay at home now all the time," wrote one of them, "having very little to do—but to think over the past and speculate on the future."[24] Another, whose two Confederate sons had died of typhoid, said, "No one who has not been similarly situated can properly understand what I am now suffering all alone." He said the death of his sons seemed a blessing because it spared them "the nightmare of defeat."

The same planter issued a bitter prophecy on his future and that of his fellow proprietors: "The owners of the soil will make nothing, the lands will be sold for taxes, and bought by Northern men, and the original owners will be made beggars—This is the result of Secession and abolitionism—Was there ever such folly since the world began.—."[25]

Another planter uttered a similar prediction:

The days (emphatically days of darkness and gloom) succeed each other bringing nothing but despondency with regard to the future.—Our beautiful Parish is laid waste and is likely to become a desert—Plantations abandoned, fences and buildings destroyed, mules, horses and cattle driven off by federals, the Negroes conscripted into the army or wandering about without employment or support, and stealing for a living—Those who remain are insolent and refractory, and in domestic, family arrangements the few who continue with their owners are more trouble and vexation than they are of use.—Their laziness and impertinence is beyond belief.—There can be no crop made in the country and of course starvation will be the dreadful consequence.—All this is fearful to consider, and if indiscriminate plunder and massacre do not supervene we may consider ourselves lucky.—The Lord help us.—Such is war, civil war.[26]

The most poignant expression from the sugar country came in response to the most dramatic and most fateful event of the war. A Unionist planter said he had received "the terrible news" that President Lincoln had been assassinated. "This is one of the most extraordinary occurrences in the history of the world," he continued, "and in my judgment one of the greatest misfortunes that could have befallen the country.—I had, since the fall of Richmond, and the surrender of Lee . . . begun to admit the hope of an early peace. . . . [Lincoln's] death is therefore, in my opinion a great loss to the whole country and especially to the South—as from him, we had a right to expect better terms of peace than from anyone else at all likely to come into power.—Oh! my poor country—What have you yet to suffer."[27]

Notes

This essay is based, in part, on the author's *Louisiana Sugar Plantations during the American Civil War* (Leiden, Netherlands: E. J. Brill, 1957), which was reissued by Louisiana State University Press (Baton Rouge, 1998) under the title *Louisiana Sugar Plantations during the Civil War.*

1. William Howard Russell, *My Diary North and South* (Boston, 1863), 285.

2. William T. Palfrey Plantation Diary, August 6, 1860, Department of Archives and Manuscripts, Louisiana State University, Baton Rouge.

3. Charles P. Roland, *Louisiana Sugar Plantations during the American Civil War* (Leiden, Netherlands: E. J. Brill, 1957), gives a full account of the subject. For a de-

scription of the plantation society, see pp. 1–9; A. Franklin Pugh Plantation Diary, January 27, 1861, Department of Archives and Manuscripts, Louisiana State University.

4. Russell, *My Diary North and South,* 260.

5. P. A. Champomier, *Statement of the Sugar Crop Made in Louisiana in 1861–1862* (New Orleans, 1862), vii–viii; Magnolia Plantation Journal, April 16, 1862, Southern Historical Collection, University of North Carolina, Chapel Hill, N.C.

6. John W. De Forest, *Miss Ravenel's Conversion from Secession to Loyalty* (New York: Harper and Brothers, 1939), 191.

7. Alexander J. H. Duganne, *Camps and Prisons: Twenty Months in the Department of the Gulf* (New York, 1865), 34, 49, 53.

8. Palfrey Plantation Diary, December 10, 19, 1862, January 22, 1863.

9. Bayside Plantation Journal, May 11, 1863, Department of Archives and Manuscripts, Louisiana State University; *New Orleans Daily Picayune,* December 4, 1862.

10. G. P. Whittington, "Rapides Parish, Louisiana: A History," *Louisiana Historical Quarterly* 18 (January 1935): 38.

11. Roland, *Louisiana Sugar Plantations,* 73; quoted in James Partin, *General Butler in New Orleans: Being a History of the Administration of the Department of the Gulf in the Year 1862* (New York, 1864), 489, 580.

12. Quoted in Barnes F. Lathrop, "The Pugh Plantations, 1860–1865: A Study of Life in Lower Louisiana" (Ph.D. diss., University of Texas, Austin, 1945), 209.

13. Quoted in Benjamin F. Butler, *Autobiography and Personal Reminiscences of Major General Benjamin F. Butler: Butler's Book* (Boston, 1892), 496–97; John W. De Forest, *A Volunteer's Adventures: A Union Captain's Record of the Civil War* (New Haven: Yale University Press, 1946), 75.

14. Roland, *Louisiana Sugar Plantations,* 75–78. For specific instances of these activities, see M. W. Minor to William J. Minor, March 21, 1864, William J. Minor Papers, Department of Archives and Manuscripts, Louisiana State University; G. P. Whittington, ed., "Concerning the Loyalty of Slaves in Louisiana," *Louisiana Historical Quarterly* 14 (October 1931): 494; Palfrey Plantation Diary, November 17, 23, 28, 1864; William J. Minor Plantation Diary (1863–1868), April 24, 1864, Department of Archives and Manuscripts, Louisiana State University.

15. L. Carroll Root, ed., "Private Journal of William H. Root, Second Lieutenant, Seventy-fifth New York Volunteers, April 1–June 14, 1863," *Louisiana Historical Quarterly* 19 (July 1936): 651; George W. Powers, *The Story of the Thirty-eighth Massachusetts Volunteers* (Cambridge, 1866), 83.

16. Lawrence Van Alstyne, *Diary of an Enlisted Man* (New Haven: Tuttle, Morehouse and Taylor Company, 1910), 193–94; Henry T. Johns, *Life with the Forty-ninth Massachusetts Volunteers* (Pittsfield, Mass., 1864), 126.

17. Magnolia Plantation Journal, January 25, 1863. James M. McPherson gives a brief, realistic discussion of the prevailing conditions among the runaways throughout the Confederacy, conditions which he estimates took a death toll of 25 percent (*Ordeal by Fire: The Civil War and Reconstruction* [New York: Alfred A. Knopf, 1982], 394–96).

18. Minor Plantation Diary (1863), September 5; ibid. (1863–1868), September 29, October 12, November 11, 14, 16, 27, 1863.

19. For such expressions, see the *New Orleans Times,* October 13, 21, November 2, 1864; Minor Plantation Diary (1863–1868), November 17, 1864.

20. The Union commander of the department in 1863 predicted with bumptious optimism that within three years the sugar crop would be four times as large as ever. Minor Plantation Diary (1863), January 8. The crop would not equal that of 1861–1862 until almost three decades after the war.

21. Caroline E. Merrick, *Old Times in Dixie Land: A Southern Matron's Memories* (New York: Grafton Press, 1901), 95–98.

22. Sarah Morgan Dawson, *A Confederate Girl's Diary* (New York: Houghton Mifflin, 1913), 226, 243, 272–74.

23. Merrick, *Old Times in Dixie Land,* 39, 89.

24. Pugh Plantation Diary, November 26, 1862.

25. Minor Plantation Diary (1863), February 5, March 2, May 20; ibid. (1863–1868), September 29, 1863.

26. Palfrey Plantation Diary, March 16, 1864.

27. Minor Plantation Diary (1863–1868), April 19, 1865.

Part Three

Civil War Leadership

Albert Sidney Johnston and the Defense of the Confederate West

According to family tradition, Confederate president Jefferson Davis lay ill in bed one day in late August 1861 when he heard familiar footsteps in the hallway below and said, "That is Albert Sidney Johnston. Bring him up." A few moments later Johnston was ushered into the president's room.

This was doubtless an emotional occasion for both men. They had been friends since their cadet days together at West Point, where Johnston, who graduated in 1826, was two years ahead of Davis. Johnston held the coveted position of adjutant of the Corps, and Davis had admired him deeply. Years later they had served together gallantly in the battle of Monterrey in the Mexican War. In the 1850s, when Davis was U.S. secretary of war, he had played a key role in appointing Johnston colonel and commanding officer of the newly created 2nd Cavalry Regiment, an elite organization that included in its roster such subordinates as Lieutenant Colonel Robert E. Lee, second in command, and Majors William J. Hardee and George H. Thomas, along with others who achieved distinction in the Civil War.

Later in the decade, the War Department selected Johnston to command an expedition to quell a threatening rebellion by the Mormons in Utah territory. He achieved the rank of brevet brigadier general in this operation. On the eve of the Civil War, Johnston was assigned to command the Pacific Department, with headquarters in San Francisco. He resigned his commission when his adopted state, Texas, seceded, and he made a Herculean journey across the southwestern region of the nation to join the Confederacy.

Davis was overjoyed with Johnston's appearance in Richmond, not only because the two were dear friends, but also because Johnston was perhaps the most distinguished field officer of the U.S. Army at that time.

A description of him published in the *Harper's Weekly* magazine during the Utah operation captured him precisely:

> Johnston is now in the matured vigor of manhood. He is about six feet in height, strongly and powerfully formed, with a grave, dignified, and commanding presence. His features are strongly marked, showing his Scottish lineage, and denote great resolution and composure of character. His complexion, naturally fair, is, from exposure, a deep brown. His habits are abstemious and temperate, and no excess has impaired his powerful constitution. His mind is clear, strong, and well cultivated. His manner is courteous, but rather grave and silent. He has many devoted friends, but they have been won and secured rather by the native dignity and nobility of his character than by his powers of address. He is a man of strong will and ardent temper, but his whole bearing testifies to the self-control he has acquired.

At the time of his promotion during the Utah expedition, General Winfield Scott, commanding general of the Army, wrote to President James Buchanan, "[Johnston] is more than a good officer. He is a God send to the country through the army." General U. S. Grant wrote in his memoirs that the Union officers at the beginning of the Civil War considered Johnston to be the most formidable opponent they would meet in the conflict.

At the moment, Davis was urgently in need of someone to command the far-flung western theater of the Confederacy. Johnston seemed to be the perfect choice; he was a native of Kentucky and had spent most of his career in Texas and other parts of the West. On September 10, Davis issued the order assigning Johnston to the command of Confederate Department No. 2, a vast area spreading from the Appalachian Mountains on the east to, and including, Indian Territory [now the state of Oklahoma] on the west. He was assigned the rank of full general, the highest field officer of the Confederacy. He proceeded at once to Nashville and took over the active command of his department.

Johnston faced a grave decision—what to do about the state of Kentucky. The Confederacy considered Kentucky to be a Confederate state. The Kentucky government had declared the state neutral, and the Lincoln administration had sent in no military formations, though Union troops were being recruited, armed, and trained in the state. Ten days prior to

Johnston's arrival in Nashville, Confederate major general Leonidas Polk occupied Columbus, Kentucky, a key strategic point located on the Mississippi River at the northern terminus of the Mobile & Ohio Railroad. Should Johnston order Polk to withdraw into Tennessee, along with a small contingent of Confederate troops under General Felix Zollicoffer located at Mill Springs, guarding the Cumberland Gap in eastern Kentucky, or should Johnston occupy and defend Kentucky for the Confederacy?

Urged by Governor Isham Harris of Tennessee, Johnston took the bolder course and ordered a contingent of four thousand troops under the command of Brigadier General Simon Bolivar Buckner from Nashville to Bowling Green, Kentucky. Johnston pointed out to the Richmond authorities that otherwise the Confederacy would lose Kentucky and invite an immediate invasion of Tennessee. But the move into Kentucky was motivated primarily by political considerations, and it was based on the hope and belief that Kentuckians would rally in great numbers to the Confederate cause. If they failed to do so, Johnston would find his situation precarious.

In some ways, Johnston's strategic views were circumscribed by those of Davis, whose policy was that of territorial defense—voluntarily yielding no part of the Confederacy to the enemy. This dictated a cordon or line form of defense and prohibited an early concentration of Confederate forces. Consequently, Johnston's small army (initially, some thirty thousand) was spread across a Kentucky front of approximately five hundred miles, with wide gaps along the line. It was anchored on the west by General Polk's troops at Columbus on the Mississippi, a position that Polk at once began to fortify in order to deny the use of the river to the Federals. The eastern flank was held by Zollicoffer's force at the Cumberland Gap. The center lay at Bowling Green, with General William J. Hardee in immediate command. Bowling Green was also the site of Johnston's headquarters, as well as the Confederate government of Kentucky.

Painfully aware of the weakness of his line, Johnston worked diligently to strengthen it. His hope of receiving thousands of volunteers from Kentucky soon vanished. He appealed for troops to the governors of the other states within his department, but their response was disappointing. He then sought reinforcements from the Confederate authorities, suggesting that these troops be sent from other parts of the Confederacy. In January 1862, he wrote to the Confederate adjutant general: "All the resources of the Confederacy are now needed for the defence [*sic*] of Tennessee." His efforts to strengthen his line were all in vain, and he faced a showdown against a Union force approximately twice the size of his own.

The most vulnerable place in this attenuated line lay where the Tennessee and Cumberland rivers ran through it in their course to the Ohio. Small forts guarded these points: Fort Henry on the Tennessee and Fort Donelson on the Cumberland. The two were only eleven miles apart. Johnston appreciated the weakness of these forts, but he was unable to remedy it; perhaps because of his preoccupation with the overall strategic situation, he did not pay sufficient heed to the vulnerability of the forts.

The opening attacks on the Confederate line came at its extremities. In early November, Brigadier General Ulysses S. Grant led a force from his base at Cairo, Illinois, and struck a small Confederate outpost at Belmont, Missouri, across the Mississippi from Columbus. Polk's troops drove off the attackers by ferrying reinforcements across the river. In mid-January 1862, Johnston's eastern force, now commanded by Brigadier General George B. Crittenden, attacked Union troops under Brigadier General George H. Thomas north of the Cumberland River in the battle of Mill Springs (also known as the battle of Fishing Creek or the battle of Logan's Cross Roads). The Confederates were defeated and driven back across the river.

These actions were preliminary to a far more serious operation, an attack by General Grant in the western segment of the Confederate front. It came at the points where the Tennessee and Cumberland rivers penetrated the Confederate line. On February 6, a joint army-navy force of seventeen thousand troops under Grant and a flotilla of seven gunboats commanded by Flag Officer Andrew H. Foote moved against Fort Henry. The gunboats alone quickly overpowered the fort's batteries, and the commander, Brigadier General Lloyd Tilghman, surrendered the position. Grant and Foote now prepared to take Fort Donelson.

The loss of Fort Henry opened an irreparable breach in Johnston's line. The Tennessee River was navigable by Union gunboats and transports all the way to the Muscle Shoals in northern Alabama. Two-thirds of Johnston's army in Kentucky was subject to being trapped within the great arc of the river.

On February 7, Johnston assembled his ranking subordinates to adopt a strategy for meeting this desperate situation. The group included General Hardee and General P. G. T. Beauregard, who had been sent to Kentucky from Virginia to serve as Johnston's second in command. Beauregard was the lowest-ranking of the five full generals of the Confederacy. At the

Bowling Green meeting, Johnston proposed a momentous plan to abandon his advanced line and withdraw to northern Mississippi outside the loop of the Tennessee River. The wings of his army were temporarily to act as independent forces until they could be united at some point there. He would command the eastern wing, and Beauregard the western wing (primarily Polk's force).

This plan assumed that Fort Donelson, on the Cumberland, was untenable, and Nashville, the capital of Tennessee and an important industrial and commercial city, would temporarily be yielded to the enemy. After the Civil War, Beauregard claimed to have opposed the entire plan and to have urged Johnston to hasten by rail and boat with his Bowling Green force to confront Grant at Fort Donelson, but there is no convincing evidence that Beauregard offered such an alternative to Johnston's strategy. Both Johnston and Hardee wrote at the time that the three generals had agreed unanimously that the Kentucky line must be abandoned.

Should Johnston, nevertheless, have fashioned and adopted such a plan as Beauregard later suggested? Possibly it would have worked. But in addition to Grant's troops at Fort Donelson, Johnston's Bowling Green troops also faced another army of more than twice their strength. It was commanded by Major General Don Carlos Buell and was advancing against Johnston from northern Kentucky. Johnston, with good reason, feared that fighting Grant and Buell together in Kentucky would expose his army to destruction or capture there. General Grant wrote in his memoirs that Johnston should have taken the risk, that the outcome could not have been worse for the Confederacy if Johnston and all his army had been captured. This is a fatuous argument. It ignores the vital role played by Johnston and, after his death, by the army throughout the remainder of the war in the West.

The wisdom of Johnston's decision is debatable. That he exhibited immense moral courage in making it is beyond cavil, in my judgment. He well understood the seriousness of giving up, even temporarily, two Confederate states. He was also keenly aware of the public furor that would be aroused by this action. An outcry of indignation greeted his retreat; a citizens' delegation appealed to Davis, demanding that Johnston be removed. But Davis rejected the demand and said, "If General Johnston is not a general, then we have none and should give up the war." Despite the uproar, Johnston took the action that he considered imperative in order to save his army.

But Johnston made a monumental mistake after deciding that Fort Donelson could not be held. He sent some eleven or twelve thousand additional troops into the fort. When Grant made his February 15 attack on it, the ranking generals there, Brigadier General John Floyd and Brigadier General Gideon Pillow, in one of the most flagrantly mishandled operations of the entire war, surrendered the fort and its troops, including those who had just arrived. Only with the greatest difficulty did Johnston get his Bowling Green army across the Cumberland River at Nashville and avoid being trapped north of that stream as well as north of the Tennessee.

Now began a race for Johnston and Beauregard to get their troops into Mississippi ahead of the Federals. Johnston first had to decide where the wings of his army were to be brought together. A glance at the map indicated that the easiest place was the town of Corinth, in northeastern Mississippi. It lay where the two major railroads of the western Confederacy—the Mobile & Ohio, running north and south, and the Memphis & Charleston, running east and west—intersected. But neither Johnston nor Beauregard mentioned Corinth in their early conversations and correspondence. They probably considered it too close to the Tennessee River, only twenty miles from Pittsburg Landing, and thus likely to be captured before they could reach it.

But for various reasons, the Federals were slow in moving a force up the Tennessee. Not until almost a month after the fall of Fort Donelson did they establish a camp at Pittsburg Landing. On March 13, General Charles F. Smith began debarking an army of five divisions there. Soon a sixth division arrived, for a total of approximately forty thousand men. Following Smith's illness a few days later from an infection (from which he eventually died), General Grant took command of the force.

Meanwhile, both Johnston and Beauregard decided independently to unite their wings of the Confederate army at Corinth. This was a relatively easy task for Beauregard; he simply transported them on the Mobile & Ohio Railroad and posted them at key points along the way. Johnston's task was extremely difficult and hazardous. He ran the risk of being trapped above the Tennessee River. Nevertheless, after a grueling march by foot from Murfreesboro, southeast of Nashville, he crossed them over the river on the Memphis & Charleston bridge at Decatur, Alabama, then shuttled them by rail to Corinth. By late March he had the two wings of his army there, plus some ten thousand additional troops under Major General Braxton Bragg brought by rail from Pensacola and Mobile, and another five thousand under Brigadier General Daniel Ruggles brought by rail and river from Louisiana, a total of approximately forty thousand present for duty.

Johnston now planned a mighty blow at Grant's army, which was still encamped at Pittsburg Landing. The night of April 2–3, Johnston received word that Buell's Union army was moving rapidly to join Grant. Johnston immediately issued orders for his force to march from Corinth and deliver the attack before Buell's arrival. He wired Jefferson Davis of his intention and indicated that his assault would be made with his three main corps, those of Hardee, Polk, and Bragg abreast, with Bragg's corps, the largest of the three, on the right, followed by a reserve force under Brigadier General John C. Breckinridge, who had replaced Crittenden at Corinth.

But Johnston then delegated to Beauregard the duty of issuing the march and attack order, and Beauregard planned a different formation from the one Johnston had indicated to Davis. Beauregard's order called for an attack in successive waves by the various corps, with the main effort on the right to shear the Federals from their base at the Landing. This arrangement would have a profound effect on the outcome of the battle. Apparently, Johnston did not learn of the change of formation until the column was on the march and at a time he considered too late to alter it.

After innumerable delays and obstacles, by late afternoon of April 5 the Confederates were deployed for the attack. At this point, Johnston suddenly found himself facing what the great Prussian military theorist Karl von Clausewitz called "the moment of truth" that usually precedes a great engagement: the breakdown of the will of the army subordinates, their loss of nerve for the undertaking. At this point, said Clausewitz, only the will and character of the commander keeps the operation alive. Beauregard suddenly began to argue that all hope of taking the Federals by surprise was lost, that they would "be entrenched to their eyes" and that the assault would be bloodily repulsed. Most, if not all, of the corps commanders agreed. Johnston listened courteously, then said quietly that he still expected to find the Federals unprepared. Then, "We shall attack at daylight tomorrow." This was the supreme command decision of the entire campaign.

The Confederates struck at dawn on April 6 in the vicinity of a small, country Methodist Church named Shiloh. They found their enemies unprepared; the surprise was complete; Johnston's judgment was fully vindicated.

How was he able to sense the situation so accurately? The renowned nineteenth-century British military theorist Colonel G. F. R. Henderson answered this question generically in discussing the attributes of great generals: "If in appearance great risks [are] run, it [is] with the full knowledge that the enemy's character or his apprehensions would prevent him from taking those simple precautions by which the critics point out that the whole enterprise might easily [be] ruined. [Great generals] penetrate . . . their adversary's brain." Grant was convinced that the Confederates lacked the will and purpose to launch a counterattack. Johnston seems to have penetrated his brain on this point.

But the Federals reacted quickly and soon established a line, which they defended stubbornly. The Confederate attack formation, Beauregard's formation, gave away much of the advantage of the Confederate surprise. The initial assault was made by Hardee's corps only, about one-third of the Confederate strength, excluding the reserves. Not until more than an hour later was Bragg's corps, the largest of the three attacking corps, committed to action. The bulk of Polk's corps was committed still later. If the full Confederate strength had made the opening assault, with Bragg's heavy corps on the right, as Johnston had originally intended, the attack probably would have overwhelmed the Federals before they could have recovered from their surprise and formed a defensive line.

By midmorning, all troops on both sides, except for the Confederate reserve, were engaged, and the entire front of about three miles was ablaze. The fighting was extraordinarily fierce; both Grant and his top division commander, Major General William Tecumseh Sherman, said years later that they had seen no more furious action during the war. Thousands of Union troops abandoned the fight and fled to the river; great numbers of Confederates broke ranks to engage in looting the deserted, well-stocked Union camps. On one occasion, Johnston personally reprimanded a young officer who was doing so, then, to soften the rebuke, picked up a tin cup and said that it would be his part of the loot.

Johnston left Beauregard to oversee the rear while he himself commanded at the front. Riding across the line from left to right, he communicated directly with corps, division, and brigade commanders and made adjustments in the formation. By late morning, he was aware that, although the general attack seemed to be going well, his thrust on the right had been stopped by powerful resistance along a wagon road in the woods and at the edge of a peach orchard. He immediately ordered Breckinridge's reserve brigades into the attack in this sector.

Still the Confederates were unable to break the Union line. At about two o'clock, Johnston personally rode along the front of one of Breckinridge's reluctant regiments, tapping the points of their bayonets with the tin cup that he had said was his part of the loot. Then, wheeling his horse, he cried, "I will lead you," which he proceeded to do, at least for a short distance. The regiment then moved forward and took its objective.

Johnston was elated with this success. He kicked up one foot to show an aide, Governor Isham Harris of Tennessee, where a bullet had ripped up the sole of his boot, and he said gaily, "Governor, they almost put me *hors de combat* that time." Then he sent Harris to bear instructions to one of the brigade commanders.

When Harris returned a few minutes later, he found Johnston reeling unsteadily in the saddle. Harris inquired anxiously whether Johnston was wounded. Johnston replied slowly, "Yes, Governor. I fear seriously." Harris steadied him on his horse, led him a few yards into a wooded ravine where they were sheltered from the shot and shell, and laid him on the ground. Johnston's staff gathered around and looked frantically for a wound on his upper body. Meanwhile, he bled to death through a rent in the main artery of his right leg. By 2:30 he was dead. His personal physician, who possibly could have saved his life, was attending wounded Confederates and Federals, ordered to do so by Johnston. Ironically, the general's humane move may have cost him his own life.

Beauregard now assumed command and ordered the attack to be continued. The fighting did continue; the Union troops in the Hornets' Nest were surrounded and forced to surrender at about 5:30; the Confederate line pressed forward in an effort to consummate a decisive victory. But suddenly Beauregard ordered the attack halted. In his report of the battle, he explained that his troops were exhausted and that he had received news that Buell's army would not reach Pittsburg Landing in time to save Grant's army. Beauregard's plan was to rest his troops and complete the victory the next morning.

This proved to be a fundamental, and near fatal, mistake. Buell's troops reinforced Grant's during the night, and the following day (April 7) the combined armies counterattacked the Confederates and obliged Beauregard to disengage his army and retreat to Corinth. The bloody battle of Shiloh (Pittsburg Landing, to the Federals) thus ended in a significant tactical and strategic Union victory, leaving a powerful invading army poised to drive down the Mississippi Valley and split the Confederacy in half.

Johnston's death at the most critical point of the battle has left two of the most enduring unanswered questions of the Civil War. First, would he have won a decisive victory at Shiloh if he had not been killed? The trend among historians today is to say that he would not have done so. But this ignores the testimony of certain knowledgeable participants to the effect that a definite lull occurred in the attack, especially on the right, following his death—a lull that enabled the Union commanders to establish a final defense line around Pittsburg Landing.

Confederate General Bragg wrote in his battle report that the delay caused by Johnston's death prevented a complete Confederate victory. Union brigadier general Stephen A. Hurlbut, who commanded the left flank division in the Hornets' Nest, wrote in his report that at about 3:00, because his position was no longer under attack, he was able to withdraw his troops from the line in order to place them in the final defensive position.

The most telling affirmation concerning the result of Johnston's death came from General Sherman. He said in his memoirs: "The rebel army, commanded by General Albert Sidney Johnston . . . beyond all question fought skillfully from early morning till about 2 P.M., when their commander-in-chief was killed. . . . There was then a perceptible lull for a couple of hours, when the attack was renewed, but with much less vehemence, and continued up to dark." The break in the fighting occurred at the very point of culmination in the battle. It is a reasonable assumption that without it, the Confederates might have consummated a victory.

Critics of Johnston find fault with the command role he took in the battle. They say he should have remained at the rear, directing the attack through his aides and couriers; that he ceased to be an army commander and became a mere regimental commander; and that he was recklessly careless in exposing himself in such a way as to be killed. Under ordinary circumstances, these criticisms may be valid.

But Johnston was not operating under ordinary circumstances. He was keenly aware that a commander's ability to inspire his troops to superhuman effort in combat is as important as the orders he gives on the field; he was keenly aware that his troops at Shiloh were virtually untrained civilians and that his appearance at the front was critical to their morale and determination. He was also cognizant that victory hung at a delicate balance by early afternoon, and that his personal conduct might tip the scale.

Military history is filled with examples of great generals who have performed acts similar to Johnston's at Shiloh and have exposed themselves to injury or death in doing so. Alexander and Caesar did so in wars of antiquity; Napoleon and Wellington did so in the modern era. Wellington's chief of cavalry was killed by a shell while standing immediately by Welling-ton's side on the line. It could just as easily have been Wellington. Rommel and Patton conducted themselves in a similar fashion in World War II. Later, a British commission studying the issue of command effectiveness reached the decision that Rommel was the most effective field commander of the conflict. This was so, they said, because he commanded at the front where he could survey the scene for himself, make judgments on firsthand observation, and convey his orders and instructions to his subordinates eye to eye, with no possibility of misunderstanding. His "electric presence" at the front added a weapon to the German attack, they concluded. Every account of the battle of Shiloh indicates that Johnston's electric presence at the front added a potent weapon to the Confederate attack.

A final question remains: What would have been Johnston's role in the war if he had survived the battle of Shiloh? My evaluation is that he would have been an incalculable asset to the Confederacy. Whereas such generals as Grant, Sherman, Lee, and Beauregard grew immensely with experience in the war, Johnston was unable to do so because he died in the first truly great encounter of the struggle. But he demonstrated in it that he was a man of towering character, unshakable will, and dauntless spirit; that he was capable of anticipating and outthinking his adversaries; and that he was a troop leader of extraordinary charismatic qualities in battle. Moreover, he enjoyed the complete confidence of his commander in chief, Jefferson Davis. Of all Confederate generals in the West, Johnston alone seems to have held the potential of a Lee.

The Generalship of Robert E. Lee

Machiavelli wrote that victory is the final test of skill in war. "If a general wins a battle," he said, "it cancels all other errors and miscarriages." Conversely, one may infer, if a general loses a battle, it cancels all other brilliance and daring. Experience in two world wars, followed by a growing insecurity in the modern age, heightens the American sense of nationalism today. Supreme excellence in all things (whether economic, intellectual, or military) must come of our peculiar political and social institutions, Americans are accustomed to believe. Rudely upset in the field of science by Sputnik, Gagarin, and Titov, this happy theme yet pervades much of the literature of American history, and especially many recent treatises on the Civil War. Provincialism and conservatism restricted the Confederate military mind, say our nationalistic scholars, and assured victory to the Union. Here are the major problems in expounding the talents of Robert E. Lee: for he fought against the Union; and he is the only American general who has ever lost a war.

Fortunately, insofar as Lee's reputation is concerned, history sometimes flouts the inference from Machiavelli's rule: occasionally a great genius in war—a Hannibal, a Charles XII, or a Napoleon—falls in defeat. These exceptions to such a law of success and failure in war demonstrate that generalship alone does not always prevail, however good it may be. Victory requires that one side overmatch the opposite in the sum of its generalship plus all other capabilities for waging war. Hence, judged fairly, a general's record must be weighed against the resources at his command.

Lee and the Confederacy opposed awesome superiority in the means of making war. "All else equal," said Clausewitz, "numbers will determine victory in combat. . . . In ordinary cases an important superiority of numbers, but which need not be over two to one, will be sufficient to ensure victory, however disadvantageous other circumstances may be." Early in the war Southern troops were outnumbered 2 to 1; before war's end they

175

were outnumbered 3 to 1.[1] In industrial strength, the decisive weapon of modern war, the Confederacy was hopelessly overmatched: in 1860, for example, the North produced 20 times as much pig iron as did the South, and 24 times as many locomotive engines. At like disadvantage today, the United States would be pitted against an adversary manufacturing annually one billion tons of steel, along with comparable quantities of automotive and other industrial wares. The United States census-taker in 1865 wrote with candor that the Confederacy fell for want of material resources, and not for lack of will, skill, or courage. Forge and lathe, plow and reaper, rail and piston: all weighed in the balance against Lee and his associates.[2]

Since the South must be invaded and conquered before Federal authority could reassert itself, the Confederacy held the strategic advantage of interior, or shorter, lines of communication. Theoretically, she was able more rapidly to concentrate troops upon points of decision than could the Union. Actually, this was seldom true. Possessing less than half the railway mileage that the North had, and virtually no facilities for manufacturing or repairing locomotives and rolling stock, the Confederacy was unable to profit significantly from interior lines. Early in the war she lost the railroads of western and central Tennessee, including a long stretch of the vital Memphis and Charleston track. Command of these roads and of the upper Mississippi River and the lower Tennessee River gave to the Union forces the interior lines of communication within the broad western theater of the Confederacy. Unable to control the seas, the Confederacy fought with flank and rear continuously threatened with invasion.

Lee and the Confederate government had also to contend with the powerful influence of localism within the Confederacy. Asserting the rights of state sovereignty, many Southern governors withheld large numbers of men from the Confederate armies, and demanded protection of all territory within their states. The institution of slavery aggravated this tendency; even the temporary appearance of Northern troops in any part of the South so disrupted the labor force and the economy that they could never be returned to normal. Hence, Confederate authorities were obliged to scatter many thousands of troops at scores of points having little strategic importance, if any.

Though Lee was not responsible for the general strategy of the defensive adopted by Jefferson Davis early in the war, Lee tacitly indorsed it. Some Confederate leaders urged a prompt invasion of the North; they called for a lightning stroke against the people of the Union, before her vast resources could be mobilized. Certain historians today support this strategy by pointing out that in a prolonged war of attrition the South was foredoomed to defeat.

Critics speak with authority in disparaging Confederate strategy; they speak with uncertain voices in saying what it ought to have been. Offensive war against the North would seem to have been futile. Four years were required for the immensely more powerful Union to conquer the Confederacy; that the South could have conquered the North is inconceivable. Through the defensive, the South could conserve her lesser strength and exact of the North a heavier toll in blood and treasure. Doubtless unwittingly, Southern leaders followed Clausewitz's dictum, "Defense is the stronger form of war." Even that implacable critic of Confederate leadership, General J. F. C. Fuller, acknowledges that the defensive was the only sound policy for the South.[3]

Exigencies of Southern politics, society, and logistics caused Davis to adopt, and Lee to second, a strategy of territorial defense. Accordingly, the Confederacy was split into departments (or theaters), each with its own army, and each to be defended against invasion, with no territory to be yielded voluntarily to the enemy. Such a design fell short of the military rule, "Unity of plan, concentration of force." Lee was aware that this strategy failed to achieve maximum concentration of force; that it thus violated the fundamental principle of war as set forth by the military theorist Henri Jomini, whom Lee is nowadays accused of following slavishly. But in fashioning this plan, Confederate leaders anticipated a principle of modern warfare not then generally recognized; they sought to provide what Cyril Falls describes as ". . . that vital factor of the most recent times, the defence of the home base and civil population."[4]

In condemning this failure to concentrate, General Fuller says that the Confederacy ought to have yielded temporarily the state of Virginia and other areas of the upper South in order to mass her forces at the key rail center Chattanooga. By harassing Union communications and drawing Union armies away from base, he opines, the Confederacy may then have struck a decisive blow with her entire *grande armée*. As military science in the narrow sense, this may be sound, though it tempts the speculation that such an initial Confederate concentration would merely have caused a like Union concentration, but in far greater strength. "Concentration *a priori* and without regard to enemy dispositions invites disaster," writes General de Gaulle in a perceptive comment on French operations in World

War I. As strategy in the highest sense, strategy that blends military science with political science, social psychology, and economics, General Fuller's plan is folly. Abandonment of the upper South to the Shermans and Sheridans of the Northern army would have undone the Confederacy without a battle. "There is nothing in [Lee's] generalship," says Sir Frederic Maurice, "which is more striking than the manner in which he grasped the problems of the Confederacy and . . . adapted his strategy both to the cause for which the South was fighting and to the major political conditions of the time." Considering the circumstances of Southern life, territorial defense was probably the only strategy open to the leaders of the Confederacy.[5]

As adviser to President Davis early in the war, Lee did not decide strategy; he was in no sense general-in-chief of Confederate armies. "Broadly speaking," says biographer Douglas Southall Freeman, "Davis entrusted to [Lee] the minor, vexatious matters of detail and the counselling of commanders in charge of the smaller armies. On the larger strategic issues the President usually consulted with him and was often guided by his advice, but in no single instance was Lee given a free hand to initiate and direct to full completion any plan of magnitude."[6]

Restricted as he was by the character of his assignment, Lee nevertheless at this time showed deep insight into the nature of the war, and urged certain measures that would greatly strengthen the South for the struggle ahead. In the early days after Fort Sumter, when many people of the South still predicted that there would be no war, and that, if it should come, it would be quickly won by Southern arms, Lee said that war was inevitable, and that it would be long and bloody. In the fall, 1861, when many thought that England was about to enter the war against the North because of the *Trent* affair, Lee warned against such hope. "We must make up our minds to fight our battles and win independence alone," he wrote prophetically. "No one will help us."[7]

When in the spring, 1862, Forts Henry and Donelson fell, and the Confederate Army in the west was threatened with destruction, Lee wisely advised stripping the Gulf Coast of troops in order to reinforce Albert Sidney Johnston and Beauregard at Corinth, Mississippi. To Johnston, Lee gave sound strategic counsel: concentrate, said Lee, and strike the enemy at your front before the two wings of his army can be joined. The battle of Shiloh, fought according to this plan, came within an inch of destroying the Union army there: neither side would again come so close to a total victory until exhaustion had overtaken the Confederacy at war's end.[8]

Lee's support of conscription to muster the manpower of the South indicated advanced military thinking and willingness to break with American precedent. As early as December, 1861, Lee recommended state conscription by the government of Virginia: after Confederate losses at Shiloh and New Orleans the following spring, Lee's indorsement of Confederate conscription helped to secure passage of the act by the Southern Congress. Lee's ideas on conscription offer proof of how far beyond Jomini he had gone during the first year of the Civil War. Jomini considered war an affair to be settled by professional armies; he refused to contemplate a people's war, and wrote, "[It] would be so terrible that, for the sake of humanity, we ought never to see it." Lee said, "Since the whole duty of the nation [will] be war until independence [is] secured, the whole nation should for a time be converted into an army, the producers to feed and the soldiers to fight." Not until the outbreak of World War I would the governments of the world grasp fully this principle of total mobilization laid down by Lee almost threescore years before.[9]

In the spring, 1862, as McClellan's powerful army moved to the Virginia Peninsula and threatened Richmond at close quarters, Davis leaned heavily upon Lee for support. Lee's talent as a strategist now began to emerge in his daring shift of Confederate troops to oppose McClellan's advance. But Lee saw the futility of meeting the Federal concentration with like concentration; he realized that the smaller Southern force must ultimately be overwhelmed if this were done. Instead, Lee adopted the more resourceful technique of weakening McClellan's army by threatening a blow at the North. "As to dividing the enemy's strength," wrote Machiavelli, "there can be no better way . . . than by making incursions into their country. . . ." From relatively unexposed points in the Carolinas and Georgia, Lee drew reinforcements piecemeal for the Confederate army on the Peninsula: meantime, Lee urged General Jackson in the Shenandoah Valley to strike the enemy there in order to divert Northern troops from McClellan. This was the genesis of Lee's later strategy for the entire Confederacy.[10]

On May 31, 1862, Confederate General Joseph E. Johnston fell wounded in the fighting on the Peninsula, and Davis named Lee to command the Army of Northern Virginia. Lee's mission was to defend Virginia, and especially the Confederate capital, Richmond. He opposed the strongest of Union concentrations, which outnumbered his own force by 2 to 1. For three years Lee would fulfill his mission against the heaviest odds ever faced by an American commander.

The wisdom of defending Richmond, to the relative neglect of other points in the South, has been seriously questioned. Defense of the capital to the bitter end cannot be justified; but there was reason for holding it as long as possible without sacrificing the army. Even if Richmond had possessed no intrinsic military value, as the capital it had great symbolic value. One may lightly disparage both Davis and Lincoln for waging long and bitter campaigns for the capture or protection of idle cities; yet both men sensed the psychological importance of being able to retain the seat of government. Winston Churchill recognized this principle when late in World War II he urged that Berlin was still an objective of great strategic importance; that nothing else would blight German morale so much as would the fall of Berlin. Moreover, Richmond was by no means an idle city: she contained the great parent-arsenal of the South, the Tredegar Works, besides many other armories and factories. To the Confederacy, Richmond was Washington and Pittsburgh in one. Aside from symbolic and material values, northern Virginia possessed great strategic value for the Confederacy. It was a dagger pointed toward the heart of the enemy, a potential base for strikes against the Northern capital and the great northeastern centers of population, industry, and communication. A powerful, mobile Southern army in northern Virginia was the most effective instrument of the Confederacy for paralyzing the mind of President Lincoln and the will of the Northern people.

Lee preferred this command to all others, since it would keep him in his beloved Virginia. Though Davis made the decision to defend Richmond, Lee unquestionably approved of it.

Once in command, Lee instantly did what he would always do as long as he had the strength for it; he seized the initiative in the campaign. His strategy for weakening McClellan's force had already borne fruit; Jackson's spectacular demonstration in the Valley (April 30–June 9) caused President Lincoln to divert McDowell's corps there. Ordering Jackson to Richmond by rail, Lee now attempted a concerted blow against McClellan. Faulty staff work and the derelictions of subordinates may have cost Lee a decisive victory. Nevertheless, in a series of fierce engagements (June 26–July 2) Lee persuaded McClellan to abandon the drive for Richmond.[11]

Blunting of McClellan's thrust enabled Lee to open what Davis called an offensive-defensive against the Union armies in Virginia. From the beginning, Lee knew that his army could not withstand a siege by the vastly stronger Northern numbers opposing it. Lee must keep the enemy forces divided; he could not afford for them to concentrate upon him. In order to prevent such concentration, he must constantly maneuver and confound his opponents with threats against Washington and with lightning blows against exposed fractions of their strength. Second Manassas was a brilliant demonstration of this technique.

In mid-July Lee learned that Federal troops were concentrating under General John Pope on the Rapidan River in northern Virginia. Lee had to decide quickly whether the next Union main effort was to be from the north or from the Peninsula. Sensing that it would be made by Pope, Lee started Jackson's corps north by rail; when on August 13 Lee learned that the Union force on the James was being reduced, he reasoned that these troops were being sent to Pope. Lee then rushed the remainder of his army up to strike Pope before McClellan's reinforcements could reach him. By dividing the Confederate army and sending Jackson around Pope's flank to threaten communications with Washington, Lee unsettled his adversary and forced him out of position. Reuniting Longstreet and Jackson on the battlefield, Lee then defeated Pope (August 29–30, 1862) and drove him back to the Washington earthworks.

Lee's decision to move his army from the James to the Rapidan showed seeming uncanny ability to anticipate the enemy; it has been called a supreme example of the manner in which judgment and boldness must supplement available information in shaping strategy. Lee's shift of force was a lesson in the use of interior lines of communication and the strategic employment of railroads. Dividing the Confederate army in the face of superior numbers violated the rules of warfare; Jomini warned against it; Lee was criticized for doing it. But Clausewitz says, "What genius does must be the best of all rules, and theory cannot do better than to show how and why it is so." Lee himself gave the explanation. "The disparity . . . between the contending forces rendered the risks unavoidable," he said.[12]

With the Federal army reeling under defeat, and his own troops flushed with victory, Lee now determined to carry the war to the enemy. He proposed to invade Maryland and Pennsylvania. Invasion of the North would extend Lee's war of maneuver; it would find provisions for his troops; and it would free Virginia of molestation during the harvest. A successful campaign across the Potomac might do much more than this; it might add Maryland to the Confederacy; it might sever communications between northeast and northwest; it might place the great cities of the east at Lee's command; and it might bring foreign recognition. It might even end the war, thought Lee; and he proposed that Davis offer peace with honor to the North at this time.

In early September Lee crossed the Potomac. Segments of his army were spread wide to cut the railroads and isolate McClellan from reinforcements. Here the fates deserted Lee. His appeal to the people of Maryland fell on deaf ears. Far worse, McClellan moved against him with disconcerting assurance. One of the traits of a great general is his insight into the character of the opposing general: the ability, as Colonel G. F. R. Henderson phrases it, "to penetrate the adversary's brain." In this faculty, Lee has had few peers. On the eve of marching into Maryland, he said, "McClellan's army will not be prepared for offensive operations—or he will not think it so—for three or four weeks. Before that time I hope to be on the Susquehanna." Ordinarily, Lee would have been right about McClellan; but something extraordinary happened on this occasion. Providentially supplied with a copy of Lee's plan of campaign, found wrapped around three cigars on the ground, McClellan struck Lee's divided army and came near destroying it at Sharpsburg on September 16–17. Lee held McClellan off and won tactical victory; but Lee was obliged to return to Virginia and abandon the campaign.[13]

In striking at the North and her capital, say some scholars today, Lee again was simply obeying the stale rules of warfare as set forth by Jomini, or by his chief American disciple, Professor Dennis Hart Mahan of West Point. Actually, Lee was using a strategy as old as war itself; and as modern, too. "If the defender has gained an important advantage," says Clausewitz, "then the defensive form has done its part, and under the protection of this success he must give back the blow. . . . Common sense points out that iron should be struck while it is hot. . . . A swift and vigorous assumption of the offensive—the flashing sword of vengeance—is the most brilliant point in the defensive." This principle was alike sound for Scipio Africanus, or Frederick the Great, or George Catlett Marshall. It was also sound for Lee.[14]

In retrospect, the grander aims of Lee's campaigns into the North seem visionary. Probably England and France would have remained neutral even if Lee had won a victory on Northern soil; that the Lincoln administration would have accepted a peace offer is unlikely. But Lee did not have the advantage of hindsight. The true goal in war, says Clausewitz, is to subject the enemy to one's will. Often this can be done only through destroying the enemy's armed forces. But this is not the sole method for accomplishing the object of war, continues Clausewitz: moreover, when one lacks the resources to destroy the enemy's armed forces, he must resort to other means; he must then attempt to destroy the enemy's will through measures short of the destruction of his military power. Among such, says the German theorist, are the seizure of the enemy's capital, or the inflicting of casualties beyond the enemy's expectations. Here was just Lee's situation.[15]

Lee knew that the South could not possibly destroy the war strength of the North, however successful in battle the South might be; that, ironically, Southern victories in the field weakened the South in men and material resources relatively more than they weakened the North. Shortly after his greatest triumph (Chancellorsville), Lee wrote to Davis, "We should not . . . conceal from ourselves that our resources in men are constantly diminishing, and the disproportion in this respect between us and our enemies . . . is steadily augmenting."[16] Only by paralyzing the Northern will to victory could the South hope to achieve her war aims. Lee was aware that Washington had no intrinsic military value. But he knew also that President Lincoln and the Northern people had invested the city with great symbolic value; and he knew that defeat at home shakes a population more than defeat in a distant land. He believed that a successful invasion of the North by a victorious Confederate army was most likely to exalt his own people and to blight the morale of the enemy. Considered in this light, his decisions to invade the North are reasonable.

In Virginia again after the fruitless Maryland campaign, Lee dispersed his army, recruited his strength, and braced for another Federal assault. It came in mid-December against the impregnable heights of Fredericksburg. Reconcentrating quickly, Lee met the attack pointblank. Bloodily repulsed, the Northern army fell back across the Rapidan to await a new commander and a new occasion.

Spring of 1863 found the lines of the Confederacy holding fast in the east but deeply pierced in the west. New Orleans was lost; Grant pressed upon Vicksburg; and Rosecrans was lodged in central Tennessee, threatening Chattanooga. Davis and his counselors sought desperately for a strategy that would restore the balance in the west. Many plans were offered. Most of them called for a shift of troops from relatively secure points elsewhere to the faltering armies of the west in the hope of concentrating sufficient strength there to win decisively over Grant or Rosecrans, or both. In early March, Lee told Davis that for some time he had hoped that the situation in Virginia would enable him to detach an entire corps of his army to the support of the west. Secretary of War Seddon strongly urged this move; and Generals Longstreet and Beauregard set forth variations of it. But the strength and activity of the Army of the Potomac, now commanded by General Joseph Hooker, prevented such an operation at this time, thought Lee. A month later, as affairs in the west grew worse, Secretary of War Seddon called upon Lee to consider sending one division there. Seddon's request for Lee's views on this measure caused Lee to formulate a general strategy for meeting the crisis.

In principle, the strategy now expounded by Lee was not new to him; rather, it was an elaboration of his ingrained philosophy of war, as adapted to the peculiar needs of the Confederacy. Lee agreed with Davis and Seddon that the situation required boldness; that the Confederate armies in the west ought at once to take the initiative. Let Joseph E. Johnston concentrate and attack Grant in Mississippi, recommended Lee; let Bragg strike into Kentucky and threaten Ohio. But Lee cautioned against weakening the Army of Northern Virginia; Hooker would not stand idle, predicted Lee, but soon would strike a powerful blow against Virginia. An advocate of the maximum concentration of force against isolated segments of the enemy, Lee nevertheless felt that, in this instance, the distances were too great and the transport facilities of the South too feeble to justify such a move. The Confederacy could not match the Union in shifting troops from one department to another, he said; to rely on that method might render Confederate reserves always too late.

To prevent the North from transferring troops in order to concentrate at a given point, Lee said that all Southern commanders ought to take the offensive upon any weakening of the enemy on their fronts. Let Confederate armies in the major departments be reinforced from the less exposed departments of the deep South, he advised—from the vicinity of Charleston, Savannah, Mobile, and Vicksburg. Lee's curious listing of Vicksburg came of an erroneous notion that Federal operations there would soon have to quit because of the pestilential Mississippi summer. Apparently Davis, whose home was but a few miles from Vicksburg, never disabused Lee of this idea.

Lee's prime recommendation was that he again strike at the North with his own army. "The readiest method of relieving pressure upon General Joseph E. Johnston," said Lee, "is for the [Army of Northern Virginia] to cross into Maryland. . . . Greater relief would in this way be afforded to the armies in middle Tennessee." To penetrate the enemy's vitals, or if this were impossible, to threaten them with Clausewitz's "flashing sword of vengeance"—this was the key to Lee's strategy.

True to Lee's prediction, in late April Hooker advanced in Virginia. Again Lee seized the initiative with great audacity. Splitting the Confederate force, Lee occupied the bulk of Hooker's powerful army with slightly above one-third of his own; at the same time Lee sent the remainder of his troops under the indomitable Jackson to fall upon Hooker's vulnerable flank and rear. Lee's victory at Chancellorsville (May 2–3), says Colonel Henderson, was one of the supreme instances in history of a great general's ability to outwit his adversary and direct the attack where it is least expected. The Army of the Potomac once more fell back across the Rapidan; Confederate leaders again took inventory of strategic resources.[17]

Anxious over the security of Vicksburg, Secretary of War Seddon again proposed the shift of troops from Lee's army to support Pemberton on the Mississippi. If necessary, replied Lee, order Pickett's division to the west. But Lee warned anew that the great distance required by the move, plus the uncertainty of employment of Pickett's troops in Mississippi, made the venture inadvisable. Weakening of the Army of Northern Virginia, he felt, might force it to retire into the Richmond defenses, where it would cease to be a formidable instrument of Confederate strategy. Davis and his cabinet met with Lee on June 16 and, with Postmaster General Reagan possibly dissenting, approved Lee's plan to invade the North again. This meant that Confederate armies in the west must fend for themselves.

Already a part of Lee's army was on the move toward Pennsylvania. As he put his troops in motion, Lee searched the Confederacy for reinforcements and pondered other measures that would strengthen his blow. Earlier he had called upon Davis to bring idle troops from the Carolinas, Georgia, and Florida to the Army of Northern Virginia; if necessary, Lee had advised, strip the coastal garrisons except for enough men to operate the water batteries. He now repeated this plea and added another recommendation. Let General Beauregard come with these reserves to northern Virginia, Lee said, and there create a diversion in favor of the advance into Pennsylvania. Anxiety of the Northern government over the safety of Washington would cause a large force to be left for protection of the capital, Lee believed. Beauregard ought to command the diversionary column in person, said Lee. "His presence would give magnitude to even a small demonstration and tend greatly to perplex and confound the enemy." A mere "army in effigy" under Beauregard would have good effect, thought Lee, if no more troops than this were available.

Thinking the North shaken by Chancellorsville and the threat of Confederate invasion, Lee again advised a Southern peace overture. The South ought not to demand peace unconditionally, he said; rather, she ought to encourage the peace party of the North to believe that the Union could be restored by negotiation. "Should the belief that peace will bring back the Union become general, the war would no longer be supported. . . ." he observed. Once hostilities ended, he believed that they would not be resumed, and that Southern independence would thus be achieved.

Gettysburg was Lee's debacle. Again fortune turned upon him; at Brandy Station, on the eve of the march into Pennsylvania, Federal cavalry seized Confederate correspondence indicating a northward move by Lee. Davis made no effort to bring up reinforcements or to create the army in effigy requested by Lee. Exceeding Lee's orders, Jeb Stuart rode amiss and deprived Lee of his "eyes," the cavalry, so that he groped his way into Pennsylvania without knowing the whereabouts of the Union army. General Ewell, recently elevated to corps commander as a result of Jackson's death, proved unequal to his responsibilities and failed to seize the key position, Cemetery Hill, early in the battle, when it probably could have been taken. Longstreet sulked and was sluggish in attacking Cemetery Ridge on the second day. Lee erred gravely in ordering the frontal assault against Cemetery Ridge on the third day, when it was impregnably held. After three days of carnage, Lee retreated into Virginia. The tide of the Confederacy was spent.[18]

That in the Gettysburg campaign Lee was below his best goes without saying. His more severe critics see in the Gettysburg decision a narrow provincialism that blinded Lee to the war as a whole. In contrast to Lee's strategy, which the critics say was primarily a defense of Virginia, they see in the plan urged by Seddon, Longstreet, and Beauregard a truly comprehensive Confederate military design. It would have been a Jominian stroke on the grand scale, they say, taking advantage of the Confederacy's interior lines of communication, and concentrating a maximum of Confederate strength for the destruction of Rosecrans' isolated army in Tennessee. Thus Lee becomes the culprit who squandered the Confederacy's one opportunity to win the war.[19]

This criticism is highly problematical. It rests upon the present knowledge that Lee's plan was tried, at least in part, and that it failed. The critics assume what cannot be known: that western concentration was more likely to succeed than was Lee's eastern offensive. Exponents of western concentration do not take into account the logistical weaknesses of the South, which Lee felt made the western venture impractical. After the war, Confederate General E. P. Alexander had a vision of a powerful Confederate "army on wheels" using the interior lines of the South to shuttle rapidly back and forth between engagements east and west. Alas for the Confederacy, this could be but a vision. Southern troops could, of course, move somewhat more quickly from Virginia to Tennessee than could Northern troops, who had more than twice as far to go. But continued shifting of a large army to and fro across the South, as Alexander contemplated, was roughly the equivalent in time and effort of a like movement across Siberia today. Lee well knew the military significance of railroads; many of his campaigns had been skillful demonstrations in the strategic and logistical use of them. But he accurately sensed that Northern railroad superiority largely nullified the Confederacy's theoretical advantage of interior lines on a grand scale. General Alexander's plan was beyond the capacity of Southern transport and industry; it probably would have exhausted the Confederacy without a battle.[20]

Supporters of the western plan exaggerate the probability of decisive victory over Rosecrans and minimize the effect of weakening Lee's army as a major strategic weapon of the Confederacy. To achieve the purpose of the western effort, Confederate forces there had to do more than win a battle; they must win so prodigiously as to cause the North to quit the war. That a western Confederate victory of any degree would have done this is questionable. Complete defeat or capture of Rosecrans' army would not have destroyed the war capacity of the Union; her major striking force was elsewhere. One may further question that a total victory over Rosecrans was likely, even granting the maximum Confederate concentration. Walter Millis has pointed out that the advent of railroad, steamboat, and telegraph ended the great battlefield decisions of finality.[21] No such victory was won by either side in the Civil War, regardless of numerical advantage, until the last stages of weakness and demoralization had come upon the Confederacy. If the South could, in any event, have won a western victory of such magnitude as to end the war, she could have done it probably only through three conditions: Rosecrans must obligingly remain exposed to destruction until the Confederacy could mass her strength against him; Hooker with the most powerful of Union armies must sit idle in the east all the while; and the western Confederate force, hastily assembled from all over the South, must operate free of the very kind of miscarriage that plagued Lee's veteran army—the varsity team—in its Pennsylvania offensive. That any of these circumstances would have prevailed seems doubtful; that all of them would have prevailed seems incredible.

Nevertheless, everything ought to have been hazarded for the west, it is said; the war was lost in the west. This would appear to be only half truth; it obscures that the war was lost in east and west, and through a long process of exhaustion. The west was not intrinsically more valuable to the Confederacy than was the east; once the east was taken, the west would surely fall. The Confederacy could not live without both east and west.

Close examination of Lee's strategy refutes the accusation that it was merely a defense of Virginia. It was a comprehensive strategy for the Confederacy, however faulty it may have been. Interestingly, it was in some ways quite like Grant's later strategy for the Union: it employed Lee's seemingly invincible army, greatly strengthened, as the major Confederate striking force; and it called for simultaneous offensives by all major Confederate armies to prevent Northern concentration upon any one of them. It was designed, in part, to nullify the Northern advantages in transportation that enabled her to shift troops swiftly from one department to another. Lee's plan for an army in effigy under Beauregard was a superbly ingenious stratagem that might well have upset a nervous foe. It anticipated by almost a century General Patton's mock invasion of the Pas de Calais coast in World War II, which helped to deceive the German high command and to free the Normandy beachheads from heavy counterattack for many precious days.[22] Lee's request was worthy of strenuous effort to fulfill it.

Finally, Lee's plan would have cured the major ill in the deployment of Southern manpower; it would have drawn strategic reserves from the minor departments of the Confederacy to the main effort. Throughout most of the war, excessive numbers of Confederate troops were scattered at relatively idle stations about the South. In early 1863, total Confederate armies were outnumbered 2 to 1: but the major Confederate armies at this time faced odds of 2.5 to 1, while Confederate garrisons along the Atlantic Coast actually outnumbered the opposing Union armies. In the departments of the Carolinas, Georgia, and Florida, 45,000 Confederates opposed 27,000 Federals. From these troops, and others at various places in Virginia, Lee could have added an entire corps to his army, with enough left over to guard the coast and form Beauregard's army in effigy as well.[23]

In a word, Lee proposed to apply to the entire Confederacy the strategy that he had successfully employed within his own department. With offensives throughout the South he would keep the total enemy force divided; with diversions in northern Virginia he would confound and divide the local enemy force; then, with the strongest, the most skillful, and the most cohesive army of the Confederacy, he would direct his main effort against the vital center of the North.

Lee asked for a diversionary force too late for Davis to create it, under the circumstances, even if he had attempted it. Lee proposed this ruse on June 23, only a week before Gettysburg. By now many of the troops from the Atlantic Coast had been sent, without Lee's certain knowledge, to Mississippi, where they would accomplish nothing. This suggests a further thought in weighing Lee's role in the Gettysburg decision. Lee was not general-in-chief of Confederate armies; he was still merely commander of the Army of Northern Virginia, with the primary mission of defending Virginia against invasion. He lacked the authority, the information, the point of vantage, and the breadth of mission for putting into effect such a plan as he expounded. The supreme weakness of Confederate operations in the summer of 1863 was not the offensive into Pennsylvania: it was the want of a unified command and strategy. As a result, no adequate strategic reserve was ever created out of the minor departments: the weak reserve that was formed was sent to Mississippi, while the main effort of the Confederacy was made in Pennsylvania. The right hand knew not what the left hand was about.

Let us deal the cards in Lee's favor, as they are often dealt in favor of the hypothetical plans that he opposed, and for a moment speculate on what might have been, had he been authentic general-in-chief in early 1863. Lee would have stripped the minor departments of troops, save for minimum defensive garrisons, and from this source would have strengthened the main effort of the Confederacy. He would have given Joseph E. Johnston full authority in Mississippi, and would have ordered a concentrated effort against Grant there. Lee would have ordered Bragg to strike again into Kentucky in order to draw Rosecrans out of Tennessee and alarm the authorities and people of the North. Lee would have placed Beauregard with an army in effigy to threaten Washington from the South and paralyze his opponent. Lee would have led the Army of Northern Virginia, powerfully reinforced, into Pennsylvania. Lee would have kept his cavalry in hand, and would have discovered and destroyed Meade's two advance corps at Gettysburg on July

1, before the rest of the Northern army could reach the battlefield. With his opponents scattered, confused, and demoralized, Lee would have struck the final psychological blow at the Northern will: he would have offered a negotiated peace with a hint that the Union might thus be preserved. Given all of these conditions, the Gettysburg campaign was perhaps as likely to end the war successfully for the South as was any other strategy.

But enough of make-believe: campaigns are seldom waged as critics afterward would have them waged.

During the months after Gettysburg, Lee continued to believe that even yet he might be able to invade the North successfully. But defeat in Pennsylvania left its mark on him: when, upon Meade's failing to press Lee, Davis again desired to send a part of Lee's troops west, Lee consented. In early September he dispatched Longstreet with 12,000 men to strengthen Bragg's army before Chattanooga. Victory at Chickamauga in mid-September was followed by disaster at Chattanooga in November. Weakened by Longstreet's absence, Lee made one unsuccessful offensive effort against Meade (Bristoe Station, October 14), then fell back on the defensive.

Lee now knew that the South was too weak to invade the North. Loss of Chattanooga moved him again to write Davis concerning the general Confederate military situation. The Union army at Chattanooga now threatens Georgia with her factories and provisions, Lee said; it must be stopped if the Confederacy is to survive. Place Beauregard in command of the Confederate army in Georgia, and reinforce him with troops from Mississippi, Mobile, and Charleston, urged Lee. To defeat the coming Federal move, he explained, "the safety of points practically less important than those endangered by [it] must be hazarded. Upon the defence of the country threatened by [the enemy march] depends the safety of the points now held by us on the Atlantic, and they are in as great danger from [a] successful advance as by the attacks to which they are at present subjected." Written four months before Sherman set forth to destroy the war support of the lower South, these words show profound insight into the deficiencies of Confederate strategy. They were a prophecy of total war uttered out of season.[24]

Spring of 1864 brought face to face the military giants of the Civil War, Lee and Grant. Now came the heaviest sustained fighting that American troops have ever experienced. True to their natures and to their philosophies of war, both men attempted to seize the initiative in order to destroy the other. As Grant advanced below the Rapidan, Lee attacked fiercely. Had the two forces been equal in numbers, Lee may have achieved his aim, for he took Grant at disadvantage on the march in a country of woods and bramble. But the forces were not equal. For two days in the battle of the Wilderness (May 5–6) the result trembled in the balance as both forces fought desperately for survival. Then the armies broke off action, neither of them victorious. Sensing his opponent's tenacity and purpose, Lee now moved unerringly to block Grant's circling advance against the flank and rear of the Army of Northern Virginia.

Failure to destroy or stop Grant in the Wilderness marked the beginning of a new phase in Lee's career. He continued to seek favorable opportunity to strike Grant, for Lee had long said that his army would be lost if ever it should be pinned down in the Richmond defenses. But the Wilderness was Lee's last general offensive action; the Army of Northern Virginia no longer had the power to attack. Hoping yet to demoralize the people of the North and place the peace party there in the ascendancy, Lee husbanded his waning strength and sought to exact of Grant the maximum toll in blood and energy. When one lacks the strength to destroy the enemy, says Clausewitz, then one ought, by skillful conservation of his own resources, to seek to exhaust the enemy's will by showing him that the cost of victory far exceeds his anticipation.[25] Lee's strategy was now the strategy of conservation.

For more than a week of fierce but intermittent fighting at Spotsylvania Courthouse (May 8–18) Grant hammered at Lee's line. Unable to break it, Grant moved again. Repeatedly he sideslipped to the left and inched forward in an effort to encircle Lee's flank, force him out of position, and destroy him. Repeatedly Lee anticipated his opponent's move and shifted athwart the flanking column. From Spotsylvania Courthouse to the North Anna River, and from there to Cold Harbor veered the deadly grapple. Earthworks went up at every position. At Cold Harbor (June 3) Grant again drove his battering-ram against the Southern line. Reinforced with troops rushed from minor Confederate victories in the Shenandoah Valley and on the James River below Richmond, Lee repulsed the Northern assault with fearful punishment. Voices of censure began to rise against Grant "the butcher" among the civil and military population of the North. After a month of bloodshed such as the American people had never seen, the Army of the Potomac was still farther from Richmond than McClellan had been in the summer of 1862: Lee's gaunt army was still apparently invincible.[26]

Lee used his great talents to the utmost during this month of remorseless combat. His ability to foresee and counteract enemy strategy has become a part of universal military tradition. Carefully fitting together the shards of information collected from the battlefield, from prisoners, and from scouts and spies, Lee supplied the gaps from his own intellect and intuition: out of the whole he created a true mosaic of enemy intentions. Then he was bold enough to trust his judgment and to act accordingly. Lee must be a great strategist, wrote a Michigan soldier; for everywhere the Northern army goes, it finds the Rebels already there. To friend and foe alike, Lee's skill seemed miraculous.[27]

With remarkable effectiveness, Lee made capital of the advantages inherent in the defense. His tactical employment of interior lines enabled him to move more quickly than did his opponent from one position to another. On a larger scale, he used interior lines to draw reinforcements from the Shenandoah Valley and the Peninsula; thus he partially offset the unavoidable handicap of fighting with flank and rear exposed to a sea controlled by the enemy. Relying upon the increased firepower of Civil War weapons, and ignoring Jomini's contempt for prepared positions, Lee developed the science of field fortification to a degree that significantly altered modern defensive tactics; he elevated axe and spade to near-equality with musket and howitzer.

Lee's choice of position was unimpeachable; his eye for ground unerring. "When his eye swept a countryside it never betrayed him," says Cyril Falls. "From the ground or the map, or both in combination, [Lee] realized how to make the best use of every feature of the country, and the trace of every defensive position from his hand was masterly." Sound position, strengthened by field fortification, enabled Lee at critical moments to flout the tactical rule that one must always keep a reserve in being; he achieved maximum firepower by placing every regiment on the line. "If I shorten my lines to provide a reserve he will turn me," Lee told an observer at Cold Harbor. "If I weaken them to provide a reserve, he will break me." Audacity thus met the summons of necessity.[28]

Students of Lee's conduct in this campaign find it a brilliant lesson in defensive warfare. "[It] is a classical example in military history of how these objects [conserving one's own strength and taxing that of the enemy] ought to be sought," says Sir Frederic Maurice. "In method it was fifty years ahead of the times, and I believe that if the allies in August, 1914, had applied Lee's tactical methods to the situation . . . the course of the World War [I] would have been changed."[29]

Having failed to break Lee at Cold Harbor, Grant on June 12–16 marched around Richmond on the east and struck at Lee's communications by attacking the Petersburg rail junction below Richmond. As Grant half-circled Richmond, Lee warily moved along an inner half circle that kept his army between Grant and the city. This enabled Grant to pass south of the James River and fall with overwhelming force upon the defenders of Petersburg under Beauregard. Grant's move was daring in concept and skillful in execution. For several days Lee lost touch with the Army of the Potomac. But Grant's attack at Petersburg wanted the skill of his march. Beauregard held the Northern army at bay, and on June 18 Lee hastened the Army of Northern Virginia into the Petersburg trenches where the great siege of the war began.

Lee shrewdly anticipated Grant's move south of the James; before Grant left Cold Harbor, Lee predicted such an attempt. Aware that he could not indefinitely withstand the full weight of Grant's numbers, which would grow with time, Lee sought again to weaken Grant's main body by creating a diversion elsewhere. Should he succeed in this, Lee hoped to be able to strike a telling blow at the force still opposing him. He hoped to repeat the maneuver that had caused a diversion of troops from McClellan's Peninsula army in the summer of 1862. Lee knew that Grant would not be shaken by this ruse. Lee's strategy was aimed above Grant's head; it was aimed at Lincoln himself. On June 13, the day on which Lee learned that Grant's army was no longer before him at Cold Harbor, Lee sent General Jubal Early with 13,000 men to threaten Washington from the Shenandoah Valley.

Notwithstanding Lee's foresight, and in spite of General Beauregard's many warnings and pleas for reinforcement, Lee responded slowly to Grant's move away from Cold Harbor. Lee's tardiness has some justification; it was the result of a narrow mission and of his want of information on the whereabouts of Grant's army. Lee's primary mission was to protect the capital; without accurate knowledge of Grant's location, Lee thought it hazardous to uncover the direct route to the city. Confederate cavalry was absent, defending the Virginia Central Railroad against a massive Union cavalry raid. Beauregard's cries for help gave Lee no accurate information about the enemy; not until June 17 did Beauregard report that the Army of the Potomac was south of the James. Nevertheless, Lee did permit Grant to make the maneuver to Petersburg without striking him while on the march and vulnerable; and Lee did fail to checkmate the move at Petersburg until almost too late. Beauregard's determined resistance there saved the vital rail junction from capture. One must conclude that Grant was at his best in the passage of the James, while Lee's performance here was below that of the Wilderness-to–Cold Harbor campaign.[30]

The siege of Petersburg lasted almost nine months. It was so long and costly that it seriously blighted Northern morale; it brought to the South a false hope of ultimate success. Sherman was now halted before Atlanta, and the end of the war appeared nowhere in sight. The peace movement in the North was growing. President Lincoln himself believed his reelection to the presidency unlikely; if his Democratic opponent, General McClellan, should be victorious on a peace platform, said Lincoln, the Union probably could not be restored. Lee now learned that Davis was about to relieve Joseph E. Johnston from command of the Confederate army at Atlanta. Again Lee offered advice on general Confederate strategy. If Davis felt it necessary to remove Johnston, said Lee, then it must be done; but Lee made clear his own aversion to the decision. "It is a grievous thing to change the commander of an army situated as [the Army of Tennessee is]," he said. He had hoped that Johnston was strong enough to fight for Atlanta, wrote Lee; which was his way of saying that battle ought to be risked in an effort to save the city. If not, he counseled, concentrate all cavalry in the west on Sherman's communications, and let the Confederate army fall back upon Augusta. This was probably as wise a move as the Confederacy was capable of making at this time.[31]

Lee's demonstration against Washington failed to break Grant's hold at Petersburg. Response of the Union authorities showed that Lee's instinct was sound. As General Early crossed the Potomac and threatened Washington during the first week of July, General Halleck called upon Grant for troops; and on July 10, President Lincoln recommended, though he did not order it, that Grant himself come to the capital with a portion of the Army of the Potomac. But Lee wanted the strength to take advantage of his opponent's dispersals. Ultimately, Grant sent into the Valley enough troops to defeat Early; but Grant kept in the Petersburg entrenchments enough men to render an attack there by Lee impossible. Either Lee must hold his lines at Petersburg to the bitter end, or he must abandon Richmond altogether.

Doubtless Richmond ought now, at all hazard, to have been given up. Atlanta was lost on September 2; its fall assured Lincoln's re-election to the presidency and doomed the Northern peace movement. Lee could not hope to destroy or seriously cripple Grant's army: Hood's effort to stop Sherman had ended in disaster. Perhaps the only remote chance of Confederate survival was for Lee to break away from Grant and attempt junction with Hood somewhere in the lower South for alternate blows, first against Sherman and then against Grant. That this would have brought deliverance to the stricken Confederacy is, of course, well-nigh inconceivable: it would have meant the immediate loss of the entire east; and Sherman's army could have been promptly reinforced to a strength that would have rendered him secure even against such combined attack. Lee saw the futility of trying to hold Richmond any longer. He had long said that a siege would destroy his army; that it must remain free to maneuver and strike if it were to live in the presence of so powerful a foe. In October, probably after the final defeat of Early in the Valley, Lee told his staff officers that Richmond was a millstone to his army. But the decision to abandon Richmond was not Lee's to make. Only Davis could make it: and Lee's exaggerated deference to the President and Commander-in-Chief would not permit him to suggest it as long as the city's defense was the first mission of his army.[32]

Hunger, cold, disease, and heartache over the plight of distant loved ones: these immeasurably assisted Grant's shells during the winter of 1864–65 to break Lee's army in flesh and spirit. Still his troops held grimly to the Petersburg defenses. In early February, under heavy public pressure, the Confederate Congress created the position of general-in-chief: though Davis rightly interpreted this as a vote of censure against his leadership, he appointed Lee to the post.

As general-in-chief, Lee held dubious rank. President Davis had once written to Lee, "I have neither the [constitutional] power nor the will to delegate" to someone else the supreme command. In appointing Grant to command all Union forces, President Lincoln said to him, "The particulars of your plan I neither know nor seek to know. . . . I wish not to obtrude any constraints or restraints upon you. . . ." Such a letter as Lincoln's is unimaginable from Davis. When General Joseph E. Johnston heard of Lee's appointment as general-in-chief, Johnston wrote perceptively, "Do not expect much of Lee in this capacity. He cannot give up the command of the Army of Northern Virginia without becoming merely a minor official. . . ." No man could with impunity trespass upon Davis' authority; for Lee to attempt it would have been futile. Through tact and suggestion Lee accomplished far more with Davis than he could have accomplished in any other way. Lee thus saved his talents, though circumscribed, for the Confederacy: others, such as Beauregard and Joseph E. Johnston, who sought through sharper methods to influence Davis, wasted their faculties during most of the war in idleness and frustration. As long as Davis was president of the Confederacy he would be commander-in-chief in fact as in law.[33]

Only by the most drastic means could Lee have made his new authority tell. Only by a passionate appeal, in his own name, to the spirit of the South; only by commandeering railroads and provisions; only by abandoning Richmond, if possible, in order to concentrate against fractions of the enemy: in sum, only by making himself dictator in the manner of ancient Rome could Lee possibly have prolonged the life of the dying Confederacy. Prolonged it for a brief season, that is; for at this stage nothing could have postponed the final outcome for very long. Lee knew what measures were required: he discussed them with his staff and others. Doubtless the Congress and people of the South would have supported him in these moves. But Lee would not take them.

In accepting the appointment as general-in-chief, Lee made clear that he would continue to operate under Davis' authority. Lee is often censured for this subordination to Davis. Lee's adjutant general admitted that this deference robbed Lee of the qualities of a revolutionary leader.[34] But it is one thing to criticize Lee as a revolutionary: it is quite another thing to disparage Lee's generalship. Subordination of the military to the civil authorities is usually deemed a virtue among Americans: George Washington shunned the temptation to grasp the reins of government at dark moments during the War for Independence; nothing in Grant's career indicates that he would have led a coup d'état against President Lincoln if he had thought Lincoln a bungler. Indeed, Grant probably was as submissive to Lincoln as was Lee to Davis. To Grant's admirers, Lee's submissiveness was servility, while Grant's submissiveness was military statesmanship. Modern scholars who condemn Lee for his subordination to Davis look with indignation upon an American general who dared defy his President and Commander-in-Chief in a recent war. Lee was too American to play Napoleon.

Nevertheless, rather through suggestion than through command, Lee as general-in-chief attempted certain broad, coordinated strategic measures. He brought Joseph E. Johnston out of idleness and sent him to North Carolina to oppose Sherman; Lee ordered Johnston to collect for this effort all the scattered troops of the Confederacy, except the Army of Northern Virginia. Lee advised the War Department that he must now unite his own force with that of Johnston, though this would forfeit the capital. Hoping to strike a concerted blow against Sherman, then one against Grant, Lee began to prepare supply depots for a march to the south.[35]

But such a move was impossible through the mud of winter and with horses near starvation: Lee must wait for the roads to dry and for his livestock to regain strength. Lee must also win Davis to the desperate plan. The President blew hot and cold on it: previously he had hinted that all of the cities of the South might have to be given up in the waging of the war; now in early March he approved Lee's strategy of joining forces with Johnston. But Davis never gave unqualified consent to the abandonment of the capital; he never fully prepared himself to leave. On April 1, the day before Lee was driven from the Petersburg line, someone asked Davis whether Richmond would be held. "[Yes] If we can," replied the indomitable Mississippian.[36]

As commander of the Army of Northern Virginia, Lee strove mightily during these last days just to keep his army alive: hunger, exposure, demoralization, and constant attack by Grant's well-fed and well-clad army rendered this a burden beyond description. That, under these conditions, Lee was able to maintain a cohesive fighting force through the winter of 1864–65 is an enduring tribute to his leadership.

As general-in-chief, Lee devoted his thought to disengaging his army from Grant's tentacles and moving south to join Johnston. To combine the armies against Sherman would be a prodigious feat. It required far more than simply moving the Army of Northern Virginia from Petersburg to North Carolina, though this alone would have taxed grievously the waning resources of the Confederacy. To accomplish the junction, Lee must free himself from Grant; then Lee's famished and exhausted troops must outmarch Grant's vigorous army. Moreover, since Grant's line enveloped Lee on the south, and the direct route to North Carolina (the Weldon Railroad) was in Grant's control, Lee had to move farther to escape than did Grant to block the escape. Lee must march west and then turn south, describing two sides of a triangle, while to intercept this movement, Grant need only proceed along the third side of the triangle. Lee intended to do all in his power to make the junction; but he rightly sensed that it was well-nigh impossible. Since the coming of winter, quite likely no man or measure could have freed the Army of Northern Virginia from the Army of the Potomac, competently led.

On March 25, Lee made his move to escape and join Johnston. In an effort to force Grant to withdraw his encircling troops from the southern end of the line, Lee attacked Fort Stedman east of Petersburg. Lee planned then to slip away and gain a march on his adversary in the deadly race.

Probably no better strategy could have been devised. But the attempt failed; Lee's army was too weak to break Grant's fortified line. Grant countered instantly with a successful thrust at Five Forks on the Southside Railroad (April 1): Lee's last line of supply was severed. The next day he abandoned Petersburg and marched west for the Danville Railroad, which would carry him roundabout to junction with Johnston's army. Lee gained the railroad at Amelia Courthouse, only to lose a precious day there because his order for rations had gone awry. Before he could move south, Grant blocked the railroad at Burkeville. Lee then pushed west again, hoping somewhere to be able to turn the corner and get south of Grant's army. All was futile: outpaced and surrounded, Lee ended the terrible drama on April 9 in the surrender of his army.[37]

At last Lee's sword was sheathed.

For near a century, most students of the art of war have looked with unqualified admiration upon the generalship of Lee. Early Northern historians of the Civil War lavished praise upon him: James Ford Rhodes attributed chiefly to Lee's talents the South's unsurpassed power of resistance; John C. Ropes said of Lee, "No army commander on either side was so universally believed in, so absolutely trusted. Nor was there ever a commander who better deserved the support of his Government and the affection and confidence of his soldiers." General Viscount Wolseley of England believed that Lee was the most skillful of American generals. Colonel G. F. R. Henderson, one of the nineteenth century's most perceptive military analysts, called Lee "one of the greatest, if not the greatest, soldier who ever spoke the English tongue." Sir Frederic Maurice, critic of strategy both ancient and modern, placed Lee among the most illustrious commanders of the ages. After studying the careers of the most renowned generals of the last hundred years, Cyril Falls concludes that Lee is the greatest of them all. "Lee alone in a century of warfare deserves to be ranked with Hannibal and Napoleon," says Falls. Denis W. Brogan, keenest of present European students of American history, says that Lee was the supreme military leader of the Civil War. Grant's solutions were adequate but seldom elegant, says Brogan; Lee's solutions were frequently elegant. The man who is perhaps today's greatest living scholar-warrior and surest connoisseur of military leadership seconds these exalted estimates of Lee. Winston Churchill writes, "Lee was one of the greatest captains known to the annals of war."[38]

Critics arise from time to time to challenge the grounds of Lee's fame. They have found human failings in him; but frequently their complaints against his generalship cancel one another out. Lee was too rash and combative, says one: Lee was excessively slow and cautious, says another. Lee did not take advantage of the South's interior lines, says one: Lee clung to the obsolete concept of interior lines, says another. Lee failed to concentrate the forces of the Confederacy, says one: Lee was preoccupied with the outworn principle of concentration, says another. Lee was a slave to Jomini, says one: Lee violated Jomini's fundamental principle of war, says another. Criticism of Lee thus often ends in a confusion of tongues.

Certainly Lee was mortal: notwithstanding remarkable accomplishments, his military leadership fell short of the abstract yardstick of perfection. Major criticisms of Lee as a strategist have already been considered in this essay: that he was too provincial to see the war as a whole, and too conservative to break the fetters of the past. Without laboring all of the minor criticisms of Lee, a few may be scrutinized here.[39]

It has been said that Lee did not see the relationship between strategy and statecraft in modern war. This is true in that Lee deferred excessively to Davis and refused to seize dictatorial authority in a belated effort to save the Confederacy. But on a higher plane the criticism is not true. Lee's foresight regarding the nature and magnitude of the war; his prescience in urging total mobilization; his prediction that Europe would remain aloof from the war; his adaptation of abstract military theory to the exigencies of Southern politics, economics, and logistics; his strategies aimed as well at President Lincoln's fears as at the weaknesses of opposing generals; his suggestions of peace overtures to encourage the Northern peace movement and split the mind of the enemy; and his advocacy of the employment of Negro troops and their subsequent emancipation: all argue that Lee saw far beyond the battlefield in waging war. Lee seasoned military strategy with a rich wisdom and insight into human affairs that transcended statecraft in its primal sense to become true statesmanship.

Lee is sometimes disparaged for the slack discipline of his command; certainly, by professional standards, or by twentieth-century standards in citizen armies, discipline in the Army of Northern Virginia was easy. Yet one may question whether any other method of managing the army would have accomplished as much. To be of value, discipline must be suited to the character of the men, says Sir Frederic Maurice. "Lee knew well that the discipline of Frederick [the Great's] grenadiers" would destroy his army of

highly individualistic Southern planters and farmers. "The object of discipline in an army is to give bodies of men both cohesion and the instinct
to suffer all for duty in circumstances of great stress and danger," explains
Maurice. Few armies, if any, have ever endured more steadfastly the stress
of privation and the danger of combat than did the Army of Northern Virginia.[40]

Lee's most unsparing critic, General J. F. C. Fuller, heaps scorn upon
Lee as being a poor provider for his army. But General Fuller offers no
promising remedy for the ills of the Confederate quartermaster and commissary. Lee kept every wheel turning, and the wires hot with dispatches;
he scattered his troops among the fields and flocks of the Southern countryside, often at the expense of combat efficiency; and he sometimes launched
invasions of the well-stocked North: all in a ceaseless effort to feed and
clothe his men. How, under the circumstances, anyone else in Lee's position could have done better is beyond convincing explanation.

Lee is sometimes taken to task for his extreme combativeness, his lust
for battle for its own sake. "It is well that war is so terrible," said Lee
while surveying the carnage before his position at Fredericksburg, "else we
should grow too fond of it." This trait perhaps unsettled Lee's judgment on
the third day of Gettysburg and caused him to attempt the impossible. But
the will to fight is a fault easily forgiven in a warrior. Too often the critics
believe that wars are won in some manner other than that by which they
must be won, says Cyril Falls, which is by fighting. "Happy the army in
which an untimely boldness frequently manifests itself," wrote Clausewitz.
Lee's "fighting blood" (as Freeman calls it) was one of the qualities that
made him formidable. If, on occasion, it betrayed him into unwise combat,
on many others it saved him. It helped to make him, in the words of an opponent, "a very thunderbolt in war."

General Fuller believes that Lee failed to stamp his mind upon his military operations. Oddly, if Lee did not stamp his mind upon his own operations, he stamped it powerfully upon the operations of his enemy. "Among
the many achievements of this remarkable man [Lee]," writes Bruce Catton, "nothing is more striking than his ability to dominate the minds of the
men who were fighting against him." Lee's campaigns were the very product of his mind. One had as well say that the frescoes of the Sistine Chapel
want the stamp of Michelangelo's mind as that the operations of the Army
of Northern Virginia want the stamp of Lee's mind.[41]

Under the travail of his command, Lee sometimes made unaccountable

errors of judgment regarding enemy capabilities outside his own department. His belief that the summer climate of Mississippi would stop Grant
at Vicksburg; and his doubt that Sherman could march through the Carolinas: these were wide of the mark. But they were offered as mere opinions.
Significantly, they did not alter Lee's strategy: notwithstanding his notions,
Lee urged that Joseph E. Johnston concentrate and attack Grant in Mississippi without delay; and later Lee ordered Johnston to oppose Sherman's
drive in North Carolina with every man available to the embattled Confederacy.

Perhaps the chief flaw in Lee's generalship came of his boundless courtesy and humility. These traits heightened his deference to President Davis;
sometimes they weakened Lee's supremacy over his army. Lee chose rather to lead through tact and orders of discretion than through iron discipline
and positive commands. Freeman believes that at times Lee even permitted
himself to be browbeaten by a stubborn subordinate. Yet the critic must be
careful in scoring Lee on this count; some of Lee's most spectacular victories were the result of discretionary instructions to resourceful corps commanders. Ideally, Lee ought to have known to give Jackson his head, but to
keep tight rein on Stuart and Ewell; to stir Gordon with quiet suggestion,
but to impel Longstreet with sharp command. Here Lee made the mistake
of attributing to all of his lieutenants his own great tactical insight and high
code of gentlemanly attitude.[42]

Lee's theory of battlefield command did not always measure up to his
other qualities of leadership. To fashion strategy and so manage his army as
to bring it with maximum efficiency to the point of decision: this, felt Lee,
was his primary function. Once the missions were assigned and the battle
joined, he sometimes permitted control to drift. He was most guilty of this
on the second day of Gettysburg: here, for a time, says Freeman, the Army
of Northern Virginia was virtually without a commander. Lee remedied this
mistake during the later campaigns of the war.[43]

In dwelling upon Lee's particular weaknesses and misjudgments,
both real and imagined, critics obscure his achievements as a whole. As
commander of the Army of Northern Virginia, Lee's sole responsibility
throughout most of the war, he earned the acclaim of history. Circumscribed in command, opposing overwhelming numbers, and fighting under
every material disadvantage known to the science of war, Lee through his
generalship largely sustained the Confederacy in one of the most prodigious military efforts of the modern age. What he could have accomplished

as untrammeled general-in-chief must remain conjecture. His actual accomplishments, all things considered, were second to none in the American military experience. His virtues as a general transcended his faults.

Lee's prime quality, according to Freeman, was intellect; it was "the accurate reasoning of a trained and precise mind"; it was a "developed aptitude for the difficult synthesis of war." Intellect of the highest order enabled Lee to look into his opponents' minds and read their intentions, doubts, and fears; then with maximum efficiency to capitalize upon this knowledge.[44]

Audacity enhanced intellect to make Lee the general. Boldness is the noblest of military virtues, says Clausewitz; it is the "true steel which gives the weapon its edge and brilliancy. . . . Boldness, directed by an overruling intelligence, is the stamp of the hero." Audacity enabled Lee repeatedly to seize the initiative from opponents commanding twice his strength; audacity moved him time and again to flout the established rules of warfare in order to strike the foe at the least expected times and places. "We must decide between the positive loss of inactivity and the risk of action," Lee once wrote in a terse but profound exposition of his theory of war. Lee's prowess came largely of a readiness to accept the risk of action.[45]

Character exalted intellect and audacity to make Lee one of the greatest leaders of men the world has known. "Alexander, Hannibal, Caesar . . . and Napoleon [had] the highest faculties of mind," says F. E. Adcock in a study on the outstanding generals of antiquity. "But . . . they possessed character in a still greater degree. To this list," continues Adcock, "I would add . . . Robert E. Lee." Character lights the moral flame of leadership, a quality indefinable and mysterious, one that Clausewitz says can be spoken of only in words vague and rhapsodical. Deep religious conviction united with the chivalric tradition of Virginia aristocracy to endow Lee with remarkable serenity and nobility of nature. "I have met many of the great men of my time," said General Viscount Wolseley, "but Lee alone impressed me with the feeling that I was in the presence of a man who was cast in a grander mould, and made of different and finer metal than all other men. He is stamped upon my memory as a being apart and superior to all others in every way: a man with whom none I ever knew, a very few of whom I have ever read, are worthy to be classed." Lee's sharpest critic eloquently tells the effect of Lee's leadership through character. "Few generals," writes General Fuller, "have been able to animate an army as [Lee's] self-sacrificing idealism animated the Army of Northern Virginia. . . . What this bootless, ragged, half-starved army accomplished is one of the miracles of history."[46]

Times are perilously late for Americans to permit the zeal of nationalism to blind them to excellence, no matter whence it may come. Lee's career
teaches certain lessons for the military leadership of today. Jet airplanes,
intercontinental missiles, and thermonuclear bombs make the weapons of
Lee's era as obsolete as the tomahawk; they bring war to hypertrophy. But
if today's "balance of terror" should continue to prevail, and mankind be
spared the fiery bolts of extinction, then Lee's strategic and tactical concepts will again prove useful in the employment of conventional military
forces. Victory through attrition, which has been the key to American strategy in the Civil War and the two world wars, is no longer possible for
this nation; nor can she hope to destroy the war strength of her opponents
without resort to thermonuclear weapons. She must again learn the skills
of swift maneuver and the delivery of paralyzing blows by highly mobile
forces upon lines of communication and points of decision. Armies of the
future must be composed of semi-independent, self-contained units, says
General Matthew Ridgway, units capable of operating over great distances on a fluid battlefield, and with a minimum of control from higher
headquarters.[47] These words remind one of Lee's discretionary orders to
the virtually independent commanders, Jackson, Stuart, Early, and at the
end, Joseph E. Johnston. In darker extremity, this nation must again learn
to wage cunning defensive war for the conservation of weaker resources:
war that destroys the enemy's resolve by taxing him beyond his anticipation.

Finally, if this people must fight again, either with conventional arms
or in the holocaust of thermonuclear war, then the nobler qualities of Lee's
generalship will offer an even brighter example than his techniques of combat. Intellect to divine and cope with enemy capabilities and intentions;
boldness to strike when the occasion demands, however grave the risk; and
above all, character to inspire purpose and sacrifice in the midst of supreme
stress, hardship, and danger: these will be the imperatives of leadership for
national survival. The art and science of war can yet profit from the genius
of Lee.

NOTES

1. Carl Von Clausewitz, *On War* (3 vols.; London and New York, 1940), I, 194–
95, III, 170–71.

2. Charles P. Roland, *The Confederacy* (Chicago, 1960), 34–41.

3. J. F. C. Fuller, *Grant and Lee* (Bloomington, 1957), 262.

4. Cyril Falls, *A Hundred Years of War* (London, 1953), 18; Archer Jones, *Confederate Strategy from Shiloh to Vicksburg* (Baton Rouge, 1961), 16–32.

5. Fuller, *Grant and Lee,* 39–40; Charles de Gaulle, *The Edge of the Sword* (New York, 1960), 93–94; Frederic Maurice, *Robert E. Lee the Soldier* (Boston and New York, 1925), 76.

6. Douglas Southall Freeman, *R. E. Lee* (4 vols.; New York and London, 1934–35), II, 6–7.

7. Ibid., I, 621.

8. Lee to Albert Sidney Johnston, March 26, 1862, in Mrs. Mason Barret Collection of Albert Sidney and William Preston Johnston Papers (Tulane University Archives, New Orleans).

9. Freeman, *R. E. Lee,* II, 28.

10. Niccolò Machiavelli, *The Art of War* (Albany, 1815), 233; Freeman, *R. E. Lee,* II, 39–50, 53–57.

11. Freeman, *R. E. Lee,* II, 199.

12. Clausewitz, *On War,* I, 100; Freeman, *R. E. Lee,* II, 302, 256–349.

13. G. F. R. Henderson, *The Science of War* (London and New York, 1905), 175; R. Ernest Dupuy and Trevor N. Dupuy, *The Compact History of the Civil War* (New York, 1960), 156–57.

14. David Donald, *Lincoln Reconsidered* (New York, 1956), 94; T. Harry Williams, "The Military Leadership of North and South," in David Donald (ed.), *Why the North Won the Civil War* (Baton Rouge, 1960), 82; Clausewitz, *On War,* II, 154–55.

15. Clausewitz, *On War,* I, 35, 174.

16. Freeman, *R. E. Lee,* III, 34.

17. Henderson, *The Science of War,* 35.

18. Jones, *Confederate Strategy from Shiloh to Vicksburg,* 211–13; Freeman, *R. E. Lee,* III, 29–161.

19. Williams, "The Military Leadership of North and South," in Donald (ed.), *Why the North Won the Civil War,* 40, 46.

20. E. P. Alexander, *Military Memoirs of a Confederate* (New York, 1908), 864–65.

21. Walter Millis, *Arms and Men* (New York, 1956), 111.

22. Gordon A. Harrison, *Cross Channel Attack* (Washington, 1951), 76; Forrest C. Pogue, *The Supreme Command* (Washington, 1954), 182–83. Both of these volumes are in the *United States Army in World War II* series, prepared by the Office of the Chief of Military History, Department of the Army.

23. Jones, *Confederate Strategy from Shiloh to Vicksburg,* 24–25.

24. Freeman, *R. E. Lee,* III, 206–07.

25. Clausewitz, *On War,* I, 35.

26. Freeman, *R. E. Lee,* III, 275–391; Bruce Catton, *A Stillness at Appomattox* (New York, 1958), 63–187.

27. Catton, *A Stillness at Appomattox,* 152.

28. Falls, *A Hundred Years of War,* 59–60; Alfred H. Burne, *Lee, Grant and Sherman* (New York, 1939), 49.

29. Maurice, *Robert E. Lee the Soldier,* 85.

30. Burne, *Lee, Grant and Sherman*, 55–61; Freeman, *R. E. Lee*, III, 392–447.

31. Freeman, *R. E. Lee*, III, 461–62.

32. Ibid., 441, 496n; Walter H. Taylor, *Four Years with General Lee* (New York, 1878), 145.

33. Jones, *Confederate Strategy from Shiloh to Vicksburg*, 232; Dupuy and Dupuy, *The Compact History of the Civil War*, 281; Gilbert E. Govan and James W. Livingood, *A Different Valor* (New York, 1956), 343.

34. Taylor, *Four Years with General Lee*, 148.

35. Govan and Livingood, *A Different Valor*, 347.

36. Varina Howell Davis, *Jefferson Davis: A Memoir by His Wife* (2 vols.; New York, 1890), II, 579.

37. Freeman, *R. E. Lee*, IV, 1–143.

38. Burne, *Lee, Grant and Sherman*, 207; John C. Ropes, *The Story of the Civil War* (4 vols.; New York, 1933), II, 157–58; Garnet J. Wolseley, *General Lee* (Rochester, 1906), 62; Henderson, *The Science of War*, 814; Maurice, *Robert E. Lee the Soldier*, 293–94; Falls, *A Hundred Years of War*, 48; D. W. Brogan, "A Fresh Appraisal of the Civil War," *Harper's Magazine* (April, 1960), 136; Winston Churchill, *A History of the English Speaking People* (4 vols.; New York, 1958), IV, 169.

39. The most sweeping criticisms of Lee's generalship are in Fuller, *Grant and Lee*. Other sharp criticisms are in Donald, *Lincoln Reconsidered*, 82–102; and Williams, "The Military Leadership of North and South," in Donald (ed.), *Why the North Won the Civil War*, 23–47.

40. Maurice, *Robert E. Lee the Soldier*, 162–63.

41. Catton, *A Stillness at Appomattox*, 48.

42. Freeman, *R. E. Lee*, IV, 168.

43. Ibid., 168–69.

44. Ibid., 170–73.

45. Clausewitz, *On War*, I, 188–91; Freeman, *R. E. Lee*, IV, 172.

46. F. E. Adcock, *The Greek and Macedonian Art of War* (Berkeley, 1957), 83; Clausewitz, *On War*, I, 178–79; Wolseley, *General Lee*, 60–61; Fuller, *Grant and Lee*, 280, 117.

47. Quoted in Millis, *Arms and Men*, 318.

Robert E. Lee and the
Leadership of Character

Robert E. Lee is America's great tragic hero, in the classical use of the expression. He was a supremely gifted soldier and a fervently devoted patriot, yet he fought for the most unacceptable of American causes, secession and slavery, and he suffered the most un-American of experiences, defeat.

Still, he holds a high place in the nation's ranks of honor. Generations after his death, President Dwight D. Eisenhower would say of him that he was an inspiring leader of selfless dedication to duty, a man "unsullied, as I read the pages of our history." Winston Churchill would say, "He was one of the noblest Americans who ever lived and one of the greatest captains known to the annals of war."

Many of the military historians and analysts of the latter decades of the nineteenth century and the early decades of the twentieth century considered Lee to have been the greatest general of the Civil War. Certainly such outstanding British military figures and thinkers as Colonel G. F. R. Henderson, General Viscount Garnet Wolseley, and Sir Frederick Maurice were of this opinion. Henderson, who may have been the keenest of the British military writers of the entire period and who studied the Civil War extensively, even went so far as to say that Lee may have been the greatest general who ever spoke the English tongue.

Who was this man who could attract such statements from such distinguished figures? Briefly, Lee was sprung from two of the most renowned families of Virginia, the Lees and the Carters; his father, Henry "Light Horse Harry" Lee, was one of the most distinguished soldiers of the American war for independence; Robert E. Lee was graduated from the U.S. Military Academy second in his class academically and served as adjutant of the Corps of Cadets (the most coveted position in the Corps at that time) his senior year.

General Winfield Scott, the brilliant commanding general of American forces in the Mexican War, identified him as the outstanding soldier of that conflict. "To Lee more than anyone else we owe our victory," said Scott. "[He] was the very best soldier I ever saw in the field." A few years before the Civil War, Scott, who was still the commanding general of the Army, said, "I tell you, that if I were on my deathbed tomorrow, and the president of the United States should tell me that a great battle was to be fought for the liberty or slavery of the country, and asked my judgment as to the ability of a commander, I would say with my dying breath, 'Let it be Robert E. Lee.'"

Scott was as good as his word. Soon, with the country in crisis, he would in fact recommend Lee for the nation's top military post; President Abraham Lincoln would offer it to Lee, who would sorrowfully reject it and cast his lot with the Confederacy. What if Lee had accepted Lincoln's offer? Two of the most renowned American historians of the present century, Professor Samuel Eliot Morison of Harvard University and Professor Henry Steele Commager of Columbia University, expressed the opinion that Lee was the one man who might have ended the Civil War in a year if he had become the Union's commanding general.

Nevertheless, through the years there has been a drumfire of criticism of Lee's generalship. Ironically, the persistence of the challenges to his fame reflects its endurance, and, in my judgment, its validity. Who today would bother to challenge the fame of Union general Samuel Sturgis or Confederate general Theophilus Holmes? Probably most of you, possibly most of everybody, have never heard of either.

Though most students of the Civil War today recognize Lee's genius as an army commander, operational planner and director, and field general, there have been many criticisms, especially in recent years, of Lee as a strategist: that is, as a creator and executer of an overall design for the most effectual employment of Confederate military resources. He is said by some to have been too old-fashioned, his mind too "fossilized," to understand the warfare of his day; too provincial, too much in love with Virginia to be able to see the war as a whole; so preoccupied with Napoleonic concepts of offensive warfare that he was blind to the military effects of the weaponry of his day, especially of the advent of the rifled musket and minié bullet (or minnie ball, as the soldiers of both armies called it). In other words, that he employed eighteenth-century tactics against nineteenth-century technology, and, as a result, spent the lives of his troops in futile and costly charges against enemy positions.

Some recent historians have resorted to psychobiography to downgrade Lee as a man so obsessed with childhood insecurities and marital infelicities that he lacked the will and character to be an effectual general.

To answer fully all of these criticisms would require several talks, each as long as the one I'm here to give tonight. Suffice it to say that, in my judgment, they ignore much evidence to the contrary. To summarize the major alternatives that have been offered to Lee's strategic operations, perhaps the one favored by a majority of the critics is the western strategy. The mantra of these critics is: "The Confederacy lost the war in the West." The remedy: put the Army of Northern Virginia, Lee's army, on a strict defensive and transfer a portion of its troops to the western theater to redress the balance there. The leading advocates of this strategy at the time were Secretary of War James Seddon, Generals Joseph E. Johnston and P. G. T. Beauregard, and Lee's senior corps commander, Lieutenant General James Longstreet. A number of members of the Confederate Congress also supported this plan.

This strategy rested on a set of theoretical assumptions, the key one being the belief that a weakened Army of Northern Virginia could adequately protect the East while a hastily thrown-together force in the West could achieve victory there. Lee objected that the distances were too great between the two theaters; he also questioned the employment of his troops if they should be sent west, a veiled way of saying that he did not trust the western generals to use them effectually. When Jefferson Davis read Lee's reply, he said he concurred with it. For what it is worth, so do I. More importantly, so does history. Later, when two divisions of Lee's troops *were* sent west with Longstreet in command, they were terribly mishandled, first by General Braxton Bragg and then by Longstreet, and the effort came to naught.

Another alternative to Lee's strategy that has been suggested is avoiding pitched battles altogether and resisting the Federals by guerrilla action alone. Sound as this may be in pure theory, it ignores the political, social, and economic realities of southern life. It would have meant permitting the enemy to occupy the South for an indefinite period, probably for years—and some modern advocates of it speak in terms of decades. It would have devastated the structure of southern life.

Even if Lee had approved such a plan, which he did not, it would have been turned down by Davis and by the southern people—in my opinion, rightly so. Parenthetically, a modern analogy to this argument emerged a

few years back, during the Cold War. A British political candidate opposing the installation of nuclear weapons there recommended this strategy for
dealing with the Russians: Let them come in, he said, and we will defeat
them by guerrilla action. His opponent, Prime Minister Margaret Thatcher,
didn't even bother to turn her main batteries on him. She fired one contemptuous round from a secondary gun and he sank without a trace. Can
anyone imagine Americans today simply allowing an enemy to occupy the
country indefinitely?

Finally, Lee's critics offer the alternative of fighting on the defensive
only, thus allegedly saving Confederate lives while inflicting so many casu-
alties on the Federals that they would lose the will to fight. This alternative
is the one that has been popularized in recent years by historians such as
Thomas L. Connolly, Grady McWhiney, Perry D. Jamieson, and Alan T.
Nolan. Nolan's book, *Lee Considered: General Robert E. Lee and Civil
War History,* is probably the most sweeping attack ever written on both
Lee's generalship and his character.

Unquestionably, with all else being equal, attacking a position is costlier than defending one. But this by no means proves that a general policy
of fighting only on the defensive would have been beneficial to the Confederacy. It would have surrendered the initiative to the enemy and allowed
him to mass his superior forces and choose the place and the time of attack.
It would have given him the option of fixing Lee in position with a portion
of his force and turning Lee out of position or enveloping his flank with the
remainder. In my considered opinion, such an a priori defensive strategy by
Lee would have been a recipe for certain defeat.

In this connection, I should like to point out that in the two European
wars that were closest to the American Civil War in time and in the general
nature of the armies and their armaments—the Austro-Prussian War (1866)
and the Franco-Prussian War (1870–1871) —the defensive side was disastrously defeated even though the numerical advantage of the victorious
attackers (the Prussians) was significantly smaller than that of the Union
in the Civil War. In the Austro-Prussian War, the Prussians held only the
slightest numerical advantage. Not only did they win; they inflicted far
more casualties than they suffered.

I would remind the critics also that the Confederacy did, in fact, wage
many campaigns on the defensive. These included the defense of Kentucky
in 1861–1862, the campaign on the Virginia Peninsula prior to Lee's taking command, the Fredericksburg campaign, the Vicksburg campaign, the

Chattanooga campaign, the Atlanta campaign, the Nashville campaign, and finally, Lee's own campaign against Grant in 1864–1865. All of them, except the Fredericksburg campaign, failed disastrously, and if the prisoners lost are counted as casualties, which in practical effect they are, the defensive campaigns cost the Confederacy more soldiers both absolutely and proportionally than did Confederate attacks.

Briefly put, it was Lee who, from the beginning, saw that the Confederacy lacked the capability of winning by the ultimate strategy set forth by Clausewitz, the great Prussian theorist on war: that is, the Confederacy lacked the resources in men and materiel to destroy the Union's capacity to make war. Lee was keenly aware that the Confederate goal of winning its independence could be achieved only by breaking the will of the northern people through measures short of absolute military victory, short of the annihilation of the armed forces of the Union.

And it was Lee who came nearest to accomplishing this feat. He did it by employing the Army of Northern Virginia—which I like to call the Confederacy's "varsity team"—to win a remarkable series of victories against adversaries who commanded far greater combat power in an area that both Abraham Lincoln and Jefferson Davis considered to be of vital strategic importance—the area containing the capital cities of the Union and the Confederacy.

To an overwhelming extent it was Lee's military prowess that kept the Confederacy alive, with its multitude of military, economic, political, and social weaknesses, and its bruising internal conflict of personalities and egos, throughout four years of the most relentless warfare the American people have ever experienced. Not only did Lee play the lead role in keeping the Confederacy alive through this ordeal, he did it with such stunning effect that Professor James M. McPherson of Princeton University, who is considered by some to be the preeminent living student of the Civil War, has said that on three occasions Lee came close to winning in his efforts to break the northern will.

In the spring and early summer of 1862, Lee employed Stonewall Jackson's force in the Shenandoah Valley to menace the line of the Potomac. This operation diverted reinforcements from McClellan's army on the Peninsula and allowed Lee to strengthen his own army with Jackson's troops and launch a counteroffensive against McClellan. Though Lee suffered disproportionate casualties in this action, especially in his attack on Malvern Hill at the end of it, he won a strategic victory of incalculable importance. The capture of the Confederate capital at this time by the Federals, coming in the wake of Confederate defeat at Shiloh and the loss of Nashville, Memphis, and New Orleans, would have dealt a crushing blow to Confederate morale; it might have ended the war then and there.

Following up his victory in front of Richmond, Lee moved to northern Virginia and defeated the Union army there under General John Pope in the battle of Second Manassas before Pope could be decisively reinforced by McClellan. This was the first of the occasions when the northern will to continue the war drooped alarmingly.

Hoping to carry the war to the enemy and at the same time bring Maryland into the Confederacy, Lee moved quickly across the Potomac into Maryland, but he was blocked at Sharpsburg (Antietam, to the Federals) after McClellan, through a bizarre caprice of war, obtained a copy of Lee's operational orders.

Back on Virginia soil, Lee stood on the defensive on the heights behind Fredericksburg and slaughtered Burnside's Union columns when they assaulted him in December 1862. Early the following May, Lee won the great victory of Chancellorsville over Burnside's successor, General Joseph Hooker, who commanded more than twice Lee's numbers.

The classic account of Chancellorsville was written by John Bigelow, a northern historian, who said it was the most remarkable engagement of the entire war. In noting the brilliance of Confederate generals Lee and Jackson, he quoted the words of British officer and military analyst Captain Cecil Battine: "In all history there is not recorded a campaign which exemplifies more fully the preponderance of skillful direction over superior numbers than this week's fighting in the forest of Virginia."

Upon receiving the news of Chancellorsville, Lincoln cried, "My God. My God. What will the country say?" For the second time the northern will to win sank dangerously.

Seeking again to carry the war to the enemy, Lee waged his ill-fated Gettysburg campaign in June and July of 1863. It resulted in a severe defeat for him and heavy casualties to his army. Historians have speculated on and debated the causes of the defeat ever since it occurred. Both Richard Ewell and James Longstreet, corps commanders, have borne the blame, but Lee himself, for reasons that cannot be determined, commanded ineffectually in the battle. His renowned biographer Douglas Southall Freeman goes so far as to say that on the second day of the contest the Army of Northern Virginia was virtually without a commander. Lee must bear the responsibility for the defeat. "It is I that have lost this fight. . . . All this has been my fault," he said to his shaken subordinates, "and you must help me out of it the best way you can."

Again in Virginia, Lee faced his most formidable opponent, Grant, in the spring and summer of 1864. Lee's fierce attack in the Wilderness, followed by his skillful defensive operations at Spotsylvania and Cold Harbor, inflicted horrendous casualties on the Union army but failed to abort its resolute drive upon Richmond. Grant now abandoned his frontal attacks and turned Lee's position in a sweeping march across the James River in an effort to seize Petersburg, the key rail center below the Confederate capital. The grim, nine-month siege of Petersburg and Richmond, after the terrible fighting and losses preceding the siege, again caused the northern will to falter ominously. Lincoln himself became so discouraged during the summer that he believed he would not be re-elected in the presidential election of 1864. However, the depletion of Lee's army, followed by his surrender in April 1865, for all practical purposes ended the war.

But, largely because of Lee, the contest had been long and bitter and the end frequently in doubt. His generalship was the crux of the extraordinary Confederate military effort. How extraordinary was this effort? Let me quote a statement made by a northern citizen in the fall of 1864, at a point when the end of the war was clearly in sight. This was no ordinary citizen—it was Henry J. Raymond, managing editor of the *New York Times*. In addition to being perhaps the nation's most distinguished journalist, he was the chairman of the Republican National Committee, known familiarly as "Lincoln's lieutenant general in politics." He was a confidant of the president. He was unquestionably one of the most perceptive and best-informed men in the nation.

Here is what Mr. Raymond said: "The rebels have exhibited a most wonderful energy and skill in carrying on their struggle. No people on the face of the earth ever made so hard a fight with such limited means. . . . They have displayed a combination of dash and endurance never before equaled in military history. All candid men, whatever their hatred of the rebellion, and whatever their admiration of our own heroic soldiers, are free to admit that the final triumph of our national armies will be due only to superiority in numbers."

All this is not to say that Lee was infallible, that he made no mistakes. All generals make mistakes, and Lee made some extremely costly ones, especially in his decisions at Malvern Hill and on the third day at Gettysburg.

I freely concede that these decisions cost him soldiers who would have strengthened his hand later, and thus, to a degree, would have prolonged the life of the Confederacy. But to jump from this acknowledgment, as some critics do, to the conclusion that he might have won the war, or come significantly nearer to winning it, by some strategy or operational mode that was radically different from the one he actually employed is another matter.

This brings us to the question, how was he able to do what he did? What were the secrets of his remarkable ability to lead an immensely outgunned and underprovisioned army to accomplish such feats? The most obvious answer to this question is that he possessed a superior intellect, and certainly Lee did possess an extremely bright mind. Everything about his career attests to this fact, beginning with his record at West Point and extending through his presidency of Washington College after the war.

Lee's biographer Freeman said, "The accurate reasoning of a trained and precise mind" provided Lee with an extraordinary "aptitude for the difficult synthesis of war." Intellect enabled Lee to read his opponents' intentions, doubts, and fears with such accuracy that he appeared at times to be clairvoyant. At the height of the fighting between Lee and Grant, a Union soldier wrote home to say that Lee must be a great strategist—everywhere the Union army went it found Lee already there.

Lee once explained this capability by saying he simply assumed his adversary would do what he himself would do under similar circumstances. Actually, Lee often did what his adversary would not have done. Lee's intelligence combined with his experience in combat and his insight into human nature to give him the seemingly intuitive ability to expect the unexpected. The British writer Colonel Henderson described this quality generically in these terms: "If in appearance great risks [are] run, it [is] with the full knowledge that the enemy's character or his apprehensions would prevent him from taking those simple precautions by which the critics point out that the whole enterprise might easily [be] ruined. [Great generals] penetrate . . . their adversary's brain." Lee often penetrated his adversary's brain. And it was intellect that enabled him to take advantage of his insights with unsurpassable resourcefulness.

Countless decisions and actions by Lee refute the accusation that he was too committed to the past to be able to adopt methods of warfare suited to his own time. He freely violated accepted strategic and tactical rules, pioneered the strategic and operational use of railroads, was preeminent in the science of field fortification, endorsed a proposal for the massing of his field artillery so as to provide maximum support at the critical points of engagement, and improvised the weapon of railway artillery. These and other actions indicate a readiness in Lee to discard outmoded ways in the field.

Even more impressive were his ideas on the very nature of war. His early prediction of the length and severity of the Civil War; his foresight in urging conscription and total mobilization of southern resources; his often-successful efforts to play upon President Lincoln's fears for the safety of Washington; his resort to psychological warfare by appealing to the northern peace party and seeking to split the mind of the enemy; his canny use of northern newspapers in the formulation of his strategic and operational plans; his proposals for supporting military campaigns with diplomatic overtures; his modification of theoretical military principles to fit the southern political, economic, and social exigencies; and his support of the employment of black troops to be followed by emancipation: all indicated a concept of military affairs that went far beyond the battlefield. These judgments and measures were hardly the products of a fossilized mind.

But Lee's intellect, outstanding as it was, was only one source of his greatness as a general. An even greater source was his character. The modern British military historian F. E. Adcock, in a study of the great generals of antiquity, wrote that Hannibal, Caesar, and Napoleon possessed the highest faculties of mind, but that they possessed character to a still greater degree. "To this list," he continued, "I would add Robert E. Lee." The German military historian Hugo Friedrich von Freytag-Loringhoven included Lee, the only non-German, in his roster of the great generals of the modern era, and he said of them, "[They] acquired the ability to inspire great effort and self-sacrifice in others by strict self-discipline and strong religious faith. The purity of their characters was so evident that they seemed to be the incarnation of the ideal leader formulated by Clausewitz."

Lee's character, I believe, derived primarily from two sources: the cult of Virginia gentility in which he was reared and the profound religious faith he acquired from his mother. Lee was ever conscious of his genteel heritage. He was aware that two of his forebears on his father's side had been signers of the Declaration of Independence, and that his mother's people had been perhaps the greatest plantation family in colonial Virginia.

Finally, Robert E. Lee lived within the shadow of another Virginia patrician, George Washington. Lee's father, "Light Horse Harry," was the one who coined Washington's immortal eulogy, "First in war, first in peace, and first in the hearts of his countrymen." Robert E. Lee's wife was Washington's adoptive granddaughter. Throughout Lee's entire life, he looked to Washington as his preeminent role model.

Reared an Episcopalian and under the influence of his mother's piety, Lee was confirmed into the Episcopal faith several years before the outbreak of the Civil War. Thereafter he attended services as often as circumstances permitted, and he read Scripture and prayed daily.

Underneath his outward manifestations of religious dedication lay an abiding faith in the wisdom and power of the Almighty to direct the affairs of men to their ultimate good. He filled his letters to his wife from camp and campaign with invocations of God's blessings and affirmations of submission to the divine will. A typical line read, "May He continue His blessings to us both and all of our children, relatives, and friends, and in His own good time unite us in His worship, if not on earth, forever in heaven."

Religion produced in Lee a sublime sense of fatalism toward the issues of life. He believed that after man had done all within his power to bring about a desired result, it would be decided by God. He was convinced that God alone could purge the world of evil, even of the curse of slavery. As the prospect of civil war became visible, Lee prayed that the nation would be spared such a dread consequence, but, in a statement that anticipated one of Abraham Lincoln's most memorable utterances, Lee said that if war should come, it would be "a necessary expiation, perhaps, for our national sins."

Finally, Lee believed that the outcome of the war itself lay in God's hands. Writing from Fredericksburg, Virginia, on Christmas Day in 1862 (just a few days after his great victory there), he said: "I will commence this holy day dearest Mary by writing to you. My heart is filled with gratitude to Almighty God for His unspeakable mercies with which He has blessed us in this day, for those He has granted us from the beginning of life, and particularly for those He has vouchsafed us during the past year. What would have become of us without his crowning help and protection? . . . For in Him alone is our trust and safety." Religious faith immensely strengthened Lee's arm in battle.

Clausewitz said character lights the moral flame of leadership, that it is a quality indefinable and mysterious, to be spoken of only in words vague and rhapsodical. He, of course, employed the word "character" for its military utility; he did not use it to mean either religious faith or moral rectitude. Though Lee possessed both of these in large measure, and I am convinced that both enhanced his stature as a general, he also possessed other traits that Clausewitz included in his identification of character as an indispensable element in military leadership.

Character embraces resoluteness under pressure and steadfastness in the midst of the danger, turmoil, and confusion of combat operations. In one of his most famous passages, Clausewitz wrote that as an army approaches battle and difficulties begin to arise ("and that must always happen when great results are at stake"), the will of the subordinate officers tends to break down and the inertia of the entire mass comes to rest on the shoulders of the commander. It is only through his courage, resoluteness, and character that the undertaking will be carried out. Certainly, one sees in Lee the personification of these attributes of leadership.

Clausewitz's definition of character in the context of military leadership laid heavy emphasis on the quality of boldness. He said boldness constitutes "the true steel which gives the weapon its edge and brilliancy." He called boldness "a truly creative power," and said, "Happy the army in which an untimely boldness frequently manifests itself. . . . Boldness, directed by an overruling intelligence, is the stamp of the hero." He went on to say that this does not consist in a downright violation of the laws of probability, but "in the forceful support of that higher calculation which genius, with its instinctive judgment, has run through with lightning speed . . . when it makes its choice." Of all the characteristics of Lee's leadership, boldness is the one that has drawn both the strongest praise and the sharpest criticism.

We can say in retrospect that Lee's decisions at Malvern Hill and on the third day at Gettysburg did violate the laws of probability, and Lee and his army paid the price for this violation. But Lee's boldness was an essential element in his greatness as a general. In battle after battle he demonstrated that boldness directed by a predominating intelligence could overcome the disadvantages in combat power under which he was obliged to operate. "The disparity in numbers makes the risk unavoidable," he said on the eve of one campaign. On another occasion he said, "We must decide between the positive loss of inactivity and the risk of action." These sayings might well be called the core of Lee's philosophy of command.

Strength of character reinforced Lee's intelligence and bearing to give him a force of presence that enabled him to exert a remarkable influence on his soldiers and all others who came in contact with him. From a single conference with him during the war, the eminent British general Viscount Wolseley wrote: "I have met many of the great men of my time [and he named Gladstone, Disraeli, and Bismarck], but Lee alone impressed me with the feeling that I was in the presence of a man who was cast in a grander mould, and made of different and finer metal than all other men. He is stamped upon my memory as a being apart and superior to all others in every way: a man with whom none I ever knew, a very few of whom I have ever read, are worthy to be classed."

An Irish member of the British parliament who traveled in the United States during the war and met Lee near its end described him in language comparable to Wolseley's. He said Lee was the idol of his soldiers and the hope of his people; was the handsomest man in all that constitutes dignity the observer had ever seen; and was one of the most prepossessing figures who had ever borne the weight of command or led the fortunes of a nation. Finally, said the Irish commentator, Lee kindled in the southern people a near-fanatical belief in his judgment and sagacity.

A vivid demonstration of the electric effect of Lee's presence on his troops occurred on the second day of the battle of Chancellorsville. As he rode forward to preserve and direct the momentum of his attack, a mighty, spontaneous ovation arose from the throats of the battle-grimed soldiers. A staff officer wrote later, "I thought it must have been from such scenes as this that men in ancient days ascended to the dignity of gods."

When General Longstreet and his divisions returned in 1864 from Tennessee, where they had reinforced General Braxton Bragg's army, Lee welcomed them with a review. When he rode onto the field and bared his head, the tatterdemalion soldiers shouted and wept and waved their battle flags. Passing slowly down the line, he seemed to search every pair of eyes; all felt the power of the bond between them. Brigadier General E. Porter Alexander described the event as being more than a review: he said it was a "military sacrament."

One of the most striking affirmations of the effect of Lee's presence came from the other side of the line, from Union general Joshua Chamberlain. Those of you who watched the television drama of the battle of Gettysburg will recognize him as the Union hero of that engagement. He was present at Lee's surrender at Appomattox and left a vivid description of that climactic event. He said that when Lee rode into view, he [Chamberlain] felt a "mysterious and powerful presence" come over the field.

The combination of Lee's qualities inspired a virtually unmatchable confidence among his troops, a confidence that enabled them frequently to accomplish what appeared to be impossible. A captain in Longstreet's command, writing from Tennessee after having fought at both Gettysburg (a severe Lee defeat) and Chickamauga (a victory by Bragg's army), gave voice to this confidence in Lee by saying: "The difference between this army [Bragg's] and Lee's is very striking. When the men move in the Army of Northern Virginia [Lee's army], they think it is the proper thing, whether it be backward or forward, and if all the success anticipated is not secured, at all events, it is not Lee's fault." No general could wish for a greater tribute from one of his soldiers.

Ironically, the most eloquent testimony to Lee's leadership of character came from one of his most implacable critics, General J. F. C. Fuller of the British army. Writing in the 1930s, Fuller judged Lee to have been deficient in his strategic, operational, and tactical dispositions, and said he "failed to stamp his mind" upon his operations. Yet when Fuller stood back at arm's length and surveyed the effects of Lee's leadership, he was moved to say, "Few generals in history have been able to animate an army as Lee's self-sacrificing idealism animated the Army of Northern Virginia." And again, "What this bootless, ragged, half-starved army accomplished is one of the miracles of history." One must wonder what General Fuller would have said if he had admired Lee's generalship!

Despite Lee's mistakes, whether actual or merely imputed, his generalship was the key to the Confederacy's extraordinary military effort. That anyone else could have surpassed it is well-nigh unbelievable.

Alan Nolan Considered:
or Lee in Caricature

Alan T. Nolan began his book *Lee Considered: General Robert E. Lee and Civil War History,* published in 1991, with a clever feint. He wrote in his preface, "I believe that . . . Lee was a great man—able, intelligent, well-motivated and moral, and much beloved by his army." Then he wrote 210 pages dedicated to proving that Lee was a villain in his character and that he squandered any chance of Confederate victory by dashing his troops against the Federal army in a reckless and hopeless bloodbath of outmoded offensive tactics. He even hinted that Lee did this as a display of his virtuosity rather than in an effort to support the Confederate cause.

In reviewing Nolan's book, Professor James McPherson, a renowned Civil War historian of Princeton University, wrote that Nolan's criticisms of Lee were not mean-spirited except in one chapter, the chapter titled "The Price of Honor." In this chapter Nolan argued that Lee ought many months before the end of the war to have urged Jefferson Davis to surrender. Nolan strongly suggests that the blood of the many thousands of soldiers killed during this period of continued Confederate resistance was on Lee's hands, that he dishonored himself as a soldier by keeping up the fight. McPherson takes strong exception, as do I, to the accusations and general tone of this chapter. My purpose in the present discourse is to show that Nolan's entire book, not just one chapter, is mean-spirited and tendentious.

Nolan sets up his assault on Lee with a brief discussion of the "mythic Lee," the Lee of the Lost Cause legend, the Lee who was apotheosized by worshipful biographers and other historians and thinkers of the generations that came after the Civil War. He quotes President Woodrow Wilson as saying that Lee "was unapproachable in the history of our country." Nolan quotes with relish a fellow critic's view of a eulogistic Civil War historian as saying that for "[Clifford] Dowdy the Civil War was a passion play, with Lee as Christ."

Certainly, many admirers exaggerated Lee's virtues and converted him into a military genius without peer and something of an immaculate construction of a man. They made him into a noble abstraction, a model of perfection that no flesh-and-blood human can possibly live up to. Scholars today have a quite legitimate right, indeed a duty, to point out these exaggerations. But what Nolan does, under the guise of identifying them, is to attack Lee, attack him relentlessly, both as a general and as a man. His Lee does not merely fall short of the abstraction of perfection, he falls woefully, despicably short of it. Nolan's Lee is a caricature of the real general and man.

Nolan assaults Lee on his views toward slavery and secession. He assaults him also on his attitude toward blacks after the Civil War. Time prohibits me this evening from addressing these aspects of Nolan's attack. My purpose is instead to analyze and respond to his criticism of Lee's military policies and practices as a Confederate general. Concerning the other part of Nolan's criticism, permit me to say only that, in my judgment, it is waged in a prosecutorial and presentist fashion. Though it disparages Lee as being simply a product of his southern culture, it fails to place him within the context of the national culture of his time; it largely ignores the attitudes of the national population and leaders on such subjects as slavery and race prior to the Civil War and on the subject of race after the war. In other words, it is comparable to condemning Abraham Lincoln because he made statements and took policy positions that today would be considered horrendously racist and politically incorrect, which he most assuredly did.

I do wish to touch upon one point before getting into the discourse on Lee's conduct as a general. This point has to do with the circumstances of his accepting an appointment as an officer of the state of Virginia immediately after resigning his commission in the U.S. Army. Though Nolan admits that there is no direct documentary evidence indicating that Lee had entered into any prior arrangement with the Virginia authorities, he nevertheless weaves a complicated web of circumstantial evidence that leads him to insinuate that Lee did just that. Without attempting to unravel this entire fabric, I would pose the question: What was Lee seeking to accomplish by doing what Nolan intimates he did? If he was jockeying or bargaining for any sort of advantage, why would he turn down the command of the Union armies in order to accept a major general's commission in the armed forces of the state of Virginia? It makes no sense to me.

But let me get into the body of my address this evening: Nolan's analysis of Lee's military strategy. Drastically summarized, it argues that because of the severe Confederate disadvantage in numbers, Lee should have adopted a general strategy of fighting only on the tactical defensive in order to conserve the lives of his soldiers. This was particularly necessary at the time of the Civil War, Nolan continues, because of the recent advent of the rifled musket, which decisively increased the range and accuracy of the infantryman's primary weapon, and which, Nolan believes, greatly enhanced the advantage of the defensive over the offensive.

If Lee had only adopted this strategy, Nolan reasons, he might have waged such a war of attrition, inflicting such heavy casualties on the Federals, that the northern population would have abandoned the war and the Confederacy would have won by Union default. Or, this strategy might at least have significantly lengthened the war. He presents as examples Lee's success in such tactics at Fredericksburg and in the final campaign against Grant's great offensive that ended in Lee's surrender at Appomattox. In short, Nolan makes victory or defeat depend entirely on the counting of casualties, and the number of casualties depend entirely on whether one is fighting defensively or offensively. I believe both propositions are false.

I would point out, as an aside, that this was by no means a new argument. A number of other military analysts had already made it, and the scholars Grady McWhiney and Perry D. Jamieson had made it the central theme of their book *Attack and Die: Civil War Military Tactics and the Southern Heritage,* published in 1982. Nolan simply dusted off this argument and appropriated it in a particularly venomous manner for his indictment of Lee.

Again, in commenting on Nolan's criticism of Lee's generalship I do not propose to attempt a specific refutation of every point. This would require far more time that we have available this evening. What I propose instead is to challenge certain of the basic premises on which his conclusions rest, because if they are destroyed, then the entire structure collapses.

I should point out in the beginning that Nolan seems to have sensed a certain weakness in his argument; he seems to have recognized that an undeviating resort to defensive operations and tactics is inherently vulnerable. It yields the initiative to one's opponent and allows him to concentrate his forces at the point, or points, and commit them at the time and in the manner of his choosing. One of the most venerable axioms of military doctrine holds that whereas the attacker must be strong only at the point of his main effort, the defender must be strong everywhere, from which it follows, as night follows day (to borrow from Shakespeare's Polonius), that the defender will be weak everywhere. This is an advantage of incalculable proportions to the attacker.

Simply standing on the defensive also gives the attacker the option of turning the defender out of position by moving around him and attacking or threatening his line of communications or his base. The defender is then subject to an attack in the open and frequently in a state of disorganization and faulty deployment. If completely turned, he may be obliged to mount an attack himself in an attempt to fight his way out of the trap that he has set for himself. The defender also is subject to a massed envelopment of one or both of his flanks.

Sensing these possibilities, Nolan resorted to a bit of CYA, which I will launder by translating to mean "cover your rear." He said that an overall defensive strategy would not preclude offensive campaigns and tactics on appropriate occasions if they were waged "in the context of [the] defensive grand strategy."

Well, hello now! Nolan's statement sounds to me suspiciously like a textbook description of Lee's very military policy: a defensive grand strategy supported on appropriate occasions by offensive campaigns and tactics. The critical element missing in Nolan's formula is: Who is to make the decisions as to when the occasion for an offensive is appropriate, or what the nature of an appropriate offensive is to be? Nolan sets forth a theoretical proposition only; he offers no hints of answers to these critical questions; he sounds as if the occasions would simply announce themselves, along with appropriate plans of action. In other words, he recommends an *a priori* adoption of a general defensive with occasional offensive tactics and no explanation of the conditions under which they are to occur.

But in real life, the commander in the field (Lee, in this instance) has to make these decisions, has to make them in the midst of the continuous, formidable military operations engulfing him—in the chaotic flux of war—assaying by a combination of judgment and intuition honed by his own experience, has to decide when the moment is right for such an operation and what kind of operation it ought to be. Lee was the one man who, with a wrong decision, could lose the war in an afternoon. I would argue that he was remarkably successful in making most of his decisions, but certainly, under such conditions, he can be forgiven for a nonfatal misjudgment now and then.

In his pursuit of CYA, Nolan concedes that two of the most risky of Lee's offensive operations "may have been justified." He identifies these as Lee's counteroffensive against McClellan's army on the Virginia Peninsula in the early summer of 1862, because, Nolan says, this may have saved Richmond; the other attack that "may have been justified," according to Nolan, was Lee's attack on Grant's army in the Wilderness in the spring of 1864.

I should like to place Lee's counterattack against McClellan on the Peninsula in a bolder strategic perspective than Nolan has chosen to place it. The capture of Richmond at that time, coming in the wake of such stunning Confederate defeats as Shiloh and the loss of New Orleans, might well have ended the war. Lee's action may have saved the Confederacy. Nobody has made this point more forcefully than Professor McPherson in his review of Nolan's book. After describing the apparently hopeless condition of the Confederacy at the point when Lee took command of the Army of Northern Virginia, McPherson says: "Within three months Lee's offensives had taken the Confederacy off the floor at the count of nine and had driven Union forces onto the ropes. Without Lee the Confederacy might have died in 1862." It is clear to me that McPherson goes far beyond believing that Lee's attack "may have been justified," as Nolan puts it; McPherson believes it literally turned the war around, at least for the moment. So do I.

Nolan does not say why Lee's attack against Grant's army in the Wilderness may have been justified, so, with your permission, I shall venture an explanation: it was the best opportunity Lee would have to destroy the threatening army or so cripple it that it would be obliged to halt its operations against Richmond for an indefinite length of time. Such a result would, of course, have exerted an electrifying effect on southern morale and a correspondingly depressing effect on northern morale. It might even have caused Grant to be relieved of his command.

To go back and pick up the chronological narrative of the war, after the Peninsula campaign in June and July 1862, Lee promptly moved to northern Virginia to strike the large army being concentrated there under General John Pope. This bold and rapid maneuver, capped by Jackson's brilliant turning movement and Longstreet's devastating flank attack, won the spectacular victory of Second Manassas. Not only was it a spectacular Confederate victory, smashing a dangerous Federal campaign for Richmond and immensely boosting Confederate morale, the casualty figures were favorable to Lee: over nine thousand Confederate, over thirteen thousand Union.

The outcome of this battle refutes the idea that the defensive always exacts more casualties than the offensive. The lesson to be drawn here is that casualty figures, and victory or defeat, are the result of a combination of many factors (including boldness, decisiveness, resoluteness, willingness to accept the calculated risk of action, ability to deceive or surprise the enemy, charismatic leadership under fire, and astute employment of terrain and mobility); victory is not the product simply of the disposition of defense or attack by the two armies or of the range of the weapons employed.

Lee then moved rapidly to invade the northern homeland. The battle of Antietam thwarted this offensive. Just how much the chance discovery of Lee's order giving his campaign plan assisted his opponent McClellan in the Antietam campaign is beyond exact measurement, but certainly it was of considerable assistance.

Nolan presents Antietam as an example of Lee's wastage of troops in his obsession for the offensive. I challenge this reasoning. It is true that in penetrating enemy territory Lee was waging a strategic offensive. But casualties do not occur as the direct result of strategic operations; they are the result of tactical operations (actual combat). Antietam was a tactically defensive battle by Lee. His army was in a defensive position with its back to the Potomac River and was under attack there by the Union army. In other words, Nolan confuses tactics with strategy in evaluating the results in casualties at Antietam. According to his thesis, Lee should have been able to inflict far heavier casualties on McClellan than Lee incurred. Yet the casualty figures at Antietam (over ten thousand Confederate, over twelve thousand Union) were more nearly equal, and less favorable to Lee, than those at Second Manassas, in which he had waged an attack.

Though Antietam was a tactical victory for Lee, a narrow one or a tactical draw, it was a Union strategic victory because it stopped Lee's advance into Maryland, prevented a possible recognition of the Confederacy by England and France, and gave Lincoln an opportunity to issue his preliminary emancipation proclamation. Yet it was not without strategic benefits to the Confederacy. It delayed indefinitely a renewal of the Union move to seize Richmond and it paralyzed McClellan. When Lincoln heard that he said his horses were too fatigued for another campaign right away, the president retorted sarcastically, asking what McClellan's horses had done that would fatigue them. Finally, Lincoln decided to remove the reluctant general from command and replace him with Ambrose Burnside, a choice that proved to be disastrous.

Next came the Fredericksburg campaign. Nolan believes that the battle of Fredericksburg was the model of what Lee should generally have practiced throughout the war. For the Confederates it was a tactically defensive battle fought on terrain that heavily favored the defender. Union casualties more than doubled those of the Confederates. If I were picking a favorite battle for the Confederacy, I, too, would look with distinct approval on Fredericksburg.

But what reason is there to believe that the Union commanders would have obliged Lee by replicating time after time their Fredericksburg tactics: frontal assaults up a dominating grade that provided the defender a long, unobstructed field of observation and fire? Not even Burnside would have done so. After his bloody defeat there, he was attempting a turning movement to force Lee out of his nearly impregnable position when the Union army became mired in the mud.

Nor did General Joseph Hooker, Burnside's replacement, launch a frontal attack on Lee, as the Nolan scenario would have had him do. Instead, he devised a clever turning movement around Lee's left flank and carried it out with genuine boldness and skill. At this point Lee had to make a decision: whether to remain in position on his comfortable heights back of Fredericksburg or mount a counterattack. Nolan does not commit himself on what Lee should have done in this situation, but his general formula would have had Lee remain in position and fight defensively. The engagement that ensued, Chancellorsville, is, presumably, one of the battles counted by Nolan as a product of Lee's faulty strategic policy.

What Lee did at Chancellorsville was to mount a counterattack, seize the initiative from the palsied Hooker, and win a sensational victory with fewer casualties than he inflicted on his opponent (over thirteen thousand Confederate, over sixteen thousand Federal). I vote for Lee's decision. In fact, had he not done what he did, he would in all probability have been forced into a disastrous retreat or would have suffered a catastrophic defeat, possibly the destruction of his army. Moreover, this battle, like Second Manassas, provides an impressive refutation of the Nolan casualty thesis.

Lee now launched the Gettysburg campaign. That he suffered a serious tactical defeat and heavy casualties there is no secret. It is easy to say in retrospect that he erred grievously in ordering an attack, especially on the third day. Gettysburg is Nolan's ten-strike; my conviction is that he bases his entire thesis on this one encounter, an encounter that Archer Jones, a highly respected student of Confederate strategy, calls an "aberration" from

Lee's customary practice. Certainly, Gettysburg demonstrated the high risk of attacking directly across hundreds of yards of open ground against a foe holding the military crest of the ridge in front.

But Lee's defeat there hardly proves the Nolan thesis even for Gettysburg, to say nothing of the rest of the war. The late Russell Weigley, perhaps the preeminent American military historian at the time of his death, says in his recently published book, *A Great Civil War,* that Lee's strategy in the Gettysburg campaign might have proven sound for the Confederacy if he had achieved a victory in the battle. Another recent study of the battle itself, Noah Andre Trudeau's *Gettysburg: A Testing of Courage,* though it faults what it calls Lee's "culture of command," offers the intriguing statement that his tactical plan was well crafted, and that if all parts had worked as they were designed to do, "the grand attack might very well have succeeded." These conclusions strongly suggest that the failure of the campaign lay not in its conception, but in its execution. They are light years removed from Nolan's sweeping condemnation of Lee's decisions to wage strategic and tactical offensives.

In discussing the Gettysburg campaign, Nolan takes two little detours to add other smears on Lee's character. He recounts the letter that Lee wrote to Jefferson Davis three weeks before the battle in which he urged the Confederate president to make an overture for a truce to talk about peace terms. Lee recommended that Davis not demand unconditional Confederate independence, but leave the subject open. He said he believed the northern people would not be willing to resume the fighting if they were under the impression that peace could be restored through negotiation, and that the Confederacy might thereby achieve its goal without expressly demanding it. He said all steps should be taken "honorably" and "consistently with truth."

Nolan believes Lee acted dishonorably on this occasion. Unquestionably, Lee's proposal contained an element of deception. He obviously meant that though he would not tell an explicit lie in this matter, he would withhold certain aspects of it. Nolan apparently is unaware that politics, diplomacy, and military strategy frequently, if not invariably, contain elements of deception by silence on certain points, by withholding information. For example, Lincoln, in writing his published letter to the newspaper editor Horace Greeley on what he intended to do about slavery, withheld the fact that he had already decided which of three courses he had chosen. He did this because he believed the time was not politically propitious for the announcement of any form of emancipation. Lee was a master of deception on the battlefield, though a novice in politics and diplomacy. Nolan has no problem with deception on the battlefield, but in disparaging Lee's sense of honor in this instance, he apparently fails to distinguish between the nuances of honor in personal affairs and in the affairs of politics and diplomacy. To employ a down-home metaphor, Nolan would have Lee reveal his diplomatic trump before the trick was played.

Nolan also insinuates strongly that Lee countenanced the seizure of runaway slaves and free blacks while in Pennsylvania. Longstreet's cavalry did seize some blacks, but there is no evidence to support the insinuation that Lee knew anything about the matter. His army was accompanied by thousands of southern slaves who served as drivers or as body servants of their owners. He had no way to distinguish among the blacks. Certainly, he had enough on his mind without bothering with this problem. It is possible that he would have countenanced the seizure of runaways because he considered them the legal property of southern owners. But this is purely speculative. It is unthinkable that he knowingly would have approved the seizure of free blacks. After all, Virginia contained many thousands of free blacks living legally and peacefully within her own population.

While I am on Gettysburg, I wish to give a comment on the strategic wisdom or unwisdom in Lee's decisions to mount offensives into the North. Nolan, of course, considers them to have been utterly foolhardy. But I am convinced that, even in failing to win tactical victories on the two occasions when Lee marched north, his offensives served an extremely valuable strategic purpose for Lee and the Confederacy. Lee was obliged to fight the entire war with his right flank and rear exposed to a turning movement by the Federals through their naval command of the Chesapeake Bay and the Atlantic. There was nothing Lee could do to control these waters. The major Union expedition designed to take Richmond, McClellan's Peninsula campaign, was just such a turning movement. By having Jackson mount his famous counteroffensive in the Shenandoah Valley, Lee drew off reinforcements intended for McClellan and crippled his campaign to the point that Lee was able to repel it.

What Lee could do to protect his flank and rear was to pose such a serious threat to Washington and other eastern cities that the Union authorities would not again risk a turning movement by water. Both Antietam and Gettysburg served this purpose.

The most serious proposal to undertake such a movement again came from Grant just before he became general in chief of Union forces. His first thought on how to defeat Lee was to land a powerful force on the Atlantic coast below Richmond and force Lee to move there in order to protect his essential line of supply and communication. Some scholars of the war believe this plan was quite feasible, and Lee himself said that if it should be attempted *successfully,* he would indeed be forced to abandon northern Virginia.

General Henry Halleck vetoed Grant's plan, saying it would split the Union army with Lee between the two wings and thus dangerously expose Washington; he said Grant's true objective was Lee's army, an accurate reflection of Lincoln's view. This obliged Grant to wage attacks directly against Lee. They were eventually successful, but only after an immense amount of bloodletting and a serious decline in northern morale. In any event, Lee's threats against Washington and the northeast prevented the turning movement by water that he feared.

A final footnote on Gettysburg: Nolan dismisses Lee's desperate need for supplies (which he found in abundance in Pennsylvania) and his equally desperate need to draw the Union army out of northern Virginia so that the farmers there could go about their work of producing the crops on which his army depended. Nolan depicts the campaign as being simply a fulfill-ment of Lee's inherent, obsessive aggressiveness. Lee actually succeeded in gathering the supplies he needed, and he succeeded temporarily in draw-ing the opposing army out of Virginia. A Confederate victory at Gettysburg would have drawn it out indefinitely.

Nolan quotes a number of historians to support his general thesis. He is guilty of distorting their true meaning by quoting them out of context in or-der to suit his thesis. I wish particularly to comment on his use of the words of one of these historians, Professor Bell I. Wiley. Professor Wiley was my major professor when I was working on my master's degree at Louisiana State University, and I served for a year as his graduate research assistant. We became close, lifelong friends, and we engaged in countless discus-sions, both formal and informal, of the Confederacy and the Civil War.

Wiley wrote: "That the South did not [achieve its independence] was due as much, if not more, to its own failings as to the superior strength of the foe." I have heard Professor Wiley say this, or similar things, on many occasions. But in this quotation he was speaking of general political and military mistakes and inherent weaknesses of the Confederacy; he was not speaking of Lee's generalship. Most of the military mistakes Wiley mentioned were made by generals other than Lee. Wiley admired Lee as an especially gifted leader. I never heard him as much as hint that Lee's faults caused the Confederacy to lose the war, and I have the strongest doubt that he ever made a remark to this effect.

Nolan also faults Lee for recommending that other Confederate generals launch offensive operations in their departments. I firmly believe that these recommendations were sound. Lee said that General John C. Pemberton at Vicksburg ought to concentrate his forces and attack Grant as soon as Grant crossed to the east side of the Mississippi River. By doing this, Pemberton could have attacked with a numerical superiority of approximately four to three. By failing to do this, Pemberton allowed Grant time to concentrate his superior force; eventually Pemberton was driven back into a besieged defensive situation and starved into surrendering his entire army.

Lee advised that General Bragg mount another campaign out of Tennessee into Kentucky. This did not occur and Bragg eventually lost the key city of Chattanooga, from which Sherman would launch his devastating campaign for Atlanta.

Lee also believed that Joseph E. Johnston ought to counterattack Sherman's advance before he reached Atlanta. Johnston failed to do so, was relieved of command by Davis, the Confederate army was turned, surrounded, and besieged in Atlanta, and the city was lost.

By now you are well aware that in judging Lee's generalship I challenge Nolan's thesis in every respect. I also seriously question his sweeping proposition concerning the superiority of the defensive over the offensive in warfare. I understand that more troops are required to take a specific position than to hold it. This was true even before the appearance of rifled weapons. The renowned Prussian analyst and philosopher on war Karl von Clausewitz, who lived before these weapons were perfected, wrote persuasively on this point; some positions are so strong, either by nature or by fortification, or a combination of the two, he said, that a numerical advantage of ten to one may be required to take them.

But most battles are not fought simply for the seizure or retention of a specific position, and seldom if ever are wars decided by such a measure. For some analogies that may cast light on the issue of the offensive versus the defensive, let us look at the two European wars that were the closest in time and the most similar in armies and armaments to the American Civil War. These were the Austro-Prussian War (1866) and the Franco-Prussian

War (1870–1871). Prussia took the offensive in both, and won both, though her numerical superiority in each was less than that of the Union in the Civil War.

The most striking example of the truth that the employment of defensive tactics does not necessarily provide an advantage is seen in the battle of Königgrätz, or Sadowa, in the Austro-Prussian War. The two forces there were virtually equal in numbers; both were armed with rifled shoulder weapons; the Prussians had the superior rifles (breach loaders), but the Austrians had superior artillery (a higher proportion of rifled cannon). The Austrian general elected to fight defensively and chose the most commanding position that lay astride the direct highway to Vienna; he deployed his force into position; his engineers established excellent fieldworks in the most critical locations; his artillery tested the ranges in advance and identified reference targets in the path over which the Prussians must advance.

Yet the Prussians won the battle and inflicted enormously more casualties than they incurred. They won it by sending heavy enveloping columns to attack both Austrian flanks while another column attacked frontally. Authorities on the engagement attribute the Prussian victory to bolder and more imaginative generalship. The Austrians might have won, they believe, if at the critical moment they had attacked the Prussian force to their direct front while the enveloping columns were still on the march to deliver their assaults. The Austrians might then have defeated the other Prussian columns by turns. According to the Nolan formula, the Austrians ought to have won a slam-dunk victory at Königgrätz, and with relatively few casualties, because they were fighting on the defensive. Instead, they suffered a catastrophic defeat and an inordinate number of dead, wounded, and captured.

Someone might reply that this was a European war with European armies engaged, and that any lessons learned from it are irrelevant to the American Civil War. Then let us return to *our* war and reflect on some of the lessons from it that have apparently eluded Nolan. One can read his book without being aware that the Confederacy did in fact wage many defensive campaigns besides Lee's in the last year of the conflict.

Here is a list of the major defensive campaigns by the Confederacy: Albert Sidney Johnston's campaign in Kentucky in the fall of 1861 and the winter of 1862; Joseph E. Johnston's campaign on the Virginia Peninsula in the spring and summer of 1862; Lee's Fredericksburg campaign in the winter of 1862; Pemberton's Vicksburg campaign in the summer of 1863;

Bragg's Chattanooga campaign in the fall of 1863; Joseph E. Johnston's Atlanta campaign in the summer and fall of 1864; Hood's Nashville campaign in the winter of 1864; Lee's campaign from the Wilderness to Appomattox from the spring of 1864 to the spring of 1865; and Joseph E. Johnston's campaign through the Carolinas in the winter of 1864 and the spring of 1865. All but one of these campaigns (Fredericksburg) resulted in Confederate defeats, many of them in disasters. Actually, if all troops lost are counted, including those captured and those who deserted, the defensive campaigns were costlier to the Confederacy than its offensive campaigns. They hardly constitute a brief for the Nolan thesis.

Let us take a final look at the effects of Lee's generalship. Nolan sets the stage for his thesis by writing that in evaluating Lee, "the key consideration is not the brilliance or boldness of his performance in a tactical or operationally strategic sense . . . the key consideration must be whether the general's actions helped or hurt the cause of his government in view of that government's grand strategy. In short, the appropriate inquiry is to ask whether the general's actions related positively or negatively to the war objectives and national policy of his government." Nolan rendered the same idea in a more contemptuous mode when he wrote, "Lee's task as commander of the Army of Northern Virginia was not to put on a martial show, a performance; it was to make the maximum contribution toward the South's chances of winning the war." I consider this reference to a "martial show, a performance" to be a cheap shot at Lee.

To my eye, it is glaringly apparent that Lee's actions did relate positively to his government's objectives and national policy. But I prefer to quote Professor McPherson on this matter because Nolan has used him also (misleadingly) as a witness for his own views. I have already quoted McPherson on the effects of Lee's generalship early in the war.

Let me quote McPherson on Nolan's general thesis that Lee ought to have fought the war defensively. "This is not to endorse Nolan's main point that Lee's offensive strategy lost a war he might otherwise have won," wrote McPherson. "It is quite true that the Confederacy had a chance to win the war—not by conquering the North or destroying its armies, but by sapping the Northern will and capacity to conquer the South and destroy Confederate armies." (Parenthetically, I agree with this view. Ironically, nobody made a more compelling statement to this effect than did Lee in his letter to Jefferson Davis shortly before Gettysburg.) Continuing the quotation from McPherson: "On three occasions the Confederacy came close to winning on these terms. Each time it was Lee who almost pulled it off. . . . Lee's strategy in the end failed to win the war. But the point is that of all Confederate commanders, Lee was the only one whose victories had some potential for winning the war. The notion that a more gradual strategy [Nolan's notion] would have done better is speculative at best." I put it to this audience, does this sound as if McPherson believes Lee's strategy lost the war for the Confederacy? Or that Lee simply put on a show, a performance?

The question of whether Lee's actions related positively or negatively to the Confederacy's war objectives was answered indirectly but powerfully by one who experienced the Civil War. This was no ordinary individual; it was Henry J. Raymond, managing editor of the *New York Times,* national chairman of the Republican Party, a friend and confidant of President Abraham Lincoln, and one of the brightest and most knowledgeable citizens of the Union. In an editorial published in September 1864, by which time the outcome of the war was certain, Raymond wrote: "The rebels have exhibited a most wonderful energy and skill in carrying on their struggle. No people on the face of the earth ever made so hard a fight with such limited means. . . . They have displayed a combination of dash and endurance never before equaled in military history. All candid men, whatever their hatred of the rebellion, and whatever their admiration of our own heroic soldiers, are free to admit that the final triumph of our national armies will be due only to superiority in numbers." Would anyone (except Nolan, of course) deny that Lee's generalship was the galvanizing force at the center of this extraordinary Confederate military effort?

By now I'm sure that my views on Nolan's criticism of Lee's military strategy are quite clear to the audience. But I should like to buttress them with a quotation from another historian who has devoted an immense amount of reflection to the issue, Russell Weigley, who writes, "if not Lee's strategy, then what strategy could have won for the Confederacy? Criticism of Lee should not evade the painfulness of his and the Confederacy's strategic dilemma, that a defensive strategy was all too likely to multiply the advantages of the Union by allowing it to concentrate men and materiel at places of its choosing, and that consequently to stand on the defensive was even less promising than Lee's offensive strategy. The Confederacy lacked strategic options. Moreover, Lee was so deadly an opponent on the tactical level that he merits his place in the pantheon of great generals whatever his flaws."

Nolan's book represents an unrelenting indictment of Lee both as general and as man.

Lee and Jackson

An Indomitable Team

In all the annals of military history, few if any other command combinations have been as spectacular as that of General Robert E. Lee and his legendary wing commander, Lieutenant General Thomas J. "Stonewall" Jackson. I would hazard the opinion that the vast majority of southerners, and a not inconsiderable number of non-southerners, have traditionally believed that had the Lee-Jackson team not been destroyed by Jackson's death, the Confederacy might well have been victorious in the conflict.

Southerners have paid homage to the two famed generals in various ways, including the publishing of biographies and essays, composition of songs and poetry, erection of statues, naming of buildings, schools, streets, and highways, and christening of children in their honor. It was through this latter means that I, as a young child, first became aware of their having lived. I had an uncle, my father's brother, who wore the evocative name, Lee Jackson Roland. Nor, in my opinion, is this acclaim unmerited. From the time the two Confederate leaders began operating together in the spring of 1862 until the moment a year later when Jackson fell, they set an unsurpassed record of military success against seemingly impossible odds. It behooves us, then, to examine their careers in search of the keys to their efforts.

Lee and Jackson shared many elements of heritage and allegiance. Both were Virginians, though they represented sharply different strains of Virginia society. Lee was the scion of two of the most revered families of the state, the Lees and the Carters. The Lees had for generations been in the forefront of Virginia public affairs. Two of Robert E. Lee's ancestors had been signers of the Declaration of Independence. His father, Henry

"Light Horse Harry" Lee, was one of the most renowned soldiers of the American Revolution; he was also the coiner of the immortal eulogy of George Washington: "First in war, first in peace, and first in the hearts of his countrymen."

Lee's mother, Ann Hill Carter, was descended from the wealthiest and probably the most influential planter of colonial Virginia. Her great-grandfather, Robert Carter, was so rich and so admired (or, doubtless by some, so resented and so envied) that he received the nickname "King" Carter.

Jackson was from plainer stock. Born and reared in western Virginia (now the state of West Virginia), he bore in his character and personality the imprint of the rugged terrain and austere lifestyle of his native region. He also carried in his heart the sorrow and loneliness of orphanhood; his father died when he was two years old, his mother when he was seven.

Reared by relatives, his early years were filled with labor: logging, plowing, working in his uncle's mill, and tending cattle and poultry. At age sixteen, a product of the meager education afforded in his time and place, he became a schoolteacher, holding lessons in a log cabin. The following year he became a local constable. Unquestionably, it seems to me, much of the force that drove Jackson the man grew out of the struggle of Jackson the youth to surmount the adversities that beset him. This struggle, and his success in overcoming the obstacles, was reflected in his great motivational axiom, "You may be whatever you will resolve to be."

When he was eighteen, through his ties with a local congressman, abetted by a stroke of luck, he received an appointment to attend the U.S. Military Academy. (His luck occurred because the first appointee to the slot at West Point promptly withdrew, leaving a vacancy that was then filled by Jackson.)

Though Lee was spared the degree of sorrow and adversity experienced by the young Jackson, he did not escape them altogether. His father, illustrious in war, was unstable in peace. Overwhelmed by debt that resulted from his speculations and by the passions aroused by his fierce Federalist political partisanship, he abandoned the family when Lee was only six and fled to the West Indies. Lee never saw him again. Most of Ann Carter Lee's inheritance was by then exhausted. The young Lee had to make his mark in a profession instead of in the role of a gentleman planter. Lacking the means to attend medical school or law school, he chose the Army, with its expense-free education at the U.S. Military Academy.

Thus, both he and Jackson were products of West Point in their formal military training, with Lee several years ahead of Jackson. Their careers at the academy were markedly different. Lee was well-prepared by private schools and tutors for the courses of the program. From the beginning he made high marks; he graduated second in his class and without a conduct demerit. His senior year he served as adjutant of the Corps of Cadets, the most prestigious position in the Corps at that time. He was so handsome and poised, so graceful in his bearing that the other cadets called him a "marble model."

Jackson was ill-prepared for the demands of the West Point curriculum. He was at the very bottom of his entering class. Only through the most strenuous exertions was he able to do the lessons, and then, perhaps, only through the gratis tutoring of a fellow cadet, William H. C. Whiting, the class leader. Jackson was so dependent upon his tutor that he became known as "Whiting's plebe," a not-so-gentle West Point slur. Jackson ignored the innuendo and strove mightily to excel. He succeeded. He graduated in the top third of his class, and many of his acquaintances in the Corps said he would have been number one if the program had lasted a year longer. Jackson, like Lee, absorbed what West Point had to offer.

Both Lee and Jackson served their main military apprenticeship in the 1840s as officers in the war with Mexico. This struggle has been called a "rehearsal for conflict" because it was the practical training ground for so many of the American officers who would a few years later achieve fame on both sides in the Civil War. Jackson served in the Mexican War as a junior officer of artillery. So bold and decisive was he in his conduct, so effective in execution, and, significantly, in light of his later reputation and nickname "Stonewall," in the words of a fellow officer of the Mexican War, so "indomitable in his sticking qualities," however hot the enemy fire, that he received citation after citation from his superiors.

But Jackson's most coveted accolade was not a formal citation. It occurred at the end of hostilities, when the commanding general, General Winfield Scott, staged a reception for his officers. Scott was a master of military command, strategy, and tactics. He was also a virtuoso of pomp and circumstance, a spit-and-polish general known by his troops, both derisively and affectionately, as "Old Fuss and Feathers." He was an enormous figure of a man, standing six feet five inches tall and weighing almost three hundred pounds.

As Jackson stepped up to him in the reception line, Scott drew himself up to his towering height and ostentatiously withheld his hand, saying in a booming voice, "I don't know if I will shake hands with Mr. Jackson. If you can forgive yourself for the way in which you slaughtered those poor Mexicans with your guns, I'm not sure that I can." Then, after a pause, while Jackson squirmed in confusion and humiliation, Scott beamed a smile of affection and admiration and thrust out his huge hand. The group burst into applause as Jackson grasped it. An acquaintance in attendance said, "No greater compliment could have been paid a young officer for courage and zeal."

Lee served in the Mexican War as an engineer officer and as the premier member of Scott's staff. He carried out the daring reconnaissances, positioned the artillery, guided the assaulting columns, and offered tactical suggestions, all of which helped make Scott's operations a model of military effectiveness. After the war, Scott would write of him, "[American] success in Mexico was largely due to the skill, valor, and undaunted energy of Robert E. Lee. . . . [He] was the very best soldier I ever saw in the field."

Later, Scott said to an acquaintance, "I tell you, that if I were on my deathbed tomorrow, and the president should tell me that a great battle was to be fought for the liberty or slavery of the country, and asked my judgment as to the ability of a commander, I would say with my dying breath, 'Let it be Robert E. Lee.'" Scott was as good as his word. Shortly, with the nation in crisis, he would recommend Lee for the command of the Union army, and President Abraham Lincoln would make the offer. Lee sorrowfully turned down that offer, with incalculable consequences for himself and for the nation.

Scott's influence on the military capabilities of both Lee and Jackson was immense. Lee expressed his boundless admiration for his commander in the following lines written to a friend from the imperial palace of Mexico. "Our general is our great reliance," he said. "He is a great man on great occasions. Never turned from his object. Confident in his powers and resources, his judgment is as sound as his heart is bold and daring. Careful of his men, he never exposes them but for a worthy object, and then gives them the advantage of every circumstance in his power. This accounts in some measure for our comparative small loss, when you consider the odds and circumstances against us."

Lee's and Jackson's combat experiences with Scott reinforced in their minds the cardinal principles of warfare, along with a deep appreciation of his personal leadership qualities and the originality of many of his military conceptions. They saw demonstrated in fire and blood the advantage of audacity in the seizure of the initiative, the imperative of careful reconnaissance before commitment to action, the supreme value of turning movements and flank envelopments in tactical maneuvers, the need for proper logistical arrangements (factors involving the mobility and supply of troops) to support the actual combat operations, and the sometime necessity of abandoning one's line of communications in order to reach the vitals of the enemy. Scott was a war mentor virtually without peer.

Both Lee and Jackson were powerfully motivated by religion. Lee was reared an Episcopalian, imbued with the earnest piety of his mother. Throughout his career, and especially after he joined his daughters in 1853 in being confirmed into the Church, he yielded himself to God's Providence. He attended services as often as circumstances permitted—though he tended to sleep through the sermons—and he read Scripture and prayed daily.

His letters back to his wife from camp and field were sprinkled with supplications for and acknowledgments of God's blessings, along with affirmations of subjection to the divine will. A typical line read, "May He continue His blessings to us both and all of our children, relatives and friends, and in His own good time unite us in His worship, if not on earth, forever in heaven." Writing to console a soldier over the death of the man's child, Lee said he also was grief-stricken by the event, but he added that he considered it "far better for the child to be called by its heavenly Creator into His presence in its purity and innocence, unpolluted by sins, and uncontaminated by the vices of the world."

Jackson followed a sterner path in his religious pilgrimage. Long interested in matters of the spirit, he was baptized into the Episcopal Church in 1849, at age twenty-five. Presently, however, he became strongly attracted to the reasoning and tenets of the Presbyterian faith, including, after a struggle within his mind, the formidable doctrine of predestination.

In 1851 he joined the Presbyterian Church, and in 1857 he became a deacon in it. He embraced its teachings completely, yielding absolutely to his view of God's will in both personal and worldly matters at large. He shunned all manner of unrighteousness, gave up such activities as dancing and attending theater as being unacceptably frivolous, and followed with virtually unique rigor the Mosaic commandment to remember the Sabbath to keep it holy. He, of course, attended services punctiliously, though he, perhaps more soundly than Lee, slept during the sermons. Jackson would not read a newspaper, write a letter, or engage in a secular conversation on

Sunday, nor would he post a letter that would be in transit that day of the week. If, as I believe, Lee represented the personification of the Cavalier myth in southern religion and life, Jackson represented the incarnation of the Puritan ethos.

The two were Christian soldiers with an intensity of conviction and dedication that is incomprehensible to the sophisticated and materialistic modern mind. This applied even to their views on the most controversial and difficult practice of the age—human slavery. Lee considered it an evil, but one that served as a temporary form of tutelage to the primitive African race, and one that could be eradicated only by God's intervention. Jackson's views were similar. He probably disapproved of slavery, though he left no explicit statement to that effect; he looked upon the blacks as children of God with souls to be saved, and he created and conducted a Sunday school class for that purpose. But, in his judgment, the blacks were children who, for God's own purposes, had been subordinated to the white race and consigned to slavery. Hence, both Lee and Jackson considered the institution to lie beyond the reach of human hands; only God in his infinite wisdom and power could remove it.

In the years after the Mexican War, both Lee and Jackson became associated with military educational institutions: Lee for a term as superintendent of the U.S. Military Academy; Jackson as the professor of natural and experimental philosophy at the Virginia Military Institute in Lexington, Virginia.

Lee had little enthusiasm for his job at West Point; he had attempted to have changed the orders assigning him there. When this failed, he undertook and carried out his work in his characteristically conscientious manner. He introduced no original programs into the Academy curriculum, but he conducted the existing program with efficiency and elegance. I suspect his most vexing task was riding herd on his unruly nephew, Fitzhugh Lee, who repeatedly seemed on the point of expulsion for some infraction of the countless rules. The cadets were impressed by Lee. One of them wrote his mother that Lee was the handsomest man he had ever seen, and he repeated the simile of Lee's cadet days, "just like a marble model," to which his mother, who was acquainted with Lee, replied, "Handsome, yes, but not like marble. Colonel Lee is very human, kind, calm, and definite." Hers was a remarkably apt analysis, I believe.

The academic subject taught by Jackson is described by Professor James I. Robertson, his definitive biographer, as having been "a loose conglomerate of physics, astronomy, mechanics, and sprinklings of other sciences"; it included excursions into electricity, magnetics, acoustics, the science of heavenly bodies, and the properties of light (or optics). Small wonder that Jackson had trouble teaching it in an engaging manner. He, in fact, taught it by memorized verbatim lectures delivered in a high monotone, and he conducted himself with more than the usual share of professorial eccentricities. To his students, he became "Old Jack," "Tom Fool," or "Old Hickory." But the more perceptive and more dedicated among them came to appreciate the earnestness, substance, and character of the extraordinary man who stood or sat at attention before them.

Both Lee and Jackson were severely upset over the bitter political controversy that erupted into secession in 1860–1861. In theory, neither was a believer in secession. Upon the withdrawal from the Union of the states of the lower South, Lee wrote in caustic disapproval, saying that the Virginia statesman Thomas Jefferson had condemned as treason an earlier threat of secession by certain New Englanders. "What can it be now?" Lee demanded. He said he hoped Virginia would stand fast and save the Union. Jackson supported Union candidates in the election of delegates to the Virginia secession convention.

Both men, however, loathed the abolitionists as bigoted and dangerous fanatics whose doctrines invited insurrection and bloodshed by the slaves. In Lee's letter to his wife expressing the view that slavery was an evil in society, he denounced the abolitionists unsparingly, saying, "The consequences of their plans and purposes are clearly set forth, and they must also be aware that their object is both unlawful and entirely foreign to them and to their duty; for which they are irresponsible and unaccountable." They intended, he concluded, to accomplish their goal "through the agency of civil and servile war." To Jackson, the abolitionists were godless men seeking to abort the will of the Almighty.

Both Lee and Jackson played a role in an event that seemed to give incontrovertible evidence to the view that the goal of the abolitionists was indeed a slave insurrection. This was the attempt in 1859 by the most implacable of abolitionists, John Brown, to incite an uprising, beginning with the seizure of the U.S. arsenal at Harpers Ferry, Virginia.

Brown's deed became the more abhorrent in the South as certain influential voices in the North praised or commended him for it. The renowned thinker and essayist Ralph Waldo Emerson called him "a new saint awaiting his martyrdom, and who, if he shall suffer, will make the gallows glorious like the cross." Emerson's friend, the writer and fellow philosopher Henry David Thoreau, called Brown an "angel of light." The passionate abolitionist theologian Wendell Phillips thundered: "[Virginia] is a pirate ship, and John Brown sails the sea Lord High Admiral of the Almighty with his commission to sink every pirate he meets on God's ocean of the nineteenth century." By an odd stroke of circumstance, Lee commanded the detail of U.S. Marines that snuffed out Brown's effort at Harpers Ferry and captured him.

Also by an odd stroke of circumstance, Jackson commanded the artillery portion of the detail of VMI cadets that helped to provide security for the occasion of Brown's hanging in Charles Town, Virginia. Jackson left a graphic account of the affair. Though he fully believed that Brown deserved to die, he said he sent up a prayer that he might be spared, because, he said, "Awful was the thought that he might in a few moments receive the sentence, 'Depart ye wicked into everlasting fire.'"

All of the emotions of love for their native state, convictions that slavery was an institution authorized by God Almighty and sanctioned by the U.S. Constitution, and fear and loathing of abolition came to a head as the two men faced their personal moment of truth when Virginia faced its collective one regarding secession. Jackson had already made his intentions clear a few weeks earlier. Even while writing that he opposed secession at the time, he said that if the free states "instead of permitting us to enjoy rights guaranteed to us by the Constitution of our Country, should endeavor to subjugate us, and thus excite our slaves to servile insurrection in which our Families will be murdered without quarter or mercy, it becomes us to wage such a war as will bring hostilities to a speedy close." By which, he would soon explain, he meant a war of the "black flag": "No quarter to the violators of our homes and firesides," he said.

Lee was more hesitant, opposing secession until the last moment and refusing to commit himself to a definite course of personal action. But when President Lincoln indicated his intention to employ military force against the seceded states and called upon all of the states for troops for this purpose, and when Virginia refused him troops and promptly seceded, Lee cast his lot with her and eventually with the Confederacy. "I cannot draw my sword against my own people," he said in sorrow. Did he perhaps recall the words spoken by his father when he made his choice to join the American fight for independence: "Virginia is my country. Her will I obey, however lamentable the fate to which it may subject me."

Both Lee and Jackson immediately accepted commissions in the armed forces of the state of Virginia—Lee as a major general commanding the forces, Jackson as a colonel of volunteers. Jackson was immensely pleased over Lee's appointment. To his wife he wrote words of the highest praise for Lee, saying, "This I regard as of more value to us than Gen. Scott could render as commander. . . . I regard [Lee] as a better officer than Gen. Scott." Shortly, Lee assigned Jackson to command state forces at Harpers Ferry, the strategic point at the confluence of the Shenandoah and Potomac rivers.

Presently, Virginia became a Confederate state, and Lee and Jackson became Confederate officers—Lee acting unofficially as President Jefferson Davis's military advisor (a position somewhat analogous to a modern chief of staff), and Jackson as a brigadier general commanding a brigade of troops. The two men were in these positions when the initial significant battle of the Civil War, the first battle of Manassas, occurred. Lee was not in the battle. Jackson and his troops, having been ordered from Harpers Ferry to Manassas, were at the very vortex of it. It was, of course, from their immovable stand at Manassas that Jackson received the everlasting metaphoric sobriquet, "Stonewall," and the unit itself became the "Stonewall Brigade."

The vital association between Lee and Jackson began almost a year later. Lee was now a full general. He had been on a futile mission to hold western Virginia for the Confederacy and on a successful mission to create a workable defense for the lower Atlantic coast. He was back in Richmond, officially in charge of Confederate military operations, actually again as Davis's military advisor.

Richmond was in dire peril. General George B. McClellan's large Union army, opposed by General Joseph E. Johnston's smaller Confederate army, was approaching the city up the peninsula formed by the York and James rivers; General Irvin McDowell's large Union corps was poised to march from Fredericksburg on the Rappahannock River to join McClellan; another Federal force, under General Nathaniel Banks, was moving from the Shenandoah Valley to reinforce McClellan. If the junction of Federals on the Peninsula should occur, their combined weight would be overwhelming and the Confederate capital would surely be lost.

The junction did not occur—the response of Lee and Jackson prevented it. Jackson, now again in the Shenandoah Valley, acting according to his most renowned military axiom, "Never take counsel of your fears," attacked segments of the Federal forces there so vigorously that the Union authorities in Washington stopped the movements of both Banks and McDowell. Lee took careful note of this reaction.

Beginning in late April, Lee sent Jackson some of the most consequential operational messages of the entire war. "I have hoped," said Lee on April 25, "that in the present divided condition of the enemy's forces, a successful blow may be dealt them by a rapid combination of our troops before they can be strengthened either in position or by reenforcements." On May 16, Lee wrote, "Whatever may be Banks' intention, it is very desirable to prevent him from going either to Fredericksburg [to join McDowell] or the peninsula [to join McClellan]. . . . Whatever movement you make against Banks, do it speedily, and if successful, drive him back toward the Potomac, and create the impression, as far as practicable, that you design threatening that line."

These messages contained the germ of the entire remarkable strategic and operational partnership between Lee and Jackson. They anticipated the merger of Jackson's troops into the main body of the Confederate army defending Richmond, but assigned Jackson a mission only, leaving him largely free to exercise his own judgment as to how the mission would be carried out. (Permit me two brief asides at this point. On the wall of the George S. Patton Museum at Fort Knox, Kentucky, hangs one of that celebrated general's favorite sayings, which reads, "Never tell a subordinate how to carry out an order. Give him the order and leave the details to him. You will be amazed at the ingenuity he will demonstrate in executing it." General Matthew Ridgway, one of the most distinguished American military leaders of the post–World War II era, wrote that the mission type of order would be imperative for success in American wars of the future.)

Lee was enormously gratified by the ingenuity that Jackson now demonstrated. His execution of Lee's wish exceeded all hopes and gave the world an unforgettable demonstration of the leadership of intuition, audacity, and will, those qualities most valued by the great Prussian philosopher on war Karl von Clausewitz. Jackson's conduct provided an equally striking demonstration of the employment of terrain, interior lines, mobility, concentration of force, and surprise, those operational and tactical principles cited by Antoine-Henri Jomini, the famed expositor of Napoleon Bonaparte's generalship.

Surrounded by three times his numbers, Jackson swept up and down the Valley, using the Massanutten Mountain along its trough as a shield, darting through the mountain's gap and around its extremities to strike his divided opponents by turns. During the month of May and early June, he marched his force four hundred miles, fought five battles, and captured as many Federals as he had troops in his entire body, besides seizing large quantities of arms and supplies.

Great as these operational and tactical accomplishments were, the strategic accomplishment was greater. In addition to tying down the sixty thousand Federal troops in the Valley, Jackson immobilized McDowell's corps. At the end of May, Lee received the word he longed to hear: McDowell's column was being withdrawn to its original location on the Rappahannock, where it would be in position to go to the defense of Washington if necessary.

Meanwhile, the battle between Johnston and McClellan for possession of Richmond had begun. On June 1, following Johnston's severe wounding, Jefferson Davis assigned Lee to the command of the army. Lee promptly gave it its historic name, the Army of Northern Virginia.

Bringing Jackson and his troops from the Valley to reinforce the army defending Richmond, Lee counterattacked McClellan's force in the Seven Days battles. In this first combined action, the Lee-Jackson team did not function well. Lee's plans were too complicated, his staff work was ineffective, his knowledge of the terrain and roads was inaccurate, his orders were fragmentary and incomplete. Meanwhile, Jackson was physically and mentally exhausted and failed to demonstrate the alertness and energy he had shown in the Valley.

The Confederates were unable to win a decisive tactical victory in the Seven Days battles, and they suffered an inordinate number of casualties. Yet, in forcing McClellan to withdraw down the Peninsula, they won a strategic victory of immeasurable proportions. In saving Richmond, they may have saved the Confederacy. Confederate morale was plummeting. The loss of the capital city, coming in the wake of defeat at Shiloh and the loss of Nashville, Memphis, and New Orleans, might well have ended the war then and there. The battles on the Peninsula turned it around. Also, despite the disappointments and misunderstandings that had occurred during the fighting, the Lee-Jackson combination held. Jackson said he would follow Lee blindfolded; shortly, Lee would entrust to Jackson a mission of stupendous daring and difficulty.

The Federals were now massing a large army under General John Pope in northern Virginia. It was being reinforced from McClellan's army on the

Peninsula. Determining to strike it before it became prohibitively powerful, Lee quickly moved his army by rail to confront Pope.

Then he put his team into action, sending Jackson on a prodigious march around Pope's right flank to move through the Thoroughfare Gap in the Bull Run Mountains and strike the Union base at Manassas Junction on the railroad. When Pope turned to meet him (as Lee expected he would), Jackson concealed his troops in an abandoned railroad cut. When Pope finally located them and attacked their position, Lee was able to strike his flank with the remainder of his army (under Longstreet's immediate command) and drive the Federals from the field with heavy losses. Second Manassas was a Confederate victory at all levels—tactical, operational, and strategic; it staggered the Union morale. This campaign exemplified splendidly the Lee-Jackson phenomenon; it demonstrated also how thoroughly they recalled the lessons learned from Winfield Scott.

The next two encounters of the Army of Northern Virginia—Antietam in September 1862, and Fredericksburg three months later—were tactically defensive battles by the Confederates that offered Lee and Jackson no opportunity for the sort of sweeping action carried out at Second Manassas. But Chancellorsville, in May 1863, demonstrated spectacularly that the Lee-Jackson formula had not been abandoned.

I shall omit the details of this remarkable Confederate victory against numerical odds of more than two to one. Let me say only that the decisions and actions of the two southern generals in that battle constitute one of the most brilliant and most daring tactical performances ever seen on a battlefield: Jackson in his inimitable flank envelopment of the Union Army; Lee in repeatedly splitting his small force to shuttle his formations back and forth on interior lines and striking his opponent at his weakest points.

In his classic account of the engagement, John Bigelow (a quintessential Yankee, by the way) extols the virtuosity of both men and concludes by quoting approvingly the following judgment by the British military analyst Captain Cecil Battine, who said, "In all history, there is not recorded a campaign which exemplifies more fully the preponderance of skilful direction over superior numbers than this week's fighting in the forest of Virginia."

In summary, then, what were the qualities in Lee and Jackson that made them into such an extraordinary team? Doubtless, in the absolute sense, these qualities were unique to the men and their situations—so subtle, so occult, that they defy identification. In attempting to present the attributes of the ideal general, Clausewitz wrote, "What genius does is the best of all possible rules, and we can do no better than record it." I have attempted this evening to record briefly the more outstanding things that Lee and Jackson did. Let me presume to identify at least some of the discernible characteristics that enabled them to do these things.

Obviously, these leaders possessed superior intellects. This superiority was demonstrated in their records at West Point and in their achievements throughout their subsequent careers. Mental superiority enabled them to analyze the moods and anticipate the moves of their opponents. In the words of the renowned contemporary British officer Colonel G. F. R. Henderson, they penetrated their adversaries' brains. "If in appearance great risks [are] run," he wrote, "it [is] with the full knowledge that the enemy's character or his apprehensions would prevent him from taking those simple precautions by which the critics point out that the whole enterprise might easily [be] ruined." Mental superiority also enabled Lee and Jackson to devise the necessary means to take advantage of their insights.

Both Lee and Jackson displayed another characteristic that is essential to great generalship—audacity. They showed an extraordinary willingness to take the calculated risk of battle. Clausewitz identified boldness as one of the most important traits of military leadership. "Boldness is a truly creative force," he said; "Boldness directed by a predominating intelligence is the mark of the hero." Once when the risk of a proposed operation was mentioned to Lee, he said quietly, "The disparity in numbers between the contending forces makes the risk unavoidable." On another occasion he said, "We must decide between the positive loss of inactivity and the risk of action." These sayings lay at the heart of his doctrine of warfare; a member of his staff truly said of him, "His name is audacity." Jackson summed up his own boldness in the axiom already quoted: "Never take counsel of your fears." I venture to say the world has never seen two bolder soldiers than Lee and Jackson.

The final characteristic I would name in attempting to explain the generalship of these two is perhaps the most important of all, but it is also the most difficult to analyze. This is the attribute called character.

Clausewitz said character is a quality that is elusive and indefinable, the quality that lights the moral flame of leadership, a quality that is best spoken of in terms mysterious and rhapsodical. A distinguished modern British military historian, F. E. Adcock, in a study on the great generals of antiquity, said they all possessed "the highest faculties of mind. . . . But they possessed character in a still greater degree." To emphasize his point, he added Lee to his list. A twentieth-century German officer and military analyst, Major General Hugo Friedrich von Freytag-Loringhoven, in a discourse on great generals of modern history, wrote, "[They] acquired the ability to inspire great effort and self-sacrifice in others by strict self-discipline and strong religious faith. The purity of their characters was so evident that they seemed to be the incarnation of the ideal leader formulated by Clausewitz." Lee was the one non-German named by this writer to exemplify his point.

Any discussion of character as a quality of leadership in the Civil War must include Jackson, for in this respect he and Lee were remarkably similar. I surmise that the origins of this attribute in both men lay in their profound religious faith, mingled with their Virginia heritage of honor, manners, and regard for their fellow men. Whatever the origins, both men possessed this quality to the highest extent, and it gave both a power of authority and inspiration that transcended their acknowledged great technical capabilities.

Ironically, the most eloquent testimony to Lee's leadership of character comes from one of his most unremitting critics, the twentieth-century British general J. F. C. Fuller. After indicting Lee for faulty strategic conceptions and unsound logistical operations, Fuller wrote this amazing statement: "Few generals in history have been able to animate an army as Lee's self-sacrificing idealism animated the Army of Northern Virginia. . . . What this bootless, ragged, half-starved army accomplished is one of the miracles of history." One must wonder what Fuller would have said of Lee's generalship if he had admired it.

What I have said of Lee's leadership of character would be equally applicable to Jackson. Professor Robertson has written, "He demanded the impossible of his men for good reason: with God's abiding help, nothing was impossible." I would add: frequently nothing *was* impossible for Jackson. The operative words here are "with God's abiding help." Both Lee and Jackson drew strength and confidence from their unshakable religious faith; both prayed to God daily for victory; both attributed their victories to His blessing; both thanked Him fervently for the victories when they occurred.

Chancellorsville was a stunning Confederate triumph, but it came at high cost—Jackson's death. Lee best expressed what this loss meant to him: "He has lost his left arm, but I have lost my right"; "Any victory would be dear at such a price. I know not how to replace him"; "Such an executive officer the sun never shown upon. . . . Straight as the needle to the pole he advanced to the execution of my purpose."

Together, Lee and Jackson forged what figuratively might be called a synergistic relationship in which the effect of the whole exceeded that of the sum of its parts, the performance of each man galvanized by the presence of the other. The Army of Northern Virginia would continue after Chancellorsville to fight with remarkable skill and valor; it would play the crucial role in sustaining the Confederacy for two additional years of relentless warfare against increasing odds. But Jackson's death broke the great team. Neither Lee, nor his army, nor the Confederacy would ever be the same again.

Part Four

The South in Fact and in Myth

The South, America's
Will-o'-the-Wisp Eden

In an address to the leaders of the Democratic Party in New Orleans, Louisiana, during the 1964 presidential campaign, President Lyndon Johnson summoned a vision of a future Southland flowing with milk and honey. "I want us to put behind the problems of the past and turn toward the promise of the future," he said. "For Louisiana, and for the South, the meaning of our victory [in the forthcoming presidential election] will be a fresh burst of progress, not a new spate of problems." Calling upon the South to forget both the Mason-Dixon line and the color line in her pursuit of prosperity, and to accept the counsel of Robert E. Lee that she lay aside old animosities and rear her sons to be Americans, the President cast a tempting horoscope for the region. "From the tip of Texas to the tip of Florida," he declared, "this crescent of the Gulf offers one of the great opportunities of the Western World. . . . I see a day when New Orleans will stand as a queen city on this crescent—a center of trade with the world—a center of culture for the nation—a terminal for waterways reaching into the heart of America . . . a good and gracious city for your families to call home." Then in conclusion, "We are not going to lose that tomorrow in division over things of the past."[1]

True enough, President Johnson spoke these words as a politician seeking votes. Yet, after full allowance is made for political motives, his remarks still have the ring of sincerity. One observer aptly said of him, "He dreams of a South rid at last of its ancient racial grievances entering a new age of abundance and gracing the whole nation with a fresh flowering of Southern achievement."[2]

Indeed, President Johnson would have been alien to an abiding current of American thought if he had not believed in the promise of an abundant South. Since the first camp was pitched by Englishmen on Roanoke Island almost four centuries ago, Southern citizens and observers alike have been predicting that the region was just about to become the garden spot of the universe. "The air is temperate and wholesome there," wrote a chronicler of Sir Walter Raleigh's venture upon Roanoke Island, "the soil is fertile. . . . and in a short time the planters may raise . . . commodities . . . [that] will enrich themselves and those who trade with them."[3]

The happy theme of Southern bounty pervaded the literature of all her early settlements. "Virginia equals, if not exceeds all others in goodness of climate, soil, health, rivers, plenty, and all necessaries and conveniences of life. . . ." wrote a booster of the mother colony of the South. He believed that the very temperament of the Virginians was superior to that of other colonists. "If New England be called a receptacle of dissenters, and an Amsterdam of religion," he said, "Pennsylvania the nursery of Quakers, Maryland the retirement of Roman Catholicks, North Carolina the refuge of runaways, and South Carolina the delight of Buccaneers and pyrates, Virginia may be justly esteemed the happy retreat of true Britons and true churchmen for the most part; neither soaring too high nor drooping too low, consequently should merit the greater esteem and encouragement."[4]

The Carolinas also were said to abound in all resources needed for the production of wealth;[5] and the marvels of Georgia prompted one admirer to turn poet in his effort to do them justice. He wrote:

The Spring, which but salutes us here,
Inhabits there, and courts them all the Year;
Ripe Fruits and Blossoms on the same Tree live;
At once they promise what at once they give.
So sweet the Air, so moderate the Clime,
None sickly lives, or dies before his Time.
Heav'n sure has kept this Spot of Earth uncurst,
To shew how all Things were created first.[6]

The supreme example of such visions was John Law's use of an overflowing horn of plenty to symbolize the inexhaustible riches said to be awaiting emigrants to Louisiana.

At the end of the colonial era, the South bade fair to fulfill her promise of prosperity for all. A gracious plantation society throve along the tidewater section, while the yeomanry of the Piedmont and back country enjoyed a rude plenty. The severing of ties with England in the Revolution opened a fair prospect of increased well-being by sweeping away the planters' debts, which, almost like heirlooms, had been handed down from father to son; by confiscating and distributing the great estates of many wealthy Tories; by removing all restrictions on westward expansion; and by freeing the planters to sell their produce in the markets of the entire world.

Then an event occurred that kindled the highest hopes yet held for Southern affluence, an event that altered all the subsequent history of the region. In 1795 Eli Whitney invented the cotton gin, and the South began that great transition which ultimately would establish her as a "Kingdom of Cotton" from the Atlantic seaboard to the plains of Texas.

Southerners among the Founding Fathers trusted the laws of nature, if left free of governmental tampering, to bring the South into a rich agricultural destiny. "Our revenues once liberated by the discharge of the public debt," wrote Thomas Jefferson from his retirement at Monticello, "and its surplus applied to canals, roads, schools, etc., and the farmer will see his government supported, his children educated, and the face of his country made a paradise. . . . The path we are now pursuing leads directly to this end, which we cannot fail to attain unless our administration should fall into unwise hands."[7]

Immediately after the War of 1812 a group of nationalistic young Southern political figures, led by John C. Calhoun of South Carolina and Henry Clay of Kentucky, briefly abandoned the earlier Southern fear of governmental interference, and embraced economic nationalism as the source of Southern plenty. Supporting a bill in 1816 to establish tariff rates that would succor domestic industries, Calhoun argued that prosperity was the result of a combination of agriculture, manufactures, and commerce. "When our manufactures are grown to a certain perfection," he said, "as they soon will be under the fostering care of government, we will no longer experience the evils [of the recent war]. The farmer will find a ready market for his surplus produce; and what is almost of equal consequence, a certain and cheap supply of all his wants. His prosperity will diffuse itself to every class in the community."[8]

But the South quickly veered away from Calhoun's economic nationalism. Within a decade, Calhoun himself had turned against the tariff; from the mid-1830's to the Civil War, the South placed its highest hopes of riches upon slavery and cotton, and an open world market. To many Southerners of this period the economic millennium seemed almost to have arrived: they glowed with anticipation and pride as they expanded their plantations, purchased additional slaves, and built new and more ornate mansions. Senator James H. Hammond of South Carolina voiced the aspirations and the boast of the plantation South when in 1857 he claimed that the wealth and strength of the entire nation—indeed, of the entire world—rested upon Southern agriculture, and concluded with the ringing proclamation, "Cotton is King."[9]

The faith expressed by Senator Hammond found its ultimate manifestation in the movement for Southern independence. Addressing a convention of delegates from the slave states in Nashville, Tennessee, in 1850, the South Carolina lawyer and political thinker, Langdon Cheves, cried, "Unite, and you shall form one of the most splendid empires on which the sun ever shone [with] a soil the most fruitful, and a climate the most lovely. . . ."[10] Ten years later the city of Charleston greeted the South Carolina secession convention with paintings of wharves piled high with cotton and a harbor bristling with masts—visions of the blessings expected of Southern nationhood.[11]

The Civil War itself stimulated a diversification of Southern agriculture and an expansion of Southern industry. A Manufacturing and Direct Trade Association of the Confederate States was organized, with the famed factory master of the Old South, William Gregg, as president. Southern editors hailed the burgeoning mines and factories as harbingers of a self-sufficient South. Chattanooga called herself the "Pittsburgh of the South"; other communities assumed comparable suggestive titles.[12] The Confederacy seemed about to fulfill the hopes of one of her citizens, a prominent Louisiana sugar planter, who had predicted that she would achieve "prosperity . . . as permanent as earthly things may be."[13]

Such a happy end was not to come. Long before the collapse of the ill-starred Confederacy, these dreams of affluence had vanished in a nightmare of privation.

There were many all along who vehemently rejected the Old South's articles of faith. Northern and European abolitionists condemned the institution of slavery as severely on economic grounds as on moral principles. The most thorough and perceptive of the outside critics of the Old South, Frederick Law Olmsted, concluded that slavery was an economic millstone around the region's neck.[14]

The few remaining Southern abolitionists agreed with the Northern critics. "Lawyers, merchants, mechanics, laborers," wrote Cassius M. Clay of Kentucky, "How many clients do you find among [the slaves]? How many goods do you sell, how many hats, coats, saddles, and trunks do you make? . . . All our towns dwindle, and our farmers lose, in consequence [of slavery], all home markets. . . . A home market cannot exist in a slave state."¹⁵ The most disparaging book written by an antebellum Southerner, Hinton R. Helper's *The Impending Crisis of the South,* indicted slavery for the impoverishment of the entire white farmer and laboring population of the South. "The North has surpassed [the South] in everything," concluded Helper, "and is going farther and farther ahead of her every day. . . . The downward tendency of the South can be arrested only by the abolition of slavery." Remove this curse, he urged, and the section would reap the blessing that God Almighty had promised to the ancient Israelites on a comparable occasion. "And the Lord shall guide thee continually and satisfy thy soul in drought, and make fat thy bones; and thou shalt be like a watered garden, and like a spring of water, whose waters fail not."¹⁶

Though Olmsted's and Helper's books were repudiated by the Old South almost as vehemently as *Uncle Tom's Cabin* was, their central theme—that all of the region's material ills were caused by slavery—ultimately would become a truism on the lips of all critics of the Southern economy.

This theme provided the North in the Civil War with a war aim almost as compelling as that of the preservation of the Union or the emancipation of the slaves. Once the blight of slavery was removed, reasoned Northern leaders, the South would blossom forth into a New England below the Potomac or a Northwest below the Ohio. "The lands of the South will rapidly appreciate to double, treble, quadruple their former values," prophesied the New York *Tribune.* "Idleness will give way to Industry."¹⁷ Not only would the downtrodden Southern poor whites and the freed slaves quicken to the energizing Northern touch; the South would receive also a transfusion of vigorous Northern blood as multitudes of victorious soldiers would remain to enjoy her fertile soil and salubrious climate. "Schools and churches will be multiplied under Northern inspiration and example," predicted one Yankee observer; "industry, production, and intelligence will follow our arms, and when our forces withdraw instead of leaving a desolate country behind them, they will point to it as a blooming and regenerated Eden."¹⁸ This was an inspiring vision: the Garden freed of the serpent, and its inhabitants and their rescuers sharing its fruit undisturbed!

Radical Reconstruction after the Civil War was, at least in part, an effort to translate into reality these Northern visions of a purged and prosperous South. Hand in hand with the mischievous schemes of Reconstruction went innumerable plans for industrializing the defeated region, for rebuilding its railroads, redistributing its land, diversifying its agriculture, overhauling its tax and fiscal structure, uplifting its poor—both black and white—vitalizing its educational system, and purifying its churches. Along with the crooks and adventurers among the Northern newcomers were countless ex-soldiers who were sincerely sympathetic toward the stricken country, who were genuinely attracted to its soil, climate, and people, and who earnestly believed in its future. Within months after the war's end, Louisiana alone was estimated to be playing host to 50,000 Northern men engaged in lumbering, planting, and a great variety of other business activities. Inflated as this estimate doubtless is, it nevertheless indicates the promise of wealth which the South held in the minds of the conquerors.[19] The authors of what the Southern people have traditionally regarded as being the foulest crimes ever committed against their section—Carpetbaggery and Negro rule—were beguiled by the image of an opulent South.[20]

Optimism soon yielded to disillusionment as the Reconstruction experiment ran afoul of the realities of Southern life and the weaknesses of human nature. Corruption and incompetence, both real and imagined, united with the South's implacable hostility toward the freed Negroes and with the apathy of the North to bring about the overthrow of Reconstruction and to make its very name a hiss and a byword on the American tongue. Yet, even in abandoning Reconstruction, its protagonists did not give up all hope of an abundant South. Writing in 1875, and urging that Southern political and social affairs be left in Southern hands, Charles Nordhoff of the New York *Herald* said: "The South contains the greatest body of unreclaimed soil on this continent. Louisiana seems to me to have elements of wealth as great as California. Georgia has a great future as a manufacturing state, and will, I believe, within a few years tempt millions of Northern and European capital into her borders to engage in manufacture. Alabama now exports iron to Europe—in small quantities, to be sure—and her coal-fields and iron ores will make her the rival of Pennsylvania at no distant date. . . ."[21] And so it went for the entire region. Nothing could altogether blot out the vision of Southern plenty.

But the South emerged from Reconstruction almost as lifeless economically as she had been immediately after Appomattox. Plantation homes still lay in ruins, railroads were scarcely passable, towns were deserted and stores empty: the region's per capita wealth was reckoned at about 35 percent of that of the rest of the nation. "Fifteen years have gone over the

South," wrote a perceptive Northern journalist, "and she still sits crushed, wretched, busy displaying and bemoaning her wounds."[22]

Not all Southerners, however, sat in the ashes of despair. Even while outside observers shook their heads over the apparently incurable lethargy and poverty of the region, a group of young Southern economic evangelists were beginning to preach a fresh hope and to exhort their people to a renewed faith. The heaven of their economic religion was called the New South.

An energetic young Georgian, Henry W. Grady, editor of the Atlanta *Constitution,* was the most compelling spokesman of this movement. Multitudes, both North and South, were converted to the New South persuasion through Grady's facile pen and tongue. Born in 1851, the son of a well-to-do merchant who had lost his life in the Confederate army, and reared amid the abortive efforts of Reconstruction to industrialize and revitalize the South, Grady combined the heritage, the experience, the personal qualities, and the timeliness required to lead a great transition in Southern outlook. His vision of the South's future was that of a community blending the virtue and grace of the Old South, minus its weaknesses, with a vigor and industry copied from the triumphant North. Grady glorified the South's past and extolled those forces that had produced a Washington, a Jefferson, a Clay, and a Calhoun; he spoke with reverence of the men who had supported the Lost Cause, and declared that the New South ought to stand dumb and motionless rather than deny the greatness of Generals Lee and Jackson. But, he asserted, the New South rejoiced over the destruction of slavery and the preservation of the Union. The New South, as he put it, was the Old South under new conditions.[23]

Grady especially deplored the economic colonialism of the Old South—her dependence upon the North for manufactured wares and foodstuffs. His travesties for exposing this colonialism—his description of a prewar Georgia funeral, and his analysis of the ills of single-crop agriculture—have become Southern classics of a sort. The marble headstone for the Georgia funeral came from Vermont, said Grady, though the grave was dug through solid marble; the pine coffin came from Cincinnati, though the cemetery lay beside a pine forest; the iron nails, screws, and shovels came from Pittsburgh, though a mountain of iron ore overshadowed the graveyard; the wagon used as a hearse came from South Bend, Indiana, though hardwood and metals abounded in Georgia; the clothing on the body came from Cincinnati, though cotton fields spread in every direction about the burial ground. "[Georgia], so rich in undeveloped resources, furnished nothing for the funeral except the corpse and the hole in the ground," Grady declared, "and probably would have imported both of those if it could have been done."[24]

Once, while traveling through a particularly rich agricultural area in Pennsylvania, said Grady, he inquired the source of the remarkable prosperity. "Tobacco," was the reply. Later, traveling through a particularly poor agricultural section of North Carolina, Grady inquired the cause of such poverty. "Tobacco," was the reply. The difference was, he said, that in Pennsylvania tobacco was made the crown and money crop of a diversified agriculture, while in North Carolina tobacco was the sole crop, and the growers were obliged to purchase all foodstuffs and household necessities at premium prices.[25] "Develop Southern industry and diversify Southern agriculture," was Grady's repeated exhortation to the South.

Other voices were almost as powerful as Grady's in preaching the Gospel of the New South. Daniel A. Tomkins of South Carolina invoked the South's industrial past as an inspiration to an industrial future. Convinced by studying the federal census records of 1810 that the South Atlantic states had then produced more manufactured wares than New England and New York combined, and that slavery and cotton had sidetracked this promising career, Tomkins devoted his life to speaking, writing, investing, and laboring to build up in the South a new cotton textile industry that would rival the industry of New England. Sidney Lanier, the Georgia poet, called for a revolution in Southern farm tenure and agricultural methods. Walter Hines Page of North Carolina—and later, New York—supported a score or more of programs for what he called the "rebuilding of old commonwealths." Francis W. Dawson, Charleston publicist and capitalist, urged his people to "bring the cotton mills to the cotton fields." Richard H. Edmonds through the columns of the Baltimore *Manufacturers Record,* Henry Watterson in the pages of the Louisville *Courier-Journal,* Major E. A. Burke of New Orleans by means of press and public addresses, and a host of lesser figures in newspapers about the countryside, all sang the praises of a burgeoning industrial and commercial South.[26]

Grady and his fellow believers were convinced that the advent of the New South was at hand, and that it would fulfill all of the promises of affluence which had so long tantalized the region. In 1890, after quoting and endorsing a wide selection of authorities who said that the South was just about to become the center of the nation's industry, Grady exclaimed in rhapsody: "Surely, God has led the people of the South into this unexpected way of progress and prosperity. . . . The industrial system of the South responds, grows, thrills with new life, and it is based on sure and certain foundations. For it is built at the field, by the mine, in the field—from which come the cheapest and best and fullest supply of cotton, iron and wood! . . . The industries of other sections—distant from the source of supply—may be based on artificial conditions that in time may be broken. But the industrial system of the South is built on a rock—and it cannot be shaken!"[27] To which the South resounded with "amens."

The half-century following the appearance of Grady and his associates was a period of vast change for the section. In the Piedmont South arose a cotton textile industry that did indeed rival that of New England; at Birmingham arose an iron and steel industry that threatened the supremacy of Pittsburgh; in the cotton country arose a flourishing cotton oil industry; and in Louisiana and Texas arose one of the world's richest petroleum and chemical industries. Even the pine barrens of the South became a source of wealth with the discovery of ways to make paper out of soft pulpwood. At the same time, Southern agriculture throve as new methods and fertilizers enabled small farmers to compete with planters in growing cotton, and as great numbers of husbandmen turned their capital and efforts to the production of cattle, fruit, or vegetables. The prophecies of a New South seemed indeed to have come true.

The major prophets of this epoch—the Gradys, Tomkinses, and Dawsons—were followed by a series of minor prophets who offered fresh and expanded visions of the coming Utopia in the Southland.[28] An English observer in 1910 captured the spirit of this group when he wrote: "[This] great agricultural, industrial, and educational revival is rapidly transmuting the South from a ghost-haunted region of depression and impoverishment into one of the most eagerly progressive, and probably one of the wealthiest, of modern communities."[29] Seventeen years later, a distinguished Southern scholar—Professor Edwin Mims of Vanderbilt University—summed up these optimistic analyses of the region's affairs in a book bearing the significant title, *The Advancing South*. Professor Mims foresaw a South balancing diversified agriculture with diversified industry, and crowning her economic victories with comparable intellectual and artistic triumphs. If the people of the twentieth-century South would but prove true to their New South forebears, he concluded, "the time is not far off when scholarship, literature and art shall flourish, and when all things that make for the intellectual and spiritual emancipation of man shall find their home under Southern skies."[30]

Although the New South philosophy did not go entirely unchallenged at any time, the major critical appraisal of it on its own terms—that is, the South's economic well-being—appeared only when the Great Depression of the 1930's obliged all Americans to re-examine the premises of their social and economic beliefs. President Franklin D. Roosevelt's National Emergency Council, including a group of selected Southern scholars, laid bare the economic facts of life in the New South. In spite of all efforts to catch up with the rest of the nation, the council concluded, the South was still woefully behind. Her per capita annual income was hardly more than half of that of the nation as a whole; her agriculture was the most archaic and wasteful in the nation; her industry the most colonial; her out-migration of human talent the most crippling; her citizens generally the poorest housed, clothed, and fed; her sick the least adequately treated; and her children the least effectively educated. "The South," declared the President after receiving the report, "is the nation's economic problem No. 1."[31]

Realistic as it was in analyzing the region's shortcomings, the council did not repudiate the ancient vision of an opulent South. Its exposition of Southern possibilities sounded like a paraphrase of Henry W. Grady's rhetoric.[32] But the South could not achieve this goal unaided, reasoned the council. The federal government must come to the region's assistance by spending federal funds on Southern public works and services, by encouraging industries to move south, by providing favorable credit facilities to farmers and home builders, and by removing discriminatory taxes and freight rates.[33]

The epoch of President Roosevelt's New Deal and of World War II, with its aftermath of booming prosperity for the entire nation, has given the South the greatest affluence of its history. Most of the implicit recommendations of the National Emergency Council have been carried out: TVA, rural electrification, soil conservation, and farmers' and home builders' credit have long been in effect. Government price support has vastly increased the farmers' income. Discriminatory taxes on Southern cotton oil products, such as margarine, and prejudicial freight rates against Southern manufacturers have long been gone. The munitions and armaments industries of World War II, and the thriving aluminum, synthetics, and petrochemical industries of the post-war years have changed the base of the Southern

economy from agriculture to industry. Cotton has been dethroned and reduced to the ranks of the minor nobility.[34]

Finally, the most persistent of all problems affecting the region's economy—that of racial accommodation—has been attacked pointblank. All
players in the Southern drama have sought a solution to this difficulty as a
key to the fulfillment of their dreams of Southern betterment. The Old South
sought a solution in slavery; the abolitionists sought it in emancipation; the
Radicals of Reconstruction sought it in political equality for the freedmen;
the New South sought it in white supremacy and racial segregation.

Ever since the overthrow of Reconstruction, however, a minority of
white Southerners has insisted that segregation and suppression of the Negro retard the South economically even as they debase her morally. In the
late nineteenth century, Louisiana novelist George Washington Cable said
this discreetly in a book entitled *The Negro Question;* the Virginia industrialist Lewis Harvie Blair said it vehemently in a book entitled *Prosperity
of the South Dependent on the Elevation of the Negro.*[35] Although President Roosevelt's National Emergency Council recommended no specific
program to solve this problem, it did again call attention to the crippling
effects of Negro deprivation on the general Southern welfare.[36]

Beginning with the United States Supreme Court's school desegregation decision in 1954, and culminating in the passage by Congress of the
civil rights acts of the 1960's the federal government—both applauded and
assisted, and damned and resisted—has sought to solve the Southern racial
problem by fiat and persuasion, and, when necessary, by coercion.

This cluster of Southern developments—economic and social—since
World War II has brought forth a fresh chorus of voices ringing with optimism over the section's future.[37] A prime example of this trend appeared in
an address entitled "The South's Call to Greatness: Challenge to All Southerners," by a renowned Texas historian, the late Professor Walter P. Webb.
After cataloging the South's unmatched natural resources—her coastlines,
rivers, water power, climate, fertile soil, and metal and mineral deposits—
Professor Webb then reviewed the region's great recent gains in industry,
agriculture, per capita income, bank deposits, and ownership of corporate
stock. The South, he asserted, was "on the threshold of a new era. Chance
and circumstance [had] conspired to offer [her] a great opportunity." He
concluded by endorsing the words of a modern Southern industrialist, who
said: "The conscientious, level-headed citizens of the South may one day
hold the destiny of America in their hands."[38]

One would be foolish indeed to deny that since the Civil War, and especially during and since World War II, the South has taken giant strides in industry and prosperity. A century ago the South possessed less than 10 percent of the nation's industry and her per capita annual income was less than half that of the nation as a whole; today the South possesses better than 20 percent of the nation's industry and her per capita annual income is roughly 80 percent of that of the nation as a whole.

But figures and statistics are not infallible. Indeed, every prophet of Southern opulence since the days of Sir Walter Raleigh has enlisted arithmetic to support his optimism. Perhaps one ought to consider the line on a certain comic card which reads, "The hurrier I go, the behinder I get." If the application of this absurdity exaggerates the economic plight of the South—and admittedly it does do so—it at least suggests a comparable problem. It is instructive, and at the same time frustrating, to consider how much the Southern economy, notwithstanding its remarkable gains, has remained the same. For the South still lags seriously behind the rest of the nation economically. A statement issued in 1964 by the Federal Department of Health and Welfare is strikingly reminiscent of the report of President Franklin D. Roosevelt's National Emergency Council thirty years ago. The Welfare Department named Tunica County, Mississippi, as the poorest spot in the nation, then went on to list among the ten states with the highest number of impoverished families the following states of the South: Mississippi, Arkansas, South Carolina, Alabama, Tennessee, North Carolina, Kentucky, Georgia, and Louisiana.[39] In 1967 the annual income of the average citizen of Florida, the South's richest state according to personal per capita income, was more than $1,000 below that of Connecticut, the nation's richest. In 1968 the annual income of the average citizen of Mississippi, the South's poorest state, was more than $1,200 below the national average.[40] Thus the South remains the nation's economic problem No. 1.

The achievement of genuine economic parity by the South would seem to require a drastic alteration in the very nature of her society and economy, and to a degree, in the nature of the national economy as well. For the Southern economy remains highly colonial. The happy statistics on Southern industry do not reveal that it is still primarily extractive—concerned with drawing out the oil, mineral ores, timber, and farm products of the South to provide fuel, metal, and fiber for the national industrial machine. Or that Southern industry is disproportionately crude, leaving the fabrication of the finished, and therefore more expensive, products to be done outside of the region. Or that a great part of Southern industry is held by national corporations that are chiefly owned and managed by outsiders.[41]

Perhaps most serious of all, the figures on Southern progress do not expose the general weakness of the Southern educational system, which is expected to serve as the very incubator of a truly superior industry and economy. Notwithstanding strenuous efforts by the Southern population to create a strong school system, the high birth rate of the region combines with the relative lack of wealth to keep its schools behind those of other sections of the country. An eminent student of the South has recently said, "The South needs some first-rate universities and graduate schools to attract and hold the best students and the best professors it produces. At present, the region does not have a one of the ten or fifteen best universities in the country."[42] The same criticism can be made of the South's elementary and secondary schools. Nor, apparently, is the educational gap being closed. Only a short time ago the United States associate commissioner of education reported that the South's public schools are losing ground instead of gaining, in relation to those elsewhere. "The present generation of Southern students is more disadvantaged than was my generation," he declared.[43]

Three quarters of a century ago Henry W. Grady used the story of a Georgia funeral to dramatize the colonial nature of the Southern economy. Let us do the same today. Suppose Grady were to return to a funeral in the present South. Would he find everything changed? Admittedly many things would be different; but many would also be the same. Chances are that he would find the corpse today dressed in a suit made in Chicago, transported in a hearse made in Detroit, and buried in a casket made in St. Louis. Moreover, Grady would find a number of innovations in economic colonialism that have been added since his day. The bereaved family of the present would be calmed by tranquilizer pills made in Philadelphia, and supported by insurance payments from a company in Hartford where most of the life savings of the departed one had been invested. Perhaps the supreme irony of the modern Southern funeral would be that the very commodities imported for the occasion—the hearse, the clothes, and the casket—had been made by the hands of Southern-born laborers now living outside of their native region.

The South has persistently been the nation's greatest economic enigma—a region of want in the midst of boundless natural riches. It has been, and remains today, a land becoming and not a land become—a garden spot that beckons only to recede like a mirage when approached. It is America's will-o'-the-wisp Eden.

NOTES

1. New Orleans *Times Picayune,* October 10, 1964. This essay was originally presented by the author in an address sponsored by the Institute of Southern Culture, Longwood College, Farmville, Va., and is published here with the permission of that organization.

2. Ibid.

3. Thomas Hariot, *A Brief and True Report of the New Found Land of Virginia* (London, 1855), quoted in Stefan Lorant, *The New World* (New York, 1946), 276–77.

4. Hugh Jones, *The Present State of Virginia,* edited by Richard L. Morton (Chapel Hill, 1956), 83.

5. John Lawson, *Lawson's History of North Carolina,* edited by Frances Latham Harris (Richmond, 1952), 80–178; Newton D. Mereness (ed.), *Travels in the American Colonies* (New York, 1916), 397–401.

6. Pat. Tailfer and others, *A True and Historical Narrative of the Colony of Georgia,* edited by Clarence L. Ver Steeg (Athens, Ga., 1960), 12.

7. Thomas Jefferson to Dupont de Nemours, April 15, 1811, in Andrew A. Lipscomb and "Others" (eds.), *The Writings of Thomas Jefferson* (20 vols., Washington, 1904), XIII, 39.

8. Quoted in Robert L. Meriwether, *The Papers of John C. Calhoun* (2 vols., Columbia, 1959), I, 350.

9. *Congressional Globe,* 35th Congress, 1st Session, Appendix, 70.

10. Quoted in Rollin G. Osterweis, *Romanticism and Nationalism in the Old South* (New Haven, 1949), 133.

11. Charles P. Roland, *The Confederacy* (Chicago, 1960), 5.

12. Ibid., 69.

13. A. Franklin Pugh Plantation Diary (Louisiana State University Archives, Baton Rouge, La.), January 17, 1861.

14. Frederick L. Olmsted, *A Journey Through the Seaboard Slave States* (2 vols., New York, 1856), I, 213–15; and *Our Slave States: A Journey Through Texas* (3 vols., New York, 1837), II, xiii–xviii.

15. Eugene D. Genovese, "The Significance of the Slave Plantation for Southern Economic Development," *Journal of Southern History,* XXVIII (November, 1962), 457.

16. Hinton R. Helper, *The Impending Crisis of the South* (New York, 1860), 33–34, 412.

17. New York *Tribune,* December 24, 1864.

18. Milwaukee *Sentinel,* February 2, 1864. For comparable statements, see Columbus *Ohio State Journal,* November 23, 1861; Terre Haute *Daily Express,* September

16, 1862; Dubuque *Daily Times,* September 28, 1862; New York *Tribune,* August 25, December 25, 1863, January 23, December 24, 1864; Indianapolis *Daily Journal,* January 24, 1865; *Congressional Globe,* 37th Congress, 2nd Session, 1495, 2196; ibid., 3rd Session, 630; ibid., 38th Congress, 1st Session, 1188; ibid., 2nd Session, 484–85.

19. John T. Trowbridge, *The Desolate South, 1865–1866,* edited by Gordon Carroll (New York, 1956), and (Toronto, 1956), 212.

20. John Hope Franklin, *Reconstruction after the Civil War* (Chicago, 1961), 127–51; Francis Butler Simkins and Robert H. Woody, *South Carolina during Reconstruction* (Chapel Hill, 1932), 147–223, 266–311; Hodding Carter, *The Angry Scar* (Garden City, 1959), 310–21.

21. Charles Nordhoff, *The Cotton States in the Spring and Summer of 1875* (New York, 1876), 23.

22. C. Vann Woodward, *Origins of the New South, 1877–1913* (Baton Rouge, 1951), 107–11.

23. Henry W. Grady, *The New South* (New York, 1890), 146–47.

24. Ibid., 188–89.

25. Ibid., 208–09.

26. George T. Winston, *A Builder of the New South: Being the Story of the Life Work of Daniel Augustus Tomkins* (New York, 1920), 20–73, 84–94, 349–67; Sidney Lanier, *Retrospects and Prospects* (New York, 1899), 104–35; Walter Hines Page, *The Rebuilding of Old Commonwealths* (New York, 1902), 107–53; Broadus Mitchell, *The Rise of Cotton Mills in the South* (Baltimore, 1921), 77–159; Woodward, *Origins of the New South,* 144–48.

27. Grady, *The New South,* 193–95, 206–07.

28. Hilary A. Herbert, *Why the Solid South?* (Baltimore, 1890), 430–42; Philip A. Bruce, *The Rise of the New South* (Philadelphia, 1905), 472.

29. William Archer, *Through Afro-America: An English Reading of the Race Problem* (New York, 1910), xiv.

30. Edwin Mims, *The Advancing South* (New York, 1927), 20–79, 80–112, 315–16.

31. Arthur Goldschmidt, "The Development of the U.S. South," *Scientific American* (September, 1963), 225; National Emergency Council, *Report on Economic Conditions of the South* (Washington, 1938), 8.

32. National Emergency Council, *Report on Economic Conditions of the South,* 5–8.

33. Goldschmidt, "The Development of the U.S. South," *Scientific American* (September 1963), 228.

34. John S. Ezell, *The South Since 1865* (New York, 1963), 438–39; Thomas D. Clark, *The Emerging South* (New York, 1961), 55–56.

35. George Washington Cable, *The Negro Question* (New York, 1890), 51–53; C. Vann Woodward, "A Southerner's Answer to the Negro Question," *The Reporter* (February 27, 1964), 41–44.

36. National Emergency Council, *Report on Economic Conditions of the South,* 19–20.

37. Ezell, *The South Since 1865,* 451; Clark, *The Emerging South,* 121–23; Gold-

schmidt, "The Development of the U.S. South," *Scientific American* (September 1963), 228–29.

38. Walter P. Webb, "The South's Call to Greatness: Challenge to All Southerners," an address to the Seventh Annual Conference, The Texas Council for Social Studies, San Marcos, Texas, June 29, 1959.

39. New Orleans *States-Item,* November 24, 1964.

40. *Survey of Current Business* (April 1968), 14.

41. C. Vann Woodward, "The New South Fraud Is Papered by Old South Myth," Washington *Post,* July 9, 1961.

42. Ibid.

43. Quoted in New Orleans *States-Item,* December 19, 1964.

The South of the Agrarians

The South of the 1920s, like the South at any other point in its long history, was something of an enigma. It was in the United States and of the United States, yet it was distinct from the rest of the United States. As late as 1941 Wilbur J. Cash would say the South was not quite a nation within a nation, but that it was the next thing to it.

Southerners did not have to be taught from books that the South's history was different from that of the nation as a whole. Everybody knew, however imperfectly, that the South had once been a Cotton Kingdom with plantations worked by black slaves; that it had attempted to become an independent nation, only to be defeated in war and forced to remain within the Union; that the slaves had been freed in the course of the struggle and then had been granted citizenship, both against the will of southern whites; that the South was occupied by federal armies and subjected to the authority of Carpetbaggers, Scalawags, and ex-slaves; and that this regime had been overthrown by southern white violence and fealty to the Democratic party.

The actual history of these events was often twisted in the southern mind, exaggerated by time and telling, by prejudice and pride. The legendary Old South became an idyllic land of kind and gracious masters and obedient and happy slaves. According to the late-nineteenth-century Virginia novelist Thomas Nelson Page, the society of antebellum Virginia was the noblest that ever lived. He believed even the moonlight shone brighter on it. The Civil War, in the romantic view, was an epic in Confederate valor against the northern hordes; Reconstruction was a tyrannical effort to impose African barbarism on an honorably defeated people. From these travails the South had emerged victorious in spirit even if held guilty of the cardinal sins in the national mythology—the sins of slavery and rebellion. Indeed, southerners still viewed themselves as guardians of the elemental American verities. A classic expression of this sentiment came from the lips of Senator Carter Glass of Virginia when in 1941 he was asked the reason for the South's strong interventionist feelings toward the war in Europe. It is, he said, because of the southerners' superior character and understanding of the problem.

Obviously the South was physically different from the rest of the country, a difference that had played a subtle but powerful role in creating a distinctive set of attitudes and code of behavior. Southern summers were unusually long, hot, and humid, without the comfort of modern air conditioning; such expressions as "ninety degrees in the shade" and "the long, hot summer" were more meaningful when spoken with a southern accent. Southern winters were relatively short and mild. Growing seasons for field crops and flowers—and for grass and weeds—were twice as long in the Deep South as in the far North. Every student of the southern scene has been impressed by the influence of the weather. The climate slowed the pace of things in the South, giving the region a reputation for easy living, or, in a more disparaging word, laziness. A historian of early colonial Virginia said the inhabitants there were "climate struck"; he explained their behavior by saying people never work hard for themselves where God has already done so much for them. One of the most famous books ever written on the region, Ulrich B. Phillips' *Life and Labor in the Old South,* opens with the line: "Let us begin by discussing the weather, for that has been the chief agency in making the South distinctive."

The distinguishing element of southern society that most quickly met the eye was the racial contrast. As the home in 1920 of some nine million Americans of African descent, the South was the nation's Black Belt. Southern blacks accounted for more than four fifths of all blacks in the United States and more than one fourth the total population of the South itself. In the Deep South the density was greater; in two states, South Carolina and Mississippi, blacks were in the majority.

Everywhere in the South the blacks were a caste at the foot of the social and economic ladder. Most white southerners looked upon them as being inferior in intellect, a childlike and emotional race placed by God or nature under the white man's tutelage and authority. To many religiously devout white southerners, the blacks, as descendants of the Old Testament figure Ham, were consigned by divine fiat to the condition of servants because their remote ancestor had shamed his father, Noah, by looking upon Noah's nakedness while he was drunk on an experimental beverage called wine.

Some southern politicians courted white approval by referring, perhaps whimsically, to the black man as the "missing link" in Darwin's scale of evolution. Racial segregation in schools, churches, cemeteries, drinking fountains, and all other forms of public accommodation was required by law—the so-called Jim Crow statutes—as well as by the mores of the society. Within this system was a great latitude for paternalism and indulgence along with contempt and mistreatment. Strong ties of affection developed among countless individual whites and blacks. But all classes of whites agreed that the blacks must "stay in their places." So apparently immutable was this determination that Ulrich B. Phillips called it the "Central Theme" of southern history.

The South was traditionally the poor cousin of the affluent American society. Its economy had always been predominantly agricultural; at the time of the Civil War the eleven Confederate states produced less than 10 percent of the nation's manufactured wares as measured by sale value. In spite of great efforts after the war to industrialize itself, the South in the early decades of the twentieth century was still largely agricultural. It still depended heavily on its historic crop—cotton. Indeed, in some ways cotton dominated the South more in the 1920s than it had on the eve of the Civil War. There were now four times as many acres in cotton as in the 1850s. The regional economy was essentially colonial. Southerners sold their farm produce and natural resources such as timber and oil to feed the national industrial machine, at the same time importing from the North the bulk of their manufactured goods such as plows, harvesters, and automobiles. Estimates in 1919 indicated that southern per capita income was 40 percent below the national average. The disparity between the southern income and that of the wealthier states of the Northeast, Midwest, or Pacific Coast was much wider. A survey taken in the late 1930s caused President Franklin D. Roosevelt to call the South the nation's "No. 1 economic problem."

Southern politics served to protect the region's traditional interests and prejudices within the national political framework. Having emerged from Reconstruction through what may be termed paramilitary means under the leadership of former Confederate officers, the southern voters long gave these men their full allegiance at the polls. Election to southern office in the late nineteenth century without the badge of honor of a Confederate battle wound was almost unheard of. When General Francis T. Nicholls of Louisiana was running for the governorship of that state, minus an arm and foot lost in the war, he was introduced to audiences with the words: "I present to you what is left of General Nicholls." A South Carolinian writing in the 1930s remembered United States Senator Wade Hampton, a former Confederate hero, as "the limping apotheosis of the Lost Cause."

To the southern people such men were known as "The Redeemers" because they had saved the South from its alleged tormentors. To less sympathetic, outside observers they were "The Bourbons," who, like the restored royal family of France, had neither forgotten anything of the ancient regime nor learned anything from the Revolution. Under whatever title, they were conservative in their political, social, and economic views. Their major commitments to the voters were to keep whites in control of affairs and to practice competence, honesty, and frugality in running their administrations. To the first of these commitments they were faithful; to the rest of them their devotion was more erratic.

An agrarian or small-farmer revolt against the Redeemers (or Bourbons, if you please) occurred near the end of the century. Led by such fiery orators as Tom Watson of Georgia and Pitchfork Ben Tillman of South Carolina, the small farmers of the South gained a more influential voice in regional politics. Early in the twentieth century the reform movement known as progressivism, championed largely by the middle classes, took control of most southern state administrations and sent many of their leaders to Congress. By 1920, southern politics had come to represent a blend of all three of these forces.

But this diversity was overshadowed by a stronger unity. Whether Bourbon, Agrarian, or Progressive, the vast majority of voting southerners were Democrats, thus giving the region the name "the Solid South." Many voters became known as "Yellow Dog Democrats" because they were said to have declared they would support a yellow dog for office rather than a Republican. To add spice to political life, and perhaps to give emphasis by humorous distortion, the story was sometimes told of such a Democrat who on one occasion was so displeased with his party's candidate that he voted for the Republican opponent. Reminded of his vow, he admitted having made it. "But," he explained, "the Democrats didn't run a yellow dog this time, and lower than that I will not go." The Democratic primaries, almost everywhere "lily white" (closed to blacks), were in effect the final elections. Frequently the Republicans declined even to put up candidates. The fundamental characteristics of southern politics were Democratic hegemony and white supremacy.

To nonsoutherners the South was a backward country area relieved here and there by the charm of a Charleston, a Mobile, or a Savannah, or of a white-columned, rural antebellum plantation mansion. The old abolitionist fantasy of dividing white southerners into two classes only—the fabulously rich and powerful lords of manors and the squalid and torpid poor whites—still had a strong influence on popular thought. The region was, in fact, the most rural part of twentieth-century America. Three out of four southerners in 1920 were classified by the federal census as being rural. Approximately half the total population made their livings as farmers, neither rich nor poor in the traditional planter or poor-white sense. The bulk of the non-farming population lived in the thousands of towns and villages that dotted the countryside. Only about 10 percent of the region's inhabitants lived in cities of 100,000 or more population. Finally, the cities themselves were more or less large country towns because they were relatively small (Atlanta 200,000, for example), and because of the strong ties of blood and culture existing between the city folk and their country kin.

Thus, despite the inroads of industrialism and urbanism, the South of the 1920s preserved in great measure the conventions and flavor of the old rural life. Along with the newfangled nightclubbing and such immensely popular spectator sports as college football, many of the more traditional diversions remained, including horsemanship and hunting and fishing. Because of the mildness of the climate, the great expanses of open fields and woods, and the countless natural streams and lakes, the South probably had more hunters and fishers than any other population of comparable numbers in the world.

The core of southern society was the family, and the South's failure to receive any significant proportion of the European immigrants who entered the United States in the nineteenth century and early twentieth century gave the entire southern population a family-like homogeneity. Actual blood ties were extraordinarily strong; outsiders said any two southerners who got together would ultimately discover they were cousins. Family reunions and community homecomings were memorable social occasions, sometimes attracting stray kinfolk from as far away as Chicago or Los Angeles. Home cooking was a source of immense family pride, featuring dishes made from the secret recipes of Aunt Nancy or Aunt Millie, ladies who, at least in some instances, were spinster casualties of the Civil War. Seasoning the food was usually done by the pinch and taste method. The hot biscuit, cornbread, and fried chicken line was as authentic a regional boundary as the Mason-Dixon line.

Though the South was the stronghold of the Prohibition movement, and the southern churches inveighed also against dancing, card-playing, and what was euphemistically called "petting," the region was known as well for its hard drinking and other weaknesses of the flesh. In New Orleans it had a community celebrated far and wide for its love of pleasure—a city of sin at the end of the big river. Someone has remarked that New Orleans was a safety valve for a people reared in a strict Calvinistic tradition; that the city provided them an opportunity for escaping their inhibitions and discharging their emotions, even if frequently it was done by surrogate. Cash said the South offered the world's greatest paradox of hedonism in the midst of puritanism.

Drawing upon the aristocratic, plantation ideal, southerners gave allegiance to the cult of manners, for they looked upon form as being indivisible from function or substance. The words *chivalry* and *chivalric,* free of any sense of derision, were not at all uncommon on the southern tongue. As late as the mid-1930s in the city of Nashville (or in other southern cities) one might see a half-dozen men rise simultaneously to offer a woman a seat on a crowded trolley. Even the poorest and least-educated southerner, said Cash, deported himself with a certain level-eyed courtesy and ease of bearing derived from the customs of the gentry. Hand in hand with the cult of manners went a cult of violence. Being a population of hunters, and perhaps also because they were votaries of a strong military tradition, almost all southerners owned firearms. Southerners more than others were prone to resort to trial by combat in settling personal disputes. The region steadily held the nation's highest homicide rates. The emphasis on manners coupled with that on violence gave rise to the saying that a southerner would remain polite until he was angry enough to kill.

Accompanying and reinforcing the economic, political, and social factors of southern distinctiveness was a set of equally distinguishing cultural characteristics. Among these, no force was stronger than that of religion in developing and sustaining a southern ethos. Church membership was more common in the South than elsewhere, and most southerners who were not on the church rolls shared the world view of those who were on the rolls. Overwhelmingly orthodox Protestant, the membership was heavily concentrated in the white and black branches of the southern Baptist and Methodist churches, the southern Presbyterian church, and the Churches of Christ. Many southerners also were attracted to the numerous Pentecostal and Holiness bodies, which were largely of southern origin.

Edwin McNeill Poteat, Jr., said the churches were arranged along class lines, the Episcopalians at the top of the social and economic scale, the Presbyterians in the middle, and the Methodists and Baptists at the bottom. Though he omitted a number of groups and, doubtless intentionally, exaggerated the class thesis for those he listed, his statement was accurate in that southern religion did accommodate itself to social distinctions. There was a saying handed down from the Old South that many roads lead to heaven, but the true southern gentleman would follow the Episcopal route.

The variety of denominations and their class arrangements failed to destroy the region's theological conformity. Regardless of church affiliation, the Word of God as revealed in the Bible continued to provide the masses of the southern population their fundamental philosophy. Southerners accepted scientific technology, but they would not yield the belief that "man holds a position in the universe under divine guidance"; they refused to convert science into a religion. Southern belief in a literal interpretation of the Bible was strong enough to cause many states to enact statutes prohibiting the teaching in state-supported schools of any idea, including Darwin's theory of the evolution of species, that contradicted the literal Genesis account of the creation of man.

An English writer traveling in the South in 1910 observed: "The South is by a long way the most simply and sincerely religious country that I was ever in. . . . It is a country in which religion is a very large factor in life, and God is very real and personal." At mid-century Hodding Carter was still moved to say: "Though the citadels crumble, the South remains the great western-world stronghold of Protestant, fundamentalist Christianity. . . . That thing called the old-time religion is in the blood of most of us, and if it is laughed at, the laughter has an accompaniment of inescapable inner, esoteric warning that the ways of God are not to be mocked by man."

Southern churches were not completely untouched by the winds of liberalism, or modernism, as it was usually called in the South. In public matters the leading denominations supported the aims of the Progressive movement, including such humanitarian measures as the regulation of the working conditions for women and children, the right of laborers to form and join unions, and the entire set of political reforms that were then being heralded as forces for the uplift of society. The churches also sponsored the building of hospitals, schools, orphanages, and homes for the outcast and indigent. Many educated southerners accepted such unorthodox teachings as the Higher Criticism of the Bible and the theory of the evolution of man.

The upper economic and social classes tended to substitute for the religious fervor and emotionalism of earlier times a comfortable reconciliation with secular ideas and worldly ways.

But the dominant religious energies of the South were directed to otherworldliness and the salvation of individual souls rather than the reform of society. Southerners were the least utopian of Americans; the teachings of the Social Gospel, popular in other areas, made slow headway in the South. The precepts of southern religion reinforced the lessons of southern history to keep the people from believing in the earthly perfectability of man. Robert Penn Warren remained true to his southern upbringing when he caused the central figure in his novel *All the King's Men* (published in 1945) to say he had thoroughly learned about the sinful nature of mankind in his childhood Sunday school training in Louisiana.

Religious conservatism touched all aspects of life in the South. It kept alive the puritanism that struggled with the natural love of pleasure among the people. It emphasized the vital role of the family in God's plan for society. It strengthened the color line both through its theological explanation of race relations and through the role of the churches, white and black, in observing social convention. Even the region's economic plight was alleged by some to be the result of its religious convictions. "In religion," said Broadus Mitchell, "the past has stretched forth her hand and held us fast. . . . We have remained like Mary enraptured at the Master's feet, and have refused to have a part in the workaday world, or be like Martha, 'anxious about many things.'" One of the most knowledgeable students of the southern mind, C. Vann Woodward, has written that the "exuberant religiosity" of the South persisted powerfully into the twentieth century and was largely responsible for the homogeneity of the people and the readiness with which they responded to common impulses; that, indeed, it explained much of the survival of a distinctive regional culture.

Southern literature also supported and reflected the region's outlook on itself and the rest of the world. Because this topic is to be thoroughly discussed by others in later gatherings of this symposium, I shall not attempt any analysis of it here. Permit me to say simply that the South has traditionally been a highly verbal society. The politicians, preachers, journalists, novelists, and poets of the Old South mobilized the language in defense of slavery and the other activities and ideas that made up the southern "way of life." In the years after the Civil War the most celebrated southern writers, the local colorists, presented a mellow view of the Old South and superimposed upon it the tragic theme of the Lost Cause of the Confederacy. Thomas Nelson Page, quoted earlier in this essay, was perhaps the most popular of this group. Finally, the entire body of southern writers and rhetoricians provided the base for the twentieth-century flowering of southern letters known as the Southern Renascence, a most significant element in which was the Fugitive and Agrarian movement at Vanderbilt University.

The South was never particularly distinguished in the fine arts. Only in its architecture, in the adaptation of European and classical modes to the southern environment, did the Old South demonstrate an outstanding aesthetic quality. The architecture of the post–Civil War South was often imitative and banal. There were, of course, exceptions. A notable one was the work of Neel Reid, an early twentieth-century Atlanta architect, who inspired a revival of the colonial Georgian style tastefully set in the wooded hills on the outskirts of his city.

The most sustained artistic effort to express overtly the region's awareness of its historic distinctiveness occurred in sculpture. The chief activity in this medium during the half-century following the Civil War was the placing of a nondescript Confederate soldier in stone on virtually every courthouse square. Sculpture of genuine merit included the recumbent statue of General Robert E. Lee at Lexington, Virginia, by Edward M. Valentine, the equestrian statue of Lee at Richmond, by Jean Antoine Mercié, and the recumbent statue of General Albert Sidney Johnston at Austin, by Elisabet Ney. In 1923 on the face of Stone Mountain in Georgia, Gutzon Borglum began the colossal figures of Lee, Jefferson Davis, and General Stonewall Jackson, but the work soon halted and would remain unfinished until after World War II.

The most original artistic contribution made by the South was its folk music. Of greatest appeal during the 1920s were the black spirituals, which in turn brought recognition to other forms of Afro-American music and its derivatives, including blues and jazz. The ancestral white folk music, ballads, and white spirituals also remained alive in the rural and mountainous areas of the South, but these styles and their offshoots, hillbilly music and ultimately country music and gospel music, would be slower in claiming the enthusiasm of the American public.

Clearly the South in the 1920s exhibited a great variety of social and cultural traits. The region was not isolated geographically from the rest of the nation. It offered no impenetrable linguistic barrier, though its differences in accent and cadence may have tempted some observers to say of northerners and southerners what Shaw said of Englishmen and Americans: that they were two people separated by a common language. The South was not impervious to outside ideas. But as David M. Potter has convincingly explained, the region's long and intimate experience as a rural society had the effect of preserving into the twentieth century strong elements of an older folk culture which tended to offset, even to repudiate, the urban-industrial culture that by now was far advanced in the other major sections of the country. In this folk culture, said Potter, the people retained a more direct and primal relationship with the land, with nature in general, and with one another. Also, one might add, a more direct and primal relationship with God.

But forces had long been at work that threatened the traditional culture of the South and sought to bring the region into the wide channel of national progress. The banner under which these forces marched was that of the New South. A title actually coined by a Union officer during the Civil War, the expression "The New South" was taken over in the 1870s and 1880s by a group of enterprising young southerners who by circumstance and timing were ready to lead an important transition in southern thinking. The most imaginative and most colorful of the group was the Atlanta journalist and raconteur Henry W. Grady.

Grady and his cohorts did not consciously assault the region's culture. These men held a vision of the future in which the virtue and grace of the Old South, now that it was rid of the burden of slavery, would blend with a vigor and industry copied from the victorious North. The New South, as they expressed it, was simply to be the Old South under new conditions. Thus, in the words of a leading present-day student of the movement, Paul M. Gaston, the original New South adherents sought to maintain a "vital nexus" between the modern impulses of material progress and the traditional values of the South. The unanswered question was: "Would the vital nexus hold?"

The New South advocates deplored the economic colonialism of the South, its dependence on the North for manufactured wares and even for many of its items of food. Grady illustrated this dependence with two stories, neither original to him, but both of which he made famous. In one of the stories he described a pre–Civil War Georgia funeral, for which, he said, the hearse, the clothing, and every other commodity had been imported from the North—except the corpse and the hole in the ground. Both of these probably would have been imported, Grady said, if it had been possible to do so. In his other story Grady told of having made two trips, one in a section of Pennsylvania grown rich through the planting of tobacco and another in a section of North Carolina impoverished through the planting of the same kind of crop. The difference was, he explained, that in Pennsylvania tobacco was the money crop of a diversified agriculture while in North Carolina it was grown to the neglect of everything else, thus obliging the farmers to purchase all their necessities from outsiders at premium cost. Grady and his associates urged the South to become prosperous through industrialization and the diversification of agriculture.

The New South spokesmen were convinced by their own rhetoric that the region was becoming the very garden spot of American abundance. Grady in 1890 wrote rhapsodically: "Surely God has led the people of the South into this unexpected way of progress and prosperity. The industrial system of the South responds, grows, thrills with new life, and it is based on sure and certain foundations. For it is built at the field, by the mine, in the field—from which come the cheapest and best and fullest supply of cotton, iron and wood! . . . The industries of other sections—distant from the source of supply—may be based on artificial conditions that in time may be broken. But the industrial system of the South is built on a rock—and it cannot be shaken."

Events during the closing years of the nineteenth century and the opening years of the present century gave the illusion of fulfilling the New South dream. In the Piedmont South arose a textile industry that threatened to replace New England as the great center of American spindles and looms; in Birmingham arose an iron and steel industry that seemed to qualify it to be called the Pittsburgh of the South; in the cotton country arose a flourishing cotton oil industry; and in Texas and Louisiana arose one of the world's richest petroleum and chemical industries. At the same time, southern agriculture throve as new methods and fertilizers enabled small farmers to compete with planters in growing cotton, and as many landowners turned their capital and efforts to the production of cattle, fruit, or vegetables. In 1910 an English observer could have been speaking for the late Henry W. Grady in saying: "[This] great agricultural, industrial, and educational revival is rapidly transmuting the South from a ghost-haunted region of depression and impoverishment into one of the most eagerly progressive, and probably one of the wealthiest, of modern communities."

Meanwhile, the Progressive political movement that swept through the southern Democratic ranks in the early years of the twentieth century was an ideal vehicle for the cause of the New South. Southern progressivism reached high tide with the election of President Woodrow Wilson, a Virginia-born son of one of the founders of the southern Presbyterian church. The South voted solidly for Wilson, and he responded by establishing the most southern administration since the Civil War. Seven southerners held positions in Wilson's cabinets, and southern senators and congressmen played a dominant role in the enactment of the body of legislation that Wilson called the "New Freedom." Southern spokesmen played a strong part also in the events leading to the American entry into World War I and in supporting the military effort when war came. The fullness of southern participation in the conflict seemed to place a final seal on the covenant of national unity that had been temporarily broken by the secession of the South more than half a century before.

On the surface, the South of the post–World War I decade was in many ways indistinguishable from other parts of the country. Southern cities had their skyscrapers even if they were dwarfed by those of New York or Chicago. Southern metropolises had their continuous snarls of automobile and pedestrian traffic and noise. They hummed with commerce and a growing industry. The booster spirit was strong. If Grady had come to life in one of the larger southern communities, he would have believed his prophecies fulfilled beyond all his hopes.

But the national image of the South emphasized aspects of its behavior and appearance other than its integration into the American political, economic, and social mainstream. Nonsouthern views on the region were not altogether different from some of those cherished by southerners. Perhaps out of a sense of need to escape the stultifying effects of a rampant urban-industrialism, nonsoutherners helped keep alive the picture of the romantic Old South—the land of moonlight, magnolias, and mint juleps. There was also a less flattering image of the South that existed along with the romantic one in the nonsouthern mind. George B. Tindall has called this other image that of the "Benighted South."

The Benighted South was old stock in the great American morality theater. It began before the Civil War with the abolitionist crusade against slavery. Certainly this zealous reform movement was right in condemning forced servitude. But ultimately the accusations went far beyond this to become a raging philippic against an entire people and their culture. No area of southern life escaped the sting of northern politicians, editors, preachers. Southern politics, according to them, was an exercise in oligarchy and conspiracy, southern religion a blasphemy, southern education a mockery, southern family life a debauchery, southern character a morass of barbarism and degradation. In an abolitionist book on the southern Methodist church titled, significantly, *The Brotherhood of Thieves,* this denomination was said to be "more corrupt than any house of ill fame in New York." The whole South was referred to as one great brothel. In blessing John Brown's attempt to incite the slaves to a general insurrection, Wendell Phillips cried: "Virginia is a pirate ship, and John Brown sails the sea a Lord High Admiral of the Almighty with His commission to sink every pirate he meets on God's ocean of the nineteenth century." Professor Frank L. Owsley, a member of the Agrarian writers, once wrote: "One has to seek in the unrestrained and furious invective of the totalitarians to find a near parallel to the language that the Abolitionists and their political fellow travelers used in denouncing the South and its way of life. Indeed, as far as I have been able to ascertain," he continued, "neither Dr. Goebbels nor . . . other Axis propaganda agents ever so plumbed the depths of vulgarity and obscenity."

After the abolition of slavery and the defeat of secession in the Civil War, followed by a turbulent and recriminatory, but brief, period of Reconstruction, the North and South turned to the task of learning to live together in a reasonable state of amity. For a half century the southern image improved in the American mind because national unity, sectional reconciliation, was the imperative of the era. The romantic picture of the Old South and the optimistic picture of the New South became predominant in the North as well as in the South. Northern readers could not get enough of the writings of the southern local colorists. Three of the most thoughtful northern writers—Herman Melville, Henry James, and Henry Adams—wrote works in which southerners in the decades after the Civil War remained virtuous amid the crassness and venality of American life, especially that in the nation's capital.

Twentieth-century America inherited strong traces of both images of the South, but by now the need for sectional comity no longer seemed so pressing. There were other imperatives, and the South was the most obvious deviant from the nation's image of itself. The South was the locale of the most visible practices of racial discrimination, religious fundamentalism, arrested cultural development, conservative politics, and retarded economy. The region was an irresistible target for the new century's outspoken social critics. It was the very favorite target of the most flamboyant of these critics, the popular Baltimore essayist, cynic, and lampoonist H. L. Mencken.

In 1917 Mencken opened fire with an essay in which he gave the South the name "Sahara of the Bozart." "One thinks of the interstellar spaces," he said, "of the colossal reaches of the now mythical ether. . . . It would be impossible in all history to match so complete a drying-up of a civilization." Later he wrote a piece calling the South the "Bible Belt," a scathing attack upon what he considered the narrowness and bigotry of its religious outlook, which he denounced as "Baptist and Methodist barbarism." "No bolder attempt to set up a theocracy was ever made in the world," he wrote, "and none ever had behind it a more implacable fanaticism." To him, Prohibition was the worst crime committed by the southern religionists. He said the passage of the Prohibition amendment to the federal Constitution caused southerners to gloat "in their remote Methodist tabernacles as they gloat over a hanging."

The occurrence in 1925 at Dayton, Tennessee, of the trial of a public school teacher for violating the state's antievolution law brought Mencken to the height of his denunciation of the South. Among other equally elegant expressions, he damned the area as the "bunghole of the United States, a cesspool of Baptists, a miasma of Methodism, snake-charmers, phoney real-estate operators, and syphilitic evangelists." Oddly, Mencken's outpourings seem to have eluded Professor Owsley's search for a parallel to the vulgarity and obscenity of the abolitionists.

All this, then, was the immediate setting for the emergence of the Agrarian authors. They lived in a South that was significantly behind the rest of the nation according to every measure of progress: a South that yet preserved a great body of its traditional beliefs and values: a South that bore a heavy burden of national scorn.

The Agrarians were, of course, scholars and men of letters in addition to being southerners. They were part of a world community of literary figures, such as Joyce and Eliot, many of whose ideas they shared. Professor Louis D. Rubin has wisely written that one should not read the Agrarians' manifesto, *I'll Take My Stand,* as a treatise on economics and politics or as a guide to regional social structuring. Instead, he says, one should read it as a commentary on the nature of man.

Yet the Agrarians *were* southerners, and their response to the world situation was unmistakably a southern response as well as a philosophical one. The issuance of their famous book was in part precipitated by the diatribes being hurled against the region. John A. Rice (a southerner, but not one of the Agrarians) once wrote that regardless of the many differences among southerners, there was a certain inner unity that became evident in the way they reacted to outside criticism. All southerners, he said, tended to boil at the same point. Various of the Agrarians have made clear that the Dayton trial and the ridicule of southern institutions caused by it brought them to the boiling point. In forming their reply, the Agrarians drew upon time-honored southern perceptions and convictions. Finally, they were responding to a mood of the South itself, because they saw that the modern advocates of a New South were about to abandon the "vital nexus" with the traditional South; that they were poised for a mighty effort to make the dream of industrial and material progress come true at whatever cost to other values. The Agrarians took this occasion to warn of the consequences before it was too late. Or so they hoped.

Happy Chandler

The 1935 Kentucky governor's election had just ended. In the flood of con-
gratulations to Albert Benjamin Chandler over his stunning victory, a former companion wrote: "Your biography up to the present would be more
thrilling and sensational than the best of Horatio Alger's works." It was an
apt comment. For Chandler is the very incarnation of the Horatio Alger tradition in American life—the tradition of rising from rags to riches through
pluck, proper conduct, hard work, and unflinching determination. Nor was
Chandler himself unaware of the parallel between his life and the lives of
the young men in the more than one hundred Horatio Alger novels. As a
youngster he was a voracious reader of these success allegories, books with
such suggestive titles as *Ragged Dick: or Street Life in New York with the
Boot-Blacks,* or *Struggling Upward,* or *Jed, The Poorhouse Boy.* The young
Chandler always identified himself completely with the hero.

Chandler was not actually born to rags, as were the Horatio Alger figures, though on July 14, 1898, he was born into a family of severely limited
means. His parents, Joseph Sephus Chandler (known familiarly as "Uncle
Joe") and Callie Sanders Chandler, lived on a small farm one mile from the
little town of Corydon in the Pennyroyal section of western Kentucky. Life
was stern for them, as it was, of course, for most small farmers in the South
during those times. When Chandler was only four years old, life became far
sterner for him. That year his mother left the family to go her own way. The
account of the parting is poignant in the extreme: how the lad trailed his
mother down to the gate on the road where a buggy waited to take her away,
followed her weeping and begging her not to leave. But leave she did; as a
child he was not again to experience a mother's love and guidance. Thirty-
two years later, when he was lieutenant governor and after long believing
his mother dead, he located her alive in Florida and brought her back to his
home in Kentucky.

One other episode of interest and possible significance occurred during the family breakup. After the father became convinced his wife was leaving him, he turned to Albert and his younger brother, and asked whether she wished to take either or both of the boys with her. She pointed to Albert and said: "I sure don't want him. He's too much like you." Both children remained with the father. What importance is the biographer to place on this extraordinarily traumatic event in his subject's early life? We live in the heyday of psychobiography, which tends to attribute to the experiences of infancy and childhood all the subsequent developments of a person's career. The behavior of Andrew Jackson, Robert E. Lee, Theodore Roosevelt, and other historic figures is often explained as being a lifelong struggle to overcome conscious or subconscious fears of inadequacy that were sown during their youth. I must confess that I am tempted to try my hand at such an interpretation on Chandler. What a spectacular example of the phenomenon sometimes identified as "overcompensation" for feelings of insecurity and insufficiency.

But I pause when I read also that children who suffer broken homes, parental abandonment, and maternal rejection (even if the rejection is merely implicit instead of the strikingly explicit kind visited upon Chandler) usually grow into adults who are withdrawn, morose, antisocial, even criminal. In the end I feel compelled to fall back on the conventional, old-fashioned wisdom and conclude that Chandler offers a remarkable illustration of the power of the individual in a free society to conquer adversity through will and character.

By almost any American standards, Albert Chandler's boyhood was extremely hard. At first he stayed with relatives. Later he lived in Corydon with his father. The young Chandler worked almost from the time he could walk, because farm life required chores even of children of tender years. In Corydon, from the age of seven or eight, he virtually supported himself by delivering newspapers, running errands, splitting kindling wood, filling firewood boxes, and whatever other jobs came to hand.

He seems also to have become something of an unofficial member of many of the town's kind families, who customarily invited him to a place at the table when he happened to be present at mealtime. One lifelong friend and admirer of his has suggested the whole little community became a sort of surrogate mother to him. In his upper teens he performed heavy labor. One of the jobs required him from daylight till dark to shoulder hundred-pound bags of corn into the rail cars for shipment. This and other strenuous work combined with athletic training at school and on the community playground to develop the wonderful physique that was to become a part of the Chandler legend. More important was the effect of the entire experience on his character and outlook. He grew up to believe he could do anything he set out to do. He grew up also with a deep sympathy for the poor, the weak, and the outcast.

Years later, writing to someone who had commented on Chandler's kindness to a group of little boys, his wife would describe his attitude in these terms:

> [His] affection for little boys is very genuine not only because of his own 2 little boys but because it brings very vividly to his mind memories of his own unhappy childhood of how he was deserted, as you know, by his own mother when he was a helpless child of 4. He had a bitter struggle with never enough to eat and never enough clothes to keep him warm. The sight of a small boy selling papers on the street never fails to remind him of his own past.

Though Chandler as a man refused to cry over his earlier hardships, he never forgot them, and the memory unquestionably helped to form his views toward public policy. In the middle of his first term as governor, he wrote a petitioner saying:

> You are correct in assuming that I am interested in the welfare of every underprivileged man, woman and child in the Commonwealth. . . . I might mention that I have known the pinch of poverty and that I have been dependent upon my own resources from my very earliest years. I would be sympathetic with any program that would give poor children an opportunity to enjoy the necessities of life.

The young Chandler did more than master the hardships besetting him. He mastered them with flair. Instead of turning inward, souring on life, wallowing in self-pity, he grew up cheerful, buoyant, self-assured. He flashed a ready smile at everyone and very early received the nickname "Irish," either because of his presumably Irish disposition or, as he supposes, because he reminded his acquaintances of the lad in Horatio Alger's novel titled *Only an Irish Boy.* It seemed everyone in town knew Irish Chandler and was fond of him. Though he was quite girl-shy and never really had a teenage sweetheart, he was popular in school, captain of the baseball team, a member of the basketball and track teams, and active in the drama club. He was also a young man of strong religious convictions; he served as superintendent of the Sunday School of the Livesay Christian Church in Corydon. Endowed with a strong, clear tenor voice which he delighted in using, he was the leader of the high school choir and an outstanding singer in his church.

These traits of character and personality made a lasting impression on Chandler's associates. The words of a high school classmate written a few years later, but before Chandler entered public life, give a measure of the esteem in which he was held. "Albert," said his friend, "of all my high school and college friends and associates, there is not one for whom I have so high a degree of admiration and honest-to-goodness respect as for the Happy Irishman from Corydon. . . . You always have been fortunate but you have always earned your good fortune." In the Corydon High School yearbook for 1917, beside Chandler's photograph as a graduating senior, are printed these words: "Irish is the 'lark' of our class. He excels in knowledge of History and English. We are certainly proud to have him with us. He goes to Transylvania University next year, and we predict for him the most brilliant future."

That fall Chandler did enter Transylvania. His inventory of the assets he brought with him is forever embedded in Kentucky folklore. He said: "I had a red sweater, a five-dollar bill, and a smile." As events turned out, the smile far more than compensated for the lack of affluence symbolized by the red sweater and the five-dollar bill. He, of course, brought many other nonmaterial assets as well. Among these were a keen mind, a willingness to work, abstemious habits (he avoided both alcohol and tobacco, and he has done so even until now), an effervescent cheerfulness and friendliness, outstanding athletic ability, a good singing voice, and a determination to acquire a college education. This determination had been severely tested even before he arrived on the campus, for his decision to come had been made over his father's objection. Uncle Joe believed a high school education was enough and that Chandler ought now to settle down to a regular job. Chandler had loftier goals in mind.

Transylvania played a critical role in molding him for the career he eventually achieved. He chose Transylvania instead of the state university because Transylvania was a small school where the students enjoyed a more intimate contact with the faculty, and because the school was associated with the Disciples of Christ Church, a kindred body to his own Christian Church. Another powerful influence on his choice was the impression left on him by his conversations with two members of the Transylvania faculty, President Richard Crossfield and Professor Homer Carpenter. During his last year in high school he heard both of them make addresses in which they said any young person who genuinely desired a college education could get it at Transylvania, regardless of whether he had the money in hand to pay for it. When Chandler questioned them in private on this point, he was assured they meant what they had said. Hence the decision for Transylvania.

Chandler made his way through college much as he had made it through his earlier life. He worked at whatever jobs came along: babysitting and performing household chores for Professor Carpenter and his wife, delivering papers, doing laundry, washing windows, serving tables at a nearby boarding house, and leading the singing at church services. He was a star athlete, captain of the baseball and basketball teams, and quarterback on the football team. His spirit on the field often carried the day. "Kill Chandler," said a Kentucky Wesleyan rooter in what may be hoped was merely a sporting figure of speech. "The rest of them won't hurt you; kill [Chandler]." As in high school, Chandler's academic interests turned chiefly to history and English. He intensely enjoyed hearing and reading about the deeds of heroic men and women; he was thrilled by poetry, which he committed to memory in long passages that even today he can quote with remarkable fidelity. His grades, though not brilliant (mostly B's and C's, with a scattering of A's and D's), were good enough to get him admitted to the Harvard University Law School. Chandler has ever afterward paid homage to Transylvania for its generosity to him and for what it supplied him both in formal education and in the larger preparation for life.

In addition to the moral, intellectual, and physical training and the life-long associations Chandler acquired at Transylvania, he acquired something else that would be of incalculable worth to him in the years to come. He gained a new nickname that was so apt, so perfectly suited to his temperament and demeanor, that it displaced both his original nickname "Irish" and his legal given name. Ultimately it displaced them so thoroughly that many Kentuckians had trouble even remembering them. Different accounts are given on how he got the new name. Here is the way he recalls getting it. One afternoon during his freshman year, as he and a group of other athletes were strolling back to the dormitory after basketball practice, one of the boys, Ollie Hawkins of Lawrenceburg, turned to Chandler and addressed him as . . . "Happy."

Chandler has long been aware of the value of his famous nickname. Some years after he got it, and at a time when he was on his way up the political ladder, his former Transylvania roommate, John Barclay, advised him to drop the name in favor of a more formal and more dignified manner of address. Chandler replied that he had the highest regard for his friend's intelligence and good sense. "But," he said, "you have very little political shrewdness. The name 'Happy' is a great asset to me. It is worth tens of thousands of votes." Musing today on the significance of the whole affair and on the role of chance in a man's life, Chandler says with a characteristic chuckle, "Just think. What if he had called me 'Stinky'?"

In 1922, Chandler entered the Harvard University Law School, but after one term there he returned to his home state to enroll in the University of Kentucky Law School, from which he graduated two years later. To support himself through law training, he coached high school athletics, first at Wellesley, Massachusetts, and later at Versailles, Kentucky.

After graduating he began the practice of law in Versailles where, with inexhaustible energy, he continued his high school coaching and took on the added duty of scouting college games for the famed Praying Colonels football team of Centre College. Chandler gained quick success as a beginning lawyer, a success purchased by hard work and an extraordinary empathy for his clients.

During the first year of his law practice he married a young woman named Mildred Watkins. She was from Virginia and was then teaching in the Margaret Hall girls' school in Versailles. He could not have made a more suitable choice. She was both exceptionally bright and exceptionally charming. As if these assets were not enough, she possessed keen political insights and instincts as well. Mrs. Chandler, whom Chandler long referred to affectionately as the "Secretary of War," but known eventually throughout the Commonwealth as "Mama," would be a devoted wife and an invaluable adviser and associate.

The gibes of Chandler's close friends when in 1931 he won the office of lieutenant governor offer a hint of Mrs. Chandler's influence. One of them said: "Regards to your wife. She doesn't know me but tell her I know she is a remarkable woman to have done so much with you. And from her picture I see you have a highly cultivated eye for beauty." Coach "Uncle Charlie" Moran of Centre College wielded a more Puckish pen:

Now don't spoil everything and try and grow a mustache. Be yourself, and another thing, it is roomer [rumored] . . . that your wife
wrote all your speeches, also has been the brains of the family, and
you know it strikes me that there has been a big change in you,
as no Shyster Lawyer from a town like Versailles Kentucky could
have pulled the wool over the eyes of the Commonwealth of Kentucky without some outside help.

Mrs. Chandler did not write all of Chandler's speeches. Nobody did,
for they were delivered largely impromptu. But she did cover home base
with great effectiveness while he was out stumping the state, and she wrote
innumerable letters, bearing her own signature, to worried, puzzled, or un-
decided voters. These letters reveal a firm grasp of the political situation
and an outstanding ability to address the issues of the campaign in language
that was at once forceful, tactful, and reassuring. She played an important
role in persuading delegates at the 1931 State Democratic Convention to
nominate her husband for lieutenant governor.

Chandler had entered politics soon after becoming well established
in his law practice. To one acquainted with his personality and character
and with the influences and interests of his youth, this move ought not to
be surprising. He grew up in reverence for the great public figures of the
South's and the nation's past: Washington, Jefferson, Andrew Jackson, Lee.
He held "Old Hickory Jackson" in especially high favor. Chandler's father
had been an admirer of William Goebel, the progressive "martyred" governor of Kentucky. A picture of Goebel hung on the wall of the Chandler
house, and the father's feelings rubbed off on the son. Even at an early age,
he and some of his high school friends often discussed political affairs.
Chandler's taste ran to men of action.

Just as he finished high school an event occurred that seems to have
had considerable influence in turning him toward a career in politics. He
attended a graduation party given by one of the girls in the class. Each
guest upon arriving was handed a slip of paper bearing a statement—like
a saying in a Chinese fortune cookie—that was supposed to apply to the
recipient. On Chandler's paper were these words: "Study hard, work while
you wait, and you'll be Governor of your State." Years later, after he was
elected lieutenant governor, the woman who had been the girl who gave the
party wrote Chandler from her home in Indiana and reminded him of the
incident. He was delighted to get her letter, but she had no need to recall

the episode to his memory. He replied: "I still keep in the Bible at my home [that] little clipping." The message itself he kept in his heart. If it did not plant in him the seed of ambition to become governor, it unquestionably nourished the thought. He says that from an early age he felt destined to hold some high office, and that while he was a student at Transylvania a prominent Lexington preacher strengthened this conviction by telling him he had the "divine spark" to achieve great things. Finally, his perceptive young wife recognized his possibilities and encouraged him to fulfill them.

Chandler became active in the Woodford County Democratic organization and, in 1929, won a seat in the state senate. Two years later he was nominated by the Democratic State Convention for the position of lieutenant governor on the Ruby Laffoon ticket, and the two were victorious in the general election. Chandler soon broke with Governor Laffoon over the state sales tax, which Chandler opposed. The Laffoon forces in the senate retaliated by enacting a series of so-called "ripper bills" that stripped Chandler of his ordinary prerogatives as president of the body. In 1935, guided by his friend and political mentor, State Auditor J. Dan Talbott of Bardstown, Chandler made the most daring step of his career. Seizing an opportunity while Governor Laffoon was temporarily out of the state, thus leaving Chandler acting governor, Chandler called a special session of the legislature for the purpose of enacting a law requiring party primaries, instead of conventions of political bosses, for the nomination of candidates. The Court of Appeals validated the call, and the legislature eventually passed the law.

In recounting this episode Chandler quotes with relish the famous line that Shakespeare put in Brutus's mouth: "There is a tide in the affairs of men, which, taken at the flood, leads on to fortune." Certainly, Chandler's key role in getting a party primary law caught a tide that led *him* on to fortune. It led him directly into the Governor's Mansion. It brought an instant outpouring of favorable mail from all over the state. The most penetrating analysis of the effects of the action on Chandler's situation came from a Newport attorney and state legislator who wrote urging him to consider running for governor in the forthcoming election, saying:

You may not realize it, but now you are a different man in the realm of reputation than you were a few weeks ago. Comparatively few people knew you well enough [then] to appreciate you; they considered you a likeable young man more or less on a political lark. They liked you, but they would not have supported you for Governor. Since your dramatic victory over the machine a few weeks ago, you have emerged as a young political leader conspicuous for courage and brains. You are a field-general now.

Though Chandler at first held back in announcing his candidacy and planned to support former Governor J. C. W. Beckham if he should choose to run, Chandler needed no spur to his ambition. An erstwhile Transylvania fellow student wrote to remind him that, even in college, Chandler had predicted he would one day be governor. The day after he was nominated for lieutenant governor, he received a telegram from Governor Harry F. Byrd of Virginia, saying this meant Chandler would next be governor of the Commonwealth. Shortly after his election as lieutenant governor, Chandler wrote an old friend inviting him and his wife to visit the Chandlers when Chandler got into the *Governor's* Mansion. "And I am planning to get there," he added.

When in 1935 Beckham, because of health and other reasons, chose not to run and instead offered his support to Chandler, the Woodford Countian captured his party's nomination in a Democratic primary. Then, in the general election, he overwhelmed his Republican opponent in a landslide victory. Widely hailed as the "Boy Governor" (he was only thirty-seven), Chandler launched a vigorous program of administrative reorganization, reform, frugality, fiscal responsibility, and sales tax relief; at the same time, he made significant improvements in the state's roads, schools, health and welfare, and penal and correctional institutions. These measures, along with his forceful address and winning personality, made him the hero of a majority of the citizens of Kentucky and gained him national recognition as well. Expressions of confidence, gratitude, and praise showered upon him from people of all areas, classes, and conditions. Typical is this line contained in a letter of 1938 from a Louisville man: "Your achievements thus far undoubtedly place you in the position of being the greatest Executive ever to serve our Commonwealth." Though I am not enough of an authority on Kentucky history either to confirm or refute this statement, my conversations with some who are, including those who became critics of many of Chandler's subsequent activities, convince me that his administration from 1935 to 1939 certainly was one of the very best in the state's entire experience.

Urged by a multitude of his constituents, Chandler now made a move that brought the first reverse of his meteoric political career. He challenged Senator Alben Barkley, the majority leader of the United States Senate, in the 1938 Democratic senatorial primary in Kentucky. Chandler lost in a campaign of accusations and counter-accusations, a campaign in which President Franklin D. Roosevelt felt obliged to come to Kentucky to speak in direct support of Barkley. Chandler had undertaken too much in his bid to oust a popular and accomplished incumbent who was also a formidable campaigner and who had the backing (including the patronage) of an adored president of the United States.

The fates nevertheless soon placed Chandler in the United States Senate. In October 1939, the junior senator from Kentucky, M. M. Logan, died suddenly. Chandler now resigned the governorship in favor of his lieutenant governor, Keen Johnson, who, by prearrangement, appointed Chandler to the vacant position in Washington. The next year Chandler won a special election to serve out the remainder of Logan's term; in 1942, in another campaign filled with recriminations, Chandler defeated a former political ally, John Y. Brown, Sr., for a full senatorial term.

In the Senate, Chandler associated himself closely with a group of southern conservatives led by Senator Harry F. Byrd, Chandler's warm friend and political model. But Chandler never wore any one political brand; he was the quintessential maverick who insisted upon following his own head. Though he never forgave Roosevelt for introducing himself into the 1938 Kentucky senatorial campaign, Chandler usually supported the measures of the Roosevelt administration, while opposing what he considered the spendthrift ways of the New Deal.

The most burning issues of Chandler's Senate years were those of military preparedness and the waging of World War II. Appointed to the Military Affairs Committee, he shared the deliberations and activities of this important body. He was one of a set of committee members who circled the globe in 1943 inspecting American bases, troops, and operations. He supported the nation's war measures with unstinting devotion.

He supported the measures, but he disagreed vehemently with the grand military strategy adopted by President Roosevelt with the other Allied leaders, which called for this country's main effort to be thrown first against Germany, and only after victory there, against Japan. Chandler was convinced this policy underestimated the Japanese threat. Also, he distrusted British and Russian promises of full participation against Japan, once

Germany was out of the war. Finally, Chandler ardently admired General Douglas MacArthur, who, he believed, was being disastrously shorted in troops and arms in the Pacific theater.

Chandler in the spring of 1943 took the floor to air his views. He failed to alter the Allied strategy, but he had the satisfaction two days later of hearing Prime Minister Winston Churchill of Great Britain assure the United States Congress of complete British support against Japan ("while blood flows in our veins," said the eloquent Churchill) as soon as the war in Europe should end. Chandler has never wavered in his conviction that only the timely use of the atomic bomb saved this nation, and Japan, from a bloodbath in the invasion of the Japanese home islands.

Shortly after the end of the war, Chandler surprised his acquaintances (and himself too, he says) by suddenly resigning his seat in the Senate to accept the position of national commissioner of baseball. He did this, he explains, out of financial necessity, exchanging $10,000 a year for $50,000, ultimately for substantially more. But this is only part of the explanation. If politics is one of his great loves, athletics is the other. After being a star athlete in high school and college, followed by successful experience as a coach, he played some minor league professional baseball. He would have enjoyed immensely a career as a major league player. The game's immortals—Babe Ruth, Ty Cobb, Connie Mack—were the shining heroes of Chandler's youth. He seemed ready-made for the job of baseball commissioner.

He served in this position almost six years (1945–51), a period that witnessed some of the most significant developments in the history of the sport. Two of the most far-reaching acts in which he took a leading role were the establishment of a players' pension fund and the admission of black players into the major leagues. The going was often rough. A strong-headed man himself, Chandler found his course opposed by many of the strong-headed men who played on, managed, or owned the teams. Every owner except one objected to his decision to admit the black players. But Chandler says: "The black people were good to me when I was a boy. They took care of me then." He recalls fondly his association with one Bill Blunder, a big black man with whom he loaded corn into the rail cars. Blunder told him he was the only white boy who had the "willie" to do such labor. "My conscience wouldn't allow me to keep those black boys off the teams," he declares. It might be noted also that black voters had strongly supported him in the Kentucky elections.

Chandler was forceful enough to suspend for an entire season one of the most aggressive and colorful players and managers of the era, Leo Durocher of the Brooklyn Dodgers. Chandler was convinced that Durocher was guilty of serious misconduct on and off the field. In March 1951, when Chandler's appointment came up for renewal, a majority of the owners voted for him, but the affirmative vote fell short, by three ballots, of the required three-fourths. Chandler resigned and came back to Versailles, where he reentered his often-interrupted practice of law.

Nobody expected him to remain very long on the political sideline, and he did not disappoint the throng of Chandler-watchers. In 1955, he successfully challenged the Democratic party establishment in the state by defeating Judge Bert T. Combs in a hotly contested primary for the governorship. Chandler then won the general election by the greatest margin ever polled in Kentucky to that time. That Chandler could return to politics and defeat the Democratic organization was unquestionably a tribute to his past accomplishments. It was also a tribute to his art as a campaigner, in which he has had few peers and no superiors. In this role, perhaps more than any other, he became a Kentucky folk figure, a living legend. His strength lay partly in his perceptiveness in identifying and elaborating those issues of deepest concern to the citizens—tax relief, for example. Just as important, his strength lay in his skill at infusing the appeal for votes with the verve and color of his own personality.

Chandler loved a campaign. There was a saying that he enjoyed running for office more than he enjoyed occupying the office. His 1955 publicity bid to the electorate was: "Be like your pappy and vote for Happy." Crisscrossing the state by automobile, loudspeakers blaring "Happy Days Are Here Again" as he rolled into town, eating quick-order meals and sleeping in catnaps, delivering a dozen or more speeches a day, he wore out his opponents with his volcanic energy.

He wore them out, too, with his whiplash wit and ridicule. Establishment leaders Senator Earle Clements, Governor Lawrence Wetherby, and State Superintendent of Parks Henry Ward became "Clementine, Wetherbine, and Henryine," pronounced with an inimitable Chandler inflection that somehow made them sound ridiculous and brought hilarious laughter from the crowds. He roasted them for allegedly wasting the taxpayers' hard-earned money in sumptuous living. He pointed especially to the rug Wetherby had on the floor of his office, a rug that Chandler said had cost the state twenty thousand dollars. "Come down to Frankfort after the election," he invited all his hearers. "You can take off your shoes and see how a rug like that feels to your feet." Candidate Bert Combs became "Little Bertie," or "the little Judge." Or sometimes Chandler would refer to him condescendingly as "that little fellow" picked by the political bosses to take the heat for their own misdeeds.

Chandler exhorted temporizing or hesitating voters and politicians to "get on the wagon while the tailgate's down." "Don't be a mugwump," which he defined as a bird sitting with his "mug" on one side of the fence and his "wump" on the other. A Louisville woman in one audience was heard to exclaim: "Ain't Chandler a sight? Can't nobody ever beat him." He vowed to "take Wetherby off the public teat and turn him out into the cornstalks," where he said he would bellow like a young bull. At that point on one occasion a lively little mountain woman in a calico dress and bonnet piped up: "Happy, you can't hardly wean a bull calf by putting him on cornstalks." "Send me back to Frankfort and I'll do it," he replied. The audience went wild.

Chandler usually mounted the rostrum of a courthouse, schoolhouse, or truckbed with a prepared script at hand, but he soon abandoned it as he warmed to his theme and audience. The gathering then began to take on a spell like that of an evangelical revival meeting: affirmation by Chandler, response from the audience, reaffirmation from Chandler. Complaints and requests from the audience, promises by Chandler. One of his truest supporters says he had a weakness for making too many promises in the excitement of the hustings. But the promises did win votes, and he did fulfill many of them once he was in office.

Chandler could move his hearers with oratory. He quoted freely from poetry or the Bible. He could move them with song, with renditions of "Sonny Boy," or "When Irish Eyes Are Smiling," or "There's a Gold Mine in the Sky." He could move them with accounts of hardship and tragedy, with grim stories of his own childhood. An admirer recalls a scene in which Chandler described one of his wartime overseas visits to a group of battleworn Kentucky soldiers, the mother of one of whom was in the crowd Chandler was addressing. "When he finished," said the narrator, "the mother was crying, the audience was crying, I was crying, Happy was crying, everybody was crying." And probably everybody voted for Chandler.

Possibly the most telling part of his campaigning occurred off the platform. With exuberant self-assurance he mingled in the crowds, radiating an

incandescent glow of familiarity and friendliness, shaking hands, squeez-
ing arms, patting shoulders, embracing women (and men) with a bearlike
hug. He seemed to know everyone in the state, and the power of his memory for people became a favorite topic in the Chandler folklore. "Hello,
Joe." "Hi there, Sam, How's your pretty girl? Has her baby come yet?"
"Hello, sweetheart." "You're a luv." "Bill, how's your hardware business
getting along?" "Jack, I'll bring my clubs next time and show you how
to get off the tee." To a Republican friend discovered in the assembly:
"Well, well, look who's here. You never know what you're gonna run into
when you're out without your gun." At times they deliberately tested his
recall with: "Hello, Happy. Do you remember me?" Often he showed he
did remember, and then some, by responding affirmatively, then asking:
"By the way, how's your mother's arthritis? Kiss her for me. God bless.
God bless." Or Chandler might reply to a tester of his memory: "Why,
partner, I'd know your hide in a tanyard." Few Kentuckians doubted him
when he said it. Away to the polls they went, to send him back to the mansion.

When I first indicated an interest in writing on Chandler, a knowledgeable Kentuckian exclaimed: "The first thing you ought to know about this
subject is that there are two kinds of people in the Commonwealth: those
who idolize Chandler and those who despise him." (He might have added
that on many critical occasions, especially on election days while Chandler
was in his prime, most of them seemed to idolize him.)

Why, you may wonder, would anyone disesteem a man of such accomplishments and attractiveness? The answer to this question, I believe,
is quite complex. Doubtless I shall never be able to determine it fully; certainly, I am not now able to attempt it at all, except in the most superficial
manner. I would observe straight away that Chandler is by no means at
all times the sweet man with the disarming grin. He is capable of flaming
anger, and many of the people who have been closest to him admit there is
a wide streak of vindictiveness in his nature.

There are also other matters to be considered. In 1940, just after the
uproar of the notorious Louisiana political scandals that sent the governor
of that state and a score of other prominent citizens to jail, Earl Long, the
younger brother of Huey and a flamboyant figure in his own right, ran for
the governorship. Earl boasted that he was obviously the cleanest of the
candidates, because, he said, he was the most investigated man in the state,
yet nobody had been able to prove anything on him. Chandler was never

the most investigated man in the state of Kentucky, but he was at times a highly accused man.

I am not going to wave a list of these accusations here. I do, however, want it known that I am aware of them and that I intend to investigate all of them to the best of my ability before reaching any conclusions on them. "Power tends to corrupt," said the great British historian Lord Acton, "and absolute power corrupts absolutely." Chandler never possessed absolute power, but he did often possess great power. It would be gratifying to find, when all the available information is assembled, that he was an exception to Lord Acton's dictum. Yet I am prepared to conclude otherwise, if convinced by the evidence. But power is of the essence to the state. The students might put it: "Power is what the state is all about." This is especially true of the modern progressive, activist state. Without the exercise of power nothing gets done, and Chandler is not the do-nothing kind. He was eminently willing to exercise power. I sense that he enjoyed it. He explains his philosophy of leadership whimsically by saying, "When they put you up in the high chair, there's nobody else to hand it to." He tackled the duties of office with the same kind of fierce energy and overflowing confidence with which he tackled the affairs of his personal life. A *Time* magazine writer described him as a person living at the peak of mental and emotional tension. Using a metaphor from his youthful experience working in the Kentucky oil fields, Chandler used to say: "If you drill a dry hole, don't fill it up with tears. Move your digger and try again."

Chandler was no Hamlet wandering in a fog of indecision. "I may be wrong," he said, "but never in doubt." He sometimes adds a corollary: "Nobody else can be blamed for the things I did while in office. I was always sober and I meant to do exactly what I was doing." Just as he had been a tenacious battler in making his way in boyhood, or later in playing and coaching athletics, he was also a tenacious battler for the measures he sponsored as governor. An admirer wrote him that he had an "uncanny ability" to persuade the legislators to support his bills. "It's not the dog in the fight that counts," Chandler liked to say when the opposition was formidable. "It's the fight in the dog." On a more somber note, he describes the problems confronting a public official in his effort to overcome the roadblocks of the various competing individuals and interest groups, by saying: "They're either at your knees or they're at your throat. You've got to cope with them." Cope with them he did—arbitrarily and ruthlessly, according to his critics; fairly and effectively, according to his supporters.

Within the ranks of his own political organization Chandler exerted power by demanding an absolute loyalty. He looks upon loyalty as the noblest human characteristic. When he talks about loyalty he chiefly means personal loyalty. He is not given to abstractions; to him, life in its entirety is an intensely concrete and personal experience. Loyalty to an ideal or a political philosophy, or to a political party, tends to fall in his estimation below loyalty to a friend or benefactor. Loyalty had to work both ways. If one expected his support and patronage, then one must give wholehearted and continuous support to him and all his policies and candidates. To a man who was long a staunch member of Chandler's legislative team, but who later endorsed a party choice Chandler did not favor, Chandler wrote a letter with a greeting that indicated sharply this feeling about permanent personal loyalty. The greeting read: "Dear Former Friend."

Chandler's second administration lacked the youthful reforming zeal of the first. It attracted a drumfire of criticism from the state's traditionally liberal voices, including the Louisville *Courier-Journal,* which had been a strong Chandler supporter early in his career. But there were many positive accomplishments, particularly in highway building and the financing of schools and other public institutions. More spectacular were Chandler's enforcement of the United States Supreme Court's school desegregation decision in Kentucky, which he did with National Guardsmen in tanks, and his preeminent role, against determined opposition, in the creation of the University of Kentucky medical school and hospital—deservedly named the Albert B. Chandler Medical Center—which he calls the greatest achievement of his entire public life.

Three times Chandler again sought the state's highest office, all in vain. In 1963, he lost to Edward T. Breathitt, Jr., in the Democratic primary, a defeat that Chandler still questions. When in 1967 he lost the primary to Henry Ward, Chandler threw his support to the Republican nominee, Louie Nunn, thus helping Nunn to gain a victory in the general election. Chandler's final bid for the governorship, as an Independent (1971), was a farewell campaign gesture by an aging but undaunted political warrior.

In national presidential politics Chandler usually supported the Democratic party choice, though sometimes with a sublime lack of enthusiasm, and he reserved the right to disagree. In 1956, he himself was a candidate, placed in nomination at the Democratic Convention as a "favorite son" by the Kentucky delegation. He received 36½ votes on the first ballot when Adlai Stevenson won the nomination with 905½ votes.

Paradoxically, Chandler had something of a leaning toward southern states' rights movements. In 1948, for example, he was so friendly to the Dixiecrat candidate, Governor J. Strom Thurmond of South Carolina, that Chandler is believed to have given him his "tacit support." In 1968, Chandler seriously considered running on the American Independent party ticket with Governor George C. Wallace of Alabama, but in the end the two could not reach an agreement on the racial issue. Needless to say, Chandler's party inconstancy gained him little love among Democratic stalwarts, and his flirtations with southern third-party movements gained him even less love in liberal circles. On the other hand, Chandler was an early and ardent supporter of John F. Kennedy for the presidency.

Chandler has been out of political office since his second term as governor ended in 1959. These nevertheless have been full years. As the recent state and federal elections have demonstrated, Chandler remains active on the political scene. He has been engaged in various business and public enterprises. He has served on, and is yet a member of, the Athletics Board of the University of Kentucky and the boards of trustees of both of his alma maters, Transylvania University and the University of Kentucky. I understand he is also Fran Curci's assistant coach. Or is it the other way around? Nor has Chandler given up on the Wildcats. The embodiment of the Kentucky spirit, Chandler is the state's most enthusiastic booster. When he says Kentucky is "God's country"—and he says it often—the words come from the heart. When he sings "My Old Kentucky Home," which he says is the most beautiful song ever written, the words, notes, and tears come from the heart.

In his own mind he is at peace with the world, including his rivals and critics of the past (most of them, at least). He is secure in the knowledge that his individual efforts will leave Kentucky and, to a lesser extent, the entire nation a legacy of better health, education, well-being, and contentment. His long love affairs with Mama and with life are still going strong. He says he lives every day as if it were his last day on earth, and sleeps every night as if he were going to live forever. His door in Versailles is open to everyone. His telephone number is listed in the directory. He is besieged with requests for favors or assistance from fellow Kentuckians, and non-Kentuckians, of all ranks and descriptions. To these petitioners, nothing seems impossible if he sets his mind to it. At eighty-two his eyes still twinkle; his handshake is still viselike; he is still ready to flex a bulging arm muscle and invite the caller to feel it. He keeps himself informed and holds strong opinions, which he will freely share, on almost any imaginable subject. Above all else, he is still . . . Happy.

NOTE

This essay was originally presented at Transylvania University on November 19, 1980, as part of the Distinguished Transylvanian Lectures.

Change and Tradition
in Southern Society

Southern society after World War II underwent the most severe stress of its entire history. Despite the trials of the Civil War and the upheavals of Reconstruction, neither of these experiences had threatened the core of the traditional southern society with the force of the recent political, economic, and social changes. Yet countless landmarks of sectional distinctiveness remained. The changes themselves took place in a manner peculiar to the South. Moreover, the primary institutions and modes of conduct survived, even where drastically modified. Every study of southern behavior and attitudes in the 1960s and 1970s indicated the persistence of the old in the midst of the new.[1]

Southern class structure endured the effects of industrialization, urbanization, and prosperity. Descendants of the antebellum planters still formed a small but select gentry even if overshadowed by others with more money or more political influence. The planter offspring usually lived on income from inherited property or by such professions as law, medicine, or the military. But tradition was the mainstay of their survival as a class. Southerners continued to draw a sharper distinction than nonsoutherners between the expressions "good family" and "good people." This was especially true in such enclaves of old southern values as Charleston, where, according to one observer, the very names of individuals tended to become genealogical incantations: for example, Pinckney Ravenel Rutledge or Ravenel Rutledge Pinckney. Though less pronounced in less historic places, the principle of guarding family name and prestige was strong everywhere. A scholar reared in New Orleans described this trait: "Even most Boston Brahmins can hardly imagine the intense awareness of the past long dead and the preoccupation with matters of family, ancestry, and local history particularly among older women of the Southern patriciate."[2]

The aristocratic tradition was not altogether the product of self-admiration. Most white southerners of all classes, and at least some black southerners, still venerated the region's plantation past and conferred a certain respect upon its heirs. At their worst, these aristocrats by popular consent represented a pretentiousness that failed to conceal their lack of wealth or power. At their best, they continued to represent a welcome exception to the mass, with emphasis upon personal honor and integrity, valor, graciousness of manners, and the perfection of "good living," as opposed to the mere accumulation of money or the cultivation of utilitarian competence.[3] They believed, said a sympathetic but critical analyst, "that who you are, if not superior to what you are, transcends at least the standard of what you have."[4]

Eclipsing the old plantation elite in everything but tradition and family pride were the wealthy businessmen, who had begun to arise before World War II and whose numbers were multiplied by the prosperity of the 1950s and 1960s. The New South ideal of progress through commerce and industry now came into its own and spread from the metropolises to the smaller cities and eventually into the towns and villages. At the top of the economic and social pyramid were the millionaire and multimillionaire entrepreneurs in mineral recovery, manufacturing, marketing, and life insurance. Oil was the source of the most sensational wealth, especially among the swashbuckling prospectors of Texas. Such men as H. L. Hunt, Sid W. Richardson, and Clinton W. Murchison stood at the head of a list of Texas "Big Rich" who would have been at ease among the Rockefellers, Vanderbilts, and Carnegies of an earlier age. Spreading down from the multimillionaires was a substructure of lesser business figures—self-made, rugged proprietors of small, independent enterprises in furniture, clothing, refining, and food processing. Serving the needs of these manufacturers and marketers was a multitude of contractors, truckers, machinery and appliance agents, employees of service firms, and wholesalers and retailers.

The blending of the regional economy into the national economy greatly increased the number of native southerners and newcomers associated with national corporations. These employees of General Motors, Standard Oil, Du Pont, Lockheed, and the like were scattered throughout the society at all levels. Corporate executives and regional managers lived in the most exclusive neighborhoods and moved in social circles with the entrepreneurs and most distinguished professional men. The corporation engineers, geologists, and lower-echelon administrators made up a significant part of the southern "white-collar" class. They together with the rank and file of the lawyers, physicians, accountants, small businessmen, and teachers populated the sprawling middle-class suburbs that grew around the cities.

Next in order were the armies of "blue-collar" workers, the mechanics, carpenters, pipe fitters, electricians, machine operators, and assembly line workers of the expanding cities and industries. Unlike many of their fellow laborers in other parts of the country, who often were from the immigrant population, these southerners were of the same origins as their superiors in the business and social hierarchy; they were chiefly new arrivals from the hundreds of thousands of surrounding small farms that were now disappearing under the economic and social forces of the times. Many of them came also from the neighboring small towns. They lived in the previously middle-class and now frayed sections of the cities, which became available to them because of the exodus of former residents to the suburbs, or in the lower priced new residential developments in the less scenic or less convenient areas on the outskirts of the cities.

But class distinctions were still observed in the midst of social flux, and the southern sense of hierarchy remained strong. The innumerable whites who rose to prosperity from humble origins quickly took on the airs and practices of the establishment and guarded their new status as jealously against the lower economic and social orders as the baronial planters of the Old South were said to have done. Many of them built houses that looked like plantation mansions and filled them with antique furniture, or with reproductions of antique furniture. If all did not become Episcopalians, as some did, they moved into the "high church" congregations of the other denominations. They began to send their children to exclusive private schools. They changed from Populist to Bourbon in their political outlook. Frequently some member of the family undertook to trace the family tree in an effort to establish a legitimate heritage from the Virginia or South Carolina gentry.

All classes retained a certain rural outlook and style, though by 1970 approximately 65 percent of the southern population was officially classified as urban. A primary reason for the rural tone was that the great majority still lived outside the large cities. Only about 25 percent of the total population lived inside cities of as many as 100,000 residents, while 40 percent lived in suburban areas or in the more than 4,500 cities and towns of fewer than 100,000. The suburbs were generally conservative in social and political attitudes and shared many of the values and beliefs of the rural and small-town population. Indeed, most southern cities themselves were hardly cities at all by nonsouthern standards; they were still more like overgrown country towns. No city in the states of South Carolina, Mississippi, and Arkansas had a population as high as 200,000. Southern cities also preserved a rural flavor because most of their residents were from the surrounding countryside and still had countless friends and relatives there. Visits back and forth kept common interests alive. Even such southern metropolises as Atlanta and Houston seemed quaintly uncrowded and relaxed in comparison with the leading metropolises of the East, Midwest, or Pacific Coast. Southern cities lacked what James Dickey called the "frenetic, urban sensibility" of a Pittsburgh or a Detroit.

Finally, better than 35 percent of the southern population was still officially classified as rural, that is, actually living in the country or in towns or villages with populations under 2,500. Though four out of five of these people now held their chief employment in the factories, stores, or offices of nearby cities or towns, driving automobiles to and from work every day, they remained country folk in outlook and behavior as well as in residence. The small portion of the population still making a living on the farm kept its division into planters, yeoman farmers, and tenants, with social distinctions to match.

An important cause also of this persistently rural outlook was the emphasis on family that survived the disruptive forces of modern life. Southern families were exceptionally cohesive; divorce was less popular than in other major areas; parental authority tended to be stronger. Domestic training and family lore, more often than elsewhere reinforced with a hickory switch, still impressed upon southern children an assortment of distinctive if not ineradicable attitudes, tastes, loyalties, and mannerisms. A southern-born scholar writing in the mid-1960s commented upon the reluctance of southerners to espouse ideas that might stir up disagreement among their extended, close-knit families of uncles, aunts, siblings, and cousins.[5]

The family was the citadel of the color line. "Family life in Brazil cannot be defined in racial terms," said a sociologist, "but this is precisely how it is defined in the South. White and Negro Southerners do have kin across the color line but they are not publicly recognized, and we may not expect the fundamental social structure of southern society to change appreciably until and unless the family finally yields to desegregation."[6] Interracial marriage was the strongest of southern taboos. Occasional marriages of this nature took place as a result of the desegregation of schools and other public institutions and of the federal courts' striking down laws against such unions. But the number was too small to have any significant effect on the color line.

To a considerable extent the entire southern community kept a familylike quality, so much so that James McBride Dabbs called it a "kinship-oriented society." This was possible because, in spite of the stream of outsiders coming into the region after World War II, the southern people retained much of their homogeneity. In 1970 the South was substantially higher than the rest of the country in the proportion of inhabitants whose parents were born in the same state as the child. In six former Confederate states more than 98 percent of the population was from "native parentage" as compared with 83.5 percent in the entire nation.

Also, newcomers into the region still demonstrated a marked capacity to "go native." Their children born in the South were hardly if at all distinguishable from other southern children; their grandchildren doubtless will be absolutely indistinguishable. Walker Percy in the mid-1960s described the "almost familial ambit" of Mississippi in terms that would have been more or less applicable to the entire South. "The whole Delta, indeed of white Mississippi, is one big kinship lodge," he said. "You have only to walk into a restaurant or a bus station to catch a whiff of it. There is a sudden kindling of amiability, even between strangers. The salutations, 'What you say now?' and 'Y'all be good,' are exchanged like fraternal signs. The presence of fraternity and sorority houses at Ole Miss always seemed oddly superfluous."[7]

All the southern traits of class and family were held by the region's blacks, along with various other characteristics derived from their own experience. Though blacks left the South in great numbers during and after World War II—approximately 1.5 million each decade between 1940 and 1970—the area still had the nation's greatest concentration of Americans of African descent. The more than 10 million blacks in the old Confederate states in 1970 accounted for almost half the nation's blacks and for better than 20 percent of the region's total population. Because of economic pressure and social preference the movement of blacks from southern farms into southern cities went on steadily. On the eve of World War II approximately 35 percent of the region's blacks were city dwellers; by 1970 approximately 67 percent of southern blacks were classified by the census taker as urban. About 56 percent of them lived in metropolitan areas, with 41 percent collected within the central cities. Blacks now made up more than half the population of Atlanta, and they were approaching the halfway mark in a number of other southern cities.

Profound changes took place in the lives of black city dwellers. The upper and middle classes expanded significantly both in numbers and in wealth, thus reflecting the growth of black insurance companies, banks, savings and loan associations, and a wide variety of small business enterprises, all primarily serving a black clientele. By 1970 the North Carolina Mutual Life Insurance Company, a black organization with headquarters in Durham, held assets worth over $118 million; in 1972 the Atlanta Life Insurance Company announced assets of better than $80 million, plus an unassigned surplus of more than $14 million. Auburn Street in Atlanta, where many of the city's flourishing black businesses were located, was called the "richest Negro street in the world." Every major southern city had prosperous black owners and managers of thriving companies, along with a professional class of successful physicians, lawyers, ministers, and professors in the black colleges and universities. Handsome and exclusive black residential neighborhoods, some of them with swimming pools and golf courses, marked the rise of the black bourgeoisie.

Employment opportunities created by the civil rights acts of the 1960s along with the rising demand for labor drew blacks into jobs never before open to them in the South. The textile mills, for example, began to hire black operatives, not only because the law required it, but because their workers were leaving for the higher wages of the new plastics and electronics factories. The many industries that had traditionally held blacks to the most menial jobs now began to upgrade a number of their positions. Fear of the adverse economic consequences of racial strife and black boycotts caused many southern business and community leaders to undertake to preserve racial harmony; by the late 1960s most of the states and many communities had created interracial committees that attempted to relieve the urgent problems of black employment, relations with the police, and general living conditions. Virtually every southern business and industry was now hiring blacks in at least limited numbers for a variety of jobs that spread from the janitorial level through the secretarial and assembly line positions and into the lower administrative ranks. Local authorities added blacks to police and fire department forces and assigned them to clerical positions in the courthouses and government offices.

Although racial friction still existed in the South, it tended to fade in the public mind during the late 1960s in comparison with the violence, arson,

Table. Population of the South 1940, 1970

	Total[a] 1970	% change since 1940	White 1970	% change since 1940	Black 1970	% change since 1940
Alabama	3,444,165	+ 22	2,533,831	+ 37	903,467	– 8
Arkansas	1,923,295	– 1	1,565,915	+ 7	352,445	– 27
Florida	6,789,443	+258	5,719,343	+314	1,041,651	+103
Georgia	4,589,575	+ 47	3,391,242	+ 66	1,187,149	+ 9
Louisiana	3,641,306	+ 54	2,541,498	+ 68	1,086,832	+ 28
Mississippi	2,216,912	+ 2	1,393,283	+ 26	815,770	– 24
North Carolina	5,082,059	+ 42	3,901,767	+ 52	1,126,478	+ 15
South Carolina	2,590,516	+ 36	1,794,430	+ 65	789,041	– 3
Tennessee	3,923,687	+ 35	3,293,930	+ 37	621,261	+ 22
Texas	11,196,730	+ 75	9,717,128	+ 77	1,399,005	+ 51
Virginia	4,648,494	+ 74	3,761,514	+ 87	861,368	+ 30
Total South	50,046,182	+ 57	39,613,881	+ 73	10,184,467	+ 15
United States	203,211,926	+ 54	177,748,975	+ 50	22,580,289	+ 76

Source: U.S., Bureau of the Census, *Sixteenth Census of the United States, 1940: Population,* vol. 2, pt. 1, p. 52; *1970 Census of Population,* vol. 1, parts for individual states.
[a] Includes white, black, and other nonwhite.

and looting of the black riots in the northern and western cities. Appalled by these upheavals, some students of racial matters, including such eminent spokesmen as Roy Wilkins of the NAACP and the sociologist Gunnar Myrdal, went so far as to predict that the South would outpace the North in establishing harmony between the races. Increased opportunities for black employment in the South joined with the relative calm of the area to cause a significant reverse migration of blacks from North to South. In the early 1970s an estimated average of about 100,000 blacks a year was reported to be moving into the region, a number that probably exceeded the rate of those leaving during the same period. But these figures were uncertain and controversial. Estimates by the Bureau of the Census showed that between 1970 and 1972 the black population of the greater South decreased from 53 percent to 52 percent of the total American black population, thus indicating a continued excess of outward movement.

In spite of the many improvements in the situation of the blacks, they remained as a class at the bottom of the regional economic and social scale. In 1966 the median income of black families was estimated to be only 51 percent as high as that of white families; in 1972 it had risen to 55 percent. Favorable as this advance unquestionably was, it brought little comfort to most blacks. Much of the gain turned out to be the result of a higher proportion of employed black wives than of white wives. Ominously, as inflation elevated the "poverty line"—defined in 1973 by the Office of Economic Opportunity as $4,275 annual income for an urban family of four—the proportion of blacks below it increased far more rapidly than the proportion of whites. And recession unemployment among the blacks was higher than among whites. The plight of rural blacks, who still made up roughly one-third of the region's total black population, was especially severe, because of their virtual peonage on the white man's land or in his shop or, worse, because of the unemployment brought on by mechanization and conversion to grazing. Thousands of black children in the isolated countryside were found to be seriously undernourished.[8]

Nor did the comparative racial harmony of the South and the collapse of legal segregation indicate the disappearance of actual segregation. The vast majority of the members of the two races lived as far apart in the 1970s as they had in the 1940s. Possibly they lived farther apart. The black influx into the cities accelerated the white exodus to the suburbs and left extensive ghettos where checkerboard neighborhoods once existed. Atlanta was the leading example of this transformation within the old Confederate states;

some observers foresaw the day when this city would be all black. The same trend was at work in most other southern metropolises.

The rural and small-town South showed a far greater amount of genuine desegregation in public places than was to be seen in the cities. But in the small towns and the countryside the rigidity of a caste system grounded upon the conjunction of race, poverty, and tradition was largely unshaken. A careful study of the blacks in South Carolina, a state of small cities and towns and a large rural population, concludes that the civil rights movement of the 1960s caused little fundamental change in the race relations of this state. At the beginning of the 1970s, the author says, blacks had little prospect "that their needs would be realized in the near future. . . . Public policy was still more concerned with neutralizing their aspirations than with helping them realize them."[9] Paradoxically, where things had changed the most they seemed to have changed the least.

If modern southerners in the midst of economic and social transition managed to perpetuate numerous traditional distinctions of class and race, they also preserved a great body of traits common to all levels of the regional population. Unconscious as well as conscious ties with the past held strong. Southerners remained conservative in lifestyle as in public attitude. Even southern liberals were scarcely so by outside standards. James McBride Dabbs said: "Northern liberals are much more typical of the modern world. Southern liberals are hardly liberals at all. . . . The Southerner retains a sense of community—he's critical, but not willing to chuck the whole thing. . . . Southern liberals are really conservatives."[10] Observation of the regional characteristics in, and outlook toward, personal and domestic relationships, manners and speech, and athletics and recreation indicates the South has kept a style of its own.

Violence was still very much a part of the regional way of life. In 1972 the southern murder rate was almost 40 percent higher than that of the West, the major area that came nearest to matching the South in this unenviable record. Some of the regional violence was accountable to racial discord and the anger stirred by the civil rights movement. But the homicide rates within the races of the South were also higher than those elsewhere. Was this the result of the southern habit of owning firearms? Most residents of the area did so; virtually every household in the rural and small-town South had a closetful of shotguns and rifles, and many had a pistol for good measure. Or did southerners own and use weapons because they were by nature or circumstance violent? Was violence impressed into the southern personality by the prevalence of corporal punishment during childhood? At least one study suggested this possibility. Was Wilbur Cash right in attributing personal violence in the South partly to the intemperance of the southern weather: the languorous heat of summer followed by the crashing thunderstorm? Whatever caused the violence, it seemed to persist.

Doubtless the regional tendency toward personal violence underlay its continued emphasis on force as an agent of national policy. Southerners exhibited a collective "military-patriotic" personality that placed them in the forefront of support for the armed services and of a strong American presence overseas. One analysis of the army's officer corps in the early 1970s estimated that four out of five of its active generals were born in small southern towns. Representing less than 23 percent of the nation's population, soldiers from the old Confederate states received better than 29 percent of the Congressional Medals of Honor awarded during the Vietnam war. This seemed a natural heritage of a people bred to revere military heroes as the greatest historic figures.[11]

Southern manners and southern violence were at the opposite poles of regional behavior; it has been said that a southerner would remain polite until he was angry enough to kill. The regional code of manners remained recognizable, though eroded by the frictions of the new industrial progress and by the "candor" of many of the young. Especially in circles away from the business centers of the major cities, or away from the more "enlightened" university campuses, one still observed a certain quaint deference of man to woman, of youth to age, of student to teacher; the attentive ear still caught the "yes sir" or the "no ma'am" that so long had been hallmarks of southern courtesy. Quite possibly the rituals and restraints of etiquette, deeply ingrained in southerners of both races, helped to keep the civil rights confrontation from becoming uglier than it was. At one point in negotiating with the segregationist members of the Board of Commissioners of Prince Edward County, Virginia, a civil rights leader commented that she was dealing with gentlemen.[12] Blacks who returned to the region from elsewhere frequently referred to the greater ease of communication and personal relationship in the South. Beset as it was on every front, the old chivalry had not yet surrendered; it was another vestige of the "culture lag" between the South and the rest of the nation.

The primary source of all southern social conventions was still the home, for it continued to be the center of most social activity except among the young singles. Dining out, nightclubbing, and theatergoing among the

married folk were largely confined to an affluent minority in the larger cities. Home cooking still presented a sharp contrast to the fare of the medio-
cre if not dismal restaurants of most southern cities and towns. Perhaps the
culinary South was no longer as clearly defined as it once was; yet southern wives still prided themselves on special family recipes. Despite many
compromises with the science of nutrition and with the convenience of the
frozen and prepackaged groceries of the supermarkets, they were yet able
to prepare such historic regional delicacies as hot breads, country-cured
ham, and pecan pie. Innumerable southern tables at frequent intervals still
served corn bread, black-eyed peas, and fried chicken or ham in the ordinary family diet. Renamed "soul food" among the blacks, and whimsically
called this by many whites as well, these dishes came to enjoy considerable
popularity in restaurants throughout the country. An entire new industry
grew up to meet the regional, and to some extent national, demand for fried
catfish. Even clay eating, a habit presumably adopted among some poor
southern whites and blacks in response to malnutrition, seemed to have
become a culture trait that refused to yield to improved diets. Stories were
told of southern migrants to the North who had friends mail them table clay
from choice locations in Mississippi.

The central figure in the southern home was the southern lady. An institution that had endured the travail of war, Reconstruction, and all the rest
of the regional experience, she refused to disappear from the modern scene.
A recent critic has attempted to destroy the image of the southern belle by
reducing her to a purely ornamental figure without brains, substance, or
even sensuality.[13] A serious evaluation of southern women would reveal
that they have never been the vaporous creatures portrayed in sentimental
lore but have always borne their share of the burdens and responsibilities
of life. The South has had its quota of mother O'Haras and Melanies as
well as its Scarlets and Aunt Pitty Pats. Southern women in the 1960s and
1970s hearkened to the practical aspects of the Women's Liberation Movement, including such demands as those for equal economic opportunities,
day-care centers for working mothers, and greater participation in the political process.[14] But they did not renounce either their femininity or their
southernness. They retained enough of what William Alexander Percy once
called a "morning-glory air" to make a southern Bella Abzug impossible
to imagine.

Southern speech in the 1970s remained as distinctive as southern manners, southern cooking, or any of the other characteristics that continued

to set the region apart from the rest of the country. In spite of the recent immigration of hundreds of thousands of newcomers, and in spite of a half-century of listening to the brisk syllables of northern radio announcers and a quarter-century of northern television commentators, southern children still grew up speaking southern. They still drawled their vowels, dropped their r's, said "creek" instead of "crick" (or brook), and addressed one another as "y'all." Blacks from the South who applied for jobs outside the region were said to be handicapped by dialectalia—the most sophisticated name ever invented for the southern accent. The region was full of expressions of strictly local coinage and meaning. More than a century ago Union soldiers from the far North could hardly believe that Confederates from the Deep South spoke the same language as they. Doubtless a northern visitor today would be less impressed by the regional differences in cadence and intonation. But he could not fail to notice them.

Southern forms of recreation also distinguished the region, though southerners enjoyed many of the same diversions enjoyed by all Americans. For example, they embraced television with the uncritical devotion of the rest of the country. Yet to the close observer there were subtle distinctions of tone and mood.

Considering the strictures of their orthodox Protestant churches, southerners were perhaps freer in indulging in many of the pleasures of the flesh. Wilbur Cash in the 1930s was struck by the South's ability to reconcile love of pleasure with the exercise of religious puritanism; forty years later he would have been even more intrigued by this paradox. Gradually the southern states relaxed their laws against the sale of alcoholic beverages; in the late 1960s Mississippi, the last state to do so, repealed its statewide prohibition statute. The hard-drinking state of Texas long kept a law forbidding the sale of alcoholic drinks in public places; but the law permitted a subterfuge whereby these drinks could be dispensed in private clubs, and so-called private clubs flourished everywhere in the Lone Star State. New Orleans with its French Quarter and Mardi Gras celebration remained an entertainment Mecca where throngs of tourists reared in a Calvinistic atmosphere vicariously discharged their pent-up hedonistic impulses. The strong influence of the Southern Baptist church and other denominations of conservative social outlook in Kentucky did not prevent this state from being a leading producer of Bourbon whiskey, cigarette tobacco, and race horses for pari-mutuel betting. The Kentucky Derby with its pageantry, gaiety, and flow of mint juleps was something of a Mardi Gras of the border South.

Southerners kept their enthusiasm for sports and outdoor exercise. The regional passion for athletics, especially college football, reached new heights during this period. Virtually all the colleges and universities either built new stadiums or greatly expanded their old ones. Southerners were convinced that their football teams played the best game in the nation; indeed, a football argument was one of the surest tests for establishing regional loyalty. Lighter on the average than opponents from other places, southern teams emphasized speed, deception, passing, and adroit ball-handling. Also, in the eyes of a northern journalist, southern football reached "levels of meaning, intensity, and violence entirely foreign to other regions."[15] Southern contenders in intersectional rivalries won often enough to give a measure of support to the boasts of their partisans. Oklahoma earned the national championship in 1950, 1955, and 1956; Tennessee in 1951; Auburn in 1957; Louisiana State in 1958; Alabama in 1961, 1964, and 1965; and Texas in 1963 and 1969. Alabama again was rated the top team of 1973 and 1974 before losing hard-fought postseason games.

Regional teams in other sports did not enjoy a comparable success and prestige. For example, Kentucky was the only school of the Southeastern Conference whose basketball teams were traditionally able to compete successfully in intersectional rivalries; they won national championships four times during the 1950s and 1960s and won National Invitational Tournaments three times. Southern basketball improved in the 1960s and 1970s, especially after the southern schools began to admit black athletes. In addition to their teams in the major sports, southern colleges and universities turned out representative and sometimes outstanding teams or performers in the so-called minor sports, including track, swimming, boxing, wrestling, tennis, golf, and gymnastics.

The regional interest in athletics, along with the growth of southern cities and the rise of southern prosperity, caused for the first time a number of major league professional teams to be located in the South. By the 1970s there were major league football teams in Atlanta, Houston, Dallas, Miami, and New Orleans; major league baseball teams in Atlanta, Houston, and Arlington (Texas); and major league basketball teams in Atlanta, Houston, Greensboro, Dallas, Louisville, Memphis, and Norfolk. The South provided its share of players to the major league teams in all these sports, whether located in the region or elsewhere.

Almost all kinds of amateur sports had their devotees in the South. All the cities and many towns had leagues of softball and bowling teams.

Thousands of golf courses and tennis courts were crowded with users. Municipal recreation departments and local chapters of the YMCA sponsored youth programs in the major sports and in many of the minor ones. Soccer enjoyed a limited popularity on southern high school and college campuses and in the major cities. Even such winter sports as ice skating and skiing made some headway in the South, though they usually required artificial ice or snow.

A remarkable increase in water sports occurred during the post-war years. Because of the long hot season, swimming in the region's countless rivers, lakes, and ponds had always been a favorite exercise and the period between the two world wars saw a great proliferation of community and privately operated swimming pools. During the 1950s and 1960s the backyard swimming pool became both a convenience and a status symbol among the well-to-do; the residential subdivision or apartment house pool served the same purposes for the somewhat less well-to-do. All motels of any claim to distinction installed pools of their own. In the earlier years boating and water skiing were largely confined to the coastal waters and the larger lakes and rivers. The postwar affluence changed this. By the 1960s the yards and garages of prosperous residential neighborhoods everywhere were cluttered with power boats and cabin cruisers. On weekends and holidays roads were jammed with boats in tow to automobiles, and waterways swarmed with craft. Even in small lakes and streams of the most remote and land-locked places one saw bronzed, bikini-clad young men and women flashing on water skis like Floridians.

The South was the acknowledged center of stock car racing—a sport matching Fords, Chevrolets, Dodges, and other passenger cars supercharged to reach speeds above 175 miles per hour in contests of as much as 600 miles. Scores of thousands of spectators gathered at the oval tracks to enjoy the ceremonial parade of pretty girls aboard floats and to cheer the daredevil antics of such favorite drivers as Glenn "Fireball" Roberts (who died in a crash in the 1960s), Robert G. "Junior" Johnson, Fred Lorenzen, and Richard Lee Petty. Tom Wolfe saw in stock car racing an authentic expression of the ethos of the rural South; he celebrated the courage of the drivers and called them the last American heroes.

The most venerable, most thoroughly native, and most widespread sports of the South remained hunting and fishing, which were pursued with as much enthusiasm in the post–World War II years as in the pre–Civil War period. The region still contained such vast areas of open field and forest that hunting was the prerogative of Everyman. Wild animals abounded from the lowly cottontail rabbit or the sulling 'possum to the dangerous wild boar or the majestically antlered deer. Hunting was open to all classes and ages of both races, from wealthy Virginians in fancy attire riding blooded horses behind pedigreed dogs in the fox chase to poor whites and blacks tramping the woods with single-barreled shotguns in the crooks of their arms and flea-bitten hounds barking up squirrel trees. Except for the poorest of the poor, game was no longer an essential part of family diet; but countless southerners still ate it as a delicacy.

Fishing was even more widespread than hunting. No other major region possessed such a combination of lakes, ponds, streams, and coastline. It would be difficult to find a spot in the entire Southeast, except in the major cities, beyond walking distance from a fishing creek or pond. The state of Florida alone claimed over 300 species of freshwater and saltwater fish. Equipment could be as simple as a cane pole cut on the creekbank, a few feet of string, a bead of lead for a sinker, a hook, and a worm or cricket for bait: total expense, a few pennies. Or it could include motorboats and elaborate tackle together costing hundreds or thousands of dollars. Every person in the entire South who liked to fish could do so, and millions took advantage of the opportunity. Perhaps no other population in the world spent so high a proportion of its time in this activity.

Examination of the South's social and recreational activities during the quarter-century after World War II reveals countless changes in and additions to the old modes of behavior. New classes rose to prominence; a revolution occurred in the situation of the black community; innovations took place in the life-style and diversions of the population. Yet these changes came no nearer to destroying sectional distinctiveness than did comparable developments in southern industry, agriculture, religion, education, fine arts, or politics. The new dominant classes inherited old customs and preferences. Official policies of racial equality and desegregation benefited the blacks but did not break the color line in the actual living arrangements of the masses of the inhabitants. The migration of population to the cities and suburbs did not destroy the rural outlook, nor did the emergence of new domestic relationships eliminate the family as the most cohesive unit of southern society or the home as the center of southern traits and attitudes. Southern courtesy, southern food, southern speech, southern athletic chauvinism, and southern sectional consciousness persisted in the midst of expanding tastes and altered mannerisms. Significantly, the immemorial sports of hunting and fishing were still the most popular and lasting kinds of southern recreation.

NOTES

1. John C. McKinney, "Continuity and Change in Sociological Perspective," in John C. McKinney and Edgar T. Thompson, eds., *The South in Continuity and Change* (Durham, N.C., 1965), p. 3. Also John Shelton Reed, *The Enduring South: Subcultural Persistence in Mass Society* (Lexington, Mass., Toronto, London, 1972), pp. 1–104.

2. Alfred O. Hero, Jr., *The Southerner and World Affairs* (Baton Rouge, La., 1965), p. 296.

3. Ibid.

4. William F. Guess, "South Carolina's Incurable Aristocrats," *Harper's Magazine* 214 (February 1957): 46.

5. Hero, *Southerner and World Affairs,* p. 361.

6. Edgar T. Thompson, "The South in Old and New Contexts," in McKinney and Thompson, *South in Continuity and Change,* p. 476.

7. "Mississippi: The Fallen Paradise," *Harper's Magazine* 230 (April 1965): 170.

8. U.S., Bureau of the Census, *Current Population Reports: The Social and Economic Status of the Black Population in the United States, 1972,* p. 18; *Time,* September 3, 1973, pp. 74–75; *Atlanta Journal and Constitution,* June 17, 1973; Steve Van Evera, "A Family Assistance Plan: 40 Acres and a Mule?" *New South* 26 (Fall 1971): 71–72.

9. I. A. Newby, *Black Carolinians: A History of Blacks in South Carolina from 1895 to 1968* (Columbia, S.C., 1973), pp. 359–60.

10. Quoted in John Egerton, "A Visit with James McBride Dabbs," *New South* 24 (Winter 1969): 44.

11. Lewis H. Lapham, "Military Theology," *Harper's Magazine* 243 (July 1971): 76; *The World Almanac and Book of Facts,* 1972 (New York, 1972), pp. 462–63.

12. Robert C. Smith, *They Closed Their Schools: Prince Edward County, Virginia, 1951–1964* (Chapel Hill, N.C., 1965), p. 246.

13. Marshall Frady, "Skirmishes with the Ladies of the Magnolias," *Playboy* 19 (September 1972): 121–222.

14. Sarah Murphy, "Women's Lib in the South," *New South* 27 (Spring 1972): 45.

15. Peter Schrag, "A Hesitant New South: Fragile Promise on the Last Frontier," *Saturday Review,* February 12, 1972, p. 55.

The Ever-Vanishing South

Most observers of the modern South emphasize the so-called transformation of the region during the last few decades. What they mean by this expression is the disappearance of regional distinctiveness: the growing resemblance of the region to the rest of the nation: the merging of the South into the American mainstream.

The prospect of a southern transformation is usually looked upon as being highly desirable, especially by the liberal journalists and college professors who do the bulk of the writing on the subject. The South has traditionally been regarded as the black sheep of the American community—a willful, delinquent child who has somehow failed to shape up to the national standards. A few years ago this idea was portrayed whimsically, but perceptively, by a *New Yorker* magazine cartoon showing a fashionably attired matron with a sour look on her face, turning down a bookstore clerk's suggestion of a volume on a certain southern state, with the comment: "I'm sorry for Mississippi, but I just don't like to read about it."[1] Clare Boothe Luce intended no whimsy when she wrote in the preface of her popular social satire *Kiss the Boys Good-bye,* saying: "We are not, perhaps, sufficiently aware that Southernism is a particular and *highly matured* form of Fascism. . . ."[2] Only a few months ago the *Manchester Guardian Weekly* chose to refer to the American South as a "neurotic region."[3]

C. Vann Woodward tells us that a major factor in the South's identity is its historic failure to share fully in the great national traditions of success, affluence, and innocence.[4] Southerners were set apart as those Americans who wore the scarlet letters of guilt for having committed the two unpardonable sins of slavery and secession. Even more ignominious, perhaps, they were the only Americans who had known the travail and humiliation of being conquered and subjected to military occupation. Howard Zinn explained what he called the "Southern Mystique" as being largely a distillation of most of the nation's worst traits, along with a few of its best, he

319

added generously.[5] Unquestionably, one of the most familiar images in the American mind has been that of what George B. Tindall has called the "Benighted South"—a land of persistent racial prejudice, religious bigotry, endemic poverty, and a cluster of other presumably un-American attitudes and conditions.[6]

What of the great transformation said to have occurred in the South in recent times? Before turning to this question, perhaps it would be worthwhile to point out that the very idea of southern transformation is not nearly so new as may be supposed from all the talk about it. In 1941, before the occurrence of any of the wartime or postwar events that are thought to be eradicating regional distinctiveness, a renowned social analyst, Wilbur Joseph Cash, felt obliged to reply to those who said the South already was a mere figment of the imagination, that it existed only as a geographical division of the United States. Cash disagreed. The South, he said, was "not quite a nation within a nation, but the next thing to it."[7]

Indeed, the idea and the fact of southern change, or transformation, are extremely old. A so-called New South was proudly proclaimed a few years after the Civil War by an entire covey of young southern boosters, chief among whom was the Atlanta journalist and raconteur Henry Woodfin Grady. Their New South was a South said to be refashioned in the likeness of the victorious North: a South of industry, commerce, and hustle—a South outdoing the Yankees at their own game yet retaining the charm and graciousness of the Old South. Or, to look a bit farther back, the North during the Civil War and Reconstruction had its own vision of southern transformation. The South, rid of the serpent of slavery, was to be remade into a Garden of Eden, or at least into a New England below the Potomac, which was another way of saying about the same thing. Actually, it seems to have been a northern army officer who coined the very expression "The New South."[8] In brief, what may be overlooked in the present enthusiasm for recent southern transformation is that at the time of World War II the South had already experienced more than three centuries of change, some of it of the most radical nature imaginable, without losing its regional distinctiveness.

Yes, the South has undergone immense change since World War II, much of it traceable directly or indirectly to the war itself. Perhaps it is no exaggeration to say the region was fated to be affected almost as much by World War II as by the Civil War. Many of the recent changes have been exactly the opposite of those wrought by the Civil War. The South emerged from that experience crushed, bankrupt, demoralized; it emerged from World War II intact, prosperous, confident. Yet some of the recent changes were remarkably similar to those growing out of the Civil War and Reconstruction, for they involved the relationship of the southern states to the federal government and of whites to blacks in the South.[9]

The South since World War II has experienced what may fairly be called revolutions in its economy, politics, and race relations. In 1940 the region was predominantly rural and agricultural; by 1981 it was heavily industrialized, and less than 5 percent of the total population actually made their livings on farms. Since World War II the South has enjoyed a prosperity beyond the dreams of former times. In 1940 the section was known politically as the Solid South: solid, that is, in its fealty to the Democratic party. In 1972 every southern state voted for the Republican presidential candidate; after a swing back to a native-son Democrat in 1976, an overwhelming majority of the region's states four years later turned Republican again. Southern blacks in 1940 were rigidly segregated from whites, except as menials, both by law and custom, and, with minor exceptions, the blacks were systematically excluded from voting or holding public office. By 1980, as the result of massive federal intervention and black protest demonstrations, southern institutions, at least officially, were thoroughly desegregated, and southern blacks were voting by the millions. Thousands of them held public office, including a few in the United States Congress and the mayoral positions of such prominent southern metropolises as Richmond, Atlanta, Birmingham, and New Orleans. A southern Rip Van Winkle, awakening after thirty years, would not believe his eyes.

This, of course, is the situation that has caused many thinkers to believe the South as an identifiable region is extinct, or almost so. This explains the utterance of such expressions as "The Vanishing South" or "The Disappearing Sectional South," and the selection of such titles as *Into the Mainstream,* "Been Down Home So Long It Looks Like Up To Me," or *An Epitaph for Dixie.*[10]

But Dixie has survived a long array of epitaphs and of epitaph writers, and many things indicate that the epitaphs being composed today may still be premature. Cash warned his readers against adopting hasty conclusions from superficial observation indicating the disappearance of the South. He drew an analogy between the South and a venerable English church with its Gothic façade and towers. Look into the nave, aisle, and choir, he said, and one finds there the old mighty Norman arches; look into the crypt, and one may even find stones hewn by the Saxons, brick made by the Romans.[11] Descend today into the crypt of the southern psyche, I suspect, and there one will discover many ancient emotions, loyalties, and traits of unmistakably southern origin.

Even in those aspects of regional affairs that have been most obviously affected by recent forces—that is, the economy, politics, and race relations—even in these, many old landmarks are still highly visible. Take the economy. Accurate as the reports of the southern prosperity are, the South today actually remains economically behind the rest of the country. The regional economy is still very much a colonial economy. Most of the stock in the great corporations dominating it belongs to outsiders; regional industry is still disproportionately extractive and subsidiary; the southern per capita income and wealth are still significantly below those of the nation at large. Much of the oil, coal, and timber of the region has always been controlled by nonsoutherners, a control that seems not to be relaxing. A recent issue of the Louisville *Courier-Journal* calls attention to the continuing engrossment of Kentucky coal rights by companies from afar. A corporation with headquarters in California, acting through a Kentucky affiliate, has consummated the largest of these recent purchases.[12]

A steady rise in southern incomes since World War II has significantly narrowed the economic gap between southerners and non-southerners. But the gap is not closed. Figures on per capita personal income in 1980 show every southern state except Texas below the national average. The poorest southern state, and also the poorest American state, Mississippi, falls almost 31 percent below the national average, and almost 40 percent below that of the wealthiest states of the Northeast, Midwest, or Far West.[13] In the late 1930s President Franklin Delano Roosevelt called the South the nation's "economic problem number one." Such a statement today would be hooted down. Nevertheless, the South has not yet attained full membership in what used to be known as the Affluent American Society.

Let us look at recent southern politics. A number of new southern congressmen elected in the early 1970s tended to be more liberal in their voting than their senior regional colleagues. The wave of congressional reform that took place then threatened to destroy one of the South's most cherished agencies of political influence, the congressional seniority system. For various reasons, some of them personal, such guardians of southern interests as Representative Felix Edward Hebert (Louisiana), Representative William Robert Poage (Texas), and Representative Wilbur Daigh Mills

(Arkansas) lost their positions as chairmen of powerful committees in the House of Representatives.

But the leopard's spots by no means disappeared. No drastic shake-up occurred in the Senate, and in a short time the new southern members of the House began to sound and vote suspiciously like the old ones. According to the *Congressional Quarterly,* the nucleus of opposition in both houses to the more liberal parts of President James Earl ("Jimmy") Carter's program still came from the South.[14] So formidable were the operations of Senator Russell Billiu Long of Louisiana (then chairman of the Senate Finance Committee) that some observers ruefully spoke of him as the "fourth branch" of the federal government. At the core of a so-called Conservative Forum of Democratic congressmen, who since the Republican successes in the 1980 elections are asserting themselves, appear none other than the once-liberal junior members from the South. Lest anyone forget their regional identity, they have taken a name that originally was conferred in derision upon their predecessors. They call themselves the Boll Weevils.[15] Most ironic of all, and most illustrative of the staying power of traditional southern politics, is the rise to the chairmanship of the Senate Judiciary Committee of James Strom Thurmond of South Carolina, former Dixiecrat, Democrat-turned-Republican, and Nixon supporter, who threatens to emerge as the South's new "fourth branch" of the federal government.

What about the role of the blacks in current southern politics? Unquestionably it has been spectacular; the blacks have made great gains and can never again be cancelled out of the regional political equation. But the limits of black political power are also visible. Except in those localities where they are heavily concentrated by de facto segregation they have usually been defeated in their bids for office. When a prominent black ran for the governorship of Mississippi in 1970 he not only failed to draw more than a token handful of liberal white votes, but he also lost an alarming proportion of the black votes. True, in presidential politics the black votes have become far more important than in local politics. In 1976 they were decisive in forming, with a portion of the white votes, a coalition that carried most of the South for Carter. But this was a precarious victory. A majority of the whites opposed Carter then, and in 1980 this majority became strong enough to defeat him in all but his native state of Georgia. This outcome, plus the omens drawn from southern history, suggests that the white-black bond in regional presidential politics is a fragile one.

Finally, race relations today. Here one sees the sharpest change of all from the way of the pre–World War II South. But legal desegregation has not by any means wiped out the color line. Only through massive court-ordered programs of busing has significant integration come about in the most desegregated of southern institutions, the public schools, and even this accomplishment has been virtually nullified in many instances by resegregation through the flight of the whites to the suburbs or the withdrawal of their children to private schools. In Atlanta, for example, where the school system a few years ago was hailed as a model of orderly desegregation, the public schools are now 90 percent black. They are approaching the condition of the Washington, D.C., schools, which are reported to be 96 percent black.

It is not, however, in economic, political, or racial affairs (at least not in official racial affairs) that the endurance of the South as a distinctive region is most pronounced. Rather, it is in the subtler areas of the mind and spirit, and even of the senses, of the eye, ear, tongue, and palate, that the South continues to affirm its differentness most effectively.

Southern religion would stand at or near the top of the list of distinguishing southern characteristics. The famed essayist and lampoonist, Henry Louis Mencken, derisively called the South "The Bible Belt." Shortly after World War II Mississippian Hodding Carter wrote more sympathetically of southern religion: "Though the citadels crumble," he said, "the South remains the great western-world stronghold of Protestant, fundamentalist Christianity. . . . That thing called the old-time religion is in the blood of most of us, and if it is laughed at, the laughter has as accompaniment an almost inescapable inner, esoteric warning that the ways of God are not to be mocked by man."[16] The South today continues to represent the nation's strongest commitment to Biblical literalism and orthodox Protestantism. The Southern Baptist church (the largest Protestant denomination in the country, with over twelve million members) is the foremost manifestation of this sectional religious outlook. It has been called the "folk church" of the South. A critic has parodied the Southern Baptists' faith in an eternal life of bliss after this life of troubles by describing their conviction in these terms: "Hang on, there's a better life coming." To which the targets of this gibe have replied with bumper stickers (or some of them have) saying: "God said it. I believe it. That settles it."[17]

Most other denominations in the South hold views similar to those of the Southern Baptists, even if they proclaim them somewhat less vehemently. Public-opinion surveys indicate that southerners are likelier than nonsoutherners to believe in the immortality of the soul and the promise of reward and threat of punishment after death and to believe that religion holds the answers to the great problems of the world.[18] A larger proportion of students in southern colleges than in colleges elsewhere consider religion a relevant part of their lives. Psychologists even detect in southerners a greater tendency to depend upon prayer rather than technology for protection against tornadoes. If anyone believes the South has ceased to be a Bible Belt, he ought to make a Sunday automobile trip across the region with his radio tuned to one local station after another as he goes.

So pervasive is orthodox religion in the South, so intimate its connection with the other elements of life, that one scholar has given it the name "Culture-Protestantism."[19] Southern churches have persistently rejected the illusion of human perfectibility, the promise of a heaven on this earth. The leading character in Robert Penn Warren's novel *All the King's Men* appropriately says he has fully understood the inherent sinfulness of man since the Sunday School training of his rural Louisiana boyhood.[20]

This Calvinistic skepticism toward human possibilities carries over into the region's attitude toward all sorts of programs for the improvement of society. Thus, it is consistent with regional theology to condemn such proposals as that of a guaranteed annual wage as a violation of the Apostle Paul's injunction: "If any would not work, neither should he eat." The religious outlook often becomes public policy, for southern churches and the state and local authorities usually form so close a liaison that neither is aware of its existence; both honestly denounce a union of church and state as a subversion of American principles. State legislatures and other governing bodies reflect more directly than elsewhere the church attitudes on sex, divorce, abortion, equal rights for women, pornography, drugs, alcohol, education, child rearing, parental authority, dress, and general behavior.[21] The celebrated Moral Majority that claimed so much media time and space during the 1980 presidential campaign spoke more often than not with a decided southern accent.

After the defeat of the Confederacy a southern preacher said: "If we cannot gain our *political,* let us establish, at least, our *mental* independence."[22] There are those today who believe this exhortation has been carried out through the region's churches.

If the southern white churches have sustained a sense of sectional independence, both they and the black churches have sustained a sense of racial independence. A British observer in the South during Reconstruction described the withdrawal of the blacks then occurring from the white churches as an extension of emancipation.[23] It has remained thus to this day. The great majority of southern congregations are still completely black or white, or almost so, apparently by mutual consent. The saying holds true that the hour from eleven to twelve on Sunday morning is the most segregated time of the week in the South. The black churches played a vital role in the civil rights struggle of the 1950s and 1960s, yet nowhere is southern religious orthodoxy stronger.

The most acclaimed form of the South's cultural expression is its creative literature. Mencken once flippantly called the region "The Sahara of the Bozart"—a literary and artistic desert. Hardly had he coined this epithet when the South flowered into a remarkable literary renascence that reached its peak in the Southern Gothic novels of Mississippian William Faulkner. Set in the imaginary Yoknapatawpha County, Mississippi, they pictured a hell on earth of murder, lynching, mutilation, rape, deceit, incest, and miscegenation. Beneath the sound and fury of Faulkner's prose was a renunciation of modern American materialism, exploitiveness, and rootlessness and a yearning for the realization of the nobler ideals of the old southern aristocracy. At Vanderbilt University a group of poets, including John Crowe Ransom, Allen Tate, Donald Davidson, and Robert Penn Warren, defended traditional southern values in a magazine entitled *The Fugitive.* In 1930 these four poets joined with eight other writers, together known as the Agrarians, to bring out the controversial volume *I'll Take My Stand,* which contained a prescient warning of the dangers lying in wait for a progressive, industrial society. Ransom captured the spirit of the work in a single brilliant line saying such a society was constantly engaged in a losing war with nature, a war in which the society won only what he called "Pyrrhic victories . . . at points of no strategic importance."[24]

Other southerners during the last half-century have enriched American literature with works that vary from the high romance of Margaret Mitchell's *Gone With The Wind* to the stark, ribald, tragic satire of Erskine Caldwell's *Tobacco Road.* The outpouring of southern letters has not diminished since World War II. Perhaps the two most distinguished figures of the postwar period are Robert Penn Warren of Kentucky (transplanted eventually to Yale University) and Eudora Welty of Mississippi. Warren has spanned more fully than any other writer the entire era from the beginning of the Southern Renascence to the present. Having interpreted the region's experience in many novels and essays and in some of the most powerful verse ever written in America, he stands with Faulkner at the summit of southern letters. Miss Welty also has been active during most of the period, producing novels and short stories that capture with remarkable fidelity the countless nuances of southern thought and speech. She exercises the region's most delicate literary touch.

Notwithstanding their diversity in mode and outlook, all southern writers share certain qualities that set them apart from others. The southerners place unusual emphasis on the very points most emphasized in southern life itself. These are family, history, race, religion, and a sense of place, of concreteness, and of the imperfectibility of man. One could never say of a novel by Faulkner what C. Vann Woodward has said of the work of a famed twentieth-century nonsouthern writer, Ernest Hemingway: that is, "A Hemingway hero with a grandfather is inconceivable. . . ."[25] Reynolds Price speaks of the influence on his own works of the surrounding North Carolinians of both races who, he says, could converse intelligibly and easily with their great-grandparents.[26] Southern fiction swarms with grandfathers and grandmothers, great-grandfathers and great-grandmothers, and so on *ad infinitum*. The strengths and weaknesses of the present generation are seen as a legacy from its forebears.

Allen Tate pointed out that regional writers reflect a sense of history as something more than what is written in books; that they see it as a force actually operating on society. Southerners, said Tate, possess a knowledge of history carried to the heart. One of Faulkner's characters puts it this way: "The past is never dead. It's not even past."[27] In discussing the career of Katherine Anne Porter—a writer of Texas birth and southern upbringing—Robert Penn Warren says her works are "drenched in historical awareness."[28] Henry Steele Commager says it is "possible to study the Civil War period in contemporary Southerners . . . [because] they retain the psychology and vocabulary of that period."[29] To the accusation that southerners continue to live in the past, the poet Miller Williams replies: "Not so, the past continues to live in southerners."[30]

So strong is the southern sense of place that the actions in southern novels cannot be imagined to have happened anywhere but where they did happen. There is an organic, symbiotic relationship between place and theme. Eudora Welty employs redundancy to emphasize the importance of place in her novels. It, she says, "is the named, identified, concrete, exact and exacting, and therefore credible, gathering-spot of all that has been felt, is about to be experienced, in the novel's progress."[31]

Another of Faulkner's characters demonstrates humorously the southern sense of concreteness by explaining the difference between how a
southerner and a northerner go about establishing a goat ranch. The southerner does it unceremoniously when his herd of goats grows so large it
can no longer be accommodated in the barnyard or on the front porch. The
northerner begins with no goats at all but with a pencil and piece of paper
to reckon how many yards of fence and how many acres of land are needed
for a given number of imaginary goats. The southerner never has the problem of making the number of goats match the length of fence or amount of
land. They never matched, and he doesn't expect them to. If, on the other
hand, after the northerner has set up his business he is unable to make
them all match, he resorts to pencil and paper again. Now, said Faulkner's
speaker, instead of a goat ranch, the northerner has an "insolvency."[32]

Katherine Anne Porter explained the southern sense of concreteness by
saying southerners cannot comprehend murder, for example, as an abstract
thing. One should note here that, according to this principle, a southerner
would never say what the young gang leader in the movie *The Godfather*
said to his distressed fiancée about a certain recent killing: that there was
nothing personal about it. "[A] good southerner," continued Miss Porter,
"doesn't kill anybody he doesn't know."[33]

Above all, southern writers dwell upon the inherent weakness and
sinfulness of man. In other words, their themes are essentially religious,
however secular they may appear to be. The critic Cleanth Brooks says of
the southern writer: "He is not disposed to dissolve evil into nothing either
by interpreting it as the temporary pressure of a hostile environment or
by transforming it into any other external thing that can be liquidated by
one's voting the right way at the polls or by paying for its removal on the
psychoanalyst's couch."[34]

The writer whose works since World War II most explicitly reveal the
effect of southern religion is the late Flannery O'Connor of Georgia. In
two novels and an assortment of short stories she used southern religious
fundamentalism of spectacular intensity to satirize the emptiness of modern rationalism. One of her characters, in a God-versus-science argument,
dismisses the marvels of the jet age with the sneer: "I wouldn't give you
nothin' for no airplane. A buzzard can fly."[35]

Miss O'Connor's tart discourses on southern literature are classics of
their own, and they aptly illustrate the regional mind. Once when asked
why southern writers are so preoccupied with the grotesque, she replied

that every southern theme is called grotesque by nonsouthern critics, unless it actually is grotesque. Then, she said, it is "called photographic realism."[36] On another occasion she wrote: "Whenever I'm asked why Southern writers particularly have a penchant for writing about freaks, I say it is because we are still able to recognize one." "To be able to recognize a freak," she continued, "you have to have some conception of the whole man, and in the South the general conception of man is still, in the main, theological. . . . I think it is safe to say that while the South is hardly Christ-centered, it is most certainly Christ-haunted. The Southerner . . . is very much afraid that he may have been formed in the image . . . of God."[37]

The most renowned southern novelist to emerge in the past two decades is Walker Percy of Louisiana. Literary critics sometimes call him an Existentialist. If he is indeed an Existentialist, he is unmistakably a southern Existentialist. According to Cleanth Brooks, Percy has consciously tried to avoid writing the "southern novel." Yet all the telltale southern literary characteristics abound in his works. ". . . I know of no present novelist who is more 'southern' in every sort of way . . . ," says Brooks. ". . . as an observer of the southern scene, . . . [Percy] can scarcely be bettered as he describes the sights, smells, and sounds of the French Quarter in New Orleans; or the chatter and posturings of a concourse of automobile sales in Birmingham; or the precise differences in manner and accent between a damsel from Winchester, Virginia, a girl from Fort Worth, and a big, strapping drum majorette from Alabama."[38]

To a reader who is familiar with New Orleans and the nearby Gulf Coast of Mississippi, Percy's first novel, *The Moviegoer,* is a haunting exercise in the sense of place. At the same time, through the experiences of an aimless young movie addict, the story points up the sense of displacement that threatens much of modern American life. Percy's later works are aimed, in part, at the sexual and general behavioral license of today. "Whether or not Percy fancies himself as a writer of the southern novel," says Brooks, "his southern heritage has stood him in good stead as he deals with his chosen theme, the alienation within man's soul." In this respect, concludes Brooks, Percy is in the direct line of Ransom, Tate, Warren, and Faulkner.[39] Also, one might add, Percy is in the direct line of his cousin and father by adoption, the late William Alexander Percy—poet, essayist, and conservative Mississippi planter-aristocrat.

The same qualities that distinguish the writings of southern white authors are also found in those of southern black authors, though they have deliberately avoided trying to turn themselves into "black Faulkners." For understandable reasons many of the southern literary characteristics, such as the emphasis on race and violence, loom even larger in black literature than in white literature. Alex Haley's universally known work of "faction," as he calls it (part fact, part fiction), his book *Roots,* is an arresting study in the sense of place and family, as well as of race, violence, and almost every other theme particularly associated with southern letters. It is, of course, possible that the author of *Roots* could have been born and reared anywhere in the United States. But Haley is, in fact, a Tennesseean. Probably, the author of *Roots* had to be a black from the South. Ernest J. Gaines, born in Louisiana, and perhaps the most prominent of the recent black novelists, explains the inspiration for his works thus: "My body left Louisiana [he lives in California] but my soul did not."[40]

Though southerners have never won critical acclaim in the visual and performing arts comparable to that in literature, they have nevertheless made their mark in these media. The works of such modern southern or southern-born playwrights as Tennessee Williams, Lillian Hellman, and Paul Green show a close affinity for southern letters. Green could well have been speaking for Faulkner in saying: "Our very existence as a people here in the South has been something of an epic tragic drama—a sort of huge and terrifying Job story, if the truth were acknowledged."[41] The southern folk arts, or popular arts, including black spirituals, blues, and jazz, and white balladry, hillbilly, Gospel, and country music, also reflect the peculiarities of the southern experience and temperament.

Innumerable traits of everyday life, desirable and undesirable, continue to distinguish southerners. For example, the South still has the highest illiteracy rate in the nation. Nor do all the illiterates object to their condition. One of them, a cantankerous eighty-three-year-old, rallied his questioner with the declaration: "I guess I made it O.K., didn't I? . . . After all . . . a man's got a right not to read, ain't that right?"[42]

Violence and widespread possession of firearms are still hallmarks of the region. It maintains the highest homicide rates in the nation. On the other hand, there remains a sense of manners that causes even the hippiest and wooliest of students to reply with a "Yes, Ma'am," or a "No, sir." One is reminded of Cash's description of the graceful manners of the old plantation gentry and how these manners were reflected in what he called the "level-eyed" courtesy and ease of bearing of the ordinary folk.[43] Someone has said, to emphasize the irony, that a southerner will remain polite until he is angry enough to kill. A heartless southern murderer in one of Flannery O'Connor's short stories apologizes for being shirtless in the presence of the women who are about to become his victims. He courteously invites them to their deaths with the words, "Would you mind stepping back in them woods there?"[44]

Southern speech still features its drawling vowels, still calls a small stream of water a creek instead of a crick, and still says "you all" when addressing more than one person. Southern speech shows little sign of surrendering to the crisp stage diction of the television announcers or to the exhortations of the speech instructors. When southern-born movie stars return home on visits, I am told, they quickly lapse into the local vernacular and inflection. Nor does southern cooking seem to have yielded to the injunctions of the nutritionists. Southern "soul food," which for centuries before it got this name was eaten by whites and blacks alike, is now challenging the national taste buds in such forms as fried chicken (Kentucky and otherwise) and even fried catfish, once considered by non-southerners to be the basest of edibles, if edible at all.

If the Redneck or Cracker of an earlier, rural South are disappearing as national stereotypes, they are being replaced by the southern Good Ole Boy: a figure who, according to a partly serious, partly whimsical, and even a partly affectionate description, is distinguishable by his uncouthness, his ruttishness, his beer belly, and his manner of mounting a bar stool—leading with the crotch.[45] Billy Carter, the Good Ole Boy, and Jimmy Carter, the born-again Christian, represented equally authentic national images of the modern South.

Finally, the South still retains a homogeneity and folksiness that seem about gone elsewhere. Having received little of the vast stream of European immigration that poured into the country during the latter half of the nineteenth century and the opening decades of the present century, the South lacks the so-called "ethnic mix" that makes up the rest of the nation. The South's two main ethnic groups, southern whites and southern blacks, are so large and so long established in the region that their homogeneity is natural and familylike. It does not need to be imposed by the public schools or by an administrative bureaucracy. Walker Percy says all "of white Mississippi . . . is one big kinship lodge."[46] The same could be said of black Mississippi; or of most of the South, white or black.

The region's folksiness defies the forces of urbanization and industrialization that are usually considered deadly to folksiness. Louis D. Rubin, Jr., identifies an extraordinary example of this quality by showing how southerners characteristically convert the impersonal artifacts of modern technology into socializing media. How the men who drive the monster tractor-trailers of American transport, "southern rednecks for the most part," he says, "good ole boys—are not merely watching the multilane road unfold before them. They are busily gossiping away with each other [on their CB radios], and with every motorist who comes along and wants to talk. . . . Driving along the interstate highway has, in short, been transformed into a social occasion!"[47]

Despite the conventions that preserve a large measure of racial segregation in the personal affairs and everyday life of the region, the relationship between the races is so ancient and so close that the sociological phenomenon known as "cultural pluralism" is hardly recognizable in the South. Indeed, a recent public-opinion survey indicates that the outlook of southern whites and southern blacks is closer together on most points than that of southern and non-southern whites.[48]

If the South is growing more and more to resemble the rest of the nation, the rest of the nation is also growing more and more to resemble the South. The humiliation of defeat in the Vietnam War and of Watergate, the revelations of the misuse of the Federal Bureau of Investigation, the Central Intelligence Agency, and the Internal Revenue Service by Presidents of both parties and of both liberal and conservative political and social persuasion, and the recognition of nationwide problems of poverty, racism, air and water pollution, and energy depletion: all have tarnished the national image of success, affluence, and innocence, have reaffirmed the eternal verity of universal human weakness, and have narrowed the philosophical gap between the North and South even as other forces are narrowing the material gap.

Perhaps the most conspicuous illustration of the trend toward a national consensus occurred in the 1976 election of a Southern Baptist from the Deep South to the Presidency of the United States, a thing that as late as a dozen years earlier would have been unthinkable, and which, incidentally, may now again be unthinkable. The nationwide popularity of such television shows as *The Waltons* indicates that a Benign South has, to a degree, taken its place alongside the Benighted South in the popular imagination. The wittiest line in Jack Temple Kirby's work, *Media-Made Dixie,* and a most perceptive line, is the one that identifies Jimmy Carter as "John-Boy Walton grown up."[49]

A frequently heard expression nowadays goes: "At last the South has rejoined the United States." Not so, says David Herbert Donald, ". . . the United States has finally decided to rejoin the South."[50] More guardedly, John Egerton says that while Dixie is being Americanized, America is being southernized.[51]

Egerton's observation is true even in the strict demographic meaning. During and after World War II millions of southerners migrated to the cities of the North and Far West, carrying their southern ways with them. There are today, for example, Southern Baptist churches scattered throughout these nonsouthern parts of the country. But for the last fifteen or twenty years also even greater numbers of northerners have been moving to the South, which seems about to become the nation's pivotal population area. Not all these immigrants are at first comfortable in their new home. There is the gasp of consternation the first time little Billy or little Jane comes in from the playground talking southern; the furrowed brow over the sudden prospect of acquiring a southern religious fundamentalist as a son-in-law or daughter-in-law. One hears of occasional efforts to establish some sort of compound to keep the natives at safe distance. You are doubtless familiar with Flannery O'Connor's story of the northerner in Atlanta who sold his house in the suburbs there to another northerner, reassuring him with these words: "You'll like this neighborhood. There's not a Southerner for two miles."[52]

But, as a rule, the newcomers and the natives soon establish amicable relations. Most of the newcomers are conservative in their political, economic, and social views to begin with, or, if not conservative, they are at least discreet in expressing their views, else they probably wouldn't have moved South in the first place. Also, the South throughout its entire history has demonstrated a remarkable capacity to absorb newcomers and convert them into southerners. Like China, it has conquered its conquerors. Many of the southern leaders in secession and the Civil War were either northern-born migrants to the Land-o'-Cotton, or their children or grandchildren. The present newcomers, or their offspring, will eventually become indistinguishable from other southerners.

It would, of course, be foolish to deny that southern attributes are being diluted or diffused at a steady rate. Many of the changes are, of themselves, good. Who would complain over the recent increase in southern productivity and prosperity? Someone has said we ought not be so fond of our disabilities that we are unwilling to give them up when the time comes. But also we ought not forget that every gain has its price. Flannery O'Connor once lamented: "The anguish that most of us have observed for some time now has been caused not by the fact that the South is alienated from the rest of the country, but by the fact that it is not alienated enough, that every day we are getting more and more like the rest of the country, that we are being forced out, not only of our many sins but of our few virtues."[53] The warnings of the Vanderbilt Agrarians have never been more timely, especially for southerners, than they are now. Southerners ought to beware of committing themselves more deeply than they are already committed to a war against nature that will bring them hollow triumphs only—"Pyrrhic victories . . . at points of no strategic importance."

Even so, the South today is still discernibly the South. Carl N. Degler concluded his recent interpretive survey of the southern experience, *Place Over Time,* with these words: "In short, neither in the realm of social fact nor in the realm of psychological identity has the South ceased to be distinctive, despite the changes of the twentieth century."[54] There is cause to believe the region's unique combination of political, religious, cultural, ethnic, and social traits, reinforced as they are by geography and history, myth and folklore, and convention and inertia, will for a good while yet keep it distinctive.

NOTES

1. Quoted in John S. Reed, *The Enduring South: Subcultural Persistence in Mass Society* (Lexington, Mass., Toronto, and London, 1972), 1. This paper is developed from an address by the author entitled "The Persistent South," given in 1978 at The Citadel: The Military College of South Carolina, Charleston, S.C.

2. [Luce], *Kiss the Boys Good-bye* (New York, 1939), x.

3. *Manchester Guardian Weekly,* November 9, 1980.

4. Woodward, *The Burden of Southern History* (Baton Rouge, 1960), 16–21.

5. Zinn, *The Southern Mystique* (New York, 1964), 218.

6. Tindall, "The Benighted South: Origins of a Modern Image," *Virginia Quarterly Review,* XL (Spring 1964), 281–94.

7. Cash, "Preview to Understanding," in Cash, *The Mind of the South* (New York, 1941), viii.

8. Holland Thompson, *The New South: A Chronicle of Social and Industrial Evolution* (New Haven and other cities, 1920), 7.

9. Charles P. Roland, *The Improbable Era: The South Since World War II* (Lexington, Ky., 1975), 169.

10. George B. Tindall, "Beyond the Mainstream: The Ethnic Southerners," *Journal of Southern History,* XL (February 1974), 3, 3*n,* 4.

11. Cash, "Preview to Understanding," x.

12. Louisville *Courier-Journal,* December 18, 1977.

13. "Revised State Personal Income, 1969–80," *Survey of Current Business,* LXI (July 1981), 31.

14. Louisville *Courier-Journal,* January 16, 1978; April 27, 1982.

15. Ibid., December 3, 1980.

16. Carter, *Southern Legacy* (Baton Rouge, 1950), 27, 28–29.

17. Roland, *The Improbable Era,* 126.

18. Reed, *The Enduring South,* 57–81.

19. Samuel S. Hill, "The South's Culture-Protestantism," *Christian Century,* LXX-IX (September 12, 1962), 1094–96.

20. Warren, *All the King's Men* (New York, 1946), 358.

21. Roland, *The Improbable Era,* 128 (quotation), 136.

22. Rollin G. Osterweis, *The Myth of the Lost Cause, 1865–1900* (Hamden, Conn., 1973), 118.

23. Quoted in Gunnar Myrdal, *An American Dilemma: The Negro Problem and Modern Democracy* (2 vols., New York, 1944), II, 860–861.

24. Ransom, "Reconstructed but Unregenerate," in Twelve Southerners, *I'll Take My Stand: The South and the Agrarian Tradition* (New York, 1930), 15.

25. Woodward, *The Burden of Southern History,* 31.

26. Price, "Dodo, Phoenix, or Tough Old Cock?" in H. Brandt Ayers and Thomas H. Naylor, eds., *You Can't Eat Magnolias* (New York and other cities, 1972), 75.

27. Quoted in Woodward, *The Burden of Southern History,* 36.

28. Warren, "The Genius of Katherine Anne Porter," *Saturday Review,* VII (December 1980), 11.

29. New York *Times,* April 26, 1971, p. 37:6.

30. Williams, "The Dominance of Southern Writers," *LSU Alumni News,* XLI (September 1965), 3.

31. Quoted in Frederick J. Hoffman, *The Art of Southern Fiction: A Study of Some Modern Novelists* (Carbondale, Ill., and other cities, 1967), 13–14.

32. Faulkner, *The Hamlet* (New York, 1940), 90–91.

33. Quoted in Hoffman, *The Art of Southern Fiction,* 6.

34. Brooks, "Regionalism in American Literature," *Journal of Southern History,* XXVI (February 1960), 41.

35. O'Connor, *The Violent Bear It Away* (New York, 1960), 173.

36. Quoted in Melvin J. Friedman and Lewis A. Lawson, eds., *The Added Dimension: The Art and Mind of Flannery O'Connor* (New York, 1966), 243.

37. Quoted in Sister Kathleen Feeley, *Flannery O'Connor: Voice of the Peacock* (New Brunswick, N.J., 1972), x.

38. Brooks, "The Crisis in Cultures as Reflected in Southern Literature," in Louis D. Rubin, Jr., ed., *The American South: Portrait of a Culture* (Baton Rouge and London, 1980), 188.

39. Ibid., 188–89.

40. Quoted in *People Weekly,* IX (June 19, 1978), 94.

41. Green, "Symphonic Outdoor Drama," in Robert W. Howard, ed., *This Is the South* (Chicago, New York, and San Francisco, 1959), 251.

42. New York *Times,* July 19, 1971, p. 15:4–5.

43. Cash, *The Mind of the South,* 70.

44. Quoted in Josephine Hendin, *The World of Flannery O'Connor* (Bloomington, 1970), 38.

45. Florence King, *Southern Ladies and Gentlemen* (New York, 1975), 91–93.

46. Percy, "Mississippi: The Fallen Paradise," *Harper's Magazine,* CCXXX (April 1965), 170.

47. Rubin, "The American South: The Continuity of Self-Definition," in Rubin, ed., *The American South,* 20–21.

48. Reed, *The Enduring South,* 83.

49. Kirby, *Media-Made Dixie: The South in the American Imagination* (Baton Rouge and London, 1978), 172.

50. New York *Times,* August 30, 1976, p. 23:2.

51. The theme of Egerton's *The Americanization of Dixie: The Southernization of America* (New York, 1974).

52. Quoted in Friedman and Lawson, eds., *The Added Dimension,* 246.

53. Quoted, ibid., 79.

54. Degler, *Place Over Time: The Continuity of Southern Distinctiveness* (Baton Rouge and London, 1977), 126.

Copyrights and Permissions

Index

Carter, Billy, 331
Carter, Hodding, 324
Carter, James Earl (Jimmy), 323, 331,
332
Carter, Robert, 236
Cash, Wilbur J.: notions of the
South, 13, 22, 269, 320, 321–22;
observations on southern behavior,
274, 312, 314
Catton, Bruce, 97, 200
Cemetery Ridge, 186
Chamberlain, Joshua, 218
Chancellorsville, battle of, 185, 212,
218, 227, 246
Chandler, Albert Benjamin "Happy":
early life of, 285–88; later life of,
301–2; law practice, 290, 296;
marriage to Mildred Watkins,
290–91; as national commissioner
of baseball, 295–96; national
presidential politics and, 300–301;
nickname acquired by, 289–90;
political campaigning and,
296–98; political career, 290–95,
296, 300–301; qualities as a
politician, 298–300; Charles P.
Roland's study of, 27–28; states'
rights movement and, 301; at
Transylvania University, 288–90;
World War II and, 294–95
Chandler, Callie Sanders, 285
Chandler, Joseph Sephus, 285
Charleston, South Carolina, 256, 303
Chase, Salmon P., 124
Chattanooga, battle of, 190
Chattanooga, Tennessee, 256
Cherokees, 104, 130
Cheves, Langdon, 256
Chickamauga, battle of, 190
Chickasaws, 130
Choctaws, 130
Christmas, 62–63
churches, 274–76, 324–26

Churchill, Winston, 75, 76, 180, 198,
207, 295
cities: blacks in, 308; in the South, 306
Civil War, causes of, 93–106
Civil War and Reconstruction, The
(Randall & Donald), 4
Clausewitz, Karl von: on boldness in
war, 200, 202, 217; on character
and leadership, 216–17; on
defense in war, 177; on genius,
181, 246–47; on the "moment of
truth" before great battles, 169; on
the strategy of conservation, 191;
on superiority in numbers, 175; on
the true goal in war, 182–83
Clay, Cassius M., 256–57
Clay, Henry, 145, 255
clay eating, 313
coal, 322
Cobb, Howell, 117, 119
Cold Harbor, battle of, 191
Cole, Hugh, 78, 80
college basketball, 315
college football, 315
Columbus, Kentucky, 165
Combs, Bert T., 296
Combs, James E., 26
*Coming of the Civil War, The: The
Repressible Conflict* (Craven), 95
Commager, Henry Steele, 208, 327
Compromise of 1850, 107, 109, 144
Confederacy, The (Roland), 4–6
Confederate Nation, 1861–1865, The
(Thomas), 6
Confederate States of America:
conscription and, 179; constitution
of, 121; defensive campaigns of,
232–33; deployment of manpower
in, 188; economy of, 256;
formation of, 119, 121–22; interior
lines of communication and, 176,
187; localism and, 176; military
strategies, 165, 176–78, 183–90,

209; Henry Raymond's praise
for military accomplishments of,
213, 234; response to Fort Sumter,
127–28; territorial defense policy
of, 165, 176–78; Union superiority
in material resources and, 175–76
*Confederate States of America,
1861–1865, The* (Coulter), 5
Congressional Medals of Honor, 312
Connelly, Thomas L., 35, 210
conscription, 179
Cooper, Thomas, 103
Cooper, William J., Jr., 19
cooperationists, 111, 113–14
Corinth, Tennessee, 168
corn, 153
Cornish, Dudley T., 6–7
corporal punishment, 62
Cotterill, Robert S., 16–17
cotton, 255–56, 271
cotton gin, 255
Coulter, E. Merton, 5
Courier-Journal (Louisville
newspaper), 300, 322
Craven, Avery O., 95
Creeks, 130
Crittenden, George B., 166
Crittenden, John J., 53n153, 118
Crittenden Compromise, 118
Crossfield, Richard, 289
"cultural pluralism," 332
"Culture-Protestantism," 325
Cumberland Gap, 165
Cumberland River, 166, 167, 168

Dabbs, James McBride, 307, 311
Dabney, Robert Louis, 143
Dalberg-Acton, John (Lord Acton), 97
Davidson, Donald, 69, 326
Davis, Jefferson, 131; biographical
overview, 119–20; James
Buchanan and, 117; as
commander-in-chief, 195–96;

Confederate war strategies and,
165, 176, 177, 209; Crittenden
Compromise and, 118; on the fate
of Richmond, 197; formation of
the Confederate States of America
and, 119, 121–22; Ft. Sumter and,
125, 126, 127–28; Albert Sidney
Johnston and, 8, 163, 167; Lee as
adviser to, 178, 228–29; and Lee
as general-in-chief, 195; Lee's
1863 invasion of the North and,
185; Lee's offensive-defensive
strategy and, 180; Richmond's
defense and, 180; Charles P.
Roland on, 5, 31, 32
Davis, Varina Howell, 120
Dawson, Francis W., 260
Dayton (Tenn.) trial, 282, 283
de Gaulle, Charles, 177
Degler, Carl N., 17, 19, 334
Delaware, 129
Democratic Party: Albert Chandler
and, 300–301; in Louisiana,
110–11; in the South, 272
desegregation, 300, 324
Dew, Charles B., 111
Dew, Thomas R., 142
Dickey, James, 306
discipline, 199–200
Divine, Robert A., 26
Donald, David Herbert, 4, 333
Douglas, Stephen A., 108, 127, 144
Dred Scott case, 123, 144
Dufour, Charles L., 3
Dumond, Dwight L., 112
Dunning, William A., 15
Durden, Robert F., 41
Durocher, Leo, 296

Early, Jubal, 193
Eaton, Clement, 5
Edmonds, Richard H., 260
education, 265

Egerton, John, 333
Eisenhower, Dwight D., 207
Eisenhower, John S. D., 82
Ellis, John M., 129
Elsenborn, Belgium, 81–82
emancipation, 102
Emerson, Ralph Waldo, 241–42
Essary Springs, Tennessee, 58, 65
Ewell, Richard, 186, 212

Falls, Cyril, 177, 192, 198, 200
Faulkner, William, 326
Fehrenbacher, Don E., 6
field fortifications, 192
1st Infantry Division, 87
fishing, 316–17
Fishing Creek (Ky.), battle of, 166
Five Forks (Va.), battle of, 198
Floyd, John, 117, 168
football. *See* college football
Foote, Andrew H., 166
Fort Donelson (Tenn.), 9, 166, 167–68
Fort Henry (Tenn.), 9, 166
Fort Pickens (Fla.), 122, 123, 126
Fort Stedman (Va.), 197
Fort Sumter (S.C.), 32; crisis of, 122–27; southern response to, 127–28
Franco-Prussian War, 210, 231–32
Franklin, Benjamin, 137
Fredericksburg, battle of, 183, 212, 227
free blacks: Lee's Gettysburg campaign and, 229; in Louisiana during the Civil War, 153–55; Francis B. Simkins's comments on, 14–15
Freed-Hardeman Junior College, 59
Freeman, Douglas Southall, 178, 201, 202, 212, 214
Freytag-Loringhoven, Hugo Friedrich von, 215, 248
Fugitive and Agrarian Movement, 277

"Fugitives," 69
Fuller, Baskin, 64
Fuller, J. F. C., 37, 177, 200, 202, 219, 248
Fuqua, James O., 113–14

Gaines, Ernest J., 330
Gallagher, Gary W., 11, 34
Gaston, Paul M., 278
"Generalship of Robert E. Lee, The" (Roland), 6–7
Georgia, 104, 254
Gettysburg: A Testing of Courage (Trudeau), 228
Gettysburg campaign and battle, 36, 185–86, 188–90, 212–13, 227–29, 230
"GI Charlie," 29
Gienapp, William E., 96, 101
Glass, Carter, 270
Glatthaar, Joseph T., 7
Godfather, The (movie), 328
Goebel, William, 291
Goering, Hermann, 87
"Good Ole Boy" figure, 331
Grady, Henry W., 259–61, 278–79, 321
Grant, Susan-Mary, 33
Grant, Ulysses S.: actions in the Western theater, 166, 168; disbanding of paramilitary clubs, 31; idea for defeating Lee, 230; on Albert Sidney Johnston, 164, 167; military campaign of 1864, 190, 191, 192–93, 194, 213; military campaign of 1865, 197, 198; relationship to Lincoln, 196; Charles P. Roland on, 40; Shiloh, battle of, 10, 168, 170; Vicksburg, battle of, 231
Grantham, Dewey W., 19
Great Civil War, A (Weigley), 228
Great Depression, 262

New South philosophy, 259–62, 278–80; northern-born migrants and, 333; post-Reconstruction, 258–59; post–World War II, 262–66; race and "cultural pluralism," 332; race relations, 263, 270–71, 323–24; Reconstruction, 257–58, 321, 325–26; recreation and sports, 314–17; religion and churches, 274–76, 324–26; Charles P. Roland's concepts of, 18; rural character of, 273, 305, 306; sentimentalizing of, 269–70; Francis B. Simkins's notions of, 13–14; social critics and, 281–82; Southern abolitionists, 256–57; southern speech and, 313–14, 331; the theme of abundance and, 253–66; transformation and, 319–34; trend toward national consensus and, 332–33; violence and, 274, 311–12, 330–31; white-collar class and wealthy businessmen, 304–5; women in, 313; World War II and, 321–22
South Carolina, 311
Southern Baptist church, 324
southern folk culture, 278
southern folk music, 277
southern food, 313, 331
Southern Historical Association, 2, 12
southern liberals, 311
"Southern Mystique," 319
Southern Renascence, 277
southern rights: the Civil War and, 96, 97–99, 102–5
southern spirituals, 277
South Old and New, The: A History (Simkins), 12, 15–16
"South's Call to Greatness, The" (Webb), 263
Southwest: the Confederacy and, 130–31

Sparks, David S., 11
sports, 315–17. *See also* baseball
Spotsylvania Courthouse, battle of, 191
Stampp, Kenneth M., 19
Stapleton, Ada Belle, 70
Starobin, Robert S., 19
Star of the West (ship), 122
states' rights: the Civil War and, 96, 97–99, 102–5
states' rights movement, 301
statues, 277
Stephens, Alexander, 31, 119, 120–21
Stephenson, Wendell Holmes, 17
Stevenson, Adlai, 301
stock car racing, 316
Stoesen, Alexander R., 25
Stoneman, George, 8
Stuart, Jeb, 186
Suarez, Raleigh A., 4
suburbs, 305–6
sugar planters and plantations, 108, 147–58
Sutherland, Daniel E., 38
swimming pools, 316
Sydnor, Charles S., 16

Talbott, J. Dan, 292
Taliaferro, James G., 114
Taney, Roger B., 123
tariffs, 255
Tate, Allen, 326, 327
Taylor, Richard, 151
Tennessee, 129
Tennessee River, 166, 167, 168, 170
Terrebone Parish, Louisiana, 154
Texas, 304, 314
Thatcher, Margaret, 210
Thomas, Emory M., 6, 34
Thomas, George H., 8, 163, 166
Thompson, Jacob, 117
Thoreau, Henry David, 242
Thornwell, James H., 94, 143

Wolseley, Garnet, 198, 202, 207,
    217–18
women: in the South, 313
Woodward, C. Vann, 5, 18, 19, 36,
    276, 319, 327
Woodworth, Steven E., 39
Wooster, Ralph A., 113
World War II: Battle of the Bulge,
    78–84; Charles P. Roland in,
    75–88; the South and, 321–22
Wright, Gavin, 26–27

Yancey, William L., 119, 120
"Yellow Dog Democrats," 272
Yoder, Edwin M., Jr., 22

Zinn, Howard, 319–20
Zollicoffer, Felix, 165